D1593756

HELLENISTIC EGYPT

In memory of
Naphtali Lewis,
in admiration for his work and grateful remembrance
of many decades of friendship.

Hellenistic Egypt

Monarchy, Society, Economy, Culture

Jean Bingen

Edited with an introduction by Roger S. Bagnall

University of California Press
Berkeley   Los Angeles

University of California Press, one of the most distinguished university presses in the United States, enriches lives around the world by advancing scholarship in the humanities, social sciences, and natural sciences. Its activities are supported by the UC Press Foundation and by philanthropic contributions from individuals and institutions. For more information, visit www.ucpress.edu.

University of California Press
Berkeley and Los Angeles, California

First published in the UK by Edinburgh University Press Ltd, 22 George Square, Edinburgh.

Library of Congress Cataloging-in-Publication Data

Bingen, Jean.
    Hellenistic Egypt : monarchy, society, economy, culture / Jean Bingen ; edited and introduced by Roger S. Bagnell.
        p.   cm. — (Hellenistic culture and society ; 49)
    ISBN-13: 978-0-520-25141-0 (cloth : alk. paper)
    ISBN-13: 978-0-520-25142-7 (pbk. : alk. paper)
    1. Egypt—History—332–30 B.C.   2. Egypt—Economic conditions—332 B.C.–640 A.D.
3. Ptolemaic dynasty, 305–30 B.C.   I. Title.

DT92.B54   2007
932'.021—dc22   2006051428

Manufactured in Great Britain

16   15   14   13   12   11   10   09   08   07
10   9   8   7   6   5   4   3   2   1

The paper used in this publication meets the minimum requirements of ANSI/NISO Z39.48-1992 (R 1997) (*Permanence of Paper*).

CONTENTS

ORIGINAL SOURCES OF CHAPTERS

Part I: The Monarchy

1. 'Ptolémée Ier Sôter ou la quête de la légitimité', *Académie Royale de Belgique, Bulletin de la Classe des Lettres et des Sciences morales et politiques* 5 ser. 74 (1988) 34–51.

2. 'I. Philae I 4, un moment d'un règne, d'un temple et d'un culte', *Akten des 21. Internationalen Papyrologenkongresses* (Archiv für Papyrusforschung, Beiheft 3, Leipzig 1997) 88–97.

3. 'Cléopâtre: l'image et le diadème', *Académie Royale de Belgique, Bulletin de la Classe des Lettres et des Sciences morales et politiques* 6 ser. 7 (1996) 235–48.

4. 'Cléopâtre VII Philopatris', *Chronique d'Égypte* 74 (1999) 118–23.

5. 'La politique dynastique de Cléopâtre VII', *Comptes Rendus de l'Académie des Inscriptions et Belles-Lettres* (1999) 49–66.

Part II: The Greeks

6. 'Les Thraces en Égypte ptolémaïque', in *Pulpudeva, Semaines Philippopolitaines de l'histoire et de la culture thrace* 4 (Sofia 1983) 72–9.

7. 'Les papyrus ptolémaïques et la diaspora achaienne', *Archaia Achaia kai Eleia: Anakoinoseis kata to Proto Diethnes Sumposio* (= *Meletemata* 13, Athens 1991) 61–5.

8. 'Présence grecque et milieu rural ptolémaïque', in M. I. Finley (ed.), *Problèmes de la terre en Grèce ancienne* (Paris and The Hague 1973) 215–22.

ILLUSTRATIONS

GLOSSARY

Achaemenids: the Persian royal dynasty.

amphictyonic: referring to a Greek religious federation or its governing body.

antigrapheis: checking clerks in Ptolemaic administration, particularly of an *oikonomos*.

apomoira: a Ptolemaic tax on produce of vineyards, orchards and similar land, of one-sixth of the net, paid (after legislation of Ptolemy II) to the cult of Arsinoe.

arakos: a leguminous crop, perhaps broad beans.

architheoros: head of a *theoria* (an embassy on sacred matters).

archon basileus: Athenian magistrate with religious functions.

archontes: principal magistrates of a Greek city.

Argeads: the Macedonian royal house to which Alexander the Great belonged.

aroura: unit of land measurement, 2,756 square metres or about two-thirds of an acre.

artaba: measure of grain introduced into Egypt by the Persians; its size seems to have varied, but 30 litres seems the most common size in the Ptolemaic period.

asyloi/asylia: exempt, a state of exemption; in Egypt mainly referring to the freedom of temples from official entry in search of fugitives.

ateleis: tax-exempt persons.

aulic: belonging to the royal court.

basilikos grammateus: 'royal scribe', head of the record-keeping department for the nome in Ptolemaic administration.

cavetto: hollow moulding with a cross-section of a quarter-circle.

chiliarch: 'chief of a thousand men', term used in Persian court (and adopted by Alexander the Great) for a high official like a vizier.

chlamys: a short mantle or cloak.

chôra: the 'country', referring variously to the territory surrounding the urban centre of a polis and belonging to it or in Egypt to the entire country outside of the territories of Naucratis, Alexandria and Ptolemais.

cleruch: soldier assigned a *klêros* for support and income rather than being paid in money.

Demotic: the Egyptian language and script used for most everyday purposes in the Hellenistic period.

dioiketes: royal official in charge of (financial) administration; in the Ptolemaic kingdom the chief royal minister, head of practically all departments of the government except the military.

diorthôma: supplementary royal proclamation correcting or revising an earlier one.

dôrea: 'gift' estate or concession of varying sorts in the Ptolemaic kingdom.

eklogistes: accountant, term used for financial official.

elaikê: the Ptolemaic tax on oil and system of contractual and administrative measures connected to it.

enteuxis: petition, usually to the king.

Epagomenai: the five days added to the twelve thirty-day months of the Egyptian calendar.

ephêbia: period of training that completed a Greek gymnasial education.

ephebic: referring to young men and their gymnastic and military training in a Greek city.

epiclesis: epithet given to kings, generally as part of the royal cult.

epigonê: 'descent, offspring', used in Ptolemaic Egypt to refer to descendants of foreign settlers in Egypt, as in 'Macedonian of the *epigonê*'. Persons with this designation are not holding military or administrative posts. The meaning of 'Persians of the *epigonê*' is controversial.

epilarches: commander of a double cavalry squadron.

epimeletes: supervisor or overseer, a financial official.

epistates: the subordinate of the *strategos* of a nome in Egypt, active at the village level, and a similar official in later Ptolemaic times at the nome level. Both had law-enforcement duties, but there was also an *epistates* of police at the nome level.

epistrategos: official like a *strategos* but of superior rank, found primarily in charge of the Thebaid.

Heraclidae: 'descendants of Herakles' in Greek mythology; the Macedonian royal house traced its lineage to Herakles.

hieroglyphic: Egyptian pictographic script.

hipparch, hipparchy: commander of cavalry or his command.

hoplites: heavily armed Greek infantry.

hydria: pottery vessel often used to hold cremated remains.

hypomnêma: memorandum.

hypomnêmatographos: official in charge of royal correspondence.

hypostyle (hall): room in Egyptian temple supported by rows of columns.

idios logos: department of the financial administration handling confiscated property and other non-recurring revenues.

katoikoi: soldiers settled on land given them in return for military service; military colonists.

klêros: plot of land allotted to someone, particularly to a Ptolemaic soldier.

komogrammateus: 'village scribe', head of records for a village under the department of the *basilikos grammateus*.

kynoboskos: raiser of sacred jackals.

logeutes: tax collector.

logistêrion: office of the *logistês*; accounting office.

machimoi: the native Egyptian warrior class.

Mammisi: 'birth temple' in an Egyptian sanctuary, where annual rites of renewal were held.

Meris: one of three administrative divisions in the Arsinoite nome (Fayyum).

metic: non-citizen free resident in a Greek city.

metrêtês: a unit of liquid measure used for wine and oil.

naos: inner sanctuary of a temple; in Egyptian temples, this room was accessible only to priests.

nauarch: naval commander, admiral.

nomarch: chief administrative officer of a nome for agricultural affairs.

nome: administrative subdivision of Egypt; there were over forty of them under the Ptolemies.

oikonomos: 'manager' of royal financial affairs at the nome level.

paides: 'boys' category in athletic competitions.

parachôrêsis: cession (of land).

pastophoroi: lower priestly group in Egyptian temples.

peribolos: enclosure wall of a sanctuary.

phylakites: guard or policeman.

politeuma: association of persons of the same origin.

pronaos: part of a temple preceding the naos.

proskynêma: inscription, typically on a temple wall, marking the presence of a person before a god and seeking to render it permanent.

prostagma: royal ordinance, usually setting forth general rules.

prostates: president or head, with widely varying reference.

rasurae: erasures in an inscription.

Saite: the twenty-sixth Egyptian dynasty, originating at Sais in the Delta.

Second Sophistic: a literary and philosophical movement under the Roman empire.

sistrum: Egyptian metal instrument like a rattle.

sitologos: royal official in charge of grain revenues and supplies.

strategos: the chief officer of military, and later civil, administration in a nome.

syngraphophylax: 'guardian of contracts', person responsible for keeping deposited legal documents.

telos: tax.

Theoi Euergetai: 'benefactor gods', epithet given to Ptolemy III and his queen Berenike and to Ptolemy VIII and his queens.

toparch: official of nomarch's bureau in charge of a section of a nome.

topogrammateus: 'local scribe' in charge of record-keeping for a district.

Uraeus: asp, representation of power on head-dresses of gods and kings.

Some definitions have been adapted from Bagnall and Derow (2004: 293–300).

Map 1 The Eastern Mediterranean in the Hellenistic period

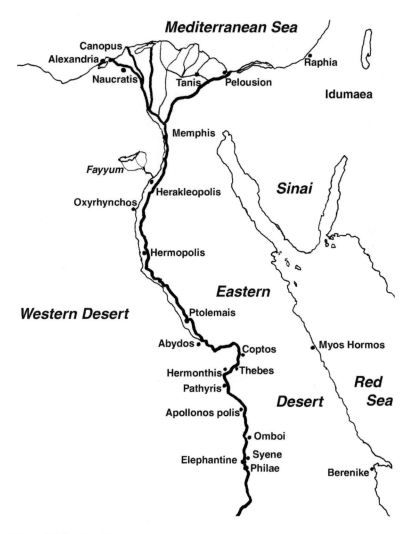

Map 2 Hellenistic Egypt

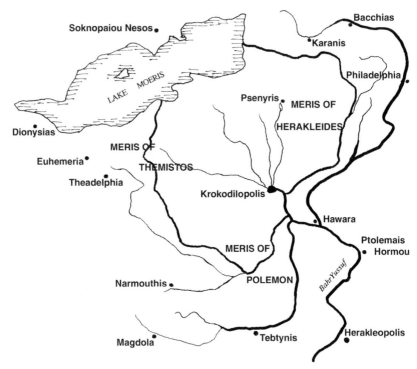

Map 3 The Fayyum (Arsinoite nome)

FOREWORD

Sixty years ago, on 8 May 1945, in our barracks, we did not perceive in ourselves much more than a never-again feeling that five years of nightmares were behind us and that, back home, things would be soon settled in the good old way. We did not realize that we were living the first day of the third millennium. I recall this here because, if the present collection offers any original features, that is due less to me than to the fact that these articles were written some time after such a break-point of history. What I had learned as a student before that from those who first guided my thinking, the works of the prestigious Wilcken and the comfortable Rostovtzeff as much as the *Économie royale des Lagides* published in 1939 by my young professor, Claire Préaux, had been elaborated on the other side of the century divide, before the crisis which forced us to think otherwise, even unconsciously – with, among others, people like Moses Finley or Pierre Vidal-Naquet.

Some weeks later, Private Bingen, on leave, defended in khaki his doctoral thesis on the so-called Revenue Laws. The dissertation was rather shy, drafted in a time when it was as difficult to find carbon paper for the five copies required by the university as to obtain free moments to concentrate on a rather untimely activity. During the discussion of the thesis, mainly a long dialogue with Claire Préaux, I perceived a rift between what I had written not so long ago and what I was proposing to my jury. I felt quickly that my essay was somehow outdated, and later I refused to have it printed when this luxury had again become possible. In 1946, at the request of Claire Préaux, I briefly marked my position on one point by publishing in the *Chronique d'Égypte* a modest article on the fiscal aspects of the monopoly of oil. With her usual sense of fair play, she had noticed the starting-point of a reflection on the economy of the Ptolemies that diverged from her own and wished it to become known. Later, we often spoke about that and other matters where Claire Préaux fully integrated the new perception of the past. One will find here (chapter 13) the synthesis of my postdoctoral reflections, which I published only in 1978. One will often perceive in some of my other papers the same need to break with certain positions considered as acquired. This only reflects the same suspicion of my generation against evidence that was too easily born in another world. These papers show too in a more timeless way the need always to go back first to the documents, in their double facet, as a testimony to be recovered in its actual existence and its mere meaning, and as the expression of a human group to be discovered in its activity and in its unconscious, but also in its incapacity to escape its own habits of thought. Maybe my remarks will also have some interest for the following generation, at least to discover how far my own thinking was in its turn unsatisfactory because also too much of its own time. I feel this already in some recent work on bicultural Egypt.

I owe the contents of this book to the epoch I lived in, to the permanent companionship of my wife in my research work, and, for the older papers, to the stimulating welcome I received in the Fondation égyptologique Reine Élisabeth with its two Graeco-Roman pillars, the austere Marcel Hombert and the smiling Claire Préaux. But, in its current shape, I completely owe this volume to the friendship, work and enormous patience of Roger Bagnall. He had suggested the publication of this collection of articles on Ptolemaic history. On the pressing advice of my regretted friend Toni Reekmans, my junior Belgian colleague as member in the École française d'Athènes, I proposed that the collection would appear in English. This was somehow overestimating my strength and my capacities. If, after too many delays, the result is, as I hope, not without value, it is due to Roger Bagnall, who even translated some of the major texts. May he be thanked for it here. Maybe he will feel this affectionate gratitude in the association with the dear beings gathered in this paragraph.

Jean Bingen
8 May 2005

Introduction

JEAN BINGEN AND THE CURRENTS OF PTOLEMAIC HISTORY

Roger S. Bagnall

The history of Ptolemaic Egypt is not among those parts of ancient history with a long past.[1] If the identification of the Hellenistic Greek world as a subject goes back to the first half of the nineteenth century, it was not until after the publication of papyri from Hellenistic Egypt began to make an impression on scholars that this part of the Hellenistic world took on a distinct identity and became an object of separate investigation. These studies, as one might expect, were strongly marked by the currents of their times. Among other parts of the outlook of the period stretching down to World War II we can hardly fail to notice the assumption that the unitary nation-state, with a single language and culture and with a deliberate policy of fostering cultural unity, was a natural institution.[2]

The European nations that were the homes of those who studied Ptolemaic Egypt had other common characteristics as well. They were colonising powers, with as yet little doubt that they had a legitimate mission in controlling and settling other parts of the globe; they were in the midst of developing a far more ambitious state apparatus than history had known before, in the service of a far-reaching sense of the proper role of the state; and they had entrenched national churches, the relationships of which with the government were of some complexity and in some cases a matter of competition for power in certain domains of life. As the twentieth century developed, the state's interests increasingly extended to the economy. Both in its more

I am much indebted to Jason Governale and Giovanni Ruffini for help in preparing this book for press.

[1] The notes to this introduction are intended only to help the reader find some of the more important currents of work on Ptolemaic history that do not otherwise figure substantially in the notes of this volume and to provide a context for how some of the main themes of Jean Bingen's work fit into the directions of Ptolemaic history in recent decades. For a more general survey of work in the subject from the 1950s to early 1980s, see Bagnall (1982) and the useful interpretative essay by Alan E. Samuel (1989).

[2] To be sure, these national languages were in virtually every case a deliberate imposition in the face of a bilingual or multilingual reality, adopted as an instrument of state-building.

extreme and deliberate form, in the communist Russian empire, and in the more moderate and reactive forms of Western state intervention, economic planning and an active government role in production and distribution came to be important parts of state activity.

In this setting, the picture of Ptolemaic Egypt sketched, sometimes in considerable detail, by the scholars of the early to mid-twentieth century took on many of the lineaments of their own setting. The monarchy of Ptolemaic Egypt was depicted as a state with a developed bureaucracy and a high level of self-conscious purposefulness and planning. With this bureaucracy, it ran a monopolistic and centralised economy, aimed at maximising production and generating economic growth as well as ensuring the public revenues. The Macedonian and Greek ruling class that had settled in Egypt was intent on Hellenising the country, bringing their more advanced culture to an archaic country that had a proud past but a backward present. In this way, their colonial domain could be turned into a more united state. The kings found themselves, however, locked in a perennial struggle with the Egyptian priesthoods and their temples, bastions of privilege and property, and as the monarchy weakened, the state lost ground to the church. Strong (and strong was always better than weak) kings reclaimed this terrain and kept the church in its place.

There is some exaggeration and caricature in this description of the state of scholarship on Ptolemaic Egypt down to World War II, and of course it would be unjust not to recognise that the scholars of the period, above all Michael Rostovtzeff, Ulrich Wilcken and Claire Préaux, laid the foundations of our understanding of this society in great monographic detail, which in many areas has not been replaced to our day and in some cases needs no replacement. Moreover, one must also take into account the ways in which the entire subject of Hellenistic Egypt – the whole Hellenistic world, in fact – fell outside the ideological framework of a classicising ancient history.[3] None the less, it is not unfair to say that the overall interpretative framework was resolutely modern in its assumptions, particularly about the nature and working of states and institutions. The views of imperialism, colonialism, the economy, the social character of religion, and the monarchic state owed little to any specific appreciation of the distinctive characteristics either of ancient Egypt or of the ancient Greek world.

The studies by Jean Bingen collected in this volume engage continually with three large themes for which the recovery of an

---

[3] See Heinen (1989).

appropriate analytic framework has been essential: the nature of the Ptolemaic monarchy, the challenges it faced, and the practices it adopted in trying to constitute and maintain power; the character of the Ptolemaic economy; and the ways in which Greeks and Egyptians did or did not encounter one another and experience some degree of cultural interaction. These three questions are interconnected in various ways; although the book has a broadly thematic organisation, many of its chapters deal with two or three of these themes, not only one. These studies were written from the late 1960s onwards, a period when the underlying assumptions of prewar scholarship were all upended or transformed by contemporary events and the development of scholarship in the social sciences. They reflect a reassessment of Ptolemaic realities as seen from a less self-confident modern world.

In this introduction I have tried to provide a sketch of the contributions the various chapters make to these subjects and particularly of the context of earlier and contemporary scholarship into which they fit. What links them all is the continuing focus on the nature of the Greek experience – Jean Bingen is a Hellenist, after all, and close reading of Greek texts figures repeatedly in these chapters – in the world brought into being by the conquests of Alexander the Great. Again and again we see how the practices of the Ptolemaic dynasty and its servants may be traced back to Greece and Macedonia. That is not to ignore the Egyptian population or its role in the formation of Ptolemaic Egypt, because the intrusion of these Greek habits and approaches into the Egyptian milieu is what constitutes the distinctive character of the society. But it is fair to say that Bingen's particular contribution to Ptolemaic history has come from the Greek side; others have made very important and different contributions that help to complete a full view of Ptolemaic Egypt, something probably now beyond the reach of any single scholar.

It is undoubtedly no accident that Belgian scholars have advanced the study of Hellenistic Egypt to a degree far out of proportion to the size of their country and its academic establishment. Belgium as a state was a nineteenth-century creation, although growing out of eighteenth-century roots, constituted with a new monarchy, a language of power and government (French), a second language spoken by a large part of the population ('Flemish', although nowadays called 'nederlands', i.e., Dutch), and a small German-speaking minority. Its institutional development thus coincided with the heyday of linguistic nationalism in Europe. Although a small country, it was an imperial power in Africa with a record of brutality worthy of Alexander the Great's bloodier moments.[4] As the speakers of Dutch became less willing to accept a second-class position, and as colonialism became a more consciously and critically discussed question, Ptolemaic Egypt came to be an interesting arena in which to explore some of the issues of the twentieth century.[5] These topics proved of special interest to the Dutch-speaking (but mainly French-writing) school developed by Willy Peremans at Leuven, beginning in the late 1930s.[6] At the same time, Préaux was publishing her great synthesis on the Ptolemaic economy and coming to view the idea of cultural fusion – that central concept of the Hellenistic in nineteenth-century thought – with suspicion. It was at this moment, under the influence of Préaux, and during the difficult days of World War II, that Jean Bingen's engagement with Hellenistic Egypt took shape. Its characteristic themes have been in part shaped by the currents I have described, but he has in his turn taken part in reshaping the direction of debate. The chapters of this book are English versions, lightly reworked and edited, of these studies written since the late 1960s and focusing on central issues and texts in the history of Ptolemaic Egypt.[7]

As the monarchy is the foundation of all else in any Hellenistic kingdom, the book begins with several studies focused on it. Chapter 1 describes parts of the challenge facing Ptolemy I Soter as he worked to turn Egypt from a satrapy held on behalf of a distant monarchy into his own kingdom. His most immediate need was to secure the continuing support of his troops, and for this purpose the legacy of Alexander was critical. Ptolemy's history of Alexander, part of the contents of which survives in the Alexander biography of Arrian, remodels the conqueror into someone congenial to Ptolemy's own self-conceptualisation, a stern judge but a generous prince. The cult of Alexander, associated with his tomb in his name-city of Alexandria, is part of the demonstration of the legitimacy of Ptolemaic rule. Ideology and propaganda thus played a large part in the acquisition and retention of power – not in opposition to the use of military power, but in part as demonstrations of the legitimacy of the holding of that military power.[8]

---

[4] See Ewans (2002).

[5] See Bagnall (1997), responding to Edouard Will (1985).

[6] Peremans (1937).

[7] The more technical of these studies have had some appendixes omitted and Greek transliterated to help make the whole available to nonspecialist readers.

[8] Other important recent studies on Ptolemaic royal ideology, treating reigns on which no essays are given here, include Hazzard (2000) and Thompson (2000).

The cultural institutions of the capital had, Bingen argues, a dual role, representing both the cultural patronage historically associated with the Macedonian kings and the Athenian tradition of learning. The Ptolemies never lost their clear sense of a link to the Macedonian past, and their court circles remained populated with those who could claim a share in that heritage, even to the point that speaking the Doric dialect of Macedonia remained a way of asserting superiority to other Greeks (the Macedonian sense of superiority is touched on in Chapter 7).[9] But the Ptolemies also had a keen sense of the political value of appropriating the cultural prestige of the dominant city of classical Greece.

By the time Ptolemy's grandson, Ptolemy III, came to power not quite six decades after his grandfather's assumption of the royal title, the monarchy was far more institutionalised than it had been earlier. Through the study in Chapter 2, in which an inscription of Philae is rescued from a neglect owed to its seeming banality, Bingen shows the shift in focus in royal ideology towards promotion of a love- and family-based monarchy, somewhat along the lines of what the British royal house attempted from Queen Victoria onwards, although with success not much more substantive than the Ptolemies'.[10] Ptolemy III's wife, Berenike, was the first Ptolemaic queen to have her own Egyptian titulature, and the cult of Isis is brought into play in support of the family ideology by stress on her son Harpocrates. This move came, as Bingen shows, at a moment of crisis, when Ptolemy Euergetes was emerging from the initial phase of his reign (247–244), with its dramatic military campaigns abroad cut short by trouble on the home front.

The figure of Cleopatra, the last Ptolemaic monarch, has fascinated scholars as much as the general public. But scholars have done no better than anyone else, generally, in seeing through the picture of the queen presented by the ancient sources, which concentrate entirely on her relationship to Roman notables (Caesar and Antony) and her dealings with the Roman state. There is another side entirely, however: Cleopatra as the last Macedonian queen – something she could not know, to be sure. It is on this side that Bingen concentrates in the two studies that make up Chapters 3 and 5. Because she did not want to be weak and thus succumb to the very visible prospect of being the last Ptolemaic ruler, she both swept other claimants aside at her accession, in order to consolidate sole power, and then, at a later point, turned to try to ensure the succession by putting her son before

[9] See Clarysse (1998).
[10] E.g., Cannadine (1998: 3–10).

her in royal titulature and having him depicted in first place in temple reliefs. He was, in her representation, already a king. What is striking is just how Macedonian Cleopatra's conception of her role still is; she is not just the last Ptolemaic ruler, but the last to attempt dynastic renewal. Her titulature uses *philopatris* ('homeland-loving'), Bingen argues, to insist on her Macedonian roots (Chapter 4). Her central concern for the political classes of Alexandria and their importance for the survival of the monarchy is also visible in the generous (and propagandistic) treatment of Alexandrian landowners in the royal edicts studied in Chapter 12, which date to the critical period between the battle of Philippi and the arrival of Antony.

Power in the Ptolemaic state was not only derived from the approval and support of others but could be exercised only with the active collaboration of a considerable number of individuals, both Greek and Egyptian. The second section of the book concentrates on the Greeks in Hellenistic Egypt, the cadres central to making it possible for the Ptolemies to have a Macedonian-style monarchy, and asks after their experience: how successful were the Ptolemies in creating an environment the Greeks would find attractive? Both the military – mostly in the form of military settlers on the land – and the civil administration figure largely in these chapters (6–12).

The omnipresence of Ptolemaic officials in the papyri has always tended to give historians an impression of a strong state. The fact that the Zenon archive was found and mostly quite swiftly published at an early stage in the development of the subject was particularly important, because the documents of this large (close to 2,000 texts) group tend to convey a sense of purpose, zeal, innovation, activity and competence. The *dioiketes* Apollonios, Zenon's employer, was, we feel, interested in everything, constantly monitoring all that went on, a model minister of state and a demanding boss. How could a government with such men fail to be purposeful, activist and effective? The so-called Revenue Laws of Ptolemy II, published in the earliest days of papyrology, only reinforced this view, for here scholars thought they saw a government of energy, purpose and system, drawing up a code for a managed economy (a subject dealt with in Chapter 13).

One of Jean Bingen's major themes has been the inaccuracy of this view of the Ptolemaic monarchy, administration and underlying society. It was, he points out, perennially short of Greek manpower to staff those numerous bureaucratic positions we see and that we love to arrange into an idealised organisational chart. It was in no position to try to run the economy in detail, and even in applying the time-tested Greek techniques of tax farming it had to make compromises in the face of its inability to have Greeks in every village to collect the taxes. Whatever initial zeal for the use of Greek methods the kings may have had was tempered by the reality of staff shortages and the complexity of Egypt. Inevitably, existing Egyptian structures had to be used, and Greek models had to be adapted to fit them.[11]

The discussion of Greeks in Ptolemaic society begins with two test trenches into the ethnic composition of that society, both originally written for conferences with a particular geographic focus. The first (Chapter 6) is about the Thracians, sometimes viewed as a kind of Ptolemaic underclass. This view turns out, in Bingen's analysis, to be almost the reverse of reality. As a major source of cavalry, they were strongly represented among the most highly endowed cleruchs, and displayed their dynastic loyalty in Greek games honouring the royal house. Cavalry settlers remained a kind of closed upper-crust society to the end of the Ptolemaic dynasty (Chapter 11), and the Thracians occupied a significant place in that population. But otherwise they are hardly distinguishable in their structural place in society from any other component of the Greek population. With the Achaeans (Chapter 7), by contrast, no distinctive characteristic can be found at any point. Like most of the Greek immigrants, they formed in the new kingdom an integrated and relatively uniform body of royal servants and entrepreneurs.

The next three chapters explore various aspects of the Greek presence in the Egyptian countryside, especially in an effort to understand just where and how Greeks and Egyptians came into contact, but also looking for what particular roles the Greeks played in most of the country. Bingen sees the two ethnic groups as relatively (but not absolutely) impermeable in the third century. The central aspect discussed in Chapter 8, and indeed a theme of several other chapters, is the land. How did Greeks satisfy their hunger for land, and what did they do with it when they got it? The royal system, with its only modest place for private ownership of land, tended to frustrate the immigrants' natural tendencies towards acquisition and, in the process, increase the pressures for the theoretically revocable military allotments to become permanent parts of a family patrimony. This impression of straightforward privatisation of the allotments is in some respects misleading, but the cleruchic land does become a kind of hereditary body of property within a closed economic class (see

---

[11] See now Manning (2003), with extensive bibliography.

Chapters 11 and 14). When the Greeks do get land, however, particularly from cleruchic holdings, they show a tendency to prefer to rent it out and live on the income from it in the gradually urbanising nome capitals (Chapter 9).

The result is a complex matrix of land-management strategies, relying heavily on mid-level managers and entrepreneurs who could free the landholders from detailed management and make a living in the space between the landholders and the actual cultivators (Chapter 10; see also Chapter 15). The 'urban milieu' in the countryside (Chapter 9) is poorly known from the documents, but Bingen makes a strong argument for the presence in these cities of a wide array of institutions and services differentiating them from the villages, and that already in the third century. These included both Egyptian components (textile production, temples, craftsmen, ports, record-keeping) and Greek (garrison, courts, bank, police, justice, prison, and the central administration of the nome). From this combination of city and village environments comes the birth, in the late Ptolemaic period, of the classes of notables who would govern both environments in the Roman period. In the villages, this class included a rising body of Egyptians at home in the royal system (especially the less wealthy Egyptian cleruchs; see Chapter 10) and in serving the business needs of the urban residents.

These issues are taken further in the chapters of Part III, particularly in Chapters 14 and 15. The inability of the Greeks to find a permanent home on the land, the result of the royal system's unwillingness to let them become true landowners on any scale, made them all too often birds of passage who added little value to the countryside. Another 'structural tension' was the zero-sum conflict between bureaucrats and entrepreneurs for pieces of the same potential profit (Chapter 14). The entire structure, in Bingen's view, was badly chosen for growth in productivity, that supposed goal of the Ptolemaic economy. Matters deteriorated further in the second century, as the government found itself unable to resolve the conflicts among the various rural stakeholders except at its own expense, by cancelling periodically the arrears of rent and taxes. Despite its chronic shortage of manpower – we return to this theme once again – the Ptolemaic state seemed unable to think economically and create true opportunities that would attract that manpower. Some wound up in the kind of middleman role delineated in Chapter 15, inventing opportunities out of the gap created by the structural tensions of the royal economy.

The royal economy itself, and its limits, are the focus of the long Chapter 13, growing out of some of Bingen's earliest research and centred on the famous Revenue Laws papyrus. This, in Bingen's analysis, proves to be two papyrus rolls, not one, each a composite assembly of several original texts amalgamated for storage. It was not a codification, but a set of annual texts addressed in the name of the king to those concerned with specific monopolies and contracts: farming the money taxes, the tax on vineyards, the oil business and banking.

The entire set of procedures described in these circulars is Greek, including the use of taxation in money (rather than produce) and the important role of sureties in providing a larger capital base for those bidding on contracts. But the system, if it can be so termed, is also a curious hybrid, for these Greek processes have been overlaid on existing tax-collection habits, without any real effort at integrating the two components into a single, rational system. Once again, the pressures of scarce manpower seem to play a larger role than general theories of management or taxation. The banking system, too, has Greek antecedents. But the oil business is Egyptian – it is oil from vegetable seeds that is at stake in most of it – and the Greek veneer is only a form of regulation and control, which does not go to the heart of the process.

Overall, then, the supposed royal economy is the result of the accumulation of many points at which traditional Egyptian practices were confronted with, and often overlaid by, Greek techniques. These regulations show an empirical, step-by-step exploitation of the possibilities for revenue, but nothing resembling an overall economic policy.[12]

The final section of the book is devoted to interactions, points where Greeks and Egyptians were brought together in the Ptolemaic system. Bingen starts Chapter 16 by thinking about the conceptual and practical problems of identifying Greeks and Egyptians, here reflecting both Peremans's practical concentration on amassing data (in the *Prosopographia Ptolemaica* project) and Préaux's more theoretical rejection of the concept of mixed cultures. But equally problematic is the supposition that Greeks and Egyptians formed homogeneous groups. The investigation proceeds to look at the various ramifications of the spread (not introduction)[13] of a cash economy under Hellenistic rule, ranging from temple operations to apiculture. The Greeks had a head start in many areas because of better access to capital through the

---

[12] Cf. the treatment of the issue of the managed economy by Rathbone (2000).
[13] Von Reden (1997).

system of sureties, but we begin to see signs of the Egyptians becoming more competitive in the capital arena in the second half of the Ptolemaic period. Still, disruptions along the way were numerous, and Chapter 17 (the earliest of the studies collected in this volume[14]) provides a microhistorical study of one disruptive moment, when the Greek penchant for advance estimation of crops collided with Egyptian agricultural practices. Even though some details of the event remain obscure, it offers a remarkable view of a group of Egyptian farmers walking away from their investment in a crop rather than accept a management technique they find inappropriate and intrusive.

In Chapter 18 Bingen turns more in the direction of cultural interaction, looking for areas of connection. On the whole, he finds little to support any notion of much integration. Alexandria remained alien to the Egyptians in this period, he thinks, and even religion, sometimes invoked as a major area in which the Greeks took on some of Egyptian culture, he finds largely a matter of superficial connection. Egyptian religion was not particularly open to foreign influences, and whatever interaction took place was essentially one way.

It is equally wrong, in Bingen's view, to suppose that the relationship of the Ptolemies and the temples can rightly be described as a zero-sum church–state conflict in which the kings gradually lost out. In a reinterpretation of a series of inscriptions from the last century of Ptolemaic rule (Chapter 19), he shows against Rostovtzeff and others that there is no evidence for a strong clergy; that the whole concept of a seesaw with king and clergy at opposite ends is an unjustified import from the medieval world; and that the late Hellenistic temples figuring in the inscriptions in question were themselves in decline. The main actors are largely Greek officers seeking to get royal protection, for temples that they are patronising, against the threats of other Greeks. It is royal strength and temple weakness that the inscriptions show, not the reverse. The right of asylum in temples, once unquestioned, now needs the king's backing to have any force.

A few central themes can be seen to underlie these studies. One is a view of the Ptolemaic economy as essentially improvised, working with existing structures rather than attempting any basic reforms. Over the inherited systems was placed a layer of control and accountability, partly in the form of bureaucracy but even more in the shape of non-government supervision underwritten by private-sector capital

[14] And the first paper by Jean Bingen that I heard, at the Ann Arbor Congress of Papyrology in 1968, when I was beginning graduate school. The present volume is in some sense a reflection of the extraordinary stimulation that it afforded me.

guarantees. This second layer was poorly integrated with the existing enterprise, but that was not of central concern. The Ptolemies and their top managers presumably viewed the inevitable cost of this extra layer as more than made up by revenues captured rather than lost, but we have no way of knowing if they were right. They did, however, create certain opportunities for Greek investors and managers.

The nature of political power in a Hellenistic state is also a pervasive concern. In keeping with other scholars of his generation,[15] Bingen recognised the imperial and colonial element in the Ptolemaic state and looked at it with a coolly critical eye. His Ptolemaic monarchy is at the start, and always remains, critically dependent on a Macedonian, and more broadly Greek, upper stratum visible in the court, the army, the higher bureaucracy and the Alexandrian political class.[16] Ideology plays a large role – alongside economic self-interest – in Bingen's vision of how that political stratum was kept loyal, and it is ideological aspects that figure most centrally in the studies of Ptolemy I and III and Cleopatra VII.[17]

This royal structure had its weaknesses, and these loom large in Bingen's view of the Ptolemaic state. Above all, chronic difficulties in staffing the bureaucracy point to a shortage of manpower willing to accept the rewards offered by the Ptolemies in return for the tasks.[18] Indeed, recent scholarship is tending to foreground the institutional weakness of the Ptolemaic state,[19] and that weakness is precisely one of the areas in which Bingen has led the way in undoing the previous idea of a mighty state with strong central planning capabilities.

Broadly speaking, it seems to me that Bingen presents to us a largely unsuccessful state and society, one without enough imagination or inner strength to get beyond the crippling constraints put on it from the start by its dual Graeco-Macedonian and Egyptian antecedents, with their largely incompatible ways of operation. The Ptolemies neither figured out ways of running Egypt as an Egyptian monarchy, without the help of tens of thousands of Greeks, nor managed to draw the logical conclusion and make Egypt into a more consistently Greek state with the property regime and economic incentives that would have created a more stable Greek society. Nor yet did they have any conception of uniting the two cultures into one,

---

[15] Will (1985).
[16] Cf., from the Leuven school, the work of Leon Mooren, especially (1975), (1977).
[17] Cf. Hazzard (2000).
[18] Cf. Samuel (1966).
[19] Manning (2003).

something neither Greeks nor Egyptians probably thought a good idea in any case.

Of course, something did come out of it, a society in which those who analysed and seized the opportunities presented to them rose to form local ruling classes, which came fully into their own only in the Roman period. The cultural and social separation of Greeks and Egyptians, so marked in the third century, was attenuated and complicated over time as Egyptians learned to work within the Ptolemaic system and as a more extensive bilingual and bicultural stratum in society developed.[20] It is by no means certain that a more determined effort to resolve the structural tensions in Ptolemaic government and society could have done better. This book is not, in the end, very optimistic about the tractability of most of these challenges that the Ptolemies faced, any more than our own society has kept its optimism about questions like the integration of ethnic minorities. In that sense it is as much a product of its times as were earlier attempts to understand Hellenistic Egypt.

---

[20] This is an area in which P. W. Pestman and his school led the way and to which Willy Clarysse has made many contributions in recent decades, in both cases generally by analysis of bilingual dossiers. See, by way of example, Pestman (1978), Clarysse (1985, 1991, 1995).

PART I: THE MONARCHY

Chapter 1

PTOLEMY I AND THE QUEST FOR LEGITIMACY

⌒

My purpose in this opening chapter is not to sketch a new biography of Ptolemy son of Lagos, the first in the series of Macedonian monarchs who, during three centuries, ruled Egypt from Alexandria as kings and as pharaohs. Friend, confidant, and later general of Alexander, the man was a part of and even an actor during a few decades full of multiple, profound changes in the Eastern Mediterranean world and in the Middle East. Our protagonist does not occupy, in the rather poor sources we have at our disposal, the place he deserves, given the importance of his reign in the history of Egypt. Our best account of his reign is found in the penetrating and original pages Eric Turner devoted to him, which I will use here as background.[1]

There is, however, still some light to be shed on certain aspects of the behaviour of the first Ptolemy as a testimony to the emergence of a philosophy of monarchic power which developed during the Hellenistic period. I have chosen some attitudes which seem to reveal how Ptolemy, a self-made man, needed and tried to justify the royal power he had seized. Indeed such an inquiry may reveal the values by which the new king felt, consciously or not, that he was able to create those ties between ruler and ruled which are the real sanctions of a new power. In the end we will better understand the whole society through its own feeling of what legitimate power is or should be.

In the history of the Western world (if one admits that this facet of history may be defined as such, and I find one reason to do so in the origins of that world in archaic Greece, so rich in specific kingdoms potentially open to evolution), one of the problems we periodically find is that of the permanent mutation of the image of kingship, the flexibility of the idea that governor and governed have of a personal power more or less felt as being sacred. The problem is coupled with that of permanent renewal, even as far as the destruction of that same power. This is because even if it evolves into absolute authority (and

---

[1] Turner (1984: 119–32).

that notion is often to be related to its specific cultural context), royal power whether in its ascending phase or in its decay is linked to the world which surrounds it by a network of more or less diffuse mutual obligations, mostly emerging from an ethical consensus. At that point, any ethical order distinguishing what is good, useful, or simply permitted, and what is a duty or simply a rule to be followed, is permanently redefined. Imagine the slow and complex development of royal ideology in France during the millennium which followed the ruin of the Carolingian imperial intermezzo. I allude to this development only because, even in the slow elaboration of a monarchic ideology under the Roman empire, there were, quite unconsciously, older paradigms such as the kings of Isocrates, Alexander and even our Ptolemy.

The last of these was a prominent member of the third generation in the huge adventure which drove Macedonia to the outer limits of the Achaemenid world and in the end ruined its own monarchy as well as those of its Eastern satellites. In the fourth century BC, the Macedonian monarchy was able to mobilise large economic resources; its opening to the new culture of the Greek cities had been a success, and it could adapt its own organisation to a panhellenic leadership destiny. Therefore Philip at first established hegemony over the greater part of geographic Greece. In the following generation, Macedonian military efficiency and economic power overwhelmed a part of Asia. Alexander followed his destiny blindly to the Indus, only to find himself master of an outsized empire, dying abruptly in Babylon. He thus left to his companions the unanticipated task of making something from an immense territory stretching from Cyrene to Afghanistan, and from the Lower Danube as far as the southern boundaries of Egypt. Some decades later, realms arose from that agglomerate, with territories and cities under the more or less direct authority of kings, *basileis*, of a new type. One of them was the realm of the Ptolemies, and eventually of some Cleopatras, with Egypt as an immediate source of wealth and Graeco-Macedonian Alexandria as the royal capital. Among the Hellenistic realms which dominated the era in the Balkans and in the East, that of the Ptolemies lasted the longest. In the end, it succumbed in 30 BC, due to the uncompromising policy of Octavian, but after having contaminated the minds of Caesar and Antony, and more insidiously Roman political thought on the eve of the empire. Alexandria continued to play a lasting and fundamental role in the further cultural and religious adventure of the Mediterranean world.

Alexander the Great was the king of the Macedonians and represented at first for his fellow travellers a Macedonian royal legitimacy, however ambiguous, based at the same time on a domestic tradition which had actually reserved the monarchy for the Argeads, descendants of Herakles and Zeus, for several generations, but always with the assent of the assembly of the nobility, which had to confirm or to establish the delegation of power. Under the successors of Alexander, many aspects of human relations in Hellenistic courts, not least in the organisation of the army and of the higher administration, had their roots in Macedonian traditions. But, at the same time, in the fourth century, Greek political thought had attempted to give rational content to the old concept of kingship. These thinkers essentially opposed the *basileus* and the *tyrannos* from the point of view of the ethics of power. At a time when, for example, rhetoricians like Isocrates, historians (including the Xenophon of the *Cyropaideia*), or philosophers, like Plato and later Aristotle, to quote only the most familiar names, had been examining the question of kingship, kingship was not merely a survival of pre-archaic Greece; it was still functional, in the double monarchy of Sparta, not to mention Macedonia. Even in the classical period, old royal responsibilities were more or less integrated into the aristocratic or democratic reorganisation of many Greek societies, for instance the *archon basileus* of Athens, with his traditional judicial and religious attributes. Numerous were the cities which had preserved a royal judiciary or a religious college of *basileis*.

For the average Greek, Greek kingship was intimately linked to a second point of reference: the *Iliad* and its images of pre-archaic kingship. Like the Macedonian monarchy, this joined the authority of the leader and the consensus of his fellow aristocratic warriors. The leader who violates this agreement falls into *hybris* and already prefigures tyranny, the corrupted form of kingship. Fourth-century political reflection on kingship was challenged by a double feeling. On the one hand, almost by definition, because the good king is a philosopher and because kingship by its nature acts according to the law, kingship either is law itself, or is the only power able to act with more efficiency and more justice than the law. On the other hand, and Aristotle expresses it best, monarchic power in the town can only end in tyranny, because it is incompatible with the equality of the citizens. Such a vision does not avoid contradictions, but, at least intellectually speaking, it changed the respectable image of the old Greek kingship into a concept of power linked with specific moral values, but eventually endangered by the weakness of human nature.

Now, in the Hellenistic period, royal ideology based itself on quite different values.[2] The king was essentially the winner, the saviour and the benefactor, the guarantor of peace and prosperity. His behaviour was essentially a *philanthropia*, an act of generosity. Furthermore, the effective exercise of power reveals the heroic and even divine nature of the *basileis*. Naturally, this new ideological basis is for the historian coupled with a substratum of complex sociological connivances: the king, at least in the Greek East, was also the symbolic link between heterogeneous components of the Greek minority power, while, among the Egyptians, as pharaoh, he was essentially the necessary intercessor between sky and earth in the only reference system of the native population, the traditional religion with its gods, its clergy and its rules.

How did the philosopher-king, the righteous king, transform himself into a victor-king who was essentially a saviour and a benefactor? In fact, the first generation of the successors of Alexander constitutes to a certain extent the missing link between the different types of kingship, as they were perceived in the fourth century, and Hellenistic monarchy. Among them, the first of the Ptolemies, the one to whom the Rhodians gave the epiclesis of *Soter*, the Saviour, can help us substantially fill the gap between the two royal ideologies.

Ptolemy was one of those future generals not at all prepared by their youth for an exceptional destiny. He was a member of the Macedonian minor nobility. The origin of his father, Lagos, as it seems, was not noteworthy, because Ptolemy did not follow the custom of giving to his eldest son the name of his paternal grandfather. The whole series of the Ptolemies was to be, until the end, Ptolemy son of a Ptolemy. In order to save appearances, opportunists easily established, probably very early on, genealogical links between Lagos and the Argeads. Some went even farther by 'revealing' that his mother conceived him during a furtive love affair with King Philip, which would make him an illegitimate brother of Alexander. But this history is too close – and not lacking in involuntary irony – to the confidence made by Ammon's oracle to Alexander that he was the son of Zeus, and not of Philip, for one to admit, with W. W. Tarn, that the legend was created by Ptolemy himself in order to be connected more directly with the dynasty of the Argeads. Such an excess of zeal was unnecessary. Through his mother, Ptolemy was descended from Amyntas I of Macedonia, thus from Herakles, son of Zeus. Under

---

[2] Walbank (1984: 61–111); Préaux (1978: esp. I, 181–293).

Ptolemy II, the official ideology, as it was sung by Theocritus, proclaimed that Alexander and Ptolemy Soter both had Herakles as ancestor. A later filiation of the Ptolemies would go back also as far as Zeus through Dionysos. Let us not doubt that this ideology of the divine ancestry of legitimate power was emphatically organised by Ptolemy Soter for himself, since his rivals Seleucus and Antigonus also justified their claims to royal power by their connections to the Argeads of Macedonia and their ancestry as Heraclidae. But this is to get ahead of ourselves.

In his youth, Ptolemy was probably part of a group which, in its proximity to the heir to the throne, made Philip anxious. At least, when he was about 25 years old, he was sent into exile by the king. When Alexander reached power, he called his friend back to his side. Nothing encourages us to believe that Ptolemy played an important role before the expedition to Asia, or even at the beginning of it. On the contrary, it ws only when the expedition got far to the East that he obtained important missions, mostly near Alexander himself. Alexander's history, written by Ptolemy and known to us indirectly through Arrian's *Anabasis*, shows, we shall see, a full approval of the policy of his leader, even in aspects which were violently disliked by his best comrades-in-arms. Anyway, at Alexander's death, this long allegiance and probably this intimacy assured Ptolemy of valuable claims, and following Alexander the Great's model was to be one of the ways that he would realise his ambitions, and later legitimise his throne.[3]

In 323, Alexander died, leaving an empire still in the stage of military occupation because there were too few people available to govern it and not enough experience in the management of such huge spaces. Facing a royal succession which fell at the worst possible moment, the companions of Alexander found a compromise solution. The throne was entrusted to the lineal heirs of Alexander's line, first to his illegitimate brother, the weak Philip Arrhidaeus, later to the posthumous son of Alexander and the Bactrian princess Roxane, the whole under the supervision of regents. The empire itself, however, was organised in 'supersatrapies' distributed among the leaders of the Macedonian aristocracy. Among these were four first-class plums: Babylonia, Asia Minor, Macedonia and Egypt.

Why did Ptolemy choose Egypt? Certainly he had recognised there the existence of wealth at hand, gold and especially wheat.

---

[3] The phenomenon is general in the world of Alexander's successors. See Goukowski (1978).

Furthermore, he realised that Alexandria, Alexander the Great's most prestigious city foundation, enabled him to obtain immediately the prestige linked with the recollection of the conqueror.

He pursued this symbolic line further. In a first episode he won a competition for the possession of Alexander's ashes against the regent Perdiccas, representing overall military power in the East. Probably arriving through Memphis, he conveniently neglected to transfer the ashes to Ammon's oasis, where Alexander had wished to find his ultimate rest. Later Alexandria was to host the grave of the Macedonian conqueror, which became the centre of a double cult, the cult of Alexander as founder of the town, a Greek tradition in full flower in Hellenistic times, and also the royal cult of Alexander. The priest of this cult, chosen among the court aristocracy, became the eponym of the royal calendar, and his priesthood was later coupled with cults dedicated to the deified kings. In our eyes, as modern historians, all this seems to conceal a worldly politico-religious preoccupation. In fact, it was surely a meaningful initiative, because Ptolemy entrusted the first priesthood of Alexander to his brother Menelaos, and that, unlike with later priests, for several years.[4]

Ptolemy chose still another way to suggest the symbiosis of his fate and that of Alexander: he wanted to be the historian of his model. We easily perceive there an ideological afterthought of political justification. Ptolemy, as a companion of the conqueror of Asia, wrote as historian a biography of Alexander, the exact title of which is unknown. It has generated a contradictory modern literature, more voluminous than what we have of the original work. Ptolemy is, naturally, present in the work that Paul Pedech has dedicated to the historians who were 'companions of Alexander'.[5] Ptolemy's book was a first-hand testimony, but it is known to us, for all intents and purposes, only from the use which Flavius Arrianus, a would-be Xenophon of the Second Sophistic, made of it in his *Anabasis of Alexander* in the second century AD.[6] Indeed, except for four fragments known from other authors, Strabo and Plutarch, and two later sources, the rest of what our collections preserve from Ptolemy consists of approximately thirty fragments in Jacoby's *Fragmente*, all passages from Arrian's *Anabasis*. It appears that they strictly follow Ptolemy's history. To this

[4] Clarysse and Van der Veken (1983), and especially for Menelaos, son of Lagos, p. 4.
[5] Pedech (1984).
[6] Vidal-Naquet (1984) admirably places the interaction of the treated subject and the complex personality of the writer and the ambiguity of his vision of Alexander's time, influenced by his own perception of the Roman empire, in the cultural context of the Second Sophistic.

historians and philologists add whatever they imagine they perceive in Arrian as coming from Ptolemy. Obviously, their points of view are divergent, to say the least. Among the most extreme, E. Kornemann (1935) considered that Arrian followed Ptolemy without any originality every time the subject of the multiple and contradictory personalities of Alexander arose. Elsewhere we find all the gradations of a more moderate judgement. One essentially refers to Arrian's passages where Ptolemy is named. Those that seem to be based on a direct participation in military operations could be easily added, especially when one assumes that Ptolemy was present, or those where one supposes that we are reading first-hand reactions to the behaviour of Alexander and his circle of acquaintances. All this means a vicious circle if one wants to establish that which concerns us here, namely, what image of his hero Ptolemy created, with more or less sincerity, and how he could have used it to justify himself in front of his subjects, his rivals, and later generations. Even one seeming anchor point does not save us. Arrian proclaims the respect which he feels for Ptolemy's history. He declares that he follows it in preference to all other sources, except perhaps Aristoboulus, who was also an eyewitness. He gives his ostensible reason in his foreword: 'It would be more shameful for Ptolemy to lie than for another historian' because he was a king. This does not help us very much, because this opinion probably reflects the idea that Arrian, a follower of Epictetus and servant of the imperial state, wished to put forward for the 'good prince' during the reigns of Hadrian or of Antoninus Pius more than it pleads for Ptolemy's truthfulness.

On the contrary, what moves us closer to our goal is Arrian's borrowings giving concrete expression to Ptolemy's idea of Alexander as a model of governance. The *Anabasis* of Arrian, and on this point there is no disagreement, depends especially on Ptolemy for technical data on routes and battles. But Ptolemy also seems to Arrian the privileged witness of the behaviour of Alexander and his Macedonian circle of acquaintances. This is doubtless clear, as Paul Pedech's analysis indirectly shows, when Arrian explains Alexander otherwise than Diodorus, Plutarch or Quintus Curtius, because the choice of a different version can be explained by the credit which he gives to Ptolemy. Alexander had moments of harsh cruelty, particularly towards some of his fellow warriors, and often under the influence of anger, even drunkenness. Now these crimes, or at least these excesses, Ptolemy, followed by Arrian, either overlooked or explained as the royal will to chastise intriguers and conspirators, of whose guilt Ptolemy was convinced.

The fact is that this justice in its severity had to remain coherent with the portrait which Ptolemy wanted to give in the course of his history of Alexander, that of an example for princes. This harshness appears elsewhere when he chastises indiscipline, breaches of trust or sacrilege. The acts of cruelty to the enemy are not hidden; Arrian tries to explain them, generally by the duplicity or the treason of the opponent. But Alexander is also the generous prince, whose severity can give way to leniency and to pity. And, in parallel, he is the leader who wages war with lucidity, logic, and concern to avoid useless losses.

Why such a divergence between Alexander's portrait according to Ptolemy and less edifying material in the other sources? Two explanations come to mind, and they are not contradictory. First let us take into account Ptolemy's old friendship for a companion of his youth. Did Alexander not include him in the most exalting part of the adventure that brought them together as far as the Indus? But friendship explains only part of the distortion. Above all, this portrait of Alexander as generally rational and fair is at the same time an indirect plea on behalf of Ptolemy's seizure of power and for the way in which he reached it, in so far as how he handled events was in accordance with the model set forth in the history. This implies that, by the end of the fourth century,[7] the public to whom Ptolemy's writing was addressed already saw Alexander in the idealised image which is inevitably attached to the successful conqueror, to the exceptional nature of his fate, and to a death as untimely as that of Achilles. This implies also that Ptolemy perceived in the minds of his potential readers a new political frame of reference. For this reason it is interesting to analyse a viewpoint wherein Alexander strangely overlaps

[7] Nothing allows us to date the work of Ptolemy to his old age. F. Jacoby, *Fragmente der griechischen Historiker* II, B, *Komm.* (1962: 499), sees there 'wohl sicher ein Werk seines Alters, wenn es sich auch nicht beweisen laszt' ('surely a work of his old age, even if this cannot be proven'), but recognises that the only *terminus post quem* would be situated around the year 310; one can date to this period the *Life of Alexander* by Clitarchus, which Ptolemy used. There is no reason to see in Ptolemy's book *Memories* (Jacoby 1962: 484) a title that would suggest a work of his later years, when it would announce a critical questioning of the contemporaneous historians of Alexander as early as the end of the fourth century, which Ptolemy's book does not seem to have been. On the contrary, it is easier to find there a book written in the period when most ancient histories of Alexander and his imperial enterprise appeared. Ptolemy could simultaneously signal his own existence for the future, justify his eminent place among the successors, and create a model of heroic kingship where the reader would discover his own personality. Cf. Goukowski (1978: 141–5) on the date and the character of the book. The way Arrian qualifies Ptolemy's testimony as a 'royal' one does not seem to me to imply inevitably that the accession to the diadem is a *terminus post quem* for the work, but even in that case it would not appreciably modify the date of its composition.

the image which Ptolemy, as diplomat, strategist and rigorous leader, wanted to give of himself in his own lifetime, even if we think that his reign could have had better justifications than as a mere imitation of Alexander.[8] His ambitious Greek enterprise of 308 was an error of judgement; but Ptolemy not only overcame that, but actually took advantage of it, in spite of the severity of his defeat near Salamis in Cyprus. It shows in an eloquent way his refusal to succumb to disaster. As a ruler and diplomat and as a strategist, Ptolemy was shrewd and rational, and, even when harsh, he found a guarantor in Alexander, or rather in his representation of Alexander, remodelled with the clear conscience of an old friendship.

Ptolemy's history after Alexander's death is that of a powerful and ambitious satrap, a satrap who at once marked his independence. From the point of view of his home policy, he immediately eliminated Cleomenes, a citizen of the Greek polis of Naucratis in the Delta to whom Alexander had entrusted the management of Egypt and the first stages of the development of Alexandria. The anonymous *Economics*, which found its way into the Aristotelian corpus, enumerates the means which this wily spirit found to fill the treasury. The Naucratite had a lot of enemies, but, as it seems, the understanding and support of Alexander, who needed a safe income rather than an ideal governor. After the death of Alexander, Cleomenes found himself naturally under the allegiance of the regent Perdiccas, wishing surely to ensure the subordinate role reserved for him following Ptolemy's arrival in the satrapy. One of the first tasks of the latter was to push aside the very man to whom he owed the wealth and the fleet he found in Alexandria. Accused probably of misappropriation of public funds – something that must have been obvious enough in the functions which he occupied – Cleomenes was executed. The new satrap showed by this that he had the makings of a king, or, not to

---

[8] One could compare with the features of Alexander as a model of kingship the admirable portrait of Ptolemy by Eric Turner (1984: 122): 'Mentally and physically vigorous (he fathered an heir at the age of sixty), he was a man of action who successfully submitted to the discipline of intelligent diplomacy and policy, and refused to be discouraged by apparent failure. As brave and skillful captain, sage judge of men and affairs, memoir-writer and hail-fellow-well-met he knew how to attract friends of both sexes and to hold their loyalty. It was an age when a man could not carve out a career for himself without carving out careers for his friends. Success depended on attracting men of adequate calibre for the tasks that were also their opportunities, on rewarding and defending them, and continually consulting them about innovations of policy. The need for a springboard to satisfy his personal ambition was what attracted Soter to Egypt. No deeper motive need be looked for.' The ambiguity which the son of Lagos created in Alexandrian opinion and in ancient historiography with the phantom Alexander–Ptolemy still exists, but in the reverse direction.

get ahead of the narrative, at least of an Alexander, a hard but pure upholder of the law.

I cannot rewrite here the history of the first years of Ptolemy as satrap. He was the soul of the coalition against the regent, who, marching against him, would in the end be murdered in Egypt by his own soldiers. Ptolemy was also the wise man who, on this occasion, refused the offer, coming from this same Macedonian army, to assume the regency for the young kings. From his foreign policy, made of wars and diplomacy, let us retain the deceptive character of his title of satrap, normally that of a simple administrator of a territory. We find indeed a royal vision in his early decision to secure at once three bastions of the Mediterranean East: Palestine, Cyprus and Cyrenaica. Already, his multiple prestigious gestures in Delos and elsewhere in Greece, his dedications, wheat or troops, represented probably not so much the first stages of a rising imperialism as an attempt to display royal behaviour. Papyrologists illustrate the ambiguity of his status by quoting the double dating that appears on the most ancient Greek document of Egypt to bear an exact date, a marriage contract of the year 311 from Elephantine. According to custom, the date is fixed by regnal year 7 of Alexander, son of Alexander and Roxane. However, what is without parallel in our surviving documents but was surely typical in Egypt of this period, the scribe added a second date, year 14 of the satrap Ptolemy. By what subtle power-play, or tacit acceptance by general opinion of a vague notion of substitute kingship, did one arrive at a formula which emphasises the importance of the year 14? Year 14 is fixed by Alexander's death and thus defines the true transmission of power, the one that privileges the man who since Alexander's death was the rescuer and defender of Macedonian Egypt. This same year 311 had been catastrophic for Ptolemy in Syria and in Palestine, but it was also the year of the treaty of 311, a mere scrap of papyrus in its territorial clauses, but actually the implicit realisation of the division of the empire into five large entities. Soon after that, in 304, after a brief interregnum and the destruction of the dynasty of the Argeads by murder (a characteristic move in Macedonian royal politics), and following the example of his main rivals, Ptolemy assumed the royal diadem, all the while continuing to reckon his Greek regnal years as if he had succeeded Alexander, his model, in 323.[9]

---

[9] On the contrary, the Egyptians, who, whatever their social status might be, had in their separate system specific connections with the pharaoh, followed a different enumeration for the regnal year in the documents drawn in their native language: year 1 in 305/304 is the one when Ptolemy officially succeeded the ghost king Alexander IV. Cf. Pestman (1967: 12–17).

There is another fruitful level of investigation into Ptolemy's search for legitimacy, as remote from classic political devices as the writings of Ptolemy as historian were: the Museum of Alexandria and the Library, its most precious section, which Ptolemy created and which his successors enriched by dedicating to it considerable financial means.[10] The Museum and the Library were not isolated creations. The royal cities and the large Hellenistic cities had their own libraries, sometimes flanked by a centre for philological or philosophical studies. Not all of them were inspired by the Alexandrian model, and some even preceded it. Still, many aspects of the enterprise make Alexandria stand out. First of all, the mobilisation of competencies and financial means indicate a scale where the phenomenon becomes a deliberate political act. Furthermore there is also the gigantic effort of assemblage of classic Greek literature, medicine and science that occurred in the Museum during its acme. No other library, not even Pergamum, made available such a universality of erudite and scientific creation. This is not the place for the history of the Museum and its Library, nor of their direct and indirect repercussions in the pre-Christian Mediterranean, and later in several religious and philosophic movements. In addition there were also the grammatical and logical foundations of literary debate, the scientific language, even the seeds of the later theological quarrels of the Western world. Certainly the cultural weight of the Museum is bound to the vitality of Alexandria, with its Graeco-Macedonian diaspora, particularly the brains drained from Greece, and other diasporas, such as that of the Jews, and later important sects coming from the East. But in our inquiry what is important is the fact that the Museum, the creation of the first Ptolemy, was a royal creation, because it came after the seizure of the diadem and was essentially an appendix to the palace. The scholars, the books and the first scientific equipment concentrated there served the prestige of the king. Scholars were also at the disposal of the monarchy: the example of Philitas shows that one of the duties of the librarians of the Museum was to provide private tutors to the royal children.[11]

The idea of the Museum arose perhaps in Cos, Ptolemy's summer residence, where the future Ptolemy II was later born. An old medical tradition and a vivacious literary movement were flourishing in the island. The philologist and poet Philitas of Cos, a prefiguration of the

[10] On the Museum, the Library and the librarians of Alexandria, one will consult, for example, Pfeiffer (1968) and Fraser (1972: esp. I, 305–479; II, 462–692).

[11] On the royal character of the institution, see Bingen (1988).

poet-philologists Apollonios of Rhodes, Callimachus and the other Eratosthenes, became the private tutor of the young heir, but also supplied the king with the first director of the Library of Alexandria, his pupil Zenodotos of Ephesos, the ancestor of modern philology. Ptolemy entrusted the organisation of the new centre to the Athenian politician and philosopher Demetrios of Phaleron. The contempt of this man for democracy and his pro-Macedonian feelings had conveniently led to his exile to the Egyptian El Dorado. We know that Demetrios became an influential adviser in numerous domains. Not only could the introduction of Athenian law (as distinct from its democratic polity) in Alexandria not have been achieved without the full agreement of the king, but it was probably an initiative of a sovereign anxious to assert and to legitimise the very real Hellenic character of his new capital. A follower of Aristotle by way of the teaching of his master Theophrastus, Demetrios brought to the Museum the encyclopedic spirit of the Lyceum and the peripatetic taste for description, explanation and classification of living phenomena, intellectual creations and institutions. Did he inspire in Ptolemy (and his own successors) the will to supply the new institution and its direction with the best people in the Greek world, one of the rare qualities which make the most prominent kings?

Why was the idea of a Museum, a sanctuary of the Muses flanked by the richest library in the world, able to seduce Ptolemy, now the king, and incite him to dedicate considerable sums to the enterprise? It is difficult to escape the conclusion that beyond the real prestige of the project (but the choice of prestige is already a political act and a social programme), the king found in this creation and its exceptional dimensions the convergence at a high level of two legitimacies: Macedonian royal legitimacy and Greek cultural legitimacy. Already, in the fifth century, the kings of Macedonia had attracted Greek writers, such as Euripides in his old age, disappointed by the rather cool reception which the Athenians gave his 'new theatre'. Other Greek intellectuals were later welcomed by King Philip of Macedonia, who entrusted the education of his son Alexander to Aristotle, symbol of the partnership of Macedonia in the new Greek cultural space. This intellectual tradition continued in the Macedonian court, with its library, poets and scholars. Some of these were encouraged by Zenodotos to join Alexandria.

But next to this royal vision, another field of prestige and legitimacy was highlighted by the creation of the large library of Alexandria: Athens and its cultural traditions, still flourishing despite the political decline of the city. There the first libraries were organised to support philosophical discussion. Aristotle gathered in the library of the Lyceum the books on which he built most of his treatises with his assistants and his students; this library was certainly the model which Philitas or Demetrios could propose to Ptolemy, a model that could be developed on the scale of the enormous funds which the expansion of the Greek world had released, especially in Egypt. Neither Ptolemy nor his first successors skimped on the means, licit or not, which would allow them to exceed everybody. 'In the house of the rich, everything is rich', said Theocritus, speaking about the palace of Alexandria. The enumeration of the Greek regions which supplied the Museum with scholars and books widens this image. It reveals that beyond Athens as the model for the concept of a polyvalent library and for Alexandria's laws, European and Asian Greece contributed to the sum of literary, medical and scientific Hellenism, which the Ptolemies wanted to offer to an elite working in the shadow of the palace. Because of it, a large part of this treasure escaped disappearance, for Alexandria, often without our knowing, was the necessary passage for most of what classical antiquity has bequeathed to us. Even if most of the achievements of the Museum are later than the first reign, what could be a more prestigious title to Greek legitimacy than to be the prince who was the patron of the search for a more authentic *Iliad*?

This remark nevertheless demands further qualification. It would be too hasty to think that Ptolemy was a 'nouveau riche' who wanted to surround himself with shelves of rare books, because he was probably himself a distinguished mind. But, for this self-made man who became a king only through his merit, the pretension that the throne took over the cultural traditions of the Macedonian court and of Greek society and its learned schools claims a supplementary legitimacy. It reveals also that, in a Greek world abruptly fragmented across three continents, people were supposed to recognise that such a process was a new manifestation of legitimacy. Surely, in his book, Ptolemy eventually displayed how little he thought of the Greeks, but this was the reflex of a Macedonian aristocrat,[12] and such feelings were perfectly compatible with an unreserved admiration for a Greek culture which Macedonia had long declared to be its own. It would be unfair to apply modern parallels to the distinction often made

---

[12] This feature is particularly highlighted in the section that P. Pedech (1984) dedicates to Ptolemy, especially pp. 257–63.

Figure 1.1   *Tetradrachm of Ptolemy I Soter (Alexandria, c. 305–285 BC).*
Bibliothèque royale de Belgique, coll. L. de Hirsch 1800 (14.87g) (enlarged)

between people from a specific culture and what their culture actually produced.

A final reflection: Alexandria was interested in the history of Egypt and, more generally, in peripheral cultures. But this was a problem of mentality and not of politics. Egypt, a distant and wise Egypt, had already been for centuries an object of admiration in Greece. In the new interest in those populations that the Greeks sometimes met in Alexandria, there was an element of exoticism, a lot of routine in the observation of the world abroad, never the desire to associate the indigenous to the work of the Greek scholars. Manetho was an exceptional answer to the need to have chronologically classified an Egypt which the Greeks had been admiring for generations. It had nothing to do with the exploited people the immigrants met in their daily activities.[13]

---

[13] In another domain, a monument as impressive as the translation of the *Septuaginta* is foreign to the basic dynamics of the Museum.

However, this quest for legitimacy did not target the Egyptian population, even though they formed a huge majority, because a majority is irrelevant when power lies elsewhere. The Egyptian clergy was offering legitimacy to Ptolemy because it was a ritual necessity. If one wanted to ensure perpetuity to the world, it was necessary that a pharaoh act as an intermediary between humanity and the gods; he must constantly carry out the gestures of worship and offering, pronounce formulae all through the year. And, not being able to do it everywhere himself, he accomplished this on the walls of the temples with the help of his uncountable reliefs, repetitive in their gestures and their texts. At his arrival, Alexander was greeted as pharaoh and was represented as such in the traditional adornments. He became a god when he died and had his own chapels. In the Demotic documents, the Egyptian scribes, as we have said, dated according to regnal years, following after the death of the pharaoh Alexander a formal succession, Pharaoh Philip, then Pharaoh Alexander, the first a half-brother and the latter the posthumous son of Alexander the Great; still later, Pharaoh Ptolemy when he had proclaimed himself king – thus for the Egyptians, and them alone, pharaoh of Egypt. The disparity we noted, which makes it such that in 304 year 1 of Ptolemy in the Egyptian document is year 19 as noted on the Greek document, is the result of the coexistence of two impervious reference systems.[14] The Egyptian system adopts a passive routine legitimacy, because it needs a sovereign. The Graeco-Macedonian one follows an aggressive dialectic of royal legitimacy based on a subjective reference, the immediate continuity from Alexander the Great to Ptolemy, a continuity later inserted into the new conception of the heroic, even divine nature of kingship.

There are other issues that might also be brought into the discussion, particularly on the religious side in Egypt and in the Aegean Sea, or on the emerging notions of deification, of royal victory, benefaction and protection. We would find there in the behaviour of Ptolemy the same effort to accumulate signs of legitimacy around the notion of actual power, born when he was put in charge of Egypt, and openly proclaimed when he decided he was a king. They had for Ptolemy, but also for us, the interest of being recognised as a king in the new world which was arising. Here, I have developed two of his strategies. First

---

[14] In Chapter 14, I have tried to define and to explain the relative impermeability of the two cultures present in Egypt, on one side a culturally closed system for the Egyptians, on the other a Greek structural system which protected the minority holders of the administrative, military and economic power.

was the model supplied by Alexander, even if the model was probably adapted to the programme of Ptolemy from the beginning; and second, the effort of the new king to create near the palace the major sanctuary of Greek culture in the reorganisation of a world where decisions were prepared and dictated in the Greek language.

Chapter 2

PTOLEMY III AND PHILAE: SNAPSHOT OF A REIGN, A TEMPLE AND A CULT

◌⟋

The famous and much-visited site of Philae is dominated by the large sanctuary of Isis, with its pylons, its Mammisi, its hybrid pronaos – simultanously courtyard and hypostyle hall – and, last but not least, in the north, its massive naos of Ptolemy II Philadelphos. The building process of this composite yet rather homogeneous complex went on all throughout the Hellenistic period.[1]

The cult of Isis in Philae was not old. The dismantling and rebuilding of the monuments in connection with the building of the High Dam at Aswan revealed the remains of a modest kiosk with the name of Psammetichus II, probably connected with the introduction of the cult of an Isis from the Delta when Saite troops were quartered at the southern frontier of Egypt.[2] And it has been possible to determine the plan of the small temple of Amasis, the existence of which is already attested in the twenty-sixth dynasty.[3] The reign of Nectanebo I is linked with other structures, among them a doorway later included in the large first pylon and the kiosk which was rebuilt in the late Hellenistic period at the opposite end of the southern esplanade.[4]

There is thus no evidence suggesting that before the reign of Ptolemy II, the cult of Isis in Philae was anything more than a modest cult honoured by the garrison and by the local population.[5] The construction

---

[1] Two recent contributions shed new light on the history of the sanctuary: Haeny (1985) takes advantage of the observations made when the monuments were disassembled and removed; Vassilika (1989), through an attentive analysis of the decoration of the temple, was able to get indirectly into more detail for the chronology of the building process. Porter and Moss (1939: 203–50) remains an indispensable tool.

[2] Haeny (1985: 202). As far as current evidence shows, when more ancient (New Kingdom, Taharqa), the stones seem to be reused building material brought from neighbouring sites (Haeny 1985: 200–2).

[3] Haeny (1985: 204).

[4] Haeny (1985: 204).

[5] Cf. Haeny (1985: 206–8), including the hypothesis, unnecessary in my view, that the decision to build the new temple was taken during the reign of Ptolemy I Soter. The reign of Ptolemy II was exceptionally long and there were still a lot of cartouches to be filled in with the name of the pharaoh when Ptolemy III succeeded to the throne.

of the large naos of Ptolemy II, a deliberate act of religious policy, marked a decisive stage in the development of the sanctuary and established the prestige of the goddess, installed at the doorway of Nubia, a region which she was to conquer in the following centuries. This impressive monument introduces us to the brief interlude in the Greek epigraphy of Egypt to which this chapter is devoted. It has the modest ambition of calling to mind two things less evident in practice than in theory: first, that it is necessary to give attention to the most modest details, in pursuit of our duty to make the edition of an inscription the true image of the original, because only this can lead us to a precise interpretation of the document; and second, that the attempt to restore an inscription to its exact archaeological context is often the only route towards giving the text its appropriate historical value.

I   The Text

OGIS 61 = *I. Philae* I 4 has not left impressive traces in the scholarly literature, hardly more than successive editions. The first edition published the inscription with some degree of vagueness, from the point of view both of the text and of the location of the inscription.[6] Nevertheless, the document is not unimportant, first because it probably constitutes Philae's oldest Greek inscription (it is at least the first of the rare Greek monumental inscriptions of the site),[7] and secondly because it is, strictly speaking, a royal inscription. Here is the text, as I read it, engraved all in one line:

Βασιλεὺς Πτολεμαῖος βασιλέως Πτολεμαίου καὶ Ἀρσινόης Θεῶν Ἀδελφῶν καὶ βασίλισσα Βερενίκη ἡ βασιλέως Πτολεμαίου ἀδελφὴ καὶ γυνὴ καὶ τὰ τούτων τεκνία τὸν ναὸν Ἴσει καὶ Ἁρποχράτηι.

---

[6] A rather hasty editio princeps in Mahaffy (1899: 199, n. 1) (from a copy of Lyons). This edition is used by M. L. Strack, *APF* 1 (1901) 205, no. 14, who erroneously divides the text into four lines, followed in this by W. Dittenberger, *OGIS* I (1903) 61, reproduced by F. Bilabel, *SB* V (1950) 8859, and Fraser (1972: II, 412, n. 567). All of them are dependent on the readings of Mahaffy. Newly edited from the original by A. Bernand (1969: 78–87, no. 4, with pl. 27) (the southern doorway of the naos; but the inscription is not visible), with a good photograph of the squeeze [paper or latex impression of an inscription], pl. 28 [*I. Philae* I 4]. Cf. my remarks in *CdE* 46 (1971) 409 (= *Pages* I, 137).

[7] In Philae 'monumental' epigraphy is something quite different from 'parietal' epigraphy, the graffiti and inscriptions which cover the great pylon and some columns of the first courtyard. The latter is a later phenomenon, which appears only after the beginning of the first century BC. On this subject, see J. Bingen, *CdE* 46 (1971) 409, and *Pages* I, 136–7, particularly about *SB* I 4087 = *I. Philae* I 14, dated 19 October 89 and not 28 October 142, a dating based on an erroneous reading of the regnal year; Totti (1985: 86, no. 26) regrettably follows the text and date proposed in *I. Philae* I 14.

τέκνα edd. | Ἁρποκράτηι Mahaffy (Dittenberger, Bilabel, Fraser; Ἁρποχράτηι Strack) Ἁρπο{πο}κράτηι Bernand Ἁρποχράτηι Bingen.

King Ptolemy, son of King Ptolemy and Arsinoe Gods Adelphoi, and Queen Berenike, sister and wife of King Ptolemy, and their children (dedicated) this temple to Isis and Harpocrates.

A very simple text, but by no means 'banal'. To the two propositions offered earlier, we may add a third: let us not decree too quickly that a document is commonplace.

I note first three elements of the formula to which I shall return. As I said, we find here strictly speaking a royal inscription, because the royal dedicants are quoted in the nominative case, as the subjects. On the other hand, the ruling couple does not yet carry the divine titulature *Theoi Euergetai*, although the parents of the king enjoy that of *Theoi Adelphoi*, 'the Gods Brother and Sister'. Finally, the queen, who is not a sister of the king, none the less carries the title of 'sister and wife of king Ptolemy'; this fiction was moreover the rule from the beginning of the reign.[8]

Mahaffy, Strack, Dittenberger and Bilabel date the inscription implicitly or explicitly 'in the reign of Ptolemy III'. André Bernand,

---

[8] As noted in the critical apparatus, the establishment of the text is problematic only in two places. The spelling of Harpocrates' name is discussed in Appendix II. The other is τεκνία. Ptolemy III Euergetes and Berenike associated their children with them in the dedication. In the inscriptions of the Ptolemaic period, the words καὶ τὰ τούτων τέκνα are the normal and very frequent formula when royal children are associated with the sovereigns. This formula has been handed down for our inscription, for nearly a century, from one edition to the next, even including the last one, that of A. Bernand, even though that is based, for the first time, on a direct reading of the document and on a squeeze. Now the photograph of the squeeze (cf. above, n. 6) does not leave any doubt about the text: Philae's inscription has καὶ τὰ τούτων τεκνία. All in all, it makes only a very slender iota of difference. Nevertheless this iota is not an insignificant detail, because the use of the diminutive τεκνία is completely remarkable in such a remote time; it is not present in the other Ptolemaic official inscriptions in Philae, *I. Philae* I 8, a dedication of the temple of Imhotep to Asklepios by Ptolemy V and Cleopatra I (186 or shortly afterwards), and *I. Philae* I 17, a dedication of the temple of Hathor to Aphrodite by Ptolemy VIII, Cleopatra II and Cleopatra III (139–132 or 124–116).

Certainly, the word is familiar to us through John's Gospel (13: 33), where Jesus addresses his followers, τεκνία, ἔτι μικρὸν μεθ' ὑμῶν εἰμι, in fact a vocative where the diminutive has only an affective value. The later success of this diminutive in Christian literature is due surely to its presence in a gospel (cf. also the other New Testament occurrences of the word, all but one in the Epistles of John and all used in the vocative plural), but that is only an aspect of its well-attested use in Greek of the imperial period, with an indisputable loss of its value as diminutive with regard to τέκνον. (For the classical period, LSJ quotes only τεκνίδιον (Aristophanes, *Lysistrata* 889) as diminutive of τέκνον. According to H. J. M. Milne, in his introduction to *P. Lit. Lond.* 84 (second century AD), a fragment of an unknown drama, 'the use of the word τεκνία [marks] the play as postclassical'.) We shall try to estimate later the weight which we have to accord to such an unexpected early use of the diminutive τεκνίον.

I. Philae I, p. 78, places it under 'Ptolemy III Euergetes' reign (246–221 BC), at least one year after the birth of the future Philopator, born towards 244'. This last assertion is contradicted by the absence of *Theoi Euergetai* in the titulature. We shall see that it is, on the contrary, necessary to place the inscription towards the end of 245 or in 244.

II   THE LOCATION OF THE TEXT

One of the reasons why the inscription has not so far sufficiently attracted the attention of historians is the rather fanciful way its editors and commentators have described the location of the inscription on the dark wall which constitutes today the back wall of the pronaos of Ptolemy VI, decorated under Ptolemy VIII. Mahaffy places the inscription 'over the north portal of the great hall of columns', true from the point of view of the modern visitor, but totally anachronistic, as we shall see, for the epigraphist and the archaeologist. Strack briefly locates the inscription 'am Isistempel über dem Nordthor' (in the Isis temple, over the North Gate);[9] this has no meaning in Philae, whether we take 'Isis temple' in the restricted meaning of 'temple of Ptolemy II' or in the broader sense of 'sanctuary of Isis' in its widest topographical extension.[10] Neither has a 'north gate'. Derivative editions follow suit.[11] For P. M. Fraser, the inscription is 'on the architrave of the temple of Isis'. The last editor of the text, A. Bernand, places it 'sur la corniche du pronaos du temple d'Isis'.[12] He even explains some hesitancies of the engraver by the fact that he was working 'in this badly lit place' ('dans cet endroit mal éclairé').

Today it is indeed true that the place is badly lit, but once more the remark is anachronistic. To be sure, a visitor wishing to visit the inner naos of Ptolemy II today comes from the south of the sanctuary, passing through the portal of Nectanebo (which was included in the

---

[9] Probably this is responsible for a misunderstanding in Hölbl (1994: 79), who, exploiting *I. Philae* I, believes that the inscription is connected with the construction of a 'zusätzliches Heiligtum für Isis und Harpokrates' under Ptolemy III near the Mammisi.

[10] I use the word 'naos' or 'temple of Ptolemy II' when referring to the actual temple of Isis, the massive building in the northern part of the architectural complex which evolved throughout the Hellenistic period. I call this larger sacred complex 'sanctuary of Isis'. I avoid referring to the 'temple of Isis', an expression which is, as I show here, quite ambiguous.

[11] Dittenberger borrows from Strack an unfortunate *supra portam septentrionalem templi Isidis* (over the north gate of the temple of Isis), which Bilabel renders as 'über dem Nordtor des Isistempel'.

[12] *I. Philae* I 78, and pl. 27.

Figure 2.1   *Philae, sanctuary of Isis, second pylon (photo Jean Bingen)*

first pylon), and crosses the courtyard of the Mammisi. Further north, the second pylon provides access to the pronaos of Ptolemy VI. At the other end of the hypostyle part of the pronaos, one perceives in the twilight what wrongly appears to be the north wall of the pronaos, in the middle of which it is possible to distinguish a doorway leading into the large naos of Ptolemy II. But the architectural complex which our visitor just went through did not exist at the beginning of the reign of Ptolemy III, except for Nectanebo's small portal. When it was built, the bare, squat mass of the temple of Ptolemy II was completely isolated, with its proper north-northeast orientation.[13] The inside of the naos, with its maze of rooms and passages, had been decorated with a profusion of reliefs explained by texts, the symbolic permanence of the saving ritual gestures of the pharaoh Philadelphos.[14] To this profusion of images the priests opposed the merciless nudity of the high outside walls of the naos. In the north, west and east, these were to be decorated only in the Roman imperial period; the south facade, by contrast, was decorated under Ptolemy VIII, after Ptolemy VI's pronaos had been stuck on the naked facade of the naos.

Naturally, the bareness of this southern facade of the naos, not in the least dark but at that time flooded with tropical sun, had been a little smoothed since Ptolemy II's reign: a gateway with a traditional cavetto cornice was opened in the centre; a string of panels with reliefs and hieroglyphs on the lintel and the jambs of the doorway framed the door, images which are a priority in the decoration of a temple.[15] In her *Ptolemaic Philae*, Eleni Vassilika strikingly studied the 'grammar of the temple', which, using parallelisms and oppositions, orders all the internal decoration of the naos and which, here also, fixed contents and motifs for the panels of the gate and their mutual connections. Speaking about the outside decoration of the south door of the naos, she declares, 'Ptolemy II did identify himself and the goddess for whom he built the Isis temple.'[16] Harpocrates does not appear there; so also, he appears only occasionally, alone and in an adventitious way, in the internal decoration of the naos.

---

[13] The only possible nearby construction was the remains of Amasis' small temple; but that structure, which masked the entrance of the new temple, was certainly demolished at the latest when the new building was opened for cult use.

[14] The internal decoration was already completed when Ptolemy II died. Some cartouches next to reliefs which are part of the global plan of the decoration and certainly represent Ptolemy II are filled with the name of Ptolemy III.

[15] Vassilika (1989: 45): 'The doorway, or at least its face visible to the entering visitor, was an early priority for the decorators, as it allowed ready identification of the building and its benefactor.' Cf. Porter and Moss (1939: 238, nos. 286–7), who correctly consider that the outside decoration of the gate is connected with the internal decoration of the naos of Ptolemy II and not with that of the pronaos.

[16] Vassilika (1989: 27).

III Two Significant Abnormalities

Two dreadful mistakes of 'grammar' were committed on this south facade, however profusely illuminated by the sun it was. The first is due to the master of the building of the temple. At the beginning of Ptolemy III's reign,[17] he had a unique relief with three figures cut at the foot of the south facade,[18] next to the lower panels of the Western post of Ptolemy II's gate. The king, followed by queen Berenike, offers land to the goddess Isis. As Eleni Vassilika showed, this relief, which begins the decoration from the bottom and not from the top, has no symmetrical counterpart on the other side of the gate and represents in this way an unusual initiative. It is, moreover, so unusual that, to save the 'grammar of the temple', the later decoration of the wall under Ptolemy VIII had to begin by producing a parallel and inverted scene on the East side of the gate: the king, Cleopatra II and Cleopatra III offer fields to Isis in the same way.[19] The other scenes on the wall were then carved on the scale of the relief of Ptolemy III.

The other hitch in the 'grammar of the temple' is situated on the rounded crown of the gate. Our Greek inscription was engraved throughout the fillet which bounds it above. For the sacred architects of Philae, one need hardly say, this traditional narrow flat space in such a space above a gate was not intended to carry an inscription, most definitely not a Greek inscription, a real solecism in the integrated vocabulary developed by the architect, the sculptor and the master of the hieroglyphs decorating the naos. How was it possible to achieve both 'abnormalities'?

IV The Royal Visit

To explain the unusual initiative which created the asymmetrical scene of Ptolemy III's offering, sculpted at the level of the eyes of passers-by, Vassilika offers the hypothesis that this relief was engraved on the occasion of a royal visit to Isis's temple early in the reign of this king. Greek epigraphy adds a series of corresponding considerations which, in my opinion, transform this hypothesis into certainty.

---

[17] Basing her conclusions on obvious stylistic arguments, Vassilika rightly concluded that the relief, strictly similar in its workmanship to the reliefs of the naos of Ptolemy II, is older than those that appear on the part of the Mammisi that was built later and decorated during the reign of Ptolemy III.

[18] Porter and Moss (1939: no. 276). See especially Vassilika (1989: 64–69, 202, and pl. XXII, D and E).

[19] Vassilika (1989: pl. XXII); Porter and Moss (1939: VI, 234–5, no. 283).

Figure 2.2   I. Philae 4 *(photo after A. Bernand,* Les Inscriptions grecques et latines de Philae I, *pl. 28, by permission of CNRS Editions)*

The relief, placed there to be seen by the king and the queen when they were penetrating into the naos, should fix for eternity the renewal by the young king of the endowment-gift of the Dodeka-schoinos to Isis of Philae. In the same way, the Greek inscription, brilliantly heightened with red, was engraved there, at the top of the gate flooded with sun, to be seen in the same circumstances. Two other features of the inscription confirm this presence of the sovereigns. The first is the syntax, which mentions in the nominative the royal couple as the originator of the inscription of the temple; it is most easily explained by the actual presence of the dedicators.[20] On the opposite assumption, the inscription would have represented a false appropriation of the royal voice and would have been difficult to explain. Even more interesting is the use of the word *teknia* (Greek τεκνία). Here, as in the case of the relief of Ptolemy III, the word must be understood as an unusual and especially contingent feature. Indeed, at this time and in such a context, the word is certainly used as a diminutive and has meaning only when referring to a concrete reality. Any inscription which quotes the king in the nominative was certainly engraved with the agreement of the royal authorities and was drafted under the control of the royal chancellery. To use in the formula *teknia*, 'the small crown princes', instead of the traditional *tekna*, an abstract notion which widens the epigraphic initiative to the totality of the royal family, is explicable only by a desire to highlight the presence in Philae of royal children of an exceptionally young age.

This is perfectly suitable for the date at which the inscription must be placed. The document is earlier than the creation of the Alexandrian cult of the *Theoi Euergetai* in the first half of year 243 or a little before, and this cult must have been created only after Ptolemy III's return from Philae to Alexandria.[21] On the other hand, the couple's

[20] In his *Recherches pour servir à l'histoire de l'Égypte* (Paris 1823), that monument of papyrology's protohistory, Letronne had already perceived the importance of this type of document: 'quand les noms du roi et de la reine sont mis au nominatif . . . il s'agit d'une opération, résultat des chefs du gouvernement' (p. 62), about the Antaiopolis royal inscription *OGIS* 109.

[21] The new eponymous formula with the Gods Euergetai appears in Philadelphia in the Fayyum on 19 August 243 BC in *PSI* IV 389, drafted in the beginning of the month of Epeiph of Macedonian year 5, if not necessarily on the first day of the month. But the creation of the cult and, probably connected to it, that of the royal epiclesis can be situated some time before

marriage took place a little while before Ptolemy II's death (in January 246); the Third Syrian War had quickly separated the couple. Announced as an expedition of support for the dynastic claims of the sister of the king, the widow of Antiochus II, the war changed after her death into a gigantic raid. Ptolemy III pushed as far as Mesopotamia, then interrupted the expedition to go back to Egypt with his booty in the second quarter of 245 or sometime later.[22] On the reasons for this return, our sources are laconic and of low quality. Was it due to an Aἰγυπτίων ἀπόστασις (as is said in *P. Haun.* 6), which means a 'desertion of the troops brought from Egypt' rather than a 'native revolt'? Or, according to late sources,[23] was it caused by a *domestica seditio*? The words suit intrigues in the palace rather than revolt. Reconciling these two hints ends in an uprising which the king would have quickly repressed;[24] anyway, it is probably on the occasion of this return or of these events that, late in 245 or next year in 244, the royal couple went up the Nile as far as Philae with their young children, probably two, and dedicated the temple of Ptolemy II to Isis and Harpocrates.[25]

V HARPOCRATES AND ROYAL IDEOLOGY

Does the presence of Berenike and her children in Philae explain another abnormality hiding under what might wrongly seem a commonplace in our inscription? The royal couple dedicated the naos not to Isis alone, but to Isis and Harpocrates. Ptolemy II's naos was a temple of the goddess Isis, as is demonstrated by all its wall decoration; Harpocrates appears in it as a secondary deity, although he is, like Osiris, a member

---

    this date, because the last eponymous date (year 4) where the mention of the Gods Euergetai is still absent dates from July 244 (*SB* XII 11059). On the other hand, the date of the priestly synod of 3 December 243 seems still to have been fixed according to the cult of the Gods Adelphoi (cf. J. Bingen, *CdE* 67 (1992) 326). This implies perhaps for the creation of the new dynastic cult a date not much before that of the synod. The beginning of Macedonian year 5 with its new Alexandrian eponyms, or the preparations for this event (May–June 243?), would supply a plausible, but still hypothetical, date for this creation. C. J. Johnson (2002: 112–16) noted that in the third century the Ptolemies did not yet, as they did later on, add their *Theos* epiclesis to their names in such dedications in the nominative. This allows a somewhat less narrow chronological approach to *I. Philae* 4 without excluding the one offered here.

[22] On all these events, see Hauben (1990), with less sceptical views than my comments here above. Cf. Hölbl (1994: 48, and bibliography on 291).

[23] Justinus XXVII 1, 9; Porph., *FGrHist.* 260 F 43.

[24] Hölbl (1994: 48, with bibliography on 291).

[25] A good occasion would be the beginning of the flood or the high waters of summer 244, but this can be only a hypothesis. One can relate to this visit the inscriptions *I. Philae* I 1, and probably I 2 (*SEG* XXIX 1665); *I. Philae* I 3 comes later in the reign.

of the divine triad, even in places where he alone accompanies the goddess. His role is not any more important than that of the numerous divinities present in the ritual decoration of the naos. This remains true in the decoration of the later parts of the sanctuary. The iconographic motive of Isis breast-feeding is ancient, but the worship of the pair of Isis and Harpocrates,[26] which must be dissociated from the theology of the Mammisi, dates from the imperial period, or at any rate not earlier than the later Hellenistic period.[27] It does not explain at all the double inscription of Ptolemy II's temple, or more exactly the inscription which was put in Greek on the entry of Isis' temple for the visit of Ptolemy III and Berenike. Even the language shows the highly circumstantial character of the carving of this text – for, except perhaps in the future Mammisi, in the later development of this sanctuary nothing confirms this consecration 'for one day' of a twin cult of Isis and the Horus child in the temple. Is not the implicit identification of the pair Isis and Harpocrates with Berenike-Isis accompanied by her *teknia* present in Philae the best explanation of this abnormality? Did not the dedication have an ideological character that it wished to underline? In fact, our inscription adds a matter of minor but real importance to what we know about the royal ideology, such as one can imagine it in Alexandria at the accession of Ptolemy III to the throne.

The main theme of this last event is well known and indeed present in our text: the exceptional excellence attributed to the royal brother-and-sister couple (and so to children issuing from so exceptional a union). Berenike was proclaimed sister of the king as part of her role as legitimate queen.[28] She has that role particularly because she and her husband are called, at least in the royal order of the world, son and daughter of the Gods *Adelphoi* and are almost a repetition of them.[29] In fact, the case of Berenike goes beyond an implicit reference

[26] Cf. D. Meeks, 'Harpokrates', *LÄ* II (1977), coll. 1002–11; Tran Tam Tinh, B. Jaeger and S. Poulin, 'Harpocrates', *LIMC* IV (1988), 1, 415–55; 2, 242–66. Note that the chapel of Harpocrates in Alexandria, which Ptolemy IV added to the Serapeum of Ptolemy III at the beginning of his reign (cf. Fraser 1972: I, 28, 269; II, 91, n. 197) is an Alexandrian phenomenon and probably essentially related to the court.

[27] I do not think that we are able to date the planning of the Mammisi of Ptolemy III to the reign of Ptolemy II (Haeny 1985: 211). In any case, this monument was built along the north-northeast axis of the doorway of Nectanebo (an axis which we find also in the second pylon and in the pronaos) and not the northeast axis of the naos of Ptolemy II.

[28] Berenike was the first queen 'of a king' who had in Egyptian an appropriate royal titulature and even in certain Demotic protocols the title of pharaoh (Hölbl 1994: 76–7).

[29] On the ideological aspects, either Greek or Egyptian, of the problem, which I cannot develop here, see Koenen (1983: esp. 157–65). On $\Phi\iota\lambda\acute{a}\delta\epsilon\lambda\phi\sigma\varsigma$ and the Theoi Adelphoi, see recently Criscuolo (1990) and Muccioli (1994).

to the couples Zeus–Hera and Osiris–Isis, which certainly coloured the notion of Sibling Gods. Now it is the new ideology of the royal couple[30] which gave to Berenike her dignity of sister of the king.

A secondary aspect of the royal ideology of these years depends seemingly on the uplifting public relations efforts of the court, but the 'loving queen' was a theme worth underlining with some insistence: Callimachus, later echoed by Catullus, sang of the doleful bride in the absence of the husband; Aphrodite had given her guarantee to this image; at the least, an astronomer of the court, a learned scholar in this particular case, proclaimed that he had found in a new constellation the lock of the queen, offered to the goddess in the hope that the beloved husband would soon come back.[31] The offering of the lock comes from a Greek tradition, but it is also very close to the same gesture of Isis in Coptos, and must easily have been taken as such in the context of Berenike's identification with Isis in other respects. The use of the diminutive *teknia*, 'the small princes', belongs doubtless to the same order of emotional ideology of the royal family, the dimension of tenderness which inscribes very young children in the image idealised by the new reign.

The inscription of the naos, in its abnormalities, is thus a modest but significant witness of an ideological development of the monarchy at the beginning of Ptolemy III's reign. Concrete mention of *teknia*, 'small crown princes', adds a new note to the monarchic domestic system, by highlighting, through its affective connections, legitimate filiation by blood. Should we see here a reaction to the chaotic character of the legitimate or illegitimate filiations which weighed on Ptolemy II Philadelphos' reign? At least, the Alexandrian dynasty seems to have continued to be inspired by the attitude displayed here until Ptolemy VI Philometor's death and even later.

Who were the two children? One of them was certainly the future Ptolemy IV Philopator. Is it perhaps too neat to think that the other *teknion* is the princess Berenike? We know that this girl, sister and potential fiancée of the heir, died five years later, still a little girl, during the priestly synod of 238.[32] For her, the decree of the upper Egyptian clergy meeting in Canopus organised an impressive cult in

---

[30] Nachtergael (1980); Hölbl (1994: 99).

[31] On the place in the royal ideology of either love between spouses or love of the couple transferred onto the child, see Koenen (1983: 161–4). The couple accompanied by their *teknia* as inscribed above the portal of the temple of Isis are a first manifestation of the new family vision, at the same time real and mythical.

[32] Cf. Dunand (1980).

the Egyptian temples, honours which seem to reveal the exceptional place which the princess-child already occupied at the Court of Alexandria. The idea is attractive and, from the point of view of the royal ideology, would give additional prominence to the use of *teknia*; but, to be sure, this is only a hypothesis.

APPENDIX I: THE DOUBLE 'RUBRICATION' OF LETTERS

The history of the inscription, as I have reconstructed it, explains also a rather surprising epigraphic peculiarity of *I. Philae* I 4. To perceive it we have to combine observations made three-quarters of a century ago by Lyons and the more recent remarks by A. Bernand. Lyons noticed that it appeared in gilt lettering when it was cleared from the layer of dust which had hidden it till then.[33] This gilt has in the meantime disappeared, scratched by eager hands or washed out by the annual flooding which followed the construction of the first dam. Bernand noticed that 'the letters are filled with white stucco, which, once scratched, lets the original red painting of the letters appear'.

This double 'rubrication', so to speak, in red and gold, is easily explained. At first, somebody engraved the inscription in the glory of the Nubian sun which floods the south facade of the temple. The letters were then painted in red, the 'rubrication' playing its double traditional role of highlighting letters and concealing any imperfections in the carving. Later, Ptolemy VI's pronaos was built leaning on the south facade of the naos. This construction put the south portal of the naos and its Greek inscription into darkness. As the text was important, somebody gilded the letters after first filling them in with white stucco, the filling seen by Bernand. Gold was more appropriate than red painting to capture enough of the dim light which still reached the south door of the naos. It is that gilt that Lyons found.

APPENDIX II: THE 'RASURAE' OF Ἁρποχράτηι

I indicated elsewhere (*CdE* 45 (1970) 409 = *Pages*, 137; concerning the stone-cutter's hesitations when inscribing the word Ἁρποχράτηι, see *Akten 1995*, 97) that we should not follow the most recent editor of the dedication, who prints Ἁρπο{πο}κράτηι; the inscription has the correct spelling with χ, as one would anticipate from the transcription

---

[33] 'Discovered by mere cleaning of the dust from the surface'. This layer of dust explains the absence of the inscription in Lepsius' *Denkmäler*.

of *Ḥr-p3-Ḫrd* (Horus the child). Mahaffy read Ἀρποκράτηι, a form adopted in the following editions, except for Strack, who probably unconsciously corrected the word without comment. The squeeze (*I. Philae* I, pl. 28, see p. 38, Fig. 2.2) allows us to clarify the reading at the end of the inscription.

ΑΡΙ → ΑΡΙ° → ΑΡΠ̄° → ΑΡΠ̄° → ΑΡ°ΧΡΑΤΗΙ

Having to complete the dedication at the end of the fillet with the last word *ΑΡΠΟΧΡΑΤΗΙ*, the engraver, after initial *ΑΡ*, initiated the following *Π* with a high left vertical. He then realized that if he continued the lettering at that rhythm, he would be short of space to write the entire word. To win some space, he drew at first a small omicron which was intended to be under the upper horizontal of the large pi. Realizing that it was not yet enough, he opted for a quite different solution: to engrave a smaller pi, squeezed against the rho which precedes, by using for its right lock part of this omicron, and to engrave then a small omicron above pi. All this mess was mended by painting in red the inscribed letters as required by the text (see Appendix I). Plaster and painting later (but not in red) were used to hide the excess engraving which is now again clearly visible on the squeeze.

Chapter 3

CLEOPATRA, THE DIADEM AND THE IMAGE

∽

Verses familiar to every young student of classics sound the refrain, *Nunc est bibendum, nunc pede libero pulsanda tellus,* 'It is now time to drink, time to strike the ground with a foot that nothing holds back any more.' But from just what fear was Rome now delivered? Horace was writing close to the imperial milieu. The ode is an immediate echo, almost live, of the birth of the foundation myth of the empire that Octavian, the future Augustus, wanted to impose on Roman opinion and on future historians. The mortal threat to Rome which Octavian averted came from a *monstrum fatale,* a 'monster capable of forcing fate', a queen who was preparing the ruin of Rome and the destruction of an empire still in embryo. Fortunately, the myth goes, Octavian defeated her in Actium, which otherwise would have been the last stage before her sacrilegious conquest of Italy. However, it was only half a victory for Octavian: Cleopatra escaped from the encircling. To chain her up, Octavian – Horace wrote – swept down upon her like the hawk upon doves or the hunter upon a hare, two at least debatable images. Horace hides neither his admiration for the queen nor his misogyny: she did not behave like a weak woman; she faced up to defeat and refused to flee from Alexandria at the arrival of the enemy. On the contrary, to escape Octavian's triumph in Rome:

ausa . . . fortis et asperas
tractare serpentes ut atrum
corpore conbiberet uenenum,
deliberata morte ferocior.

She bravely dared to handle disgusting snakes, to have all her body soaking up their black poison, finding back her energy by choosing her death herself. (*Odes* I XXXVII, 25–29)

The only parameter the poet gives us to judge this *monstrum fatale* is Cleopatra's femininity. She is not a weak woman, but she is still a woman. Across the centuries, this disturbing femininity developed both in literature and in painting a mythology of the behaviour of the queen; this was a semiotic of her body also, that of a woman subtle or depraved in love, a merciless seductress who failed only when she came up against Octavian's stern virtue. Naturally the true scandal in Rome was not the rather free manners that Cleopatra was credited with – one could find more spectacular cases right there in the capital city – but the fact that she was a woman, because there was no place for a woman in the strictly patriarchal Roman system of power. Even when the poet calls her a queen, he only adds to the condescension for the woman the contempt which Romans held for kingship. Strangely, in the ode of Horace, somebody is significantly absent: Antony, the rival of Octavian, the other potential heir of the political destiny of Caesar.

Some years later, in the *Aeneid*, another poet near to the imperial court used different words about Actium from those Horace had. In book VIII, on Aeneas' shield, the god Vulcan had depicted the naval battle of Actium as the last of the glorious hours of Roman history. Antony is no longer spared. 'On one side', sings the poet, 'Caesar Augustus drags to the fight Italy with the Senate and the people; on the other side, there is Antony, with his barbaric troops.' *Sequiturque nefas Aegyptia coniunx*, 'behind him, o scandal, his Egyptian wife'. On Aeneas' shield, the fight of the leaders is coupled with that of the gods of Rome against those of Egypt. The foundation myth of the empire had finally found all its constituent parts.

Many Roman historians and poets, taking the same tack, found new grievances and new insults for the sorceress who had diverted some distinguished Roman leaders from their duty. Propertius for instance offered to his readers two visions of Octavian's victory. In two elegies to Maecenas, he places the conflict at the level of rivalries around the future victor. He opposes in the background the loyalty of Maecenas and Antony's breach of duty. In II, 1, 17–42, the poet declares himself unable to meet the wish of Augustus' confidant to have him singing the victory of Philippi (which in fact was won by Antony), the conquest of Egypt and Actium's *rostra* – a skilful excuse to enumerate them. In IX, victory in Egypt evokes only Antony's suicide. In these two elegies, no allusion is made to Cleopatra. On the contrary, in the second perspective, Propertius, adopting the tone of solemn poetry (IV, VI, 21–4), strictly develops the subject of Octavian's propaganda: in Actium, 'on one side Augustus' vessel navigating under full rigging' – 'on the other side, a cursed fleet and weapons which a feminine hand shamefully shakes'. Elsewhere the poet describes with grandiloquence the threat that Rome might have been enslaved by a prostitute who offered her body to her slaves, to have Jupiter overcome by Anubis, the Tiber by the Nile, the Roman *tuba* by the crackling sistrum, supreme opprobrium if *mulier patienda fuit* (III, XI, 29–46).

Centuries later, Horace, Virgil and the same Propertius deeply influenced the rediscovery of antiquity by the Renaissance. However, reading Plutarch, humanists found events cast in a somewhat different light. The essayist of Chaeronea, in approaching history through the psychology of leading personalities, chose Antony as one of them, and he portrays him with more than a little sympathy. So Plutarch conferred on the tragic couple a more human dimension, exploited later by more modern writers and artists. This woman, whose name was not given the honour of a mention in the texts, was an Egyptian who almost destroyed Rome – Cleopatra VII, the last queen of the Ptolemies. In 304 BC, a Macedonian nobleman, Ptolemy son of Lagos, had proclaimed himself king, *basileus*, of the territories that he was administering in the name of the dull (and now murdered) heirs of Alexander the Great. For almost three centuries, from their royal capital of Alexandria, the Ptolemies reigned over Egypt, but also over a Mediterranean empire which, in its years of magnificence, extended from the Middle East and Anatolia to the Aegean Sea, especially including Cyrenaica and Cyprus. Among the Hellenistic realms, that of the Ptolemies was the last to survive the pressure of Rome. Alexandria had discovered Rome very early, treating this strange Western capital as an equal at first. But, from the beginning of the second century, Rome assumed in Egypt the role of a more or less discreet protector of the Ptolemies.

In the first century BC, Ptolemy XII, who proclaimed himself New Dionysos – people called him the Flautist behind his back – was in fact a vassal of Rome, but also a supplier of funds to bribe the various political factions who confronted each other in Italy. A cynical diplomat, he was able to buy off all the protagonists (Pompey as well as Caesar), with the result that every party preferred to defer the annexation of Egypt, with its gold and wheat, to avoid the possibility that their rivals might gain an advantage from it. When he was driven from the throne by the Alexandrians, Ptolemy XII took refuge in Rome, where he ruined himself by attempting to satiate a corrupt political class. However, he skilfully obtained from Julius Caesar proclamation as 'friend and ally of the Roman people'. Thus, the realm was protected and the miserable king was sent back to Alexandria with the help of a Roman army, which would not leave the Nile valley for seven centuries. Meanwhile a girl, Cleopatra, was born to the king. She was 18 years old when Ptolemy XII died, bequeathing to her the diadem. But he stipulated in his will that she had to share the royal diadem with one of her younger brothers, Ptolemy XIII. Rome was asked to take care of the execution of his last will. Perhaps, although this seems doubtful to me, Ptolemy XII had even associated his elder daughter with him on the throne during the last months of his life. At least, the royal administration immediately recognised her as sole queen. Nevertheless, Cleopatra rapidly met difficulties. A powerful faction of the court, which was supporting the rights of the child Ptolemy XIII, soon forced her to share the throne, then to exile herself to escape death. For her sake, the Roman civil war for the first time stretched as far as Egypt. Pompey, beaten in Pharsalus by Caesar, tried to seek refuge in Alexandria, but he was treacherously murdered by the faction of young Ptolemy. Julius Caesar soon arrived, and Cleopatra's time had come. She secretly joined the Roman in Alexandria and obtained from him agreement to implement the will of her father. Whatever judgement one can pass on this decision of Caesar – an error of assessment, the weakness of an old man, or on the contrary a political stroke of genius – the execution of the royal will was in any case the choice Caesar could most easily justify in Rome as in Alexandria. The young queen occupied again the palace of her ancestors, this time wisely not alone but with a still younger brother, Ptolemy XIV, the other one having perished. Egypt recovered Cyprus, occupied by the Romans some ten years earlier. Cleopatra, now 22 years old, bore a son, the sole son whom Caesar – then a man in his fifties – ever had. Caesar was already by that time back in Italy. He invited Cleopatra to join him there. Cautiously she took her young coregent and potential rival with her. As her father had laid down, and with the help of Caesar, the queen obtained that she and her brother would be officially recognised as *reges socii* and *amici populi Romani*, as 'allied kings and friends of the Roman people'. The spectre of the annexation of Egypt was pushed aside once again. But the Ides of March were near, when Caesar was murdered.

Cleopatra went back to Alexandria. With her princely blood, she honoured one of the more dramatic of the Macedonian royal traditions: she was probably the instigator of the death of her brother, killing off at its root any possible new rebellion of a hostile faction. She completed the seizure of the diadem by associating with her on the throne her 3-year-old son as Ptolemy XV Caesar, with the official title 'the God who loves his father and his mother'. This association of a queen and a king-son already existed among the pharaohs; it was not an innovation of the Ptolemies. The royal couple, mother and son, were to reign over Egypt till the dramatic end of the dynasty.

Once again, however, Cleopatra was caught in the internal fights in Rome. After Caesar's death, two leaders asserted themselves as the successors of the *dictator perpetuus*, his lieutenant Mark Antony, by the force of his personality, and young Octavian, because Caesar in his will had adopted him as son and as his main heir. The two men first joined forces to beat the republicans near Philippi in Macedonia, and they decided to entrust the organisation of the Mediterranean East to Antony. The latter summoned Queen Cleopatra to Tarsus in Cilicia, to ask her, it seems, for some justification for her actions. Indeed, the Roman army of Egypt and the fleet of Cyprus had momentarily joined the republicans. Cleopatra was 28 years old. She immediately agreed to the invitation, the more easily in that Cilicia is close to Cyprus and had been for a long time a possession of the Ptolemies. The interview at Tarsus, where she impressed the Roman by displaying her wealth and the refinement of the court of Alexandria, soon became an inexhaustible subject of literature and painting. Antony went to Alexandria soon after and enjoyed the splendours of the court, doubtless finding there, more as initiator than initiated, new fields for his unbridled life. The queen had once again saved her realm but knew that she needed a firm support; and Antony was certainly interested in the wealth of Egypt, if he wanted to make out of the Eastern Mediterranean a platform for his conquest of Rome. Probably perceiving the deep political game which animated the two protagonists, Octavian's propaganda amplified the scandal of what, for a Roman, was a cohabitation outside legal matrimony with a foreigner.

In 37/36 BC – Cleopatra now 33 years old – the Greek documents, papyri and inscriptions reveal a deep change in the formal definition which the queen seems to give to her royal identity. Until then, dating was drawn up in regnal years of Cleopatra and Ptolemy Caesar but counted from the sole accession of the queen to the throne, which was the normal way in the kingdom. The year 16 – and this could only have been a royal decision – became 'year 16 which is also year 1'. This double dating continued in Egypt till the end of the reign and appeared on some coinages of the Syrian coast. Such double dating, as evidenced in the Hellenistic period, is now better explained than it once was. The second date does not mean the addition of a new computation which concerns a coregent, but a new policy of the ruler, a new phase of a reign. Furthermore, it does not mean that the relations of the royal couple within the territory of Egypt had changed; those received a concrete expression in the first part of the date. The double date, by its second numeration, asserts new relations between Cleopatra and the rest of the Oriental world subjected to Antony. A long way from Italy, Antony needed to be helped by his vassal realms in the East to gain a prestigious victory over the Parthians, to rally Roman public opinion, and to conquer Rome. Cleopatra entered into the system as a privileged vassal. She joined Antony in Syria, and he recognised the twins whom she bore to him and added to their name a second one suggesting that Alexander Helios and Cleopatra Selene would reign outside Egypt under the protection of their mother. At that time too Antony began to entrust Cleopatra with important territories from the former empire of the Ptolemies. Let us hesitate to say that, added to the traditional dating, year 1 reveals an eventual decision of Cleopatra to reconstitute a Ptolemaic empire at the cost of Antony and of Rome as the price of her love and her gold. It is more likely that Antony, for whom the former Roman order in the East was not satisfactory, entrusted the surest of his vassals with the essential elements of the new organisation of his power. Octavian's propaganda attacked Cleopatra from then on, declaring her an enemy rather than a friend of Rome.

Antony missed the symbolic expedition against the Parthians he launched in the hope of rallying Roman opinion. In 34, he once again came to Alexandria and his wife Cleopatra (now 36 years old). Their Greek marriage made sense neither for Egypt (no more than Caesar did Antony ever enter into the royal titulature), nor for Rome, where it constituted at least one scandal more without any legal consequences. The initiative could partially be explained by a real affection, blessed by several children, that the 'unique lovers' of Alexandria felt one for the other. She had a more plausible motive, however, to confer on Antony and on the small princes whom he had with the queen a sort of parallel royal legitimacy of a purely Hellenistic type in the outer regions of her *basileia*. There, for example, monetary issues combined profiles of Antony and Cleopatra (p. 75, Fig. 5.2). When the rival of Octavian decided to move gradually closer to Italy, Cleopatra, acting as a powerful vassal, accompanied him and put her wealth and her fleet at his service. From now on, there was one candidate too many to exercise supreme power at Rome.

Horace, Virgil and Propertius tell the rest of the story. Brought back in a hurry to Alexandria after Actium, Cleopatra, now 40, committed suicide not so as to follow her husband in death, but because she knew what was waiting for her in the triumphant procession of Octavian and after the triumph. Her suicide inspired Propertius, in book IV, VI, 63–6, to a new version of the fable of the fox and the grapes. After some rather doubtful flattery (the poet proclaims the admiration of the deified Caesar contemplating from the planet Venus the bravery of his 'blood'), Propertius comforts the emperor:

> *Illa petit Nilum cumba male nixa fugaci,*
>   *hoc unum, iusso non moritura die.*
> *Di melius! quantus mulier foret una triumphus,*
>   *ductus erat per quas ante Iugurtha uias!*

> Taken on an escaped boat, she reaches the Nile with difficulty, only gaining it not to die on order. The gods had made a better decision! What a triumph would have been a single woman in those avenues along which Jugurtha had been dragged.

A woman only, and not Antony.

Octavian annexed Egypt on behalf of Rome. Adopted son of Caesar, he soon got rid of the natural son of the dictator. Cleopatra had vainly tried to put her son out of reach.

In his *Dames du XIIe siècle*, Georges Duby underlines how much, for the historian, the ladies of the past have neither face nor body. They remain for us indecisive shadows, without outline, without accent. We may like to doubt that this is really true for queens, especially for those queens who behaved as kings. But I am tempted to believe that it is true for Cleopatra, because her person was so much diluted in a profusion of contradictory images from the sixteenth century onwards. Certainly, we have some contemporary monetary portraits of the queen. They betray a profile with more energy than grace, but those coins were produced in inferior workshops and have nothing to do with the brilliant tradition of the Hellenistic royal portrait. The modern polymorphous imagery of the queen arose much later. Literature, music and painting extrapolated in all directions the luxurious body of the woman, queen and mistress, her ambitions, her tragic death. From Giovanni Boccaccio or the admirable *Antony and Cleopatra* of Shakespeare to the *Nuits de Cléopâtre*, warm nights indeed, of Théophile Gauthier, or to the *Caesar and Cleopatra* of Bernard Shaw, she was a grand lady, a bloodthirsty tyrant or a prostitute, delicate mistress, shrewd partner, even sadistic creature, either a culprit or a victim, or both. The Egyptomania of the nineteenth century remodelled her and was continued in the twentieth by films strangely influenced by the discovery of Tutankhamun's tomb. Cecil B. de Mille forced poor Cleopatra to imitate Claudette Colbert; and I hesitate to evoke how cruel it was to this queen of high Macedonian lineage to entrust her role to Elizabeth Taylor.

The artistic or simply commercial exploitation of Cleopatra's myth and its more or less doubtful vicissitudes should not be of any help for the historian. In a recent excellent book, *The Signs of Cleopatra* – a work, however, spoiled in my opinion by excessive lacanian analysis – Mary Hamer tackles Cleopatra's multifaceted portrayal. Hamer examines how, throughout the centuries, Cleopatra's phantasmagorical appearance posed problems of conflict between power and sex and revisited the wickedness of the woman. These were not problems for the native Alexandrians of Cleopatra's time, but of later societies which created each new avatar of the queen. Nevertheless, art and history have the same sources, and painters and writers conditioned historians. Who among us reads Plutarch without Shakespeare as a discreet companion? For the cover illustrations of their recent books, three authors chose an image of Cleopatra which is not innocent at all. Mary Hamer borrows, from the luxurious series which Tiepolo dedicated to the interview at Tarsus, the episode where Antony welcomes the queen. In the middle of onlookers who compose a baroque 'Turquerie' in the Venetian style, an imposing lady, very strictly dressed, gazes with somewhat disdaining eyes upon the man or, rather, the portentous panache of a helmet which is humbly bending over her hand. At the same time, Édith Flamarion puts on the cover of her *Cléopâtre: vie et mort d'un pharaon* a queen with the severe Egyptian profile and dress of Isis and a rather long nose which suggests the Pascalian meditation at which you can guess. In 1995, for the jacket of his *Kleopatra, Herrscherin und Geliebte*, 'Cleopatra, ruler and mistress', the essayist Joachim Brambach adopts a nude of heavy sensuality, bewitching, almost aggressive; but, under a black mop of hair, the glance is turned towards the sky, as if the young lady was anticipating that she was destined to suffer martyrdom. In this painting of his youth, the Italian impressionist Mosè Bianchi is a contemporary of Manet's naked *Olympia*, who aroused such tremendous scandal. If Manet had called the picture *Cleopatra*, he would have been applauded, or perhaps at most, people would have uttered some reservations about the iciness of the body. Cleopatra, like Greek mythology and the Turkish harem, was then for the painter the permission to develop with full respectability the ambiguous message of the feminine body. However, such images of Cleopatra are quite anachronistic. Even when Plutarch says that Cleopatra appeared as Aphrodite in the vessel which brought her to Tarsus, where Antony was waiting for her, she was surely luxuriously and heavily dressed, as Tiepolo rightly understood, with some symbolic detail to evoke the goddess of love; and especially she did not display that courtesan's nudity or semi-nudity which might still disturb some historians. Even among them, Cleopatra's myth does not stop growing rich in new colourings, developing in whatever direction the general problems of our society may suggest. I will only briefly mention a new Cleopatra, as heroine of feminism, because I am afraid that this Macedonian sovereign and goddess, even as the head of something like a large single-parent family, would have some difficulty in understanding what Women's Liberation could mean.

A recent avatar of the myth is situated in a current of ideas felt as historically well founded in some black intellectual circles and especially in certain American or African universities. In Afrocentrism or *Black Athena*, from the title of Martin Bernal's best-seller, we find the conviction that the wisdom of Egypt has an African origin – the ancient Egyptians, moreover, become blacks – and especially that this African culture, discovered in Egypt by the Greeks, was the foundation of Western civilisation. Whatever sympathy one feels for people who rightly ask that one finally recognise fully their dignity, history matches facts and good feelings poorly – and this is not the monopoly of Afrocentrism. *Black Athena* has at least the merit of forcing us to rethink the values of civilisation on which we accommodatingly build our own historic judgements. But could a Western mafia of professors actually succeed in hiding the fact that Cleopatra was black? It is true that there are some obscurities in the pedigree of the queen. The Ptolemies were of Macedonian princely blood and were surrounded with a court aristocracy, Macedonian and Greek, which, like all privileged classes, certainly developed in a closed and protected social environment. The Ptolemies even practised princely consanguine marriage, often the marriage of real or declared siblings, presented as the royal union of divine right par excellence, just like that of Zeus and Hera, Osiris and Isis. In the first century BC, the last century of the Ptolemies, the system was more complex. Ptolemy XII was a son of Ptolemy IX, who had successively married two of his sisters in the best royal tradition, but his son was born from an unknown woman, in fact unknown to historians probably because she was a woman without a major scandal. It cannot have been just some princely passing whim, because this lady, certainly an important lady, bore three children to the king and two of them reigned. Respecting the tradition, Ptolemy XII married his sister from the same union. But next to this royal union, perhaps now purely ritual, he also had his Montespan, another unknown lady for us. She gave him four children in ten years, and then this prolific phantom disappears from history when Ptolemy XII was expelled by the Alexandrians. But the three younger children, two Ptolemies and Arsinoe, momentarily wore the diadem with or against Cleopatra, their elder sister. Werner Huss supported recently, not without interesting arguments, the proposition that Ptolemy XII had contracted this parallel marriage in the priestly aristocracy of Memphis. But I am persuaded that the Romans would not have missed the occasion to treat Cleopatra as the daughter of an Egyptian native, even of a black, if her complexion had betrayed something else than a maternal ancestry from the best Alexandrian society. The hypothesis of Huss would not, moreover, lead to the conviction that Cleopatra was a black woman, because she would have been the daughter of a high Egyptian priest.

I do not wish to dwell upon *Black Athena*, which is of interest only as a contemporary phenomenon. But this intermezzo introduces, from the point of view of the legitimacy of the succession, the question, fundamental for me, of the continuity or breach of the traditional royal behaviour of the Ptolemies which marks Cleopatra's administration. Without the disaster of Actium, those features of her reign would at least have made her an efficient transition queen capable of ensuring the realm to her son – king Ptolemy Caesar. One of the difficulties of the historian, especially for antiquity, when studying a king or a queen, is that their record at the same time includes both a personality that we glimpse only vaguely, and the symbolic bearer of a power that others, often more remarkable or more depraved than the sovereign, actually practised in the shade of the ruler. A distinction between the two factors is almost always imperceptible for us. I said earlier that, behind Cleopatra and her young brothers, there were rival factions at the court. When a king is still a child – as was true at several moments in the history of the Ptolemies – the power of those groups is total; at least, they supplied the throne with excellent ministers, who saved the dynasty. But even when, for Cleopatra, features of her personality seem to be passed on to us, it is not by direct testimony, but through stereotypes marked from the beginning by hostile propaganda. The image of Cleopatra, an eternally young grown-up, responsible and conquering, who pays with her body the price of the power she wants to keep, the safety of the realm, even the conquest of Rome, is a reduced image and, in many points of view, completely falsified.

One of the peculiarities of the Alexandrian royal system was the isolation, almost the imperviousness, of the different functions which the sovereign simultaneously assumed. The king was the *basileus* of the *Hellênes* of the countryside,[1] the pharaoh of Upper and Lower Egypt for the Egyptians and their priests, the master of Alexandria, a capital with which the palace maintained ambiguous relations. He had to handle the expansion and administration of his empire or the pressure which it continuously experienced from abroad. Documentary evidence shows that Cleopatra assumed, like her predecessors, this multiplicity of functions. Later periods retained practically only a single register, her connections, which were certainly important, with Rome, what Octavian's propaganda reduced to two scandalous affairs and to a monstrosity in history, a woman threatening the Capitol.

As soon as one observes the queen in other domains of her responsibilities, the picture changes. Let us take the functions which she performed for the Egyptians. For them, on the religious plane, the pharaoh, even if Macedonian, had an essential role: he was the intercessor between humanity and the gods whom he would join after his death. The walls of Ptolemaic temples are covered with the images of the king praying and carrying out the ritual offerings every day. These reassuring images of the king are purely conventional; but they are no less essential and significant. Cleopatra performed this function. The most prestigious relief on the rear of the temple of Dendera presents the queen drawn up in the ritual slightly veiled nudity of the Egyptian goddesses. Her round face is exactly similar to those of the two Isis figures which appear among the gods to whom the queen and the young king make offerings. In the temple of Hermonthis, now no longer visible, Cleopatra officiated in the same way, alone or followed by her son-king Ptolemy Caesar. In Dendera, the order of precedence was modified, certainly with the agreement or more probably as a decision of the queen. She now follows her son, represented as slightly taller than she, and he wears the ritual crown of Upper and Lower Egypt. This monumental relief seems to me an official programme, important from two viewpoints. First, it reveals that the clergy recognised Cleopatra and her son completely, and that, for the priests, the continuity of power and royal intercession was ensured by them.

---

1 See pp. 94–5 below on *Hellênes*.

Secondly, through the place she reserved to herself in Dendera, Cleopatra also gave evidence of dynastic continuity as organised by her: the son-king with the double crown is the king, and she, in a sense, is only a queen. In her multiple Greek and Alexandrian functions, Cleopatra completely exercised the other continuities, particularly when she mercilessly pushed aside her brothers and her sister, possible sources of opposition in Alexandria.

Documents are scattered and fragmented. Some of them suggest that in the first century the sovereigns had to tolerate an increasing autonomy of the highest servants of the state or of certain priestly families in distant Upper Egypt, but nothing proves that this decentralisation – in a sense a reorganisation of the political space in Egypt – was made against the monarchy, even though it could weaken it and modify the Hellenistic scheme of kingship. However, the most tangible proof of her solid takeover of royal power is the fact that the queen was now able to leave Egypt, even for a long time, without any fear of a palace revolution in Alexandria or an uprising in the *chôra*. Here was at least an illusion of a recovered perpetuity warranted to the diadem of the Ptolemies. In the titulatures and the Greek dates, the double permanent presence of Cleopatra as queen and goddess 'who loves her father', and of Ptolemy Caesar as king and god 'who loves his father and his mother', shows, as in Dendera, the continuity of a dynastic policy. However, behind this picture, so remote from the fantasies of our Cleopatra's modern myth, the historian knows the weight of a nearby shadow power, the permanent presence of a Roman army, the shadowy weight of history which never stops changing the face of the world.

A last problem of continuity and break leads us back towards the mythical Cleopatra and to the nature of her relations with Caesar and with Antony, who, as I said, never appeared as partners in the royal titulature of Cleopatra and her son. I mentioned the right that the Ptolemies had taken upon themselves, ever since Ptolemy II, to define what is a royal couple of siblings, but I indicated also the dichotomy which was established later between the princely marriage of divine status and the parallel union which produces heirs. Those children – Romans could not understand it and historians misunderstand this phenomenon when speaking of bastardy – established a legitimate descent, because the prince and not the rules defined legitimacy. In her unions with Caesar and with Antony, Cleopatra had a dynastic reference, her half-sister Berenike, who had usurped the throne during the exile of Ptolemy XII. For lack of any possibility of resorting to royal endogamy, she had looked outside of Egypt for two successive husbands, in the event two disasters. For the couple Cleopatra and Caesar, at least for her and on the dynastic level, such a precedent already legitimised her behaviour, even though, perhaps, under the pressure of foreign affairs, for the queen a Roman was also a broader political choice. From the time of the first Ptolemies, the legitimacy of the succession was a decision of the prince. Ptolemy Caesar was not the small illegitimate child whom some opponents to Cleopatra mocked, as we do too often, following the Romans; he was the young king, the future of the dynasty, who appears in all his power on the Egyptian temple and in the Alexandrian titulatures. With Antony, the problem arose only partially on the same terms as for Cleopatra. She escapes us here more than ever. Whatever were the strange conditions in which this couple was constituted and flourished, or whatever the part love or affection might have had in their decisions, a double calculation, for him as for her, gave a considerable historic weight to their relations. The exploitation of the continuities which marks Cleopatra's Egyptian policy might appear as being in the hope of eventually restoring the empire of her ancestors. But the queen was, at least, quickly engaged in new ways, unpredictable ways like the project of virtual realms for the children she had from Antony. Which part is due to her in those characteristic fancies of Antony? We will never know. She behaved certainly as a faithful and generous vassal. Did she more or less inspire the last political action of Antony? It is improbable that she ever dreamed of reigning in Rome. Antony would have been the first to explain to her that such an idea was foreign to all the Roman institutional context of the moment and was also irreconcilable with the popularity Antony was still enjoying in Rome. To her misfortune, she would lose in this adventure the diadem she had remarkably strengthened in Alexandria by stabilising Egypt for the benefit of her son. Conditions in Rome had changed: the rivalry of the parties, which Ptolemy XII had been able to exploit, had given way to a merciless duel for the empire. Cleopatra followed and even had married the more brilliant of the two rivals, but he was the one who was defeated.

Chapter 4

CLEOPATRA VII PHILOPATRIS

⸎

During the year 37/36 BC, regnal 'year 16' of Cleopatra VII and Ptolemy XV Caesar was officially renamed 'year 16 which is also year 1'. The double dating that was introduced at that moment was to be used until 30 BC, with 'year 22 which is also year 7' marking the tragic end of both the double reign and the Ptolemaic era.[1] The consensus is now well established, I believe, that the introduction of this double dating is more or less directly connected with what are generally called the first territorial concessions of Mark Antony to Cleopatra, an explanation which is confirmed by Porphyry's *Chronicle*. Michel Chauveau showed that it is necessary to look for the origin of such a double dating – surely a royal initiative – not in the adoption of a coregent, but in a political reorientation considered important enough to mention in a second starting-point for the count of the regnal years.[2] More precisely, I believe that such a move was initiated by a change in the Alexandrian royal ideology, and not by the concomitant territorial extensions. The latter are more a consequence of the new policy which Cleopatra VII planned to carry out with the help of Antony.[3]

The palace of Alexandria modified Cleopatra's titulature as well as the regnal numbering. This change is also significant because it reflects a political choice which comes from the upper levels of the hierarchy of the royal administration. *BGU* XIV 2376 from

---

[1] We have to keep in mind the difference between such double reckoning, where two datings are running parallel year after year, and the double dates which pair the last incomplete year at the end of a reign with the fractional first year of the reign which succeeds it. Cf. Skeat (1962). Formulations of this last type occur twice in Cleopatra VII's early reign. The earlier follows the commonplace type for a succession, with year 30 = year 1, after the death of Ptolemy XII. The later one with the mysterious year 1 = year 3 is doubtless linked with the imbroglios of the beginning of the reign of Cleopatra and Ptolemy XIII. The victorious comeback of Cleopatra is expressed by the reuse of year 3 of her reign. Using year 1, Ptolemy XIII probably at first ignored the beginning of the reign of the young queen or pretended to succeed her. I return to this point in Chapter 5.

[2] Cf. Chauveau (1997a) with Chauveau (1990, 1991).

[3] I develop this in Chapter 5.

Herakleopolis, drafted in double copy, is the first to adopt in 36/35 the new double numbering 'year 17 which is also year 2'. It also has the new titulature of the reigning monarchs.[4] It is significantly different from what preceded,[5] at least for the queen: βασιλευόντων Κλεοπάτρας Θεᾶς νεωτέρας Φιλοπάτορος καὶ Φιλοπατρίδος καὶ Πτολεμαίου Θεοῦ Φιλοπάτορος καὶ Φιλομήτορος. The young child and king remains 'God who loves his father and loves his mother'. By contrast, the queen is proclaimed Θεὰ νεωτέρα Φιλοπάτωρ καὶ Φιλοπατρίς, ' the goddess νεωτέρα who loves her father and loves her πατρίς'.

The first novelty is the presence of νεωτέρα, 'the younger', next to Θεά, 'goddess', as the first epiclesis of the goddess Cleopatra. I argue elsewhere (Chapter 5) for the only reasonable explanation: the epiclesis proclaims Cleopatra VII as spiritual heir to Cleopatra Thea, the great queen of Syria.[6] One finds here a real manifesto of the new dimension which the queen wishes to give to her dynastic policy, adding from now on the inheritance of the Seleucids to that of the Ptolemies.

The second new epiclesis, Φιλοπατρίς, is as unprecedented as the other.[7] Confronted with this unusual epiclesis, 'the one that loves her homeland', William Brashear, the editor of *BGU* XIV 2376, sees a political message – as we would expect in royal titulature. But he at once discards as groundless two possible explanations on the basis of contemporary events, first the idea that this novelty might be bound to the first donation of territories to Cleopatra, and secondly a possible connection to the birth of the twins whom Cleopatra bore Antony.

---

[4] *BGU* XIV 2376. Cf. Schrapel (1996: 223–5).

[5] Βασίλισσα Κλεοπάτρα Θεὰ Φιλοπάτωρ καὶ βασιλεὺς Πτολεμαῖος Θεὸς Φιλοπάτωρ καὶ Φιλομήτωρ.

[6] *Status quaestionis* in Schrapel (1996: 225–34). The epiclesis was already known from coins probably struck in Phoenicia, cf. A. Burnett, M. Amandry and P. P. Ripollès, *Roman Provincial Coinage* I.1 (London and Paris 1992: 601–2, nos. 4094–6, pl. 155). The legend βασίλισσα Κλεοπάτρα Θεὰ νεωτέρα is added on the obverse to the bust of the queen, whereas the reverse represents the bust of Antony, *imperator* and *triumvir*, Ἀντώνιος Αὐτοκράτωρ τρίτον τριῶν ἀνδρῶν. Such a coupling places this coinage outside the Alexandrian sector of the new double policy of Cleopatra, because Antony never had any place in the Ptolemaic system of power. For Fleischer (1996), the monetary 'Alexandrian and Syro-Roman' portraits of Cleopatra VII represent respectively the queen as legitimate heir of the Ptolemaic diadem and as 'friend of Antony'. I would rather see there the two new fields of the policy of the queen, even though the Seleucid programme is strictly allied with Antony's aims.

[7] A contemporary use of the word for a king, but in an informal context, is the dedication *I. Olympia* 315 (36 BC–AD 17): ἡ πόλις ἡ τῶν Ἠλείων βασ[ιλέα Ἀρχέλαον] | φιλόπατριν ἀρετῆς ἕνεκεν κ[αὶ εὐνοίας τῆς εἰς αὐτήν].

According to him, the 'homeland' which Cleopatra claims to love is Egypt, and the new epiclesis seeks to assert the loyalty of the queen to her Egyptian fellow countrymen irritated by the long collaboration of the queen with the Roman invader and by the 'scandalous liaisons with Caesar and Antonius'. But this supposes a strange irritation among an 'Egyptian population' which needs more accurate definition. Pro- or anti-Roman feeling was an Alexandrian problem rather than an Egyptian concern and was not a pressing actuality in 36 BC. Were the good people of Egypt really shocked by the queen's love affairs? Most of the Egyptians were living far from the propaganda of Octavian, meant for Roman public opinion, and could not know that great invention of the future, a popular press devoted to the sentimental affairs of royalty and celebrities. I have the impression that for the humble fellahin and even the priests, the love affairs and pregnancies of a woman pharaoh were ruled by some divine inspiration; scandal arose only when the tax collectors and granary officials of the queen were pressing too hard.

W. Huss, consistently with his conviction that Cleopatra was born, like her brothers and sister, from a stable union between Ptolemy XII and a lady from the highest priestly class from Memphis, shares Brashear's opinion.[8] Michel Chauveau recently took up this idea in a wider perspective by seeing in *philopatris* a declaration of principles which renews the entire philosophy of the Ptolemaic monarchy: kingship is from now on to be based on an almost mystic link with the country of the Nile and all its inhabitants, whatever their culture and their language.[9] Dorothy J. Thompson, noting Cleopatra's more personal involvement in Egyptian religious life than her predecessors', observes that 'as the goddess Cleopatra the younger, *philopator*, "father loving", and *philopatris*, "patriotic", she was indeed queen of Egypt'.[10]

There is no obvious reason to suppose an evolution in the political connections between the queen and Egypt at this moment.[11] Moreover, the notion of 'homeland' which is postulated by such an exegesis of $\Phi\iota\lambda o\pi\alpha\tau\rho\acute{\iota}\varsigma$ seems to me quite anachronistic, surely when

[8] Huss (1990: esp. 202), where, by contrast, the epiclesis serves as evidence for a narrow link between the queen and Egypt. On the hypothesis of a union contracted by Ptolemy XII with a woman of the priestly class of Memphis, see Will (1982: 529–30).

[9] Chauveau (1998).

[10] *Cambridge Ancient History*, 2nd edn, IX (Cambridge 1994) 321.

[11] Schrapel (1996: 225), without proposing a solution, is right to emphasise how difficult it would be not to link the entire titulature with the new Mediterranean policy and the adoption of the double reckoning of the regnal years.

applied to Egypt for a Ptolemy or a Cleopatra. Certainly, the religious Egyptian recognised the pharaoh, even Macedonian or now Alexandrian, as the momentary intercessor between the gods, on the one hand, and the people and land of Egypt, on the other. But, in the Macedonian view of Hellenistic monarchy, kingship was not physically connected to a territory which constituted the 'homeland' of the king. The only source of legitimacy was his recognised nature as *basileus*, and it applied to the territory under his authority. It did not emanate from this territory, which was not a source of royal identity. The Ptolemies are kings of Egypt for the foreign historians; Cleopatra is *Aegyptia*, 'Egyptian', for Romans who wanted to offend or stigmatise her. The royal titulatures and their epicleseis, including *philopatris*, are situated on another level, that of the political philosophy of power conceived in the court milieu of Alexandria. There the king is 'king', *basileus*, not 'king of', but king in the unstable grouping of territories over which he reigns, and which for the Ptolemies was never confined to Egypt. Furthermore, I do not believe that the epiclesis 'the one who loves her homeland' could have referred to Egypt precisely when Cleopatra was beginning her opening towards the Greek East.

The adjective *philopatris* is frequent in Greek epigraphy, but most particularly during the imperial period; generally it indicates the exceptional public-spiritedness of a person who served his native town well, for example by his generosity.[12] Such a civic context does not offer any solution for our problem. In Egypt's metrical inscriptions, *patris* has its conventional sense of 'home town'. So, in Alexandria, for example, πατρὶς Ἀλεξάνδρεια Μακηδόνος Αἰγύπτοιο (*I. Métr.* 19) in the early empire or, in the early Hellenistic period, πατὴρ μὲν Εἰρηναῖος, ἀ δέ τοι πατρὶς | Μέμφις (*I. Métr.* 63).[13] In all these examples, moreover, φιλοπατρίς is granted at the initiative of other people and in a banal context; it lacks the exceptional programmatic character asserted in our case by the queen herself in her titulature.

Another context in the Hellenistic Greek language supplies us with the solution. Under Ptolemy II, in certain official Ptolemaic texts, like

---

[12] Among numerous others, see an inscription from Cos (Claudian period), Paton-Hicks 84, Θεοῖς Πατρῴοις ὑπὲρ ὑγείας Γαΐου Στερτινίου Ἡρακλείτου υἱοῦ Ξενοφῶντος, φιλοκαίσαρος, φιλοσεβάστου, φιλοκλαυδίου, δάμου υἱοῦ, φιλοπατρίδος, εὐσεβοῦς, εὐεργέτα τῆς πατρίδος.

[13] For example, Weissenow (1976) shows that, in Polybius, *patris* generally has a meaning restricted to a locality rather than to a region or a confederacy.

the collection of regulations called *P. Revenue Laws* or a *prostagma* like *C. Ord. Ptol.* 21, it is prescribed that identity, when a full name was required, should be established πατρόθεν καὶ πατρίδος, which means that one has to add to the name of a person the name of his father and that of his 'homeland', which, in this particular case, is often the homeland of his ancestors. It is the transfer in the diaspora of the formula for the full Attic identity πατρόθεν καὶ τοῦ δήμου ('by father's name and deme'), or when elsewhere than at Athens, of the formula πατρόθεν καὶ τῆς πόλεως ('by father's name and by city'), which identifies the foreigner. The obligation to define identity by the *patris* remained throughout the Ptolemaic age; the death penalty would punish any 'change of homeland and names' (μεταβολὴ πατρίδος καὶ ὀνομάτων, *BGU* VI 1213 and 1250). In Egypt hundreds of regularly formulated identities allow us to draw up an extraordinary picture of immigration: someone is a son of so-and-so, Cretan or Polyrrhenian from Crete or Achaean or Athenian, Thracian, Jew or even Persian, and in the most prestigious case, Macedonian. The Egyptian will note the nome from which he comes. On the strict plan of personal identity, one is as a rule neither Greek, Ἕλλην, nor Egyptian, Αἰγύπτιος, because these two terms mark a very wide social status, the opposite of a specific *patris*. One would perhaps acquire one of these broader statuses because of the *patris* he gives in his full identity. The Macedonian contingent was particularly important in the first cleruchic settlement, and access to this prestigious group was certainly jealously protected. The socially preeminent place of the Macedonian cavalry *katoikoi* in the *chôra* explains why *Makedôn* would, quite exceptionally, survive as an individual and private marker of identity during the first half of the first century AD. It is the only identity mark with a *patris* connotation that did not disappear with the Ptolemaic dynasty.[14]

Let us abandon, then, the idea that the homeland for which Cleopatra proclaims her love could be Alexandria. This would make no sense. Obviously Cleopatra gives prominence in her new titulature to her Macedonian ancestry and her links to the Macedonian aristocracy, jealously preserved during three centuries by the consanguineous marriages among the descendants of Lagos and by a closed onomastic repertory. The queen implicitly alludes to her ancestor, the Macedonian Ptolemy, who first reigned from Alexandria over a vast empire, in which Egypt was not a homeland, but a strategic base and

---

[14] See Bagnall (1984); Montevecchi (1997).

a land to be exploited economically.[15] She calls attention to the relationships of blood, specifically of Macedonian blood, that united Ptolemies and Seleucids. Here we connect to the epiclesis *Thea neôtera*, introduced at the same time into the titulature.

The word even echoed the prestige of the Macedonian hero par excellence, Alexander the Great, the conqueror who opened Egypt to the Macedonians and who was buried in Alexandria but was also the founder of a broader but more ephemeral Macedonian empire. I believe that this complex message, directed to the Hellenistic world and not to the Egyptian people, inspired the modification of the titulature, particularly the adoption of the epiclesis *Philopatris*. Soon other titles and other initiatives would confirm Cleopatra VII's opening to the new Greek East as it was reorganised by Antony.[16]

---

[15] Bearzot (1992) does not help us here, because it concerns only the short period which precedes Ptolemy Soter's taking of the diadem, particularly with reference to the inscriptions of Olympia and Delphi from which Pausanias (6.3.1 and 10.7.8) noted that the king wanted with some pride to be called Πτολεμαῖος Μακεδών (this is true outside of Egypt), while elsewhere he is king of Egypt (this is an error of Pausanias). I would not follow Bearzot when she considers that the Macedonians, because of their small number, merged with the Greeks. As we have just said, in Egypt, *Makedôn*, ethnic, and *Hellên*, social qualification, are semantically and juridically situated on two different levels.

[16] The absence of the epiclesis *Philopatris* next to *Thea neôtera*, both in Amathous in the Cypriot dedication *SEG* XLVII 1866 (cf. *CdE* 78 (2003) 236–40) and in the Demotic stele of Coptos (as read by M. Chauveau 1998: 114–15), reveals that the epiclesis, known only through a unique reference, was perhaps an occasional, short-lived assertion of the Macedonian ancestry of the queen or that it did not survive the later creation of the new, more impressive epicleseis of 'Mother of the Kings' and 'Queen of the Kings', as *Thea neôtera* could do, linked as it was with the divine nature of the queen.

Chapter 5

THE DYNASTIC POLITICS OF CLEOPATRA VII

၆

For nearly half a century, the confrontation between literary testimonies and new documentary evidence about the end of the kingdom of the Ptolemies has continually revised the history of Queen Cleopatra VII. Its perspective is now more appropriate to her actual destiny as a queen, and in this way, on the dynastic level, it has come to be treated less as an aspect of the heavy-handed interventions of Rome in the fate of Alexandria and Egypt. I think, for instance, of Heinz Heinen's work or more recently Thomas Schrapel's or Linda Ricketts's contributions.[1] Lucia Criscuolo (1989) shows that historians have wrongly imagined marriages by extrapolation between Cleopatra and her two young brothers, who were momentarily associated with her as *basileis*. Michel Chauveau established the political meaning of the royal dates which show a double numbering of the year.[2] Every day, we find – to take inspiration from a recent title[3] – Cleopatra further upstream from her myth.

Let us put aside, hard as it is, the uncountable Cleopatras generated either from the hostile propaganda of Octavian or, since the Renaissance in the Western world, from theatre, painting, novel, film or comics, along with the recent no less imaginary Cleopatras, the militant of women's liberation or the black princess reigning in Alexandria.[4] But the historian should never forget how much his own unconscious is marked by the weight of this luxuriant bimillenary tradition, which has seen the continuous production of contradictory

---

[1] Heinen (1966); Schrapel (1996); Ricketts (1980); Chauveau (1997b), and other contributions of the same author quoted in notes 2 and 3.

[2] Chauveau (1997a, 1990, 1991).

[3] I shall repeatedly quote Chauveau (1998), who proposes several new solutions. Even where I do not follow his conclusions, I have benefited from the progress we owe to him.

[4] Modern literature, even serious, is inexhaustible. Let us quote here, for example, J. Brambach, *Kleopatra und ihre Zeit: Legende und Wirklichkeit* (Munich 1991); Édith Flamarion, *Cléopâtre: vie et mort d'un pharaon* (Paris 1993); Mary Hamer, *Signs of Cleopatra: History, Politics, Representation* (London and New York 1993); J. Whitehorne, *Cleopatras* (London and New York 1994). Cf. Chapter 3.

value-judgements even among scholars. The influence of the Rome-oriented source tradition in ancient and modern historiography may make us feel a little deprived, arranging and rearranging the all-too-rare documents, often isolated and badly distributed in time and space, results of a process of discovery as unpredictable as their subsequent evaluation. The first century BC in Egypt in fact is relatively speaking an impoverished time in this treasure-house of inscriptions and papyri.

In the learned monographs mentioned above, two objective ancient types of information drawn from papyri, inscriptions and coins are more or less constants in any argument: the royal titulature and the formulae used for dating the documents. I shall mainly limit myself to the analysis of those documentary data and to their possible use as objective evidence for the dynastic policy which we might reasonably attribute to Cleopatra. In the Greek, hieroglyphic or Demotic sources, the complete titulature of the Ptolemies solemnly identifies the sovereign or the couple ruling in Alexandria. For instance, for the last sovereigns that reigned in Alexandria, the queen is officially called 'Queen Cleopatra Goddess who loves her father'; her son is 'King Ptolemy also called Caesar, God who loves his father and who loves his mother'.

Three basic elements appear in such titulatures. The first, at least since Ptolemy III, is the definition of the divinity of the sovereign or of the royal couple, a development of the Graeco-Macedonian hero cults, a development all the easier in Hellenistic Egypt in that it is close to the notion of the pharaoh as son of a god, called to become a god after his death. The second element, the epiclesis, confers on the king an aura bound to the virtues manifesting the royal essence of the sovereign. For example, the title of Saviour or Benefactor asserts a significant domestic source of legitimacy. Cleopatra VII as 'Goddess who loves her father' reminds us that she assumed the royal diadem in accordance with the will of her father. The teenager Ptolemy Caesar is 'God who loves his father', his father Caesar, dead and deified, who restored the traditional monarchic order in Egypt. He is also 'God who loves his mother', Cleopatra, who has restored through him the normal order of transmission of the dynasty. The third significant element of the titulature appears only when kingship is shared; it gives the hierarchical order in which the coregents are mentioned. For the historian, the value of such titulature is considerable, because we find there a message coming directly from the palace to be circulated through the entire realm and therefore an aspect of the royal ideology considered to be of central importance.

The second objective type of evidence which will hold our attention is the way documents are dated by a year of the reign of a king and, on occasion, a queen or even, for part of the reign of Euergetes II, a royal trio. Normally documents are merely dated 'year 3' or 'year 17'. Sometimes, however, the date combines two figures for one year, 'year 17 which is also year 2'. But it is necessary to distinguish here two types of double numbering, because they have quite different significances. In the first case, an Egyptian calendar year begins in the last months of a reign and ends with the first months of the successor; such a year will sometimes be referred to, during the period after the accession of the new ruler, as 'year x, which is also year 1'.[5] The formula in this case is more or less an optional[6] convenience of dating without any political message, and the formula disappears at the end of this year 1. On the contrary, the other type of double dates has a quite different meaning, because an official double numbering abruptly appears during a reign and develops in the course of time. So, after 'year 15' of Cleopatra VII and Ptolemy XV Caesar, 'year 16 which is also year 1' leads to 'year 22 which is also year 7', the last year of the Ptolemaic realm, the year of the queen's suicide. Michel Chauveau has convincingly shown that the origin of such a double numbering should be sought not in the adoption of a coregent, but in a new political orientation considered important enough to be the basis of a parallel numbering.[7]

The father of Cleopatra, Ptolemy XII, who was officially proclaimed the God New Dionysos, familiarly called Ptolemy Auletes, the 'Flautist', died in 51 BC after a rather animated reign. For more than a century, the Romans had already been exercising a more or less effective protectorate over a realm the resources of which made them greedy. Expelled from the throne by the Alexandrians, Ptolemy XII, a corrupting vassal and unscrupulous diplomat, had obtained in Rome from Julius Caesar recognition as 'friend and ally of the Roman people'. Ptolemy XII was brought back to Alexandria by a Roman army which in the event stayed in Egypt for centuries.

[5] This mechanism was best described by Skeat (1960).

[6] The double dates '30 = 1' were concurrently used with 'year 1' during the first months of Cleopatra VII's reign. It happens that the dating by the former year is used after the death of the previous king or that, in retrospective dates, people were dating 'year 1' by anticipating the last months of the previous reign; cf. Skeat (1960: 93).

[7] See note 3.

When her father died,[8] Cleopatra was 18 years old, but she was not the only heir of the realm. During the exile of Ptolemy XII in Italy, his throne had been usurped by Berenike, the only daughter he had from his royal marriage, that is, from his ritual marriage with his sister Cleopatra. Back in Alexandria he had this daughter executed. But Ptolemy XII had his own 'jardin secret', a stable union with a lady who, in my view, came from the highest Macedonian aristocracy. She had borne him two daughters and two sons, children whom Ptolemy XII presented as his rightful offspring. In year 29, the year preceding Ptolemy XII's death, a man named Nepheros, a good Egyptian name, dedicated a sacred area for the sake not only of king Ptolemy but also of his children, who are called the 'New Gods *Philadelphoi*'.[9] Even though this collective epiclesis might be quite unofficial,[10] it is remarkable because the royal children are deified and because the choice of the adjective *Philadelphos*[11] ('brother- and sister-loving') for this set of brothers and sisters seems to seek to avert what would become a tragic reality: the bloody confrontations of those brothers and sisters. All of them would reign; but only Cleopatra would survive.

In fact, the legitimacy of the four children, well prepared through their unofficial or official deification,[12] was never placed in doubt either in Alexandria or in Egypt after the death of their father. When

---

[8] Probably mid-May 51 or somewhat earlier. From Rome, Cicero is told about the death of the king on 30 June. In Egypt, in Thebes, people do not know it even on 3 June (cf. H. De Meulenaere, *CdE* 42 (1967) 297–305), whereas in Herakleopolis a dating '30 = 1' of the new queen appears as early as 24 May (*BGU* VIII 1829).

[9] *OGIS* II 741; cf. Heinen (1966: 179–80); Criscuolo (1990: 91–2).

[10] Chauveau (1998: 24) sees there an *initiative* of the king which tried 'de prévenir les dissensions familiales par le ciment du culte dynastique en réunissant toute sa progéniture au sein du collège des "dieux Nouveaux Philadelphes"'. Cf. note 13.

[11] I do not believe that, here as in other cases, the epiclesis *Philadelphos* makes any allusion to the married couple Ptolemy II and Arsinoe. They were deified as *Theoi Adelphoi*. On the contrary, *Philadelphos* as an epiclesis was reserved in that couple for Arsinoe alone; it summarises the ideological justification which surrounded the last union of that queen and the unprecedented incestuous character of the royal marriage. Later on, the epiclesis *Theos Philadelphos* was based on concrete brother-and-sister domestic relations and must be interpreted, as I said above, in the first degree. Cf. Criscuolo (1990), who rightly warns against the idea that the epiclesis is bound to a royal brother–sister marriage.

[12] The inscription *I. Louvre Bernand* 21 (Hawara?) is dated Epeiph 1 year 1 = 2 July 51 BC. Ptolemy XIII's absence and Cleopatra's sole presence in the titulature cannot be explained by the idea that the inscription of the Isiac association was made 'for Queen Kleopatra Thea Philopator' because she was revered as 'new Isis'. Such an approach appears neither on the relief nor in the text and is unthinkable only a few weeks after her accession to the throne. On the contrary, the stele was first dedicated to Ptolemy XII, as shown by the relief and by what remains of the ruling of the underlying inscription that was hollowed out. The

factions of the court violently attacked each other concerning the royal succession, they always chose the pretender among one of these four princes and princesses. Moreover – and we shall find here one of the aspects of the dynastic policy of Cleopatra – in Ptolemaic Egypt, it is the prince who always decreed the legitimacy, even authoritatively creating family links when required.[13] In this particular case, the notions of bastardy or of morganatic union which are sometimes associated with the descendants of Ptolemy XII are pure anachronisms.

In his will, Ptolemy XII had bequeathed the diadem collectively to Cleopatra and to her elder brother, his very young son Ptolemy XIII. He had also committed Rome to taking care of the execution of the will. With the supreme skill of an old fox, he mobilised in this way the only force capable of imposing the succession in Alexandria as foreseen by him, and in doing so he was automatically cancelling any previous document which would have appointed Rome as heir of the throne of Egypt. Now, against these clauses of the will, for a while Cleopatra reigned alone. She was recognised as ruler by her administration, in any case in the Fayyum, where the royal titulature is limited to three words, *Kleopatra Thea Philopator*, attested by two excellent sources, the contract *PSI* X 1098[14] and the inscription *I. Louvre Bernand* 21. This sole reign of Cleopatra has been a debatable point, but I am convinced that the documentary evidence which we have is decisive.[15] Moreover, could the court have developed hostile reactions

dedicant, after the unexpected death of the king, erased the original inscription and replaced it by one honouring the new queen. It makes no sense, given the state of the reused support, to consider that the relief represents Cleopatra as pharaoh; cf. [R. S. Bianchi] in *Cleopatra's Egypt: Age of the Ptolemies* (Brooklyn 1988) 188–9, no. 78. The pharaoh making an offering to Isis Sononais is not a theological subtlety but the carelessness of the stone-cutter who was asked to inscribe the new inscription, unless indeed he did not feel himself capable of feminising the relief.

[13] Even though the deification of the royal children could be nothing more than the result of excessive zeal on the part of the Egyptian dignitary who drafted this inscription, the document assures at least that the preparation of the duly legitimised children for a precarious succession was an actual political reality which somebody could easily evoke.

[14] *PSI* X 1098 (Tebtynis; year 1, Mesore 29 = 29 August 51) is a contract with solemn forms (eponymous dating with Macedonian and Egyptian months, and six witnesses, three of whom are 'Macedonians' and three *katoikoi*).

[15] Chauveau (1998: 27) points out that the two documents could be equally assigned to Cleopatra Berenike III, who reigned six months after the death of her father Ptolemy IX (summer 80). But it is impossible to assign *PSI* X 1098 to the reign of Berenike III. Indeed, this contract from Tebtynis (see note 14) would have been signed in a well-informed cleruchic milieu six days before the end of the year 1 of Berenike III. Into these six days – let us add ten days to meet ourselves in Alexandria – it would be necessary to pile up the two weeks of the joint reign of the queen and Ptolemy Alexander II, the murder of the queen, that of her murderer, Ptolemy XII's recall (he was not in Egypt at the time) and, last but not least, the

against Cleopatra if the succession had taken place on the terms Ptolemy XII had fixed?[16]

This 'usurpation' of the throne has sometimes been explained as the continuation of a coregency which Cleopatra supposedly exercised at the end of the life of Ptolemy XII. The traces left by this coregency, however, are very vague.[17] As pointed out earlier, some documents are dated 'year 30 which is also year 1', namely: the thirtieth year of Ptolemy XII which becomes year 1 of Cleopatra. But these dates, as I observed, cannot help us, because they represent not a continuing double numbering, but an empirical solution[18] for dating documents after the death of the king. Jan Quaegebeur, in his inquiry on Cleopatra's presence in the reliefs of Dendera, was intrigued by an anonymous woman who accompanies Ptolemy XII in the crypts of the temple and is said in one case to be 'the daughter of the King' and in another 'the elder daughter of the King'.[19] He recognised in her Cleopatra as coregent. But Cleopatra called the 'daughter' or 'the elder daughter' of the king could appear there simply as the elder daughter of the king and the only one of his children old enough to assume a visible role in the official life around the king. Let us remember moreover that Nepheros' dedication,[20] which is contemporary with the construction of the crypts, did not make any distinctions among the four young deified princes.

---

beginning of the new reign whose *second* year would actually begin after those six days (cf. for example, Hölbl 1994: 193–5). Constraints are hardly less evident for the inscription dated Epeiph 1 (see n. 12), sixty-five days before the end of the year. It would be very difficult to place in such a narrow span that series of events, but especially, in that case, how could we explain the two successive texts of the document (the second dating from the end and not early in the beginning of the reign of the queen in question), and simultaneously the fact that the stele was first dedicated in favour of a king, as shown on the relief (see n. 16)?

[16] On Ptolemy III and Berenike II affirming the dynastic legitimacy both through legitimate filiation and through the self-proclaimed divine character of kingship, see Chapter 2.

[17] Let us set aside for this question as for many the others the stele of Bucheum (R. Mond and O. H. Myers, *The Bucheum* (London 1934) 11–13, no. 13, which wrongly played an important role in establishing the train of events in 51. Chauveau (1998: 26, 113) showed that the document (year 1 of Augustus) is considerably later than those events and that it cannot be taken into account to fix the chronology of the end of Ptolemy XII's reign and the nature of the beginning of Cleopatra's.

[18] Let us note, for example, the clumsy way the double date was formulated in *BGU* VIII 1828 (ἐν τῶι ἐνεστῶτι λ τῶι α ἔτει). In this marginal note, drawn up by the *strategos*, answering a complaint introduced by some farmers, the dating reveals not an official formula coming from higher up in Alexandria, but a local improvisation. The context explains why the double numeration was used: the cultivation was engaged before the death of the king, when the year was still called 'year 30'.

[19] Quaegebeur (1991: 60–1).

[20] See note 9.

The seizure of power by Cleopatra as sole ruler was controversial in Alexandria, and there was a powerful faction at the court supporting the justifiable rights of the child Ptolemy XIII and aiming to force Cleopatra to share the throne. On 27 October 50 BC, at the beginning of year 3, Ptolemy XIII and Cleopatra promulgated together an edict severely punishing the transport towards the Thebaid of wheat and dried vegetables intended for Lower Egypt.[21] The decree is interesting because it reveals a state of scarcity which threatened Alexandria and such a crisis of the harvests that it brought the two parties to work temporarily together. The introduction of the edict 'by order of the king and of the queen' establishes the hierarchy of power: the young king is mentioned before his elder sister. This fact may betray one of the motives of the palace revolt: the presence of a woman alone on the throne probably scandalised the court more than the violation of their father's will. Cleopatra would not forget that lesson.[22]

However, the crisis broke out soon. In November 49, the senators gathered with Pompey in Thessalonike recognised only one sovereign in Alexandria, Ptolemy XIII. In fact, news may have suffered some delay between Egypt and Macedonia, because a very unusual double date furnishes a new puzzle. This time it is drawn up as 'year 1 and 3',[23] and in an even more precise version, 'year 1, which was additionally called "year 3"', $\dot{\epsilon}v$ $\tau\hat{\omega}\iota$ a $\pi\rho o\sigma a\gamma o\rho\epsilon v\theta\dot{\epsilon}v\tau\iota$ $\delta\dot{\epsilon}$ γ $(\ddot{\epsilon}\tau\epsilon\iota)$.[24] This has generated a lot of contradictory hypotheses.[25] In my opinion, we are not dealing with a double numbering of the continuous type, and surely not with a double numbering marking a coregency.[26] In this case, as a rule only year 3 would be mentioned, as is now established. We meet here once more an unofficial subtlety in a formula similar to the one we found in 'year 30 which becomes year 1' of Cleopatra. However, it has a quite different import: the double date translates, in an optional way and maybe only in part of Egypt, the passage after the beginning of 'year 3' of Cleopatra, presumably now

---

[21] *BGU* VIII 1730.

[22] Note the order in which the sovereigns are cited in the Demotic documents which Chauveau (1997b: 168–70), rightly assigns to the joint reign of Ptolemy XIII and Cleopatra VII.

[23] Cf. Skeat (1962).

[24] *SB* VI 9065, for which Criscuolo (1989: 326) rightly emphasises that the document is later than Ptolemy XIV's accession to the throne (the actual date is lost). The date which concerns us here is a retrospective one.

[25] See Criscuolo (1989: 326); Chauveau (1997b: 168–9).

[26] Chauveau (1997a: 30–1; 1997b: 170), but he assigns year 1 to Cleopatra VII.

with Ptolemy XIII, to a regime 'year 1', probably ignoring Cleopatra
for a time, and thereafter back to the previous regime 'year 3'. It is
evident that 'year 3' belongs to the counting of Cleopatra's regnal
years beginning in 51,[27] because one cannot see why the queen would
have interrupted a dating system which legitimised her power.
'Year 1' in such a sequence is most easily interpreted as indicating a
brief period of Ptolemy XIII as sole king, an intermezzo which ended
quickly as the result of a new agreement between the parties.[28] After
this return to the initial count of Cleopatra's regnal years, somebody
found it convenient to record retrospectively that at a certain moment
the current 'year 3' had been called 'year 1', probably referring to
documents dated 'year 1' which concerned his affairs.[29]

The Alexandrian imbroglio was not settled by the arrival of
Pompey the Great after his defeat in Pharsalus. He indirectly added a
new Roman dimension to the Alexandrian dynastic competition. The
events are well known. Cleopatra had disappeared. Her younger
brother had gathered an army to prevent her return. When Pompey
arrived in Egypt to ask for protection, the king's counsellors had the
Roman murdered. Julius Caesar, in pursuit of his rival, arrived at
Alexandria. Cleopatra reappeared in the palace. Julius Caesar imple-
mented the royal will: Ptolemy XIII and Cleopatra were confirmed in
their joint kingship. It is the only attitude he could justify in Rome.
Under the cover of a concession to her brother, who kept his hierarchical priority in the titulature, Cleopatra inaugurated a more stable
dynastic policy. Indeed, the presence of the Roman army gave her an
overwhelming advantage in armed manpower – it had been up to then
the weak point of the queen's faction. During the difficult war
between Caesar and the Ptolemaic army, Arsinoe, the younger sister,
proclaimed herself queen. She was defeated and shunted aside, to
appear at Caesar's triumph in Rome. Ptolemy XIII died during a

---

[27] Cf. Heinen (1966: 30–3), but in a perspective other than the one I propose here.

[28] It is difficult to place this secession in the series of documents dated 'year 3', but it is earlier
than the conclusion of the loan agreement *SB* VIII 9764 (date lost) and a lot earlier than the
month of Pauni (June 49), the point foreseen for the refund. It is later than the beginning of
'year 3' of Cleopatra (5 September 50). The double date '1 = 3' could be used concurrently
with dates 'year 3' after the return of Cleopatra, and 'year 3' might have been used all
through the year in the regions of Egypt not affected by the secession.

[29] In the petition to the queen and Ptolemy XIV *SB* VI 9065 (see note 24), the reason why the
widow Herakleia quotes the double date is evident: the will of her husband was probably
dated 'year 1' of Ptolemy XIII (the short period when Cleopatra was no longer recognised
as queen in Herakleopolis), but it was useful for her to situate the will chronologically
through a double date in the succession of Cleopatra's regnal years used in the rest of the
file.

military operation. Whether it was Caesar's caution or Cleopatra's wisdom, she took a new coregent, her youngest brother, now Ptolemy XIV. But she immediately triumphed on one point: she now had priority in the titulature, a new dimension of the royal authority she kept until her tragic end. Later, for example, in 41, at the royal court of justice, in an action brought by Alexandrian landowners in the *chôra* against the civil servants of the queen, mother and son – Ptolemy XV Caesar – appear in this order in their full titulature in the highly political verdict which preserved the fiscal privileges of their good subjects in Alexandria.[30] When she was reigning with her brother Ptolemy XIV, or more probably with her son Ptolemy XV, the head of a synagogue obtained confirmation of the right of asylum of his sanctuary by a royal *prostagma*, 'by order of the queen and king' (βασιλίσσης καὶ βασιλέως προσταξάντων), and he added in Latin to be read by the actual police force in Egypt, *regina et rex iusserunt*.[31] We shall see that, on the Egyptian level, the queen would later suggest an inversion in the royal hierarchy in favour of the young prince, when on the walls of the temple of Dendera she proposed him as the future of the dynasty.

Meanwhile, indeed, a new element had modified the perspectives of succession to the throne. Politics do not exclude love, especially when they are tied for the two parties to solid reasons for love. When Caesar, leaving a considerable Roman army in Egypt, left his queen (whose king he never was) to dash towards Asia Minor, Cleopatra was pregnant with Ptolemy XV.[32] Later she joined Caesar in Rome with their infant, her young coregent Ptolemy XIV practically held hostage.

From this sojourn in Italy, only two facts need to be stressed. First, this travelling of Cleopatra follows the model of the sojourn of her father twelve years earlier and ends with the recognition of the royal couple as friend and ally of the Roman people. Secondly, what seems to me deserving the most attention, Cleopatra gets away from Egypt for a long time without fearing some reversal at court or of Alexandrian public opinion. She would be repeatedly absent for a

---

[30] C. Ord. Ptol. 75–6. Cf. Chapter 12.

[31] Bingen (1982). The king named in the second place could be her brother Ptolemy XIV or her son Ptolemy XV Caesar. One should not follow the attempt of Bowersock (1984) to restore this decree to Zenobia and Vaballathus. The lettering, Greek and Latin, of the inscription as well as the formula indicates a date towards the end of the Hellenistic period; cf. *Bull. épigr.* (1988) 982.

[32] The birth is situated in year 5, on 23 June 47, according to the stele of the Serapeum 335; cf. Pestman (1967: 82–4).

long time. Her capital is no longer a trap, but a base. She is from now on working for the long haul, and she would soon base this continuity beyond her death on the legitimacy of her child. She had protected herself from any surprise by having her brother at hand in Rome. After Caesar's death and the return of the royal pair to Alexandria, she had the young Ptolemy XIV murdered, a traditional Macedonian solution for any dynastic competition. Maybe Cleopatra had the conviction that new intrigues in the palace or a revolt of the army for the benefit of her brother remained a strong possibility. But the queen had another reason to clear the situation, a reason which would mark the rest of her reign: the future of her son, and, through him, the definitive revival and survival of the dynasty.

Soon the child was associated with the throne as Ptolemy XV Caesar. At once, as I said, the palace fixed the titulature of mother and son: Cleopatra remained the 'Goddess who loves her father'; the child was called 'Ptolemy also called Caesar, God who loves his father and loves his mother'. The first of the two epicleseis legitimised the birth of the successor by an authoritative decision of the queen, a tradition (as we have seen) among the Ptolemies, and promoted his official paternal filiation to an object of worship.[33] The second underlined the Ptolemaic legitimacy of her child and the promise of rightful succession. From then on the young king participated officially in the royal power.

Cleopatra went still further in the promotion of this son. Dendera's temple famously unfurls on its south outside wall a grandiose double scene of royal offerings. Last in the series of the large Ptolemaic sanctuaries of Upper Egypt, the temple of Hathor represents the most impressive architectural realisation of Cleopatra's reign, a construction which like previous ones created a space of cooperation between the monarchy and some important Egyptian priesthoods. Begun under Ptolemy XII, the naos was built under Cleopatra, who is widely present in the internal decoration;[34] it was completed soon enough to have the south facade decorated to the glory of the royal mother–son

---

[33] About the dedication to Souchos *patropatôr* in favour of Cleopatra VII, Ptolemy Caesar and their ancestors, see Heinen (1998: 345), who reckons that the rare epiclesis *patropatôr* given to Souchos puts the god forward as 'the paternal grandfather' of Cleopatra and 'father' of Julius Caesar, making of Ptolemy Caesar the 'first representative of a Hellenistic-Roman dynasty such as aimed at by Cleopatra'. Without reserving such a precise place for Caesar in a new dynastic ideology, I would find there in any case a document more of Ptolemy Caesar's legitimisation by Cleopatra, as it might have been perceived in the Egyptian *chôra*. Cf. *Bull. épigr.* (1998) 552.

[34] Quaegebeur (1991).

Figure 5.1 *Dendera, Temple of Hathor, south exterior wall of naos. Ptolemy XV offering incense, followed by Cleopatra VII shaking the sistrum (photo Jean Bingen)*

couple. It presents a double antithetical scene on both sides of the large mask of the goddess Hathor-Aphrodite, mistress of the sanctuary. Turned towards this mask and addressing the divinities of Dendera, the young pharaoh Ptolemy Caesar, king of Upper and Lower Egypt, offers incense to these divinities, whereas behind him the queen shakes the sistrum and presents the *menat* necklace [a heavy necklace used as a rattle]. Mother and son are of the same size, but the queen gives the young Ptolemy the priority in access to the gods, and it is over the head of the infant king that Horus spreads his wings, a sign of power and divine protection.[35] Quaegebeur noted that the figurative representation of the mother–son couple creates a hierarchy different from the one we find when the couple is mentioned in the string course of the base: there the queen is named first.[36] But a text could only follow the official Alexandrian titulature. On the contrary, the reliefs, which for the safety of humanity fix for eternity the permanent intercession of the sovereigns before the gods, lie on a quite different conceptual level. With the freedom which strictly

---

[35] On the right-hand counterpart of the scene, it is Nekhbet who protects the young king.
[36] Quaegebeur (1991: 63).

traditional representations left to the designer of the south facade, he put the male element of the couple, bearer of the future of the dynasty, deliberately in evidence.[37] Surely this was in accordance with tradition, but, to display such a political programme, the clergy must have had royal assent.

Meanwhile the foreign policy of Cleopatra underwent a reorientation significant enough to be the occasion of a new formulation of the date: regnal year 16 became officially 'year 16 which is also year 1'.[38] This reckoning, as I remarked, was used until 30 BC, the end of the double reign, with 'year 22 which is also year 7'. Such a continuous count represents exactly the political nature recognised by Michel Chauveau in the double counting accompanying a major royal initiative. Today there is a rather wide agreement on the fact that this change coincides with the first donations to Cleopatra by Antony of territories outside Egypt. This explanation is fortunately supported by Porphyry's *Chronicle*. Following the reorganisation of the triumvirate in 43 and the victory at Philippi, Antony was entrusted with the East. He summoned Cleopatra to Tarsus to clarify her position with regard to Rome, or more exactly with regard to the Roman policy which the *triumvir* planned to inaugurate in the Near East. In the Antonian project, Cleopatra progressively became a political partner with considerable resources. She became also a partner who, well into her thirties, gave three children to the master of the East, another way for the queen to obtain from Antony the recovery of the former empire of the Ptolemies. And there is even a third reason, because Antony had accumulated at this point some setbacks and defeats in Armenia and in Media. The adoption of the double dating indicates that Alexandrian policy had adopted a project at a more ambitious level than the transfer of some territories in 37, a marginal aspect rather than the core explanation of the new political order announced with the new double dating.

The double date, which was adopted for some coinages outside Egypt, seems to me to be less an assertion of authority organising two

---

[37] For the other representations of the royal couple in the temple, see Quaegebeur (1991: 49–72).

[38] In an official document drafted in double copy from Herakleopolis, *BGU* XIV 2376, dated 'year 17 = 2', there is an allusion to a court order dated Thoth 10 'year 16 = year 1' (cf. Schrapel 1996: 211). If one admits that this last date was mentioned because it appears on the original copy of the order, the reform of the dating was proclaimed at 'new year' of year 16 (Thoth 1, 1 September 37). But retrospective dates must be handled with caution and we cannot exclude the possibility that the reform of the regnal year was announced later in 37/36.

Figure 5.2 *Cistophoric tetradrachm of Antony and Cleopatra (Asia Minor [Ephesos?], 39 BC). Bibliothèque royale de Belgique (12.17g) (enlarged)*

geographic zones, Egypt and the queen's changing foreign possessions, than Cleopatra's combination of two Macedonian successions,
the lineage of the Ptolemies and that of the Seleucids. The second
factor was a crucial aspect of her complex relations with Antony. He
needed manpower, money and reliable vassals to build in the East the
prefiguration of an imperial system which survived for a while his dis-
astrous personal fate: an agglomeration of provinces directly administered by Rome and protectorates more or less tightly controlled.
Outside Egypt, coinage did not hesitate to represent Antony and
Cleopatra together. This shows how much the queen separated, or
better, accumulated as two different responsibilities, the succession of
the Ptolemies (which went considerably beyond Egypt) and that of the
Seleucids. In Egypt, the double date testifies only to the new ambitions
of the royal mother–son couple, because Antony, like Julius Caesar,
had no place in the Alexandrian royal system, or in the titulature or
the legends of the coins.[39]

---

[39] Even after his marriage with Cleopatra, a marriage which has nothing to do either with the
dynastic ideology as reconstructed by Cleopatra in Alexandria, or with Roman law, for
which it is only a scandal. I believe, but I shall not linger on this here, that the marriage must
be understood as aiming at some legitimacy of the Hellenistic type in the Seleucid world.

In the same perspective of political renewal, Alexandria modified Cleopatra's titulature.[40] The queen was proclaimed *Thea neôtera Philopator kai Philopatris*, 'Goddess *neôtera* who loves her father and loves her *patris*'. By contrast, the young king is still 'God who loves his father and loves his mother'.

First the queen is called *Thea neôtera*, the 'younger', the 'newer' Goddess.[41] Before the publication of the Berlin papyrus which supplies the new titulature in its entirety, *Thea neôtera* was already attested as an epiclesis of Cleopatra on coins from Antioch, Chalkis (the first territory donated by Antony to Cleopatra) and Cyrene.[42] I shall not recall here the various exegeses which the epiclesis *Thea neôtera* aroused as a a divinity entirely foreign to Egypt, by means of adducing some links with local cults.[43] But why would Cleopatra have added to her cult, which already existed in itself and was of universal reach, an identification with some peripheral and obscure divinity? The existence of either form of an independent cult of Cleopatra Neôtera in Egypt is not attested with certainty.[44] Here also an identification with a particular goddess is not compatible with the idea of a religious profession ample enough to have been adopted as a major political orientation in the titulature. If there is a survival later in the imperial period of a cult of a Neôtera in Egypt in Dendera and if this cult had some link with Cleopatra,[45] it would be necessary to

[40] The change of the formula appears in the official document *BGU* XIV 2376 (see note 38), dated 'year 17 = year 2', simultaneously with the new titulature (for which see Chapter 4); cf. Schrapel (1996: 209–11).

[41] Schrapel (1996: 225–34).

[42] On Cleopatra's coinage outside Egypt, see Schrapel (1996: *passim*). The epiclesis *Thea neôtera* is particularly attested on coins probably issued in Phoenicia, cf. A. Burnett, M. Amandry and P. P. Ripollès, *Roman Provincial Coinage* I (London and Paris 1992) 601–2, nos. 4094–6, pl. 155. The legend *Basilissa Kleopatra Thea neôtera* accompanies on the obverse the bust of the queen, whereas the reverse shows that of Antony, *imperator* and *triumvir*, *Antonios autokrator triton triôn andrôn*. Such a combination places this coinage out of the Alexandrian sector of the new double policy of Cleopatra, Antony having never held any place in the Ptolemaic power system. On the iconographic plan, for Fleischer (1996) Cleopatra VII's 'Alexandrian' and 'Syro-Roman' monetary portraits present the queen respectively as the rightful heir of the Ptolemies and as 'friend of Antony'. I would rather see there the two aspects of the new policy of the queen, even if the Seleucid field was strictly bound to Antony's strategy.

[43] For the details of the question, see Schrapel (1996: 225–34). For him, *neôtera* is spelled with a capital letter and has an autonomous religious value.

[44] Quaegebeur (1988).

[45] For example, a quite doubtful connection between Cleopatra and Hathor, adducing *Aphroditê Thea Neôtera* in *I. Louvre Bernand* 28 (Dendera, AD 98) with mention of the *hieron tês Neôteras*. For different attempts to identify this Neôtera, see the commentary of the most recent editor of the inscription, Étienne Bernand.

admit that such an epiclesis does not result from a cult existing before the reign of Cleopatra, but, on the contrary, that it could only be the survival of the cult of Cleopatra. The Demotic stele of Coptos (30 BC), recently revisited by Michel Chauveau,[46] illustrates the influence of titulatures on the pervading religious mentality. According to a hypothesis formulated long ago by numismatists, the epiclesis *Thea neôtera* on the contrary presents Cleopatra as a new incarnation of Cleopatra Thea, the Ptolemaic princess who was queen of Syria as the wife successively of three Seleucids. I would add to their argumentation that in the plain language of Greek Egypt – a context that one cannot neglect – *neôteros* has a commonplace meaning, that of the 'younger child'. A *neôteros* or a *neôtera* has, for instance, the same name as an elder brother or sister. Under the patronage of the famous Seleucid queen, 'the younger Cleopatra Thea' suggests moreover the queen's aims in the Seleucid sphere. It is with good reason that Michel Chauveau, basing his argument on this interpretation of *Thea neôtera*, had originally attributed the starting point of year 1 in the new double count to Cleopatra's desire to assume the mantle of the Seleucids.[47]

I propose elsewhere a new interpretation of the second addition made to Cleopatra's titulature, the epiclesis *Philopatris*, 'the one who loves her *patris*' (cf. Chapter 4). It diverges from a certain consensus, built on William Brashear's comment in the edition of *BGU* XIV 2376. The political message implied by the extension of the royal titulature is bound, according to him, neither to the first donations of territories to Cleopatra, nor to the birth of the twins Cleopatra had by Antony, but to an attempt of the queen to assert her loyalty to an Egyptian people irritated by a too narrow collaboration with the Roman invader, and by the scandal of her rather provocative affairs with Caesar and Antony.[48] Michel Chauveau enlarges Brashear's interpretation: by adopting the epiclesis *Philopatris*, the queen renewed the entire political philosophy of a kingship that would from now on be based on an almost mystic link between the queen and the country of the Nile and all its inhabitants.[49]

---

[46] Chauveau (1998: 114–15).

[47] Chauveau (1990: 151).

[48] Huss (1990) particularly supported this idea of Brashear as corresponding to his own hypothesis that Cleopatra was born, like her brothers and her sister, of a stable union between Ptolemy XII and a lady from the Memphite high sacerdotal class. For different views of *philopatris* see Chapter 4.

[49] Chauveau (1998: 113–14).

I question in Chapter 4 how we could imagine such an attitude on the part of a supposed 'Egyptian public opinion'.[50] This conception of a territorial homeland is equally anachronistic. Hellenistic kingship is bound not to a territory constituted as a *patris*, but to a space of power assumed by a king. Cleopatra is 'Egyptian' only for foreigners, especially if they were as hostile as Octavian. In Alexandria at the court, the royal titulatures and their epicleseis are devised as political messages in which the king is *basileus*, lord of the unstable set of territories over which he actually reigns, which, for the Ptolemies, were never confined to Egypt. I show that the laudatory term *philopatris* is not rare at all in Greek epigraphy, particularly in imperial times, but that it enlightens us only on one point: it evokes a restricted space connected with birthplace or ancestry. Furthermore in the official Greek language of Ptolemaic Egypt, the identity of an individual is fixed 'by father and *patris*', and the *patris* is the ethnic origin of the individual, often that of his ancestors. If one is Egyptian, the term indicates the nome where one resides. In Hellenistic Egypt, the most prestigious *patris* is that of *Makedôn*, which for a while survived the elimination of ethnic designations in the reorganisation by the Roman conquerors of the official means of expressing identity. Cleopatra's *patris* was neither Alexandria nor Egypt. It was obviously her Macedonian ancestry – Macedonian aristocratic ancestry – jealously preserved by the consanguine marriages of the Ptolemies, by their stereotyped onomastics, that Cleopatra highlighted in her new titulature. *Philopatris* refers implicitly to her ancestor, the Macedonian Ptolemy, who first reigned in Alexandria over a vast empire where Egypt was not a homeland, but a strategic base; she invokes the Macedonian blood of both the Ptolemies and the Seleucids.[51]

Two years after the provisions of year 36, new measures increased the territories under Cleopatra's authority and were intended to ensure the future of the children of Antony by creating considerable satellite realms, in fact a virtual future. From now on Cleopatra carried the title of 'Queen of the Kings', even 'Queen of Kings, whose sons are kings', upon certain coins. Antony proclaimed Ptolemy Caesar 'King of the Kings' and at the same time recognised him as the son of Caesar. One guesses Cleopatra's influence in this ascription by Antony to Ptolemy XV Caesar of the firstborn's birthright to the constellation of territories

---

[50] Schrapel (1996: 225) points out how difficult it would be to dissociate the new titulature taken as a whole from the new Mediterranean policy of Cleopatra and from the creation of a double numeration for the regnal year.

[51] Chapter 4, pp. 61–2.

of the new Ptolemaic empire. The children of Antony would form in the future a subordinate echelon in the new Greek East. Alexander Helios received Armenia and the territories beyond the Euphrates, his twin sister Cleopatra Selene received Cyrenaica.

To the youngest child, Ptolemy Philadelphos, two years old and clearly favoured, was awarded the Seleucid part of the virtual complex built by Antony: Syria, Phoenicia, part of Asia Minor. This new Seleucid destiny of the young boy is symbolised by the Macedonian insignia of his power, the chlamys of purple, the diadem and the Macedonian head-dress, the *kausia*. A limestone head of the prince wears the *kausia* decorated with a small uraeus, signs of his Alexandrian and Macedonian royal ancestry.[52] Choosing the epiclesis Philadelphos for her last child, Cleopatra doubtless wanted to put him under the protection of his brothers, but especially of his elder brother and suzerain, the King of Kings Ptolemy XV Caesar. A Demotic stele from Coptos gives evidence that the titles of the royal mother–son couple were acknowledged as far as Upper Egypt. In the inscription which precedes by a few months the death-agony of the Ptolemaic monarchy (19 January 30), weavers call Cleopatra 'the Mother of the Kings, Queen of the Kings, the youngest goddess',[53] omitting only in this addition of epicleseis of the queen the one that hints at her Macedonian nobility, a notion which did not have a claim on the attention of her humble Egyptian subjects.

This triumph of Cleopatra's dynastic policy was only a rough draft of an unpredictable future. Not much later, Cleopatra, the most powerful and reliable among Antony's vassals, accompanied him in his careless expedition towards Rome. The disaster of Actium forced Cleopatra to return to her realm. But the fate of Egypt was sealed. Antony's suicide, that of Cleopatra, the murder of Ptolemy Caesar by Octavian – he was more dangerous as half-brother by adoption than as last king of Egypt – are only dramatic vicissitudes of the disappearance of the last powerful Hellenistic dynasty, as dictated by the winner of a contest which had Rome at stake.

---

[52] Josephson (1997: 21) rectifies the attribution of this head of whitish limestone, first assigned to Alexander the Great by Bianchi (1992).

[53] Quoted by Chauveau (1998: 114–15, amending the reading of the editio princeps in A. Farid, *Fünf demotische Stelen* (Berlin 1995) 32–76.

PART II: THE GREEKS

Chapter 6

THE THRACIANS IN PTOLEMAIC EGYPT

℘

Papyrologists wishing to deal with Thracian immigration in Graeco-Roman Egypt find their task made easier by a series of preliminary studies,[1] and especially by a monograph that V. Velkov and A. Fol dedicated to the subject in 1977.[2] This book quotes earlier research and raises questions of method connected with the existence of Thracians of the first generation or 'of the descent' in our papyrological documentation. On Velkov's responsibility a catalogue was drafted of the Thracians whose presence in Graeco-Roman Egypt may be traced more or less with certainty. Finally, Fol offered an attempt to synthesise the mechanisms and nature of Thracian immigration in Ptolemaic Egypt, and eventually under the Roman empire. My discussion owes much to their work, from which it diverges largely in the matter of the relatively low place they attribute to Thracians in the social hierarchy of Hellenistic Egypt. There are numerous and difficult problems of documentary criticism both on the level of the identification of Thracian immigrants and on that of the interpretation of their presence in a document. The inventory of those problems was established by the aforesaid authors, and, thanks to Velkov and Fol, the papyrologist feels less perplexed confronting the problem of identifying a Thracian or at least facing the contradictions we find on the subject among the specialists.

We know how embarrassing for nonspecialists the ambiguities surrounding the notion of 'Thrace/Thracian' can be: is this an ethnic expression, a geographic expression (with the Bithynian onomastics creating one more problem), a political expression (as for instance in Lysimachus' short-lived kingdom of Thrace), or simply the denomination of a military unit with servicemen from heterogeneous

---

[1] For instance, Mihailov (1968).

[2] Velkov and Fol (1977). I refer the reader to that work for previous research. The methodological part of the book was summarised by the authors in Velkov and Fol (1978). See the comprehensive review by G. Mihailov, *Philologia* (Sofia) 5 (1979) 65–70.

origins?[3] But, on a statistical level, ambiguity is already produced by the existence, starting from heuristics onwards, of two non-cohesive approaches to the phenomenon. On the one hand, the ethnic $Θρᾷξ$ (Thrax) or the preposition $ἀπό$ ('from') qualify as Thracians individuals with Thracian or Greek names; on the other hand, where the ethnic is not mentioned, only Thracian onomastics are at our disposal, with the consequence that we arbitrarily exclude from the evidence all Thracians with non-Thracian names. This way we blindly emphasise the 'Thracianness' of people whose Thracian name may be a family tradition in a milieu that had been completely Hellenised for two or more generations. As a result of an external and purely formal element, then, because the ethnic is required in some types of documents and not in others, we are perforce selective in different ways. However, the Thracian sampling borrowed from the Greek documents from Egypt by Velkov and Fol is already significant and rich in lessons.

In this chapter I do not intend to amend[4] or to complete[5] their catalogue according to the latest publications.[6] Such a catalogue implies an initial methodological frame, requiring that such a survey, to be coherent, be carried out globally, and not by a succession of alterations due to various hands, which would soon deprive the list of any coherence.

Ptolemaic evidence occupies the largest part of the catalogue, 362 persons of the 525. However, this contingent must be increased by a not unimportant number of Thracians identified by their names and classified as living in the imperial period by virtue of the date of the papyri in which they appear. Friedrich Zucker (1964), however,

[3] There is, for example, the problem raised by people identified as belonging to a unit $τῶν$ $Θρακῶν$, 'of the Thracians'. The authors (pp. 15–16) neglect those in this group who do not bear a Thracian name. However, I would not apply this rule to the petition *P. Tebt.* III 779 (towards 175 BC), where the genitive plural (without article) is due simply to the accumulation of three persons each of whom in another context would have had his name followed by the mention 'Thracian'. They belong to the category of the Greek names identified as belonging to Thracians by the mention *Thrax*.

[4] Some marginalia: in 516, $Ταλαώ$ is a place-name; 517 duplicates 479; cancel 411 for the benefit of 128, and 312 for the benefit of 520.

[5] See, however, below *SB* XVI 12221. And let us quote, all the same, among the recent additions to the list, the Thracian $Ταρυσίνας ὁ ἐπὶ τῆς πέτρας$, at the head of a quarry (*P. Lond.* VII 2098.2, third century BC). Diazelmis (no. 85) now appears on the funerary stele *SEG* XXVIII 1492 (Terenouthis, 31 BC).

[6] If we except the mention of a $Τήρης$ in *P. Tebt.* IV 1137, Thracians are totally absent even from such a considerable increase in our Ptolemaic cleruchic evidence as *Tebtunis Papyri* IV, published in 1977 by J. G. Keenan and J. C. Shelton. This point emphasises the localised, thus specific, character of the Thracian cleruchic settlements.

discovered that in early Roman Egypt numerous place-names of the type '*klêros* of so-and-so' do not indicate a present-day holder of the *klêros*, but are permanent names bound to an old settlement. Zucker found that the practice of giving a permanent name to some *klêroi* goes back at least to the beginning of the first century BC; I think it is probably much older in a lot of cases. Now, many of these toponyms which perpetuate the name of one or two cleruchs, former holders of the estate (sometimes probably the first ones), show Thracian onomastics. For instance we find, to take only the best assured examples, as the eponymous cleruchs of such *klêroi*: Amatokos, Bithys, Ebruzelmis, Spartokos and Teres in the Oxyrhynchite; Amatokos, Bithyzelmis, Zazelmis, Isazelmis, Metokos, Seuthes and Sitalkes in the Hermopolite; Satokos in the Herakleopolite. Those Ptolemaic *klêroi* names occurring in papyri from the imperial period confirm the existence of Thracian cleruchic settlements in regions where Ptolemaic cleruchic evidence had already revealed their existence during the Hellenistic period.[7] This is particularly true in the cases of the Oxyrhynchite and Hermopolite nomes, which seem to have had a relatively important Thracian cleruchic presence. As the arrival of Thracian mercenaries had ceased, or, at least, must have declined when the Ptolemies lost their North Aegean possessions,[8] those place-names recording a Thracian anthroponym seem to me to indicate that the toponymic mechanism identified by Zucker has its roots already in the early Hellenistic period.

Finally, and this goes to the heart of my observations, even if these additions to our Ptolemaic prosopography do not reveal much new on the cleruchic character of the known Thracian settlements in Hellenistic Egypt, they place those eponymous cleruchs at least at a social level high enough to have the recollection of their landholdings retained in a place-name. Fol (Velkov and Fol 1977: 97–9) noted that Thracian penetration into Egypt was essentially military, and that for Thracians, putting down their roots in the cleruchic system was relatively easy because of their rural origin. But should we situate this process, as he believes, at a very low social level as a result of the generally more elementary socio-economic level of the Thracian regions? Or are we to follow Fol even more closely (p. 99), when he concludes that 'Thracians line up among those who occupy the third place from bottom to top in the Hellenistic society of Egypt, after the slaves and the Egyptian farmers of the royal domains'?

---

[7] Cf. Fol in Velkov and Fol (1977: 90). Note, however, the absence of the Arsinoite nome.
[8] Cf. Fol in Velkov and Fol (1977: 97).

I reject this last conclusion; it is not at all in accordance with the social hierarchy in Egypt as I perceive it (there is no servile class as such, for instance). At least, the general conclusions of our Bulgarian colleagues must be qualified. This is the main object of this chapter.

I would therefore open the discussion by quoting two documents, a papyrus and an inscription, which were only fully available after Velkov and Fol (1977) was published.[9] The first is *SB* XVI 12221, of unknown origin, to be dated from the mid- or late third century BC.[10] It contains a list of eight cavalrymen and their servants. This is not the place to try to define the nature of this list, interesting because of the first published mention of the Ptolemaic *basilikê ilê*, the royal squadron of pure Macedonian tradition. The document merits close and direct attention because, among these eight cavalrymen, probably all *hekatontarouroi*[11] (100-aroura landholders) and cleruchs or members of the royal squadron, we find no fewer than four Thracians, identified by their name or patronymic or both: Satokos son of Satokos (l. 1), Polyainos son of Satokos (l. 7), Bithys, member of the *basilikê ilê* (l. 13), Satokos son of Diizaporeus (l. 26). The fact that at least half of those cleruchs are Thracians may be owed only to local conditions, but the proportion is impressive all the same. It involves four Greeks (including perhaps 'invisible' Thracians with Greek names and patronymics) and four patent Thracians at the same level – a relatively high level in the cleruchic order – and those four Thracians join at that level other Thracians we already knew as officers of a certain rank.

The inscription is the agonistic dedication *SEG* XXVII 1114, available to Velkov and Fol (1977) only through a prosopography. Since then, the text has been published by L. Koenen, who dates the document to 8 March 267 BC.[12] The clandestine discovery of the stone

---

[9] The inscription was indexed in advance in *Prosopographia Ptolemaica* VI (1968), and quoted from there in the catalogue of Velkov and Fol (1977).

[10] Published by Geraci (1979). I would prefer for the date a wider span than the 'c. mid 3rd century' of the editio princeps.

[11] This qualification is certain for the first two Thracian cavalrymen, but we do not know if it applies to the rest of the list. Anyway, the third Thracian, a member of the royal squadron, had an allotment at least as large, if not larger (cf. Geraci 1979: 19).

[12] Koenen (1977). Bibliography: *SEG* XXVII 1114 + 1305. Photograph (inscription and squeeze) in *I. Fay.* III, pl. 42. P. M. Fraser, *Ancient Macedonia* V 449–51, with photograph, assigns the stone to Middle Egypt, since it is of basalt. P. Gauthier, *REG* 108 (1995) 585, proposes the Memphite nome with a query mark. Koenen (1977: 27–8), in a generally unnoticed comment, had already found 'eine Stütze für die Vermutung dasz die Inschrift aus dem Herakleopoliten stammt' in the existence of an Aminokles son of Mnesimachos, Boeotian, of the katoikic cavalry, holder of a *klêros* in Tebetnoi (Herakleopolite) and probably resident in Herakleopolis in 61/60 (*BGU* VIII 1814). The man is apparently a descendant of Mnesimachos son of Ameinokles, Boeotian, winner in the contest of the 'hoplites' in the *Basileia* of Amadokos. It

Figure 6.1 Stele recording victors in local Basileia, 267 BC (photo courtesy of Ludwig Koenen)

does not allow us to fix the exact find-spot of this unique agonistic catalogue; but a Herakleopolitan provenance is practically certain. This uncertainty is a pity since the inscription considerably enriches the scant evidence we possess on the early phase of Thracian immigration in Egypt.

would be a remarkable – but quite possible – instance of stability, 200 years or six generations, both in the continuous possession of a *klêros* in a cleruchic dynasty and in the custom of giving to the eldest son the name of his grandfather on the father's side.

The preamble of the list runs as follows:[13]

βασιλεῖ Πτολεμαίωι Σωτήρων Ἡράκλειτος Λεπτίνου Ἀλεξανδρεὺς
ἀγωνοθετήσας καὶ πρῶτος ἆθλα προθεὶς χαλκώματα
ἔτους ὀκτωκαιδεκάτου Δύστρου δωδεκάτηι γενεθλίοις,
Βασίλεια τιθέντος Ἀμαδόκου, τὴν ἀναγραφὴν τῶν νικώντων.

To King Ptolemy, son of the Saviours, Herakleitos son of Leptines, Alexandrian, who acted as agonothetes and first offered bronze prizes in the eighteenth year on the twelfth of Dystros, at the birthday festival, when Amadokos offered the *Basileia*, (dedicated) the list of the victors.

The catalogue of the winners of gymnastic, equestrian and military contests is dedicated to the king by Herakleitos, son of Leptines, a notable Alexandrian courtier.[14] Herakleitos had presided over and endowed the first celebration of the *Basileia* founded by Amadokos. I am inclined to see in this last man a Thracian prince who emigrated to the El Dorado hymned by Theocritus; at the very least, prince or not, a Thracian condottiere who reached the high social standing where one has simultaneously the means to organise games in honour of the birthday of the king and the permission to call them *Basileia*.[15]

The nature of the competition reveals at a high level an activity developing along the lines of the royal court, in what I call the Greek register of the cultural dichotomy which characterises Hellenistic Egypt. In this register βασιλεῖ Πτολεμαίωι Σωτήρων ('To King Ptolemy, son of the Saviours'), the first words of the inscription, means the king in Alexandria, not the pharaoh of Egypt.[16] Ptolemy II is here

[13] I mainly agree with the arrangement of the preamble proposed by Koenen and adopted in *SEG* [*contra* J. Ebert, *Stadion* 5, 1 (1980) 1–9 = *SEG* XXVII 1305], but I suggest a slightly different interpretation. From the epigraphic point of view we may not neglect the basic formula: Βασιλεῖ . . . Ἡράκλειτος . . . τὴν ἀναγραφὴν τῶν νικώντων (sc. ἀνέθηκεν). The sentence isolates the absolute genitive Βασίλεια τιθέντος Ἀμαδόκου, where I see a reminder of the foundation (and not of the organisation) by the Thracian Amadokos of these local games celebrated for the first time in 267. As a consequence, I put a comma at the end of l. 3 after γενεθλίοις, and not after l. 2, or, as Ebert wants, after Βασίλεια. At first sight, one could wonder at the modesty of the mention of the 'founder' coming after that of the president and sponsor of the games. However, this order simply reflects a hierarchical order, putting an Alexandrian powerful protector before his Thracian protégé, however rich the latter may be.

[14] Cf. Koenen (1977: 19–21), on the 'aulic dynasty' of the Chrysermoi to which Herakleitos probably belongs.

[15] For Koenen (1977: 1), the competitors are 'nichtalexandrinische Kleruchen', and I offered some reservations about this statement in *SEG* XXVII, p. 200. Perhaps we are both mistaken in wanting to find later cleruchic standards in an early military milieu, where the use of the patronymic with the name of the winner is in fact a purely agonistic tradition.

[16] I refer to Chapter 18 as well as to some of the papers of the symposium of Berlin published in *Das ptolemäische Ägypten* (Mainz am Rhein 1978).

'king' for all the competitors – and not a single Egyptian among them, but Macedonians, Greeks and Thracians together in the melting pot of immigration.[17] Among the Thracians are the trumpeter[18] and five of the winners. In spite of the relative commonness of their patronymic 'son of Amadokos', I am inclined with Koenen to identify in three of the winners sons of the founder of the games. If this is true, the nature and succession of the names of the sons are interesting. The eldest brother, victorious in the boxing contest, in the adult category, is called Bastakilas, a good old Thracian name. The second, the brightest athlete of the family, accumulates the laurels in the category *paides*: individual torch race,[19] stadion race and contest for the fairest horse ($ἵππωι$ $λαμπρῷ$); his name is Ptolemaios. The third, Chrysermos, whether younger than Ptolemaios or not, won the boxing contest in the same age category. The onomastics, anyway, gives for the father evidence of both dynastic loyalty (when he calls his son Ptolemaios) and familiarity with the highest court milieu through Chrysermos' name.[20]

Even though Amadokos may be an exceptional case, the roles attested in this inscription are an element which we must not neglect when we want to locate the Thracian immigrants in Ptolemaic society. Nothing encourages us to believe that the two other winners of these gymnastic contests who have a Thracian ancestry, Ainesis[21] son of Patamousos (-ses?) and Amadokos son of Satokos (two Thracian princely names), do not belong to a rich family circle.[22]

---

[17] In fact, in the documents *Hellênes* are not opposed to Macedonians or Thracians (such a scheme would be anachronistic in Ptolemaic Egypt). When the ethnic is needed, Greeks are designated by a Greek local origin at the same level as the Thracian or Macedonian generic ethnics. The notion of 'Greek register' which I use above is only a shortcut of the modern historian, and has no ethnological character, but reflects only socio-political allegiance to the *basileus* and membership in the immigrant structures – as opposed to the socio-religious Egyptian system and its own religious feelings about the nature and the role of the king as pharaoh.

[18] Cf. J. and L. Robert, *Bull. épigr.* (1977) 566.

[19] As opposed to the traditional relay torch race, according to the interpretation proposed by J. Ebert for the expression $λαμπάδι ἀπὸ πρώτης$. Cf. P. Gauthier, *REG* 108 (1995) 580–5.

[20] Cf. the hypothesis of Koenen (1977: 19–21) that Amadokos became related to the clan of the Chrysermoi and, through his son Chrysermos, is probably the origin of a well-known branch of Alexandrian worthies (stemma: Koenen, p. 20).

[21] In l. 14a, the stone has $ΑΙΝΗΖΙΣ$ $Παταμούσου$ $Θρᾷξ$ and not as expected $Αἰνῆσις$, as I noted in the Museum of Cairo. Z is clearly legible. As the voicing of s, frequent before b or m, is unknown in the third century between vowels, the letter is a misreading of the engraver rather than a linguistic Thracian peculiarity in the pronunciation of this name. Cf. Teodorsson (1979: 190).

[22] We cannot precisely estimate Amadokos' prosperity (although he was surely comfortable), because we do not know the actual importance of the *Basileia* of the inscription. However, Herakleitos' patronage does not suggest a short-lived creation by Amadokos for his three muscular sons, and surely not with such a presumptuous title.

If we go back to the Thracian prosopography of Velkov and Fol, we are able to isolate two quite different groups: Thracians who are cleruchs, and those that are called *Thrakes tês epigonês*, 'Thracians of the descent'. It is not easy to distinguish qualitatively the Thracian constituent inside the general phenomenon of the Ptolemaic cleruchy. Does it show particular features? Were the Thracians discriminated against on the ground of their origin? Did they evolve otherwise than the other groups of cleruchs did? I have tried elsewhere (see Chapters 8, 9 and 11) to establish some trends of the Greek population in Egypt: even if we should not generalise the trend, the Greek civil servant or the cleruch were often just passers-by in the countryside, and thus an important contribution to the progressive urbanisation of the metropoleis of nomes. Was the Thracian cleruch, with a supposed peasant ancestral history, urged or inclined to settle more readily on the farmland than his fellow Macedonian or Greek cleruch? In fact, our documentation is not rich enough to allow firm conclusions about such matters, because it is dangerous to use silence as evidence in that case. The soundings which I have made do not reveal any trend among Thracians to move or not to move to the metropolis, because, if a first analysis sometimes leaves the impression that the Thracian cleruch was more attached to the soil, it may be an illusion that newer and richer sources could dispel.

Are Thracians 'of the descent' a more illustrative case? I shall not enter the debate on what the determinative *tês epigonês* placed after an ethnic implies.[23] There is no doubt about the fact that it is more than a mark of filiation from a cleruchic environment. Moreover, the structural study of the Egyptian economy in the third century dissociates the cleruch and the 'descendant'. Thracians *tês epigonês* are not numerous, but they speak for themselves. First, they supply the oldest mentions of the expression.[24] And, when it is possible to know with certainty, they always have a Greek name, whereas their patronymics are equally divided into Greek and Thracian names. In every case, they practise private activities in the economy.

One Thracian 'of the descent', Aristolochos, son of Stratios, has a particularly well-supplied dossier, eleven papyri from Tholthis, a dossier which fits into a larger collection of contracts concluded in

---

[23] For previous solutions to the problem, see Oates (1963). For him (pp. 31–71), in the early Ptolemaic period, *tês epigonês* is used for persons who have no governmental or military position and actually means 'civilians' who, just like *Persai*, have some claim to 'Hellenic' status – I would say, some claim to the privileged status of 'non-Egyptian'.

[24] *P. Hib.* I 30 (300–271) and 90 (263).

a cleruchic milieu.[25] About 216–212, Aristolochos acted sometimes alone, sometimes with a partner, a cleruch without assignment who would before long leave his military status to take that of the *epigonê*. We find Aristolochos signing various contracts where he leases parcels of grain land from cleruchs. But these contracts contain peculiarities which, as I have observed (Chapter 15), show that they invert the traditional balance of power between the owner, normally the stronger party, and the tenant, traditionally the weaker one. The most demonstrative peculiarity is the fact that the tenant pays beforehand the rent in wheat to the cleruchic holder of the parcel and that he is free to get back this advance on the harvest of the *klêros*, as he wishes, during the two or three years which follow. In other words, this pseudo-tenant is the stronger party, advancing the future rents to cleruchs who are sometimes hard pressed (they are not equipped or trained to exploit their lands themselves), and in this way he takes a long-term option on arable land. The Tholthis file shows that those *tês epigonês*, whatever their origin, do not rent those lands to exploit themselves, but instead to have them cultivated by Egyptian sub-tenants. One of the documents shows that Aristolochos as middleman has to search for cash.

However interesting, the case of Aristolochos is not necessarily the prototype of a Thracian 'of the descent'. But it could be, and conversely, if we refer to the model of Macedonians or Greeks 'of the descent' in the third century, we notice that this model is exactly superimposable upon Aristolochos' profile. Furthermore, the other Thracians 'of the descent', even if their dossiers are rather poor, do not show a profile at variance with the aforesaid model. At the same time, there is no Egyptian socio-economic profile comparable to this same 'Greek' model.

Thracians were involved in the explosion of the mercenary economy which occurred in the second half of the fourth century under Alexander and his successors. For the Thracians, it was nothing but the development of a well-established tradition of mercenary service in the Greek cities or in Macedonia. As Velkov and Fol indicated, the stream of Thracians towards Alexandria and the Nile valley was temporarily favoured by the special relations of the Ptolemies with Lysimachus and later by their own possessions on the north coast of the Aegean Sea. Did Thracians meet in Egypt with

---

[25] I analyse some social aspects of the problem in Chapter 15; see particularly for Aristolochos pp. 208–9.

unfavourable prejudice? Surely they were called or accepted on the basis of abilities useful to the Ptolemies. The papyri know them as soldiers, as cavalrymen. The aulic milieu, the senior command in the army and the upper class of the civil servants were perhaps recruited from closer or more specialised circles, such as the court of Macedonia or the elite of the trading cities of Greece or Asia Minor. A high-level career like that of Seleukos son of Bithys, *strategos* of Cyprus and nauarch at least from 142 to 131 under Ptolemy VIII Euergetes II,[26] is not necessarily typical; but neither is it a glorious exception. At such a late date, however, the Thracian patronymic of this Seleukos might be nothing more than an old family tradition in the distant descent of a Thracian successfully integrated into the Greek world of the Seleucids and the Ptolemies.

Actually the fate of the Thracian immigrants and of their descent does not seem to be different from that which the mercenaries coming from the less urbanised regions in Greece or Macedonia met in Egypt. This spot has nothing in common with this 'third place from bottom to top in the Hellenistic society of Egypt, after the slaves and the Egyptian farmers of the royal domains', proposed by Velkov and Fol.

The survival of a Thracian autonomous group in Egypt met *a priori* evident impediments. Even in the close circle of domestic life, the lack of density of the Thracian population probably put in danger the linguistic specificity of the group after two generations. The religious structures of the community had no character sufficiently esoteric to isolate the Thracians. In Egypt even the Jewish minority, constituted by immigrants of a quite different cultural type, was in the main Hellenised. The cultural dichotomy of Ptolemaic Egypt, the global character of the cultural organisation of each of the two major constituents of the population, could only accelerate the merging of Thracians into the Alexandrian royal system. As mercenaries they formed one of the major components of that Hellenophone power structure, and such a situation created mutual solidarity between the king, Greeks and Macedonians.

Moreover, as soon as they arrived in Egypt, Thracians were in a state of lesser cultural resistance towards Hellenisation. I do not say this because of some unverifiable hypothesis that their recruitment would have taken place in uncultivated rural classes. To be a mercenary was probably traditional in some Thracian groups or families, and it created early contacts with the Greek world. Moreover, Thrace

---

[26] Cf. Bagnall (1976: 258–9).

had its belt of Greek cities, permanent sources of cultural exchange. And, on a more general level, if we focus on the advanced types of Greek urban society or Macedonian aulic organisation, we should not neglect the wide socio-cultural affinities and influences which existed between the populations of the southern Balkans, not only at the level of more or less underdeveloped rural communities, but also in more sophisticated levels of those populations. Paintings in Kazanlàk give in their manner of drawing and colours evidence that we must not forget high-level interculturation when analysing the position of the aristocrat Amadokos and his muscular sons in the early Thracian immigration to the Nile valley.

The factors which facilitated the reception of such an immigration in Hellenistic Egypt made any autonomous survival of such a scattered group unpredictable. More than a specific cultural behaviour, the ethnic *Thrax* embodied for a long time some continuity in the existence of an immigrants' *politeuma*, at least in a less organised community. The preservation of Thracian onomastics, which is less constant, suggests domestic traditions which we would like to know better, just as we would like to be able to estimate the contribution of this Thracian population to the development of the composite Alexandrian cultural world. A Thracian cult surviving in Egypt in the onomastics of the Roman period, the theophoric name Heron and its derivatives (mostly in the Arsinoite),[27] supplies us with only a weak reflection of what was perhaps more central in the Thracian diaspora of the Hellenistic period.

[27] See Bingen (1994).

Chapter 7

PTOLEMAIC PAPYRI AND THE ACHAEAN DIASPORA IN HELLENISTIC EGYPT

ૐ

Achaea holds only a modest rank among the countries which supplied immigrants to Egypt in the Ptolemaic period. This is even more true of neighbouring Elis (see the appendix to this chapter). Few papyri and inscriptions from Alexandria or the Nile valley in that period testify that an individual is a native of Achaea or descended from an Achaean immigrant.[1] Such examples are, however, precious material for an eventual prosopography of Hellenistic Achaea.[2] Still, one cannot hope to find in so reduced a sample significant help for a type of research which attracted my attention, the differential study of the ethnic constituents of Hellenistic Egypt.

I shall retain here as a general frame for this chapter the immigrants that the administration of the Ptolemies called more or less officially, but in fact very rarely, *Hellênes*, a term which is much more complex than one could believe at first sight. In a papyrological dossier from the third century BC in the Vienna collection,[3] the epithet *Hellênes* applies to a group with a particular fiscal status, members of which have not only Macedonian or Greek names,[4] but also Thracian and

---

[1] A list in Emanuela Battaglia, *Aegyptus* 69 (1969) 7 (see further note 26). Cf. now W. Clarysse, *P. Petrie*², p. 18, notes 10–11.

[2] Unfortunately, the recent collection of literary and epigraphical testimonia on Achaea, A. D. Rizakis, *Achaïe I: sources textuelles et histoire régionale* (Meletêmata 20, Athens 1995), entirely ignores the papyri among the testimonia; in the prosopographical index Egypt is present only through a handful of inscriptions.

[3] *Corpus Papyrorum Raineri* XIII, *Griechische Texte* IX (1987), particularly in papyri 1, 2, 4 and 11.

[4] Valid from the point of view of onomastics (the particularism of Macedonian traditional names is well known), this distinction, trivial in our studies, is anachronistic and does not correspond to the feeling that the Macedonians of Egypt had of their unquestionable Greek cultural identity. In one of the rare examples where the label *Hellênes* is used in the singular, it is claimed by a Ptolemaios who declares elsewhere he is *Makedôn* (*UPZ* I 7 and 8). *Makedôn* was felt as a particular Greek ethnic. Perhaps on the social and emotional level, however, the word could have had some aristocratic flavour for the *Makedônes*, who probably perceived themselves as an elite among the other *Hellênes*, enjoying privileged links with the dynasty, the court, certain military traditions, and the epic of Alexander the Great, founder of the new Greek order in the East.

Jewish ones. They live in a village in the Fayyum and are in fact more or less active elements of the Alexandrian royal system on the military, administrative or economic level. Roughly, in this document, the *Hellênes* are simply everyone who is 'not autochthonous'. This papyrus consolidates moreover the image of what the notion of *Hellênes* represents in the documentation of early Hellenistic Egypt.[5] When we try to distinguish the different constituents of the group that the Vienna papyrus calls the *Hellênes*, we are faced with two questions. (1) What could each subset of those immigrants independently bring on the cultural level to the new Egyptian society, and especially to its Greek component and the service of the king? (2) Can the specific contributions of a Greek subgroup settled in Egypt reveal to us a particular cultural profile of its own region of origin?

To clarify my methodological approach, I will begin with a non-Achaean parallel example, the Thracians (Chapter 6). When I was first attracted by the problem of the Thracians settled in Egypt, a then recent study had concluded that Thracians occupied a very low social and economic standing in the population of Ptolemaic Egypt, just above the Egyptian farmers and the slaves, and that this situation was explained by the essentially rural culture of Thrace.[6] Putting the problem under the light of the two questions I formulate above (abilities and origin) and by means of the onomastics and of the prosopography, I concluded, on the contrary, that the Thracian immigrants, at least in the army, are encountered in Egypt at all the levels where one meets Macedonians or Greeks.[7] This is true at least in the countryside; we lack any evidence to widen the inquiry to Alexandria, the royal court or the senior military command which was located there. On the other hand, the onomastics in the papyri revealed the ease with which the Thracians were assimilated by the Greek social environment. Furthermore, the documents which allow us to personalise the fiscal status of the *Hellênes* in the Egyptian countryside[8] list Thracians among them. And, from the other side of the problem – their Thracian origin – I noticed that our evidence implied in Thrace not a rough, isolated agricultural environment, but steady relations with the Greek world, and that by no means only through the hiring of mercenaries.

Conditions are much less favourable for an inquiry of the same type for the Achaeans who emigrated to the kingdom of the Ptolemies. The

---

[5] On the notion *Hellênes*, see Mélèze-Modrzejewski (1983).
[6] Velkov and Fol (1977), particularly Fol (pp. 97–9).
[7] On those two non-exclusive terms, see note 4.
[8] See note 3.

instances where they are identified by their ethnic *Achaios* form only a
small subset of the group of the *Hellênes* taken in its broadest meaning,
even a small fraction of what we used to call Greeks *stricto sensu*.
Regrettably, in contrast to the Thracians, where the distinctive names
of many of them allow us to detect their origin even when the ethnic is
not mentioned, in Achaea the specific personal names, if they really
existed – the matter has never been studied – would be too rare to allow
us to extract from the documents of Ptolemaic Egypt any significant
addition to the list of Achaeans identified by their ethnic.[9] This is all
the more regrettable in that it excludes any possibility of estimating the
Achaean presence in the administration of the Ptolemies, because it was
not the habit (as a result of royal regulations on self-description) for
people in the civil service to indicate their origin after their name.

There is a further problem of heuristics for the papyrologist: the
ambiguity of the word *Achaios*. Unlike the evidence originating from
Greece, where an Achaean is normally identified by his citizenship,
Achaeans settled in Egypt, as far we know, mention only their region
of origin (i.e., Achaea), never their native or ancestral city (e.g.,
Dyme). In short, I believe that it is reasonable to admit, as for example
Launey did in his prosopography,[10] that in the third century and the
beginning of the second, the word when used in the papyri refers to
coastal Achaea in the north of the Peloponnesus, excluding Achaea
Phthiotis (Central Greece) or the broader Achaean league.

To widen the Achaean evidence from the Greek East and to have
at my disposal as a concrete starting-point a quite related case, I shall
evoke the personality of a brilliant Achaean of the Diaspora who was
in the service of the Seleucids. For that reason his name does not
appear in any papyrus and I must admit that in this case my methodological approach is perhaps somehow driven by a purely sentimental motive: Hagemonidas from Dyme takes me half a century back to
my first epigraphic discoveries in Achaea.[11]

Hagemonidas is known to us from two inscriptions from Dyme
and a passage in *2 Maccabees*. We owe to Christian Habicht the discovery of the link between the epigraphic evidence and the Bible and
the establishment of the true historic and chronological data.[12]
Towards the end of Antiochus IV's reign Hagemonidas – did he ever
return for a while to his birthplace? – simultaneously had two

 9 As is easily done for the Cretans, for example.
10 Launey (1950: 1123–4).
11 *BCH* 78 (1954) 395–8, nos. 7–8.
12 Habicht (1958).

honorary inscriptions engraved,[13] possibly in connection with the erection of statues. Anyway, these inscriptions give an impressive look to the profile of Hagemonidas son of Zephyros: we are entitled to guess that he enjoyed the favour of the Seleucid king not only because, as he recognises, he received benefactions from the king, but also because he was authorised to proclaim such prestigious links with this royal family.[14] One of the inscriptions was drafted in 170–164 in honour of Antiochus IV, to whom the queen Laodike and their son Antiochus the young are associated:

βασιλῆ Ἀντίοχον βασιλέως Ἀντιόχ[ου]
καὶ βασίλισσαν Λαοδίκαν καὶ τὸν υἱὸ[ν]
Ἀντίοχον Ἁγημονίδας Ζεφύρου ἀρε[τᾶς]
ἕνεκεν καὶ εὐνοίας τᾶς εἰς αὐτὸν Θεοῖς.

King Antiochus son of King Antiochus, and Queen Laodike, and their son Antiochus, [dedicated by] Hagemonidas son of Zephyros, on account of their virtue and loyalty to him, to the gods.

The second inscription, closely parallel, reveals that in Syria the town of Laodikeia, whose name refers to Queen Laodike, considered that Hagemonidas was a man to be honoured as a benefactor of the city:[15]

ἁ πόλις ἁ τῶν Λαοδικέ[ων]
Ἁγημονίδαν Ζεφύρου
Δυμαῖον ἀρετᾶς ἕνε-
κεν καὶ εὐνοίας τᾶς
[ε]ἰς αὐτὰν Θεοῖς.

The city of the Laodikeians [erected the statue of] Hagemonidas son of Zephyros, from Dyme, on account of his virtue and loyalty towards it, to the gods.

Later the young prince Antiochus became king under the name of Antiochus V and entrusted Hagemonidas–with the title of *strategos* – with the responsibility of a vast, strategically difficult zone, Palestine, stretching from Ptolemais as far as the Egyptian border.[16]

---

[13] The slabs, made from the same limestone, have the same shape, the same height and thickness, the same writing. Cf. *BCH* 78 (1954) 396.

[14] It is unthinkable that an honorary inscription such as *SGDI* 1622 would have been drawn up and displayed without the more or less explicit agreement of the sovereign. Furthermore, we should not forget that such an epigraphic document was intended to immortalise not only the honouring person but also the honoured one, in this case the royal Seleucid trio.

[15] *BCH* 78 (1954) 396–8, no. 8 (*SEG* XIV 369).

[16] *Macc.* II 13, 24: ('The king [sc. Antiochus V, 162] received Maccabaeus, left Hagemonidas behind as *strategos* of the area from Ptolemaios to Gerrhai, and came to Ptolemais.') Cf. Habicht (1958).

I mentioned Hagemonidas' figure only to place an Achaean emigrant in the perspective of his connections with the world to which he emigrated and with his native country. In fact Hagemonidas is not an isolated example. Two generations earlier the Achaean Xenoitas had been a *strategos* of Antiochus III.[17] And epigraphy reveals at the same time the activity of Achaean officers in Rhodes, in Macedonia, in Carthage, and in the empire of the Ptolemies in Cyprus. In all those cases, these people do not follow the rule that the kings prefer to recruit their mercenaries and their cleruchs from their own outside possessions. The presence of Achaeans in those places is probably due to their renown as senior officers, and, for some of them, as far we can judge, as condottieri supplying mercenaries.

This publicly visible aspect of the Achaean diaspora contrasts with the Achaeans we meet in the papyri. The reason is that those documents restrict our field of observation to a more modest level – as is true in most of the papyrological evidence. Here the occurrences of Achaeans are provided not by inscriptions, ostentatious material by definition, but more or less at random from documents which were not intended for the open publicity of the epigraphic monument or of the historiographical or even biblical tradition.

I briefly quote two documents which are situated in between epigraphy and papyrology and which have here only a prosopographical significance. Indeed, the first is not really part of my inquiry because the Achaean we find there is a passer-by in Alexandria. The inscription painted on his funeral urn reveals to us the name of an eminent person from Dyme who visited Ptolemy IV in 215 as leader of a delegation of *theoroi* or sacred ambassadors: '(the urn of) Anaxilaos son of Aristeas, Achaean, *architheoros* from Dyme'.[18] The epitaph places him in a series of diplomats, known through their inscribed urns, the so-called Hadra hydriae, diplomats who met their ultimate fate during a mission in Alexandria.

---

17 Polybius V 45–8.
18 *SEG* XXIV 1179, 3–6 (Hadra hydria, Cook, *Metrop. Mus.* no. 7). From Alexandria also comes the funeral stele *SB* I 449 (third century) of Lysixenos from Achaea, of whom we cannot say if he was an unlucky traveller passing through Alexandria or an Achaean immigrant settled in the town. The Achaean who wrote his name upon the great pyramid of Giza, Δαμίων Πελλ[α]ν[εὐ]ς Ἀχαιό[ς] (*SB* III 7212 = *SEG* VIII 522, first century), was probably a citizen of Pellana travelling in Egypt as a tourist and not an immigrant, as the mention of his Achaean polis suggests. For the same reason Θεόδοτος Ἀγησιφῶντος Ἀχαιὸς ἀπὸ Πατρῶν, author of the *proskynêma* OGIS I 191 = *I. Philae* I 55 (55–51 BC), is another non-resident passer-by.

The other case is more interesting, because with this graffito we come across an Achaean immigrant deep in the heart of Egypt, in the Osireion of Abydos, where, in 247 or in 132, he decided to leave a testimony of his pilgrimage:

(Ἔτους) λη Μεχεὶρ ι | Ἡράκλειτος | Πολεμάρχ[ου] | Ἀχαιὸς ἀφίκετο.[19]

Year 38, Mecheir 10, Herakleitos son of Polemarchos, Achaean, came here.

Papyrological documents which concern my subject more directly originate in the cleruchic world and all except two mention only cleruchs as Achaeans. They are servicemen or former servicemen to whom the king gave as revocable benefit a more or less substantial plot of farmland to keep them within reach for an eventual mobilisation in Egypt. The sole exceptions, moreover, are Achaeans τῆς ἐπιγονῆς, immigrants with a status I shall clarify farther on.

A first group of texts has an evident prosopographical bearing but does not enlighten us much in our inquiry. Achaean cleruchs appear there only as witnesses signing various acts which do not concern them personally. Still, it is worth pointing out that these acts were all drawn up in the same cleruchic milieu. In the first two papyri, our Achaeans are merely bystanders at the procedure. The first contract is concluded in Theogonis in the Arsinoite nome in 236/235,[20] with as witness Aristodemos, Achaean, of the men of Andriskos, 100-aroura man; the other was entered in Krokodilopolis, the metropolis of the nome, in 226/225,[21] with as witness Iason, Achaean, of the first men from the Her[mopolite], of the fourth hipparchy, 100-aroura man. We learn incidentally that Aristodemos was 'of average size, with a honey-coloured complexion, non-curly hair and a scar partially hidden by his hair', whereas Jason has 'a white complexion with a deep receding hairline and a scar on the forehead'. We shall never know if those scars are the souvenirs of glorious fighting in the service of the king, or the vestige of a drunken brawl, a fall from their horse or a domestic scene.

At the same time, in the third papyrus, the Achaean cleruch countersigns as witness a contract to operate a plantation of sesame. Here also the contract is concluded in the administrative centre of the Arsinoite.[22] The man is one [– – –]nes, Achaean, of the men of Hippokrates, of the second hipparchy, 100-aroura man. One

---

[19] *SB* I 3766.
[20] *P. Petrie* III 12 (*P. Petrie*² 18), 13.
[21] *P. Petrie* III 19 (a) (*P. Petrie*² 24), 2–3.
[22] *P. Hamb.* 24, 21 (Krokodilopolis, 223).

observation is equally interesting and disappointing: both the cleruch who concludes this contract and the witnesses who countersign belong to the same division of cavalry, the second hipparchy. Among them is one Thracian, but no fellow countryman of our Achaean. The economic solidarity of the cleruchs and their social confinement in a restricted area are clear here as in numerous documents. But our Achaean, here as elsewhere, seems quite isolated on the ethnic level in this Greek environment, perhaps a likely sign of the low density of the Achaean immigration. Does that mean that we find here cleruchs of recent arrival in Egypt?[23] Or, on the contrary, are we dealing in the 220s with the residue of an ancient arrival of Achaean mercenaries which was not continued or renewed? An answer is not yet possible, but this already outlines a first profile of the Achaean diaspora.

Two Achaean cleruchs appear in fiscal documents. Philotheros son of Sopatros, Achaean, of the men of Andriskos, [100-aroura man],[24] pays the full range of taxes in wheat and silver which a man of that status, despite being relatively privileged, had to pay for the land tax and for the poll tax. He probably operates his *klêros* either directly or by means of Egyptian farmers. Sosibios son of Xenophantos, Achaean, one of the 70-aroura cavalrymen,[25] pays the *chômatikon*, the *halikê* and the *phylakitikon* (dike tax, salt tax and police tax). All this produces good evidence for the cleruchic tax system in the *chôra*, but these occurrences, like the others, do not reveal a particular profile for the Achaeans in comparison with the other *Hellênes*.

Two mutilated texts supply us with the latest mentions of Achaeans from the cleruchic milieu, both cavalrymen, as is indeed always the case when this point can be established for an Achaean cleruch: in the beginning of the second century, a Herakleitos, Achaean (the name of the father is lost),[26] and, in the middle of the

---

[23] I do not think, here as in the other instances which we shall meet, that we are dealing with scattered arrivals, because, with the exception of Nikanor son of Antiochos (see note 35), all our Achaean cleruchs are settled in the Fayyum; they are totally absent from other cleruchic settlements as familiar to us as those of the Oxyrhynchite. We are probably dealing with more or less small, early, grouped arrivals, but not sufficiently numerous to avoid being immediately scattered in different units from the same area.

[24] P. Petrie III 111.16 (Arsinoite, 237/236). The quality of *hekontarouros* is established by the payment of 16 dr. 4 ob. (= 100 ob.) of *chomatikon* (dike -tax), for which cleruchs are rated at 1 ob. per aroura.

[25] P. Petrie III 112 (g) 11 (Arsinoite, 222/220).

[26] SB XX 14083 (editio princeps Emanuela Battaglia, Aegyptus 69 (1989) 5–8, pl. 2). In l. 8, I would restore κατ' Αἰγυπ[τίους or κατ' Αἰγυπ[τον.

same century, a Nikanor son of Antiochos, Achaean, owner of a horse used in the royal cavalry.[27]

With Areios son of Theon, Achaean of the *epigonê*, we meet the most interesting case in my small collection of texts.[28] In a study dedicated to the role of those men 'of the *epigonê*' (τῆς ἐπιγονῆς), Greeks who seem, in the early Hellenistic period, to have given up the cleruchic status or the possibility of entering the civil or the military service of the king,[29] I was able to show (see below, Chapter 15) that they played an active role in the undertaking of independent agricultural activities by leasing land allotted to the cleruchs.[30] These last were often not capable of or interested in running their *klêros* or preferred to live in the urban areas which gradually developed in Hellenistic Egypt. Therefore those 'of the *epigonê*' men constituted a sort of new social class in rural Egypt. Our Achaean fits this scheme exactly. Under the reign of the third Ptolemy he leases all the plots of arable land which a cleruch, an Athenian, probably by descent rather than recent immigration, living in another village of the Arsinoite, possesses in Kerkeosiris in the south of the Fayyum. Areios cultivates wheat and sesame there – this last activity is particularly profitable for its production of oil seeds – or more probably has the plots cultivated by Egyptian sub-lessees.

All the examples which I have gathered do not allow us to detect a particular flavour to the Achaean immigration different from the rest of the Greek population in Egypt. To a certain extent this is a disappointment. But papyrologists meet here again a phenomenon which the parallel study of the Thracian immigrants (Chapter 6) revealed in a more significant way: the ease of integration and standardisation in the Ptolemaic cleruchic milieu. Such assimilation is less amazing for Achaeans than for Thracian immigrants, who were coming from a non-Hellenic peripheral zone. But it is likely that the heterogeneous mass of the immigrants very soon created a social community of Greek immigration in Egypt, at least on the cleruchic level. And it strengthens the view that the status of the Greek in Egypt is less influenced by his origins in a Greek city[31] than by the particular

---

[27] *BGU* X 1939 (Herakleopolis), frg. C.3; cf. note 35. To be complete, add the anonymous Achaean cleruch mentioned in *P. Lond.* inv. 573 (2) recto (Arsinoite, 244/242).

[28] Arsinoite, 222. *P. Tebt.* IIIa 815, frag. 3 recto, col. II.

[29] I do not quote here the plentiful and contradictory literature on this subject.

[30] *P. Köln* VII 314 adds a new occurrence of an Achaean of the *epigonê*, interesting for its early date (257) and the activity of the man: Νίκαιος Χαριξένου runs a garden of 3¾ arouras of sacred land and pays to the temple of Herakles (Harsaphes) in Herakleopolis the tenth for the cult of Arsinoe Philadelphos on an estimated revenue of 200 drachmas.

[31] Mostly by descent.

social link – let us call it the Greek royal system – which unites the king and the immigrants in Egypt, actually or indirectly an institutional link based on the cumulative effects of the individual abilities of those immigrants as servants of the kingdom.

Another feature emerges from these first observations. It seems that Achaea is absent in the new arrivals of officers and Greek mercenaries in late Hellenistic Egypt, as far as we are able to perceive such phenomena in the inscriptions and the papyri. Maybe we find there an echo from the general history of Achaea and a confirmation that the king in Alexandria was inclined to recruit in his own possessions,[32] or at least not in territories that were becoming progressively less accessible as Rome moved to the East.

Documentary criticism generates a last query for the historian of the Peloponnesos. Does the cleruchic character of the papyrological sources which I was able to collect substantiate the idea that the Achaeans, attracted by the Egyptian El Dorado of the third century, were able to serve only as mercenaries or, in the best circumstances, as officers or even condottieri? This limitation, especially if it is linked to the absence of Achaeans in other governmental or economic activities, would imply a predominantly rural character for Achaean society, a rather unexpected conclusion given the polis-based structure of the region. But caution is necessary, because the sample is not at all significant, for two reasons. First, the circumstances of the discoveries of papyri for the early Ptolemaic period resulted in an abnormally high proportion of cleruchic texts. Secondly, as I have already explained, a purely formal reason causes other official activities as well as private life to be less visible, because documents referring to them do not produce names followed by their ethnic. Actually we cannot measure how far the political and economic experience of Achaea's cities could have been a factor of immigration to Alexandria. All that one can say is that as large a find of Ptolemaic documents as the archives of Zenon does not include, to my knowledge, a single identifiable Achaean.

Among the uncountable Greeks who appear as royal civil servants or as businessmen, engineers or doctors in Ptolemaic Egypt, there could be a lot of 'invisible' Achaeans. But it seems unlikely that the experience acquired by Achaeans in civil and economic matters in their cities or in the Achaean league could have represented a major contribution to the construction of the Hellenistic royal regime, or

---

[32] Cf. Bagnall (1984: 7–20).

something comparable in influence in the organisation of the realm, for example, to the immigration of elites coming from Athens, the islands or the Greek cities of Asia Minor.

APPENDIX: ELIS

For Elis, the evidence is so poor that it is in no way representative. Let us note simply that it is consistent with the overall picture suggested by the papyri which mention Achaeans and that it awakens the same reservations due to the fact that our documents are strictly cleruchic.

In the year 252, Kephallen of Elis, of the men of Demetrios, cleruch of 21 arouras, leases out his rather modest allotment to a Macedonian *hekatontarouros* cleruch.[33] Later, in the mid-second century, a document concerning horses of the royal cavalry[34] mentions a unit 'of the men of Polemarchos and Dionysios', after which appears the phrase 'of which, Limnaios'. On the next line, we find a reference to Pyrilampos son of Ergophilos of Elis.[35] The Elean who appears in the list is probably the owner of 'Amyntas', a horse from the stud farm of Kleopatra, a Macedonian lady, and now ridden by the Macedonian cavalryman Dioskourides.

---

[33] *P. Col. Zen.* I 49 (Memphite).
[34] *BGU* X 1939 (Herakleopolis), frg. A.8–9.
[35] In l. 8, the mention ὧν Λιμναῖος, whose nature is not clear, must be dissociated from the following item in l. 9; one does not see why the ethnic should relate to the father or to the grandfather of a cavalryman. Cf. the parallel mentions in the genitive frag. C.3: Νικάνορος τοῦ Ἀντιόχου Ἀχαιοῦ, and elsewhere in the list, as in G.4 and 8.

Chapter 8

GREEK PRESENCE AND THE PTOLEMAIC RURAL SETTING

How far Greeks were present in or absent from the Egyptian countryside is no minor aspect of the organisation of rural space in Ptolemaic Egypt. Perhaps the problem would be unimportant if it were limited, for instance, to the mere study of some of the more extensive agricultural enterprises. But it is fundamental as soon as we remember that one of the underlying elements in any structural analysis of Ptolemaic Egypt is the coexistence of two groups, a dominant Graeco-Macedonian minority and an Egyptian majority, the more so in that the zones of mixture or transfer between the two groups were relatively restricted. Its fundamental character comes to the fore, also, as soon as one realises that the organisation of rural space and the relations between any form of more or less urbanised centre and the surrounding country appear in our case different from those in Greek archaic or classical societies, for instance where the town organised around itself a self-managed space or organised exchanges by using a nearby space, the management of which was left to other people. We are also far, and not only geographically, from situations such as have been described for some parts of the postclassical Black Sea coast.

Indeed, in Hellenistic Egypt the problem is on quite another scale. If there was reorganisation of rural space (we are not able to quantify the dimensions of this reorganisation, but it was important), it was a matter of measures of wide application, often linked with the royal treasury, with modalities foreseen for all the realm. Furthermore, where our evidence reveals something of the organisation of rural space, particularly the recovery and increase of the network of irrigation in the Fayyum, this especially concerns the royal domain or cleruchic settlements, also due to royal initiative. One never finds in our papyri a mutual and autonomous action of more or less urbanised entities, a nome metropolis or a village, affecting their own rural environment. For the papyrologist, the estimate in *P. Lille* 1, with its checkerboard drawn on papyrus of dikes and canals for a holding of some 2,500 hectares (see p. 230, Fig. 17.1), doubtless calls to mind modern aerial photography and the organisation of space in the archaic or classic period. All of the evidence, however, suggests that we have in this papyrus a preliminary step in the creation of the new *dôrea* of the *dioiketes* Apollonios in Philadelphia, in fact only one out of several economic interests the powerful minister possessed scattered around Egypt.[1] The *dôrea* was not run from a nearby urban base; orders came rather from the offices of the *dioiketes* in Alexandria and partially, in all likelihood, in Memphis. At least potentially, the management was located at the level of the realm.

Nevertheless, the 'royal' definition of the *chôra* poses at the outset a problem for the papyrologist, because we know that the eventual outcome of the process in the imperial period was, on the contrary, the small office-holder settled in the village or the society of small local Greek worthies and magistrates in the metropolis, all of them largely dominating the countryside and later the councils of the metropoleis (created by Septimius Severus) with a new configuration of those relations, resulting finally in the municipalisation of the nome in the late empire. Now, one of the causes of this evolution was the initial character of the Greek settlement in the *chôra* as well as the evolution of the status of arable land, a status which after all would condition the appearance of a new social order in Roman Egypt.

Regrettably, as rich as it is, papyrological documentation supplies us only with a very partial image of the relations between the urban centres and the countryside under the Ptolemies. It is concentrated on some scattered points in space and time for the third century, and Zenon's archive illustrates an artificial and short-lived environment. Much of the documentation has a cleruchic origin, particularly the Petrie and Hibeh papyri and other similar finds, at Tebtynis in the second century and Herakleopolis for the first century. There are in addition some isolated groups like the Serapeum papyri or, for Upper Egypt, ostraca or the Graeco-Egyptian dossier from Pathyris. Neither the Delta nor most of the cities of the valley are really represented in the documentary evidence for the Ptolemaic period.

When the Macedonians invaded Egypt, they found in the Delta and the lower valley of the Nile a Greek town, Naucratis, and Greek settlements inside Egyptian communities, of which the most dense was probably that of the Greeks in Memphis. A Graeco-Macedonian

---

[1] Cf. Préaux (1947: 16–17). Her description of this exceptionally dynamic but rather artificial creation should be compared with the first global study devoted to a village in the Fayyum for the period after the (hypothetical?) 'golden age' of the third century, the monograph of Crawford (1971) on Kerkeosiris.

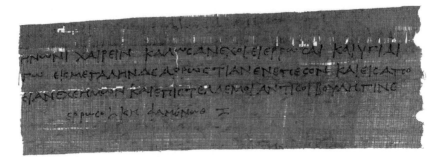

Figure 8.1 P. Col. Zen. 10, letter of Menestratos to Zenon (photo courtesy Rare Book and Manuscript Library, Columbia University)

minority then settled down in Egypt, with the dynamism natural to immigrants, based probably at first on their military occupation, gradually coupled with a network of royal administration. Many Ptolemaic institutions have a Graeco-Macedonian origin, and Claire Préaux's investigations into continuities from Greece to Hellenistic Egypt are particularly suggestive in this respect. The economy follows Greek schemes and is conceived in Greek monetary terms. Administration, as soon as it reaches a certain level, is Greek in language and thought. Greek mental customs and behaviour left their mark on human relationships and were a source of solidarity in an environment where the Greeks were a heterogeneous minority, and they formed a source of efficiency in concerted action.

On the other hand, the immigrants met an Egyptian population about which we do not know a great deal for the fourth and third centuries BC. It was, however, no more homogeneous than the Greek element. I discuss in Chapter 18 how much this environment seems to have been disrupted by the Persian occupation, and indeed the peasant class is sometimes not far from the Bronze Age, with traces of regressive archaism in a group of displaced farmers, particularly deprived of social structures and traditional ties. By contrast, some privileged groups had sources of countervailing power in dealing with the Greeks. The Egyptian clergy had all the weight of its prestige, its organisation and a certain economic power, and the Greeks needed the help of Egyptian scribes, high-ranking or not, for their relations with the native population. A century of cohabitation of the privileged minority and the subdued majority was needed to have the latter showing some awareness of common interests and character, what we call – probably erroneously – its nationalism. Historians repeat too easily the generalisation that there was no racial policy under the

Ptolemies. Even if that is correct, it is of limited interest. More evident and important is the fact that there were racial and linguistic situations (two conditions of the same type) involving discrimination embedded at the basis of the organisation and the evolution of the Ptolemaic world. Other inquiries, like that of Samuel (1970), have shown how much in the third century the two groups were discrete and impenetrable, even though it is necessary to note at the same time that some Egyptians, like royal scribes and nomarchs, had access to very high responsibilities. But to this there is a corrective: this Egyptian administrative elite carried out passive tasks rather than real management; such higher activities are always in Greek hands and are conceivable moreover only in the 'Greek dialectic' of power, administration and economy. And this brings us to the heart of our problem. It is evident that at the highest level of the realm and at the level of the nome, physical presence in the rural space was generally less of a constraint for many Greeks than for Egyptians living there.

Only onomastics can be used on a wider scale as an ethnic criterion. Personal names are omnipresent in our documentation and are generally characteristic (few names can be either Greek or Egyptian). The criterion has been debated, and it has often been denied that names still had any significant discriminating value from the second century BC onwards. This is, in my opinion, an error of perspective. To give a name to a child or to modify the name of an adult is a deliberate act, but it fits into a whole domestic or local context, cultural and religious, which is more concrete than any racial definition of an individual. Everything suggests that, taken as a body, the criterion is valuable for any period. The inquiry carried out by Louise Youtie in *P. Petaus* (pp. 46–53) showed how clearly, during the imperial period, in the rural society of the Fayyum, every village had its own onomastic profile. There were exceptions on the level of individuals, but they were not predominant, and every case (for instance, double Greek and Egyptian names; names deriving from one language with a patronymic from the other; names which crossed over from one language to the other) was probably the result of a particular situation. It would be interesting if we could always discover what kind of situation explains each case and could discover in this way the rather limited zones of contact and osmosis between the two groups.[2]

This Graeco-Egyptian environment with a double onomastic register was very unevenly distributed throughout the Egyptian rural space.

---

[2] Cf. on this limitation Préaux (1961).

It also participated, but with an importance inversely proportional to its presence, in the evolution of this rural space towards forms of hereditary and alienable private occupation of the arable land. The history of this evolution is a basic question in papyrology.[3] Private property, when this means houses and their dependencies, is well attested from the beginning, both in the Greek papyri and in Demotic documents. And it is even attested, as Préaux emphasised, in Demotic contracts dating from before the arrival of the Greeks; even types of private ownership or stable tenure of sacred land became transferable. But all this seems in the Egyptian countryside a marginal phenomenon. More important in this rural space are three categories of lands: (a) crown land administered directly or rented by the royal administration; (b) sacred land, the management of which is controlled by the king; and (c) the crown or sacred lands granted, for instance, as a *dôrea* or as a *klêros*,[4] at least in the beginning, as a revocable right. The largest part of the farmland belongs to these categories. It is there that the phenomena of the Greek and Egyptian presence, and of the evolution of relations between the rural environment and the administrative centre of the nome, are quantitatively interesting to study.

The evolution of the cleruchic grip on crown land is well known, especially thanks to the papyri from the Fayyum and Herakleopolis. In the beginning, the possession of the *klêros* was not transferable and was subordinated to military obligations and to the payment of certain taxes bound to the tenure. It was an essentially precarious benefice, but this revocability would follow the course of all private claims on a royal or a public domain, namely the continual effort to assure more stability to the tenure and eventually its heritability, even finally the right to alienate the holding. Already in the third century, the *klêros*, revocable by definition, passed to male descendants under the condition that these be registered, but *P. Lille* 4, of 218–217, shows that this heritability, even subject to conditions, was already recognised as a right. When, with the Herakleopolis papyri from the first century BC, we are able to reopen the file of cleruchic tenure, the alienability is a given, at least subject to conditions. For certain types of holdings, the process did not continue as far as turning the land into free private property, that is, with the right to use a tenure becoming the right to sell a title deed on the tenure. Doubtless, this was a non-problem: thinking of private property as an ultimate end in the

---

[3] Cf. Préaux (1939: 463–80; 1961: 218–19).
[4] On the cleruchies, see Uebel (1968).

process is probably a modern approach which creates an artificial hierarchy in the right to possess land.

Could the evolution of the cleruchy towards a stabilised and even alienable tenure have encouraged Greek settlement in the rural environment? Or, on the contrary, by a paradox, did it prepare the way for the appearance in the Roman period of a rural class, whose origin was predominantly Egyptian, people more or less dependent on the Greek bourgeoisie living in the metropolis of the nome?

We may mainly divide the Greeks who stayed in or passed through the *chôra* into three groups: the royal agents, the cleruchs, and the Greeks operating in the *chôra* in a more or less independent way. In this last case, qualifications as 'cultivators' ($\gamma\epsilon\omega\rho\gamma o\iota$, $\gamma\epsilon\omega\rho\gamma o\hat{\upsilon}\nu\tau\epsilon\varsigma$) could easily suggest a settlement in the *chôra*. But documents quickly warn us not to be too hasty. For instance, *P. Tebt.* III 782 (towards 153) is short but points out a lot of things. Two Greeks, Heliodoros and Zenon, are in conflict about plots near the village of Boubastos; the plaintiff boasts that he has made a considerable effort in the irrigation of the 13 hectares of which he says 'with me cultivating 55¾ arouras of royal land'. Nevertheless, our two 'farmers' live in the administrative centre of the nome, just like the *epimeletes* Chaeremon to whom the plaintiff addressed the document. But a note at the foot of the papyrus shows that the people who will investigate and act on the spot are called Eriemounis, Thoonis and Sokmenis – all Egyptians. And this document, so symbolic in the dichotomy of the names, deserves credence, because our documentation abounds with parallel situations.

The problem appears in much the same way for the cleruch and, in the second century, more precisely for the Greek cleruch. Now this is interesting, because the cleruchic network might seem to us to be precisely the location of a process of stable settlement of a Greek population in a rural environment, for the reason that, in our documentation, the cleruchy is largely attested in regions of the Fayyum or elsewhere that had recently been opened to agriculture. The Ptolemaic cleruchy, however, seems to have had other purposes, above all that of maintaining in Egypt a reserve of military recruitment at the disposal of the king, and also, doubtless, of distributing this reserve over the whole territory and making it self-supporting. Classical Greece, for instance in Lesbos in the fifth century, was already acquainted with cleruchs who were getting an income from their parcel of land without exploiting it themselves.[5] The second of

---

[5] Gauthier (1966).

the so-called Revenue Laws, in 259, reduces the *apomoira* tax for a category of mobilised cleruchs, 'those who have planted their own *kleroi*' – in this case, vineyards and orchards (col. 24.5–10). It implies, at least, different degrees of occupation of allotments and indicates that, from the beginning, the granting of the *klêros* was not bound to personal operation of the holding. I would quote here, among many other similar texts, *P. Enteux.* 55, of the year 222, the complaint of the Macedonian *epilarches* Polemaios, an officer who was endowed with a tenure of about 18 hectares in the Fayyum. He stayed away for a long time in Alexandria, kept there, he says, by a lawsuit. As the plot was not exploited, Polemon, a cleruch of more modest rank, together with another Greek, Aristomachos (a middleman between this cleruch and Egyptian farmers?), leased from the royal treasury half of the *klêros*, possibly because the treasury kept a right of initiative on half of abandoned holdings. The cleruch sowed the whole *klêros*, without signing a contract for the other half with the absent officer, then sowed it the next year, while doing that without any agreement with anyone. What is interesting in the complaint is that Polemaios does not protest because he was practically removed from his holding, but, very weakly, because he did not draw up an agreement with his irregular tenant, and, more strongly, because the latter did not pay any rent on his land 'at the rate at which he leased it out in the past'. The lawsuit quoted in the beginning of the complaint did not excuse the absence from the *klêros*, but it explained the prolonged absence from the region and the loss of contact with the local cleruchic administration.

From the same time another significant document reveals simultaneously that the documentary evidence for the presence of the Greeks in the rural space must be used with caution and that this presence was doubtless less dense than it seems at first reading. Fragment 4 of *P. Tebt.* III 815 (228–221), a series of abstracts of contracts, summarises in ll. 30–7 the leases by which a high-ranking officer, the Boeotian Trochinides, rented out part of his holding to Ptolemaios, son of Demetrios, a 'Prienean of the descent', for the rent of 10 drachmas 2 obols for each aroura. The document could leave the impression that this was just a matter of one Greek rather than another living on the arable land. But the abstract is followed by the summary of another contract from the same day, executed by the same *syngraphophylax*. There our Ptolemaios sub-lets to an Egyptian farmer, an 'Arsinoite cultivator', that part of the *klêros* he had rented from Trochinides, but now the rent amounts to 11 drachmas 4½ obols per

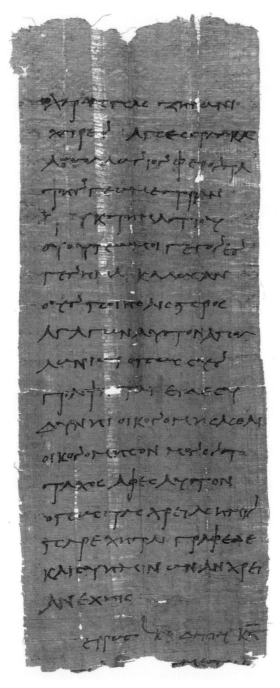

Figure 8.2 P. Col. Zen. 16, *letter to Zenon about a vine crop survey (photo courtesy Rare Book and Manuscript Library, Columbia University)*

aroura. The difference of 1 drachma 2½ obols is not great, but, even at the microeconomic level of such activities, the sub-leasing practised by Polemaios must have been more extensive to have been profitable, and it postulates the absences of other cleruchs. Anyway, the man who is present on the soil is the Egyptian farmer. In the same document, the renting of Greek *kleroi* by Greeks is so frequent that the conclusion seems unavoidable that a large part of those documents do not imply the more or less permanent presence of a certain number of Greeks in the villages. However, the actual absence of an important fraction of the Greek holders of the land and of their Greek subcontractors becomes more obvious in the second century.

For example, in the remarkable 'land-survey', *P. Tebt.* I 63, a list of owners of granted land, two groups of cleruchs emerge. In the first (ll. 95–111), we find ten cavalry settlers (*katoikoi*) who were endowed with parcels from 2½ to 12 hectares. They all have Greek names and patronymics of good quality. The document is eloquent: either those *kleroi* are not cultivated or they are cultivated by an Egyptian. There is an exception for one of the two smallest parcels (the other being uncultivated). Melanippos is said to be 'cultivator himself' (αὐτὸς γεωργός) of a plot sown with wheat. In the other sampling, ll. 147–79, we find a very homogeneous group of thirty *machimoi* with small tenures of 7 arouras, all bearing Egyptian names and patronymics. Except in some cases where the *klêros* is not cultivated (mobilisation of the holder?), all those Egyptians are the actual cultivators of their plot. Such a contrast suggests the intensity of a phenomenon which nothing allows us to think was limited to the Tebtynis area. A final text may bring an additional nuance. In the contact *P. Tebt.* I 107 (112), Menches, son of Petesouchos, the secretary of the village, takes a lease on 2½ hectares from a Greek *klêros* of 6 hectares. The lease would be commonplace, if we did not know that this *klêros* already belonged to the father of the cleruch, that the son had difficulties in paying his taxes when he took the *klêros* over (*P. Tebt.* I 61a.44), and that some months earlier Menches himself settled the fiscal arrears (in wheat) of several Greek cleruchs, among them our Ptolemy (*P. Tebt.* I 75.3–14). The fact of being on the spot sometimes made Egyptians the stronger party in transactions, whenever a cleruchic tenure encountered difficulties and the fiscal responsibility of the cleruch made his position as absentee all the more vulnerable. Probably such 'Egyptian' success led to rapid social and later cultural Hellenisation of those who gained economic 'power' in this way. It was possibly the case with Menches, but we do not know what names he gave to his children, if he had any after his ascent, and the other only criterion of his Hellenisation (it is not a good one) is the bulk of the Greek documents he discarded to the benefit of some crocodile mummies and even more of papyrologists.

We could undertake a similar inquiry about the royal civil servants who were living in or passing through the rural space. It would only confirm the image revealed by the analysis of the cleruchic presence, that of Greeks who are often there only on missions of varying duration or for personal affairs.

All the same, the evidence does not permit us to suppose an Egyptian rural space where all Greeks were only occasional actors; there were Greek villagers, and the phenomenon of the poor foreigner appears in some documents. But there clearly existed among the Greeks a tendency to stay in an urban environment, a nome metropolis or the administrative centre of a toparchy, for instance, or to go to one whenever possible. And the process must have been accentuated by the numerical inferiority of the Greek population and by permanent staff shortages. In the long term, this tendency would not be without consequences. The techniques of administrative or private management of rural space, for instance the methods of accounting for incomes and investments, were bound to the Greek language, which was the basis of the 'dialectic' of the royal organisation of the country or the monetarised economy. Knowledge of the language conferred implicitly a right to participate in the exploitation of the country. At the end of the Ptolemaic period we discover an Egyptian man, integrated into a Greek social type (two of his sons and he himself are cavalry settlers), drawing up in the Egyptian language a cleruchic document of Greek law which shows him acting as a Greek. But such a will, foreign to the Egyptian tradition, is an exception, a phenomenon without a future.[6]

The grouping in an urban or semi-urban environment of Greeks and Hellenised people explains the evolution of the social order from the 'royal' Egypt of the Ptolemies towards the regime of the Greek notables under the early Roman empire. This order created links of more or less direct exploitation between the administrative centre of the nome and its immediate rural environment, links which had, it seems, only a secondary importance during the early Ptolemaic period.

---

[6] Malinine (1967); cf. E. Seidl, *Studia et Documenta Historiae et Iuris* 33 (1967) 567–8, and J. Bingen, *CdÉ* 43 (1968) 421–3.

Chapter 9

THE URBAN MILIEU IN THE EGYPTIAN COUNTRYSIDE DURING THE PTOLEMAIC PERIOD

☙

The title of this chapter might be misleading in its breadth; it is actually aimed at developing some methodological considerations and summary conclusions. Any effort to describe the constituents and socio-economic structures of the population of the *chôra* during the Ptolemaic period is impeded first of all by the deficiencies of the sources. Inscriptions are scarce. Papyri sometimes offer very rich series of data, but they are intermittent in time and space, ignore certain periods and regions, and reflect unevenly the various population groups living in the *chôra*. Dorothy Crawford (1971) was able to give a very sophisticated image of the village of Kerkeosiris for a period of some decades; we know almost nothing about it for the two preceding centuries. And how far are we allowed to generalise from the picture of this village the author gives to us? The loss is especially considerable for the nome metropoleis. For none of these do we have, even for a brief period, a documentation with any consistency. And this condemns us to work with extremely narrow samplings.

In Chapter 8, studying an aspect of the structures of the Ptolemaic rural society, I observed that, in the countryside and its villages, Greeks, and more specially the cleruchs, are much less present than the sources would suggest. In our papyri Greeks are often an element passing through, or merely the names of absentees, even though new installations of cleruchs and new arrivals of immigrants would tend at first sight to strengthen the idea of dense Greek settlements in some parts of the *chôra*. But, if those Greeks were often somewhere else, where were they? Sometimes in Alexandria; sometimes in the *chôra* as an itinerant agent or a mobilised element. But Greeks often appear from the third century onwards fixed in a more or less permanent way in a nome metropolis. It is this milieu that I think it most important to scrutinise. In the event, however, the inquiry is doubly disappointing, first as a result of the poverty of sources already mentioned above, but then also because of the weight of some of the ideas we tend to repeat, which are mainly the product of the fact that the urban milieu for which one is misguidedly looking in Ptolemaic Egypt is often that of the imperial period. Some scholars have been led so far as to deny the existence of an urban milieu 'as such', even of the least organised sort, before Augustus' reorganisation of Egypt.

The urban milieu of the *chôra* I would like to evoke briefly is not that of Naucratis or Ptolemais. As a matter of habit, these cities, together with Alexandria, automatically condition studies of the urban milieu in some works which deal with the cities of Egypt, from Jouguet's pioneer *Vie municipale* in 1911 to Braunert's excellent *Binnenwanderung*, for instance. I shall not here evoke cosmopolitan Memphis or Egyptian Thebes, poorly known for the early Ptolemaic period.[1] These two cities were important communities, two different types of an Oriental urban milieu, and we find there on an impressive scale the characteristics of what an administrative centre of a nome was on a more modest scale; it is, rather, this latter milieu that is the object of the present chapter. Such metropoleis seem to extend and enlarge pre-existing Egyptian communities of a certain size and vitality. I think we are nearer a natural development of history when we search in such a perspective for the yet inchoate germ of the future Roman metropolis. Our documentation, at least the Greek documentation (again, leaving aside the problem of early Ptolemaic Memphis or Thebes), is based almost exclusively on some cross-checking of what we are able to make out from the references to Krokodilopolis in the third and in the second century. One would like to fill out the picture with the evidence from the Hibeh cartonnage, which seems to give an image, a rather negative image from my perspective, of a countryside where things either are purely local or are settled by reference to Alexandria. But in reality this documentation lacks sufficient density to be representative.

For the Arsinoite, let us see what we can discover by using a sort of method of random sampling, all that is left to us, for the study of the population of the nome metropolis. The most favourable example for the third century (and even so it is not very good) is constituted by the series of *enteuxeis* (petitions to the king) gathered in 1931 by Octave Guéraud (*P. Enteux.*). Just twelve texts out of the hundred in the collection hint at the metropolis. A paltry six or seven are really interesting in this regard. They are not without their humorous and even dramatic side. There is the story of a courtesan diverted from her filial duties towards her mother, and *P. Enteux.* 49 is practically a

---

[1] For Memphis see Thompson (1988); for Thebes, Vleeming (1995).

piece of a Krokodilopolitan Menander, with a fooled father attacking
the courtesan Demo, who, with some accomplices, managed to
extract the hefty sum of 1,000 drachmas from a young man, his son
Sopolis. Here we are in the urban milieu with its fatal temptations
endangering honourable families! But there is some more interesting
evidence, on two different levels. On the one hand, there are, among
these texts of the third century, some that show us Greeks having their
residence in the administrative centre of the nome and owning buildings in the city or having direct interests in the countryside, for
instance in a *klêros* which they exploit through farmers. Two documents that seem at first sight to have no significance alert us to their
importance on second reading, being petitions of Egyptians of a
certain social standing. In one, an Egyptian woollen trader, associated
perhaps with a Greek financier, is in conflict with a Jewish sheep
farmer (*P. Enteux.* 2); in the other, two Egyptian owners of linen-
weaving mills ask to be allowed to demolish their old installations in
order to replace them with two new workshops, which will allow
them to give better service to the king (*P. Enteux.* 5). Commonplace
texts, doubtless, but ones that make us regret more than ever that
we have such a scanty knowledge of the Egyptian milieu in the
metropoleis, a milieu surely better organised and better culturally and
economically equipped than the average, often deracinated, Egyptian
farming community of the Arsinoite, which is described in Greek
sources older than the *enteuxeis* (cf. Chapter 18).

And this brings us back to my previous remark: the Ptolemaic
metropolis must be considered as a specific collective element, rather
than denied an identity simply because there was at this period no
urban administration of a municipal or other type. Historians have
not been kind to the Ptolemaic metropolis. Jones writes that
metropoleis 'had been in Ptolemaic times mere villages, that is mere
aggregations of population, distinguished from the other villages only
in being the seat of government for the surrounding region'.[2] The
words 'other villages' are particularly cruel, but let us take them *cum
grano salis*, along with the 33,333 cities Theocritus ascribes to the
Egypt of the Ptolemies. Braunert gave us a brief but interesting analysis of the evolution of the metropolis, but his analysis is centred on
the problem of the movements of population.[3] Braunert does not hesitate to quote Jones and to insist on the similarity of the ways of life

in the villages and metropoleis, particularly in the Fayyum. For both of these scholars, as earlier for Jouguet (1911), Ptolemaic metropoleis were characterised by the fact they lacked the more or less autonomous organs of self-management of the metropoleis found in the Roman period, and Jones, like Braunert, situates the rapid flourishing of cities under Augustus or shortly after him in a broader phenomenon of urbanisation based on a generalised access to a controlled autonomy throughout the entire Roman empire.

In fact, this theory of the Ptolemaic metropolis-village and of the Augustan birth of the metropolis-city is a view which rests only on the ambiguity of the notion of city or of polis. As far as our ignorance of the management of Ptolemaic metropoleis allows us to decide, such a view is true only if we decide that a city exists only where an urbanised group is more or less responsible for its own fate. But surely it is an error to use in this case a purely institutional and formal definition – and a very limited one at that – of the existence or non-existence of an urban centre. I am afraid that we are conditioned by an image familiar from our education, that of the medieval city which arises from the granting of political or economic privileges of autonomy, conceded under pressure by the prince. But socio-economic realities often precede the institutional organisation which gave to the cities of the Middle Ages and modern times a certain image, one which we in turn too easily attribute to the ancient cities or to the Roman *municipia*. In fact, what distinguishes city and village is that the city is a catalyst in economic, cultural or political exchanges which go beyond the immediate environment of the town and the horizon of personal exploitation of its soil, a catalyst all the more active as the dimensions of the town or the diversification of its economic and cultural potential become more substantial.

Looking at Ptolemaic metropoleis through that lens, a first point is that the nome metropoleis were nowhere creations of the Ptolemies. They were imposed on the new rulers by their mere existence, a major parameter in Egyptian history. Krokodilopolis, Herakleopolis, Oxyrhynchos, Hermopolis, the metropoleis of the Delta and the others had their own, often prestigious, past. One can debate the importance of the political and religious role which those cities still possessed at the time of Alexander the Great's arrival, but they existed, for they were adopted as a group as the basic pattern for the first organisation of Macedonian Egypt, when the country passed from the regime of military occupation to that of a royal administration. What is striking is that there was no hesitation; the choice was based not on a general planning of the space, but on the existence of traditional nome capitals, old settlements which were not products of chance. There was a main religious centre which seems to have assured a certain unity to the nome's temple life. But the rather large built-up area which made the religious centre prosper was not there accidentally. It was connected to a certain number of economic possibilities and created a certain number of administrative traditions, rules of community life, and modes of interactions between the members of the groups that were settled there. These administrative traditions of the temples and of the community seem to have been important, because it is probably in this milieu that the Ptolemies found the class of Egyptian high-ranking servants, the royal scribes and the nomarchs, to whom they delegated important tasks, even if these were only tasks of execution rather than of policy formation. These towns were often river ports or a privileged jetty on a canal. The harbour, the temple, a garrison and the courts, along with the professions housed in the city (however lethargic they may have been), all contributed to making the city a catalyst. There, people from all around found a broader range of commodities than in the closed rhythm of the village economy.

Let us consider the Zenon 'archive', even though the *dôrea* was strongly oriented towards Alexandria and Memphis and thus characteristic of the royal dimension of the management of Egypt. Krokodilopolis and Philadelphia appear on quite different scales. In the capital, the bank extends larger loans; there, the village authorities find the police force needed to find runaway farmers or artisans; the royal court of justice and the central prison are located there; irrigation is organised there. A royal oath or a will would be put there on a papyrus sheet to give more authority to the deed. At the same moment, *P. Rev.*, which distinguishes *kômai* (villages) and *poleis* (cities) in the nomes, marks the three levels of the economy in the business of the distribution of oil: the village, the city and Alexandria (47.10–48, 18). In this period, it is true, local power delegated by the Macedonian king had already been installed. What is interesting is that it is in the cities that it was established and that without hesitation the king settled his garrisons and his scribes in the pre-existing Egyptian centres. Jouguet's reaction, which was mentioned earlier, did not so much ignore this fact as underestimate how much it was characteristic. He compared to the Greek Philadelphia, with its checkerboard pattern of streets, 'old towns with their heaping up of narrow houses in mud bricks, their sinuous alleys, their heaps of garbage near the walls or even in the corner of the walls' (Jouguet 1911: 47). It is true that Jouguet immediately admits that Naucratis was no better. For that matter, what would one say of Paris, London or Bruges in the early Middle Ages? But, he continues 'Philadelphia or Krokodilopolis, where is the city, where is the village?' – Philadelphia, conceived by a town planner, or the malodorous Krokodilopolis?

We must not fall with him and others into what I call the mirage of the village gymnasium, an element often cited in the study of connections between city and village in the *chôra* during the Ptolemaic period, but often wrongly and with the same error of perspective. The simultaneous presence of gymnasia in metropoleis and in what one calls Ptolemaic villages was often held up as an important proof that the metropolis was only a village. The disappearance of the rural gymnasiarch at the beginning of the Roman period was considered a consequence of the municipalisation of the administrative centre. Certainly, we find in villages – in Philadelphia, in Samaria and in Theadelphia, for instance – gymnasia, an ephebic organisation and Greek religious associations. These are even a major source of Greek epigraphy in the Ptolemaic Fayyum. But we would be using a negative criterion in considering the existence of the village gymnasium as proof that metropolis and village did not differ from one another. In fact, these gymnasia and associations in the villages must be regarded in quite another perspective than the purely theoretical opposition of village and polis, an anachronistic speculation foreign to the settlement of Greeks around and in the Fayyum. These foundations *sui generis*, inspired certainly by Greek urban models, are only an imported schema of social organisation proper to an ethnic group which was creating its own new living environment in Egypt. More significant is the fact that what was not viable in this schema artificially implanted in a agricultural landscape did not stand up to the test of time. The normalisation of the villages in time eliminated their gymnasia and some other organisations of an urban type like the *ephêbia*. This evolution has nothing to do with a late birth of an urban milieu. Certainly such phenomena are to be connected with the progressive concentration of a bourgeoisie of landholders in the metropoleis, but this concentration only accelerated the evolution.

Indeed, already in the third century BC we find the first direct testimonies to the exploitation of a *klêros* by a farmer for the benefit of a Greek who has taken up residence in the metropolis. In the *P. Rev.* a privileged rate of the *apomoira* tax of only a tenth is foreseen for the cleruch absent for military duty, if he at the same time exploits his vine-yard himself (24.1–10). This recognises implicitly a more general exploitation of the *klêros* by a non-privileged third party. Examples soon multiply, and in the middle of the second century a term like 'cul-tivating' (γεωργοῦντες) sometimes identifies agricultural entrepre-neurs who were actually living in Krokodilopolis and exploiting public lands through tenant farmers, generally Egyptians. We know, as Pavlovskaja[4] has emphasised, that in Hellenistic Egypt exploitation by tenant farmers was, for people who had land at their disposal, a more profitable means of using their land than direct farming by slaves or by employees. In the Tebtynis papyri from the end of the second century, this type of exploitation competed widely with direct exploitation by the Greek cleruch. And this tendency grew with the evolution of the tenure towards a stable or even free disposal of the granted land. It accelerated with the appearance of the Alexandrians, particularly asso-ciations of Alexandrian farmers in the *chôra* in the first century BC, a phenomenon which appeared to Braunert as one of the elements of the alteration of the city/village (*kômê/polis*) connections.

In the second half of the Ptolemaic period, the constituents of the future Roman metropolis were regrouping into the metropolis, sta-bilising the opposition *kômê/polis*. It would be an error to reduce this opposition to one between the farming community and the people of the city, or an opposition between Greeks and Egyptians, because nothing would give a more erroneous idea of the evolution of the nomes. Indeed, at the same moment, on the one hand, a class of village notables emerges (Menches of *P. Tebt.* is an example), which perform the small rural liturgies of the early empire, and, on the other hand, the class of the city notables, among them the *archontes* and the *strategoi*. But the social structures of the nome and of the new metropolis which those magistrates symbolise were for the most part acquired before the wave of urbanisation of the Julio-Claudian period. They joined what was altogether an evolution and a return to Hellenistic or even Hellenic standards, with such constituents as the right of ownership of the soil or the habit of living in an urban milieu on the product of farm rents. This was not the only normalisation at work, but others reinforced it: the reversion of sites like Philadelphia to a purely rural type which was natural for them; the attrition of the royal administrative structures, which led to greater autonomy in the organisation of the nome; the inevitable development through this

---

[4] Pavlovskaja (1973).

autonomy of a certain number of more or less conscious political mechanisms, which created, with the aid of Roman power, the stereotyped metropolis of the *archontes*, all the more viable in that the system served Rome while protecting the interests of the privileged minority.

These tendencies, latent from the third century BC onwards, explain the profound evolution of the urban phenomenon of an Oriental type that the Greeks found in Egypt at their arrival in the fourth century. Nothing compels us to see the metropolis of Roman Egypt as a contribution from outside or even as the result of an alteration incited from outside. It is the outcome of the evolution under the Ptolemies which led the religious and administrative centre of the nome from being an indisputable urban milieu with its major temple, its handicrafts and its *politeumata* to becoming the metropolis managed by the local *archontes* and their supporting cast, halfway between late Greek cities and imperial *municipia*.

Chapter 10

KERKEOSIRIS AND ITS GREEKS IN THE SECOND CENTURY[1]

ہ

Two themes of research which seem to me important for any structural analysis of the population in Ptolemaic Egypt have particularly preoccupied me. The first developed the hypothesis that Greeks, the driving element and protagonist of our documentation (a documentation which is predominantly Greek and rural), seem often to be in fact, in the agricultural environment, 'absentees' or 'passers-by' even though they are absentees or passers-by whose actions influence this rural environment.[2] A second hypothesis, which is correlative with the first, was that this tendency of the Greek population of Egypt (it is a tendency, and not a rule) to settle in a more or less urbanised milieu already brought, during the Ptolemaic period, a relative density to the urban character of the nome metropolis.[3]

For my first investigations on the Greek presence in the rural environment, I made use largely of papyri found at Tebtynis. Certainly, this site produced a documentation unique in papyrology, because it supplies rich series of papyri for various periods, illustrating the third century BC, then the second and the beginning of the first BC, and finally the Roman period. There is, however, no coherence among these dossiers from the point of view of onomastics, or from that of the occupation of the soil between the Ptolemaic village and later Tebtynis. Part of my argumentation in Chapter 8 is based on the 'archive' of the *komogrammateus* Menches, one of the loveliest finds of Ptolemaic papyri. However, even though those documents come from crocodile-mummies buried in Tebtynis, they concern in fact the village of

---

[1] This chapter was mainly based on the following works concerning Kerkeosiris in the meris of Polemon in the second century BC, particularly for the economic and social history of the village: Crawford (1971), with the reviews of T. Reekmans (1971) and F. Uebel (1973); Chapter 8 of the present volume; Shelton (1976) (later published as *P. Tebt.* IV 1103 = 1110 verso); *P. Tebt.* IV. We should not forget the work of the pioneers of Fayyum studies, B. P. Grenfell and A. S. Hunt in *P. Tebt.* I (1902), Appendix 1, 538–80: 'The Land of Kerkeosiris and its Holders'.

[2] See Chapter 8.

[3] See Chapter 9.

Kerkeosiris.[4] Not only does the latter represent an independent socio-economic type probably different from that of Tebtynis, but the papyri from Kerkeosiris are quite chronologically isolated,[5] and they are both fascinating and controversial. The dossier is too rich not to have been an attractive target for synthesis and generalisation, but first analysis can be deceptive, and the documents have not produced any unanimity about their representativeness for a rural community in late Hellenistic Egypt. In 1971, Dorothy Crawford exploited the evidence already used in 1902 by Grenfell and Hunt. Her detailed study, consciously innovative, covers far wider subject matter than the present chapter about the presence of Greeks in Kerkeosiris. Like Grenfell and Hunt before her, Crawford wrote the history of Kerkeosiris' cleruchies and connected it with the history of the internal politics of the Ptolemies. Coming relatively late in the context of the Arsinoite (at least as far as the current state of our sources allows us to see), *katoikoi*, 'colonists', appeared in Kerkeosiris only under Ptolemy IV Philopator. Under the following reigns, the total number of the granted areas increased considerably and eventually occupied one third of the land, because *klêroi* encroached soon on the arable soil. A final distinctive feature, from 130/129, was the granting of allotments in Kerkeosiris (albeit smaller ones) to *machimoi*, or cleruchs of Egyptian origin. The tables at the end of Dorothy Crawford's work illustrate the distribution of allotments and their status according to the onomastics of the farmers, among others the beneficiaries of *klêroi*. This is of direct interest for the discussion here.

But in a village, there are not only cleruchs and farmers of royal, cleruchic or temple land. Reekmans (1971: 387) rightly noticed that the documentation of Kerkeosiris is essentially centred on quantification and on the identification of the status of agricultural parcels; it neglects part of the population of the village, particularly that which is occupied 'in local industry and in the service sector', or (as I would rather put it) the 'craftsmen, small businessmen, and rural proletariat'.

On the other hand, Uebel (1973: 537) offered a very different observation not to be neglected by anyone wanting to analyse the structures of the rural population (and, this time, more specifically of

---

[4] See n. 1.

[5] Reekmans (1971: 585–6) indicates that Kerkeosiris appears in our papyri in other periods than the second half of the second century BC (the period which is by necessity the main subject of Crawford 1971), but he admits that nothing can be said with certainty for the previous or following history of the village. Cf. S. Daris, 'Toponimi dell' Arsinoite: Kerkeosiris', *CdÉ* 52 (1977) 337–41.

Figure 10.1 *Gharaq basin, Fayyum (photo Roger S. Bagnall)*

the Greek population). He pointed out that the differences of area between the *klêroi* of the *katoikoi* from the cavalry and the other holders of an allotment (for instance 100 arouras (cavalry) versus 30 arouras (infantry) for Hellenic *katoikoi*, or 20 arouras versus 7 arouras in the case of the Egyptian cleruchs) must be explained by the cost entailed in maintaining a horse and do not reflect the true difference in net incomes between the cavalrymen and other cleruchs. These differences are already partially marked by the more or less cultivable state of the allotments. However, the contrast in area between the holdings of the *katoikoi* and those of the *machimoi* is one of the most visible elements of the documentation from Kerkeosiris.

In his preliminary paper in the volumes in honour of H. C. Youtie, and later in *P. Tebt.* IV, John Shelton made new and decisive material available concerning the crown land in Kerkeosiris. He was able to modify the image we had of the quality of life in the farming community and of the way sacred land was operated. Like Reekmans and Uebel, Shelton had reservations about some results of the statistical analysis made by Crawford (1971: 122–31) about Kerkeosiris' land in terms of the nutrition of the population. Did she not find in second-century Kerkeosiris 'poverty and despair', 'a standard of living, consistently low, that dropped even further'?[6]

---

[6] I believe that it is very difficult for a Western scholar, when referring to antique rations or salaries in kind (cf. Crawford 1971: 130), to realise what can be the daily ration of a well-fed or underfed domestic unit in a rural zone. What is, for instance, the role of occasional food supplements with regard to wheat? As for the children, one might not count them as half-units. The excellent remark of Diodorus I 80, 5–6 (quoted by Crawford 1971: 131), on

All this is only seemingly distant from our problem, the 'presence or absence of the Greeks in Kerkeosiris'. For instance, the considerations which I have just evoked confirm the idea that the term *georgos* (cultivator) is in no way synonymous with misery or with the economically weakest part of the village population. The rural proletariat is, moreover, as we said above, invisible in our documentation from Kerkeosiris, unlike the *georgos*, a basic element of the surveys, who cannot be likened at all to them. But my brief evocation of recent studies on this village is particularly justified by a remark of John Shelton's which seems, at first reading, opposed to the views I summarised earlier. He writes (*P. Tebt.* IV, p. 10), 'Cleruchs were for the most part not absentee landlords, but present and active in Kerkeosiris, as may be seen not only in that many of them tilled their allotment personally (cf. index IX, *s.v.* γεωργὸς αὐτός), but also from complaints against individuals recorded in numerous petitions.'[7] The new documentation did not change the data bearing on this problem for cleruchic land. But is there any actual disagreement between my hypothesis that Greeks were not naturally disposed to settle in a rural environment, and Shelton's indisputable remark that numerous cleruchs operated their allotments personally?

The problem is rooted in the use in the Kerkeosiris 'land surveys' of references of the type he mentions (γεωργὸς αὐτός, 'with himself as cultivator'), taken *exempli gratia* in *P. Tebt.* IV 1110 (a doublet of *P. Tebt.* I 63), the survey by crop of crown, cleruchic and other allotted land for 116/115:[8]

the feeding of children with cheap vegetable foods throughout the day corresponds to the current situation in vast regions of the world (it is one of the major causes of infant mortality after weaning). The proportion of the underfed population in Kerkeosiris depended directly on the royal levy on the wheat, and this might affect individuals in a single rural community very differently. And, whatever the comfort level of a village, there existed, as now in the third world, a more or less large fringe of permanently underfed people. They are mostly ignored in our documents, as they are now in our newspapers, and particularly by the types of documents at our disposition for Kerkeosiris. Probably it did not move or upset very much either the contemporaneous authorities or the well-fed people, because the phenomenon seemed probably quite natural to them.

[7] This calls to mind Grenfell and Hunt's energetic remark (*P. Tebt.* I, p. 547) on *katoikoi*: 'the baselessness of the view that they were chiefly inhabitants of towns'. However, these words concerned in fact a disagreement of these two pioneers with views, today obsolete, which had been advanced about the difference between cleruchs and *katoikoi*. But the fact that *katoikoi* are landholders does not necessarily imply their presence on the land.

[8] A comprehensive table of this documentation appears in Crawford (1971: 148–59), 'using the following translations: *abrochos*, dry; *embrochos*, flooded; *halmyris*, salted; *chersos*, desert; *hypologos*, derelict; *asporos*, unsown'.

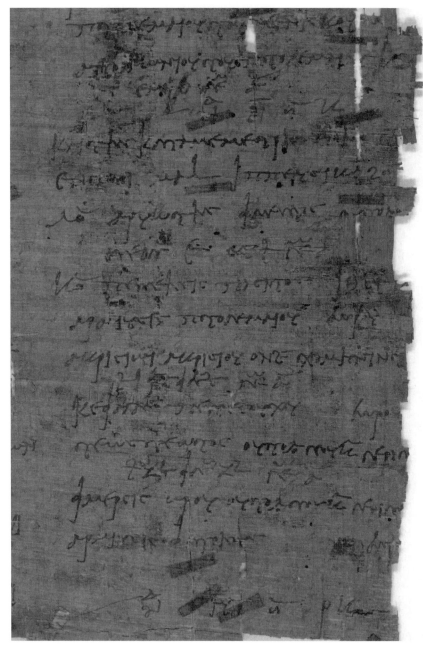

Figure 10.2 Tebt. IV 1110, col. 5, section of land register with geôrgos autos entries (photo courtesy of the Center for the Tebtunis Papyri, University of California, Berkeley)

1. ll. 37–8: 70-aroura holders: Aphthonetos son of Hebdomion, 70 (ar.), of which 10 in wheat, 30 in *arakos*, total 50; derelict salted land 20; cultivator, Petermouthis.
2. ll. 61–3: Lysimachos son of Pyrrhos, the remainder of whose *klêros* is in Ibion Eikosipentarouron, 40 (ar.), of which 15 in wheat, 15 in *arakos*, total 30; flooded 10; cultivator, Marres.
3. ll. 68–9: Leon son of Leontiskos, 40 (ar.), of which 15 in wheat, 10 in *arakos*, total 25; flooded 15; cultivator, himself.
4. l. 106: Apollonios son of Dionysios, unsown, 50.
5. l. 115: Leptines son of Stratonikos, desert, 25.
6. ll. 155–6: 7 aroura *machimoi*: Poregebthis son of Apynchis, 6½, of which 4½ in wheat, 2 in lentils; cultivator, himself.

The indications supplied by these documents present an initial dichotomy: parcels are operated by the *katoikos* or the *machimos* himself (*georgos autos*) or they are leased to another person, normally a tenant or a middleman, although no distinction between these is made. This is in fact a very vague dichotomy, because there is a third term to this choice: the allotment remains uncultivated because of various circumstances or through the simple incapacity of the holder. The term *georgos* is seemingly free of difficulty on one point: considering the importance which the surveys attach to this example, the word does not indicate someone receiving wages from the holder of the *klêros*, but indeed an operator responsible to a certain extent for the allotment, as owner or as leaseholder, whether this last operates the land directly or has it cultivated by subtenants.[9] As far as we are able to decide, *georgos autos* seems to indicate in our Kerkeosiris documents a cultivator who lives on the spot or in a nearby village.[10] Naturally, to lease out a katoikic allotment or to leave it uncultivated does not necessarily imply that the *katoikos* was absent. But this last situation must have been the most frequent.

The problem of the presence of Greeks and Egyptians in the cleruchies is regrettably complicated by all of the ambiguities that human destiny and local realities could accumulate in a community. Absence can be due to a mobilisation of the cleruch rather than to the

---

[9] Cf. for discussion Crawford (1971: 77–83).

[10] The term *georgos* can on occasion indicate the running of a plot of somebody who is absent by means of hired farmworkers. Cf. *P. Tebt.* III 782 (towards 153), where the *georgos* of an important allotment of crown land is a Greek who lives in the metropolis (cf. Chapter 8). It is reasonable to admit that the *georgoi* of our land surveys are mainly actual operators, cleruchs or farmers, especially when the last have an Egyptian name.

decision to live somewhere else on the rents of the *klêros*. On the other hand, a cleruchic population is not homogeneous and is for instance composed of successive age-cohorts (two, even three generations might live on the *klêros*), and this could generate a lot of differences in behaviour or in links with the *klêros*. At the time of these registers, the most recent cleruchic layer was a more or less homogeneous population of Egyptian *machimoi,* whereas in the older strata we find Hellenes – Macedonians, Greeks, Thracians and other ethnic groups in the service of the king – and later progressively Hellenised people in more modest posts. Are the differences in behaviour concerning the actual occupation of the land features specific to each of the two constituents of the population or the more or less recent creation of the cleruchies? Here a new ambiguity appears: the social layers from which Greek *katoikoi* come are presumably not the same as those in which *machimoi* were recruited. These peculiarities could have induced different behaviours when people were faced with living in the countryside, even if that had been the life their ancestors in Europe led or sought to lead. One can imagine, indeed, that *machimoi* not only were from peasant origin but also came from the same agricultural environment with its traditional techniques, certainly more often than was the case with the *katoikoi*. There is another element which makes a global assessment rather hazardous: as I said, allotments, even within each group, are of different sizes. Eighty arouras and seven arouras do not offer the same problems of cultivation or have the same possibilities for living on the rents. All those elements probably contributed to the choices cleruchs made, quite apart from their Greek or Egyptian social conditioning.

Our approach to the problem, then, should be limited to identifying actual situations revealed by documents towards the end of the second century and to taking into consideration the social developments that those situations seem to have brought about, without trying to define with too much precision why and how this very complex phenomenon developed.

One significant feature of the documentation was mentioned rather than exploited by Dorothy Crawford (1971: 84–5) and has not been modified by the new finds. In 117/116, with one exception, all the *machimoi* who had an allotment suitable for cultivation operated it themselves, whereas for the Greek *katoikoi*, there were twice as many allotments leased out as allotments operated by the cleruch, and the proportion of uncultivated parcels was considerable. New documents have shed some light on the situation in the following years.

They show the same massive presence of *machimoi* on their small allotments of 6½ arouras: all of them except one are still designated as *georgos autos* in *P. Tebt.* IV 1115. A more characteristic feature: while in 116/115 BC the allotments which *machimoi* left uncultivated were relatively numerous (a quarter of the whole), in 111/110 or somewhat later, this situation seems to have disappeared. Indeed, where the state of conservation of the same *P. Tebt.* IV 1115 allows us to trace the allotments left unsown some years earlier, these are now cultivated by the *machimos* himself. We find there a generalised behaviour among Egyptian cleruchs. Certainly, it can be explained, as I remarked, by the smallness of the holding and the greater familiarity of the Egyptian *machimoi* with the local conditions of agriculture, but we discover that the Egyptian *machimoi* are actually present on the soil; their neighbours, the crown farmers, also present, are Egyptians too as shown by their onomastics.[11]

These same documents show as well that, in the years which follow 116/115, the proportion of Greek *katoikoi* who lease out their allotment to a third party (generally Egyptians) remained the same. In *P. Tebt.* IV 1114 (113/112) they are nineteen, compared to seven who are described as *georgos autos*, but this is an incomplete text, which leaves the impression that the ratio 2:1 remained probably constant.[12] Thus only a minority of Greek *katoikoi* ran their allotments themselves, probably in many cases as gentlemen farmers. The new documentation does not modify my views of 1973 (now in Chapter 8) on a 'relative' absence of the Greeks in the Egyptian countryside. When Shelton, as I noted earlier, underlined the real character of the activity of 'many of the cleruchs', it is because he took together *katoikoi* and *machimoi*, groups which I have argued we must dissociate. There is no contradiction between his 'many' and the 'lesser' number of Greeks who, according to my analysis, were effectively settled on the land.

The proportion between direct operation of the holding by the two groups (almost the totality of the *machimoi* against one third for the

[11] I can only mention here the importance in a village of such settlements of exogenous Egyptian elements, particularly from the point of view of onomastics. It is doubtless one of the factors that explain why in the Ptolemaic period onomastics does not yet have the degree of local colouring that we see in Roman Egypt, particularly in the Arsinoite (cf., for instance, *Das Archiv des Petaus (P. Petaus)*, 1969, 46–53). But this is a subject where a lot is still to be done.

[12] The figure of seven is a little too low because of the gaps of *P. Tebt.* IV 1114. By comparison with 1115 and other 'surveys', one can put forward for this document the approximate figures of ± 21 and ± 10 for the two methods of running *klêroi* of *katoikoi* in 113/112. The total of the two figures is unusually high due to the low percentage of unsown allotments.

katoikoi) takes on particular visibility if one compares this with the situation in 119/118, while dynastic war was raging.[13] While in 116/115, 98 per cent of *machimoi* practise self-exploitation, the label *georgos autos* appears in 119/118 only for 44 per cent of them, and more than one third were leasing out their small *klêros*.[14] In a very convincing way Dorothy Crawford connects this situation with a more or less general mobilisation among *machimoi* because of unrest in the *chôra*. In 119/118 *katoikoi* were probably mobilised in the same way, but the ratio of 2:1 (rent/self-exploitation) appears again as 16:8,[15] compared to 12:7 in 115/115[16] and 19:7 in 113/112.[17] Mobilisation, if there was one as we may expect, hardly troubled the Greek *katoikoi*. On one hand, they had a long cleruchic tradition; on the other hand, with a rental income, they were economically much less affected by mobilisation. Dorothy Crawford writes too modestly that the figures that I took from her for 119/118 and 116/115 and completed here above 'are not very informative'. The new documents published by John Shelton show them to be on the contrary very significant. Certainly, these statistics could be refined, but even as they are, they shed light on some aspects of the different behaviour of Greeks and Egyptians in the country. Of the latter, only a few exceptions are absent; for the former, this is a permanent tendency, little affected by political contingencies.

It would be premature to develop here a comparison between the cleruchies in the third century, as we know them from the Petrie papyri (which still lack a synthesis) or from the texts from Tholthis,[18] and those of the second century. I would rather like to end by warning against a misunderstanding which the present chapter, like Chapter 8,

---

[13] Crawford (1971: 84–5).

[14] The figure of 44 per cent is uncertain. Because of the lacunae in *P. Tebt.* I 62, for nearly one third of the *machimoi* we do not know if there is self-exploitation or a leased *klêros*. But it is characteristic that in 119/118, one third *at least* of the *machimoi* lease the allotment to another Egyptian, twenty-two *or more* of them against 1 in 116/115. Here the new documents published by Shelton complete and confirm the figures established by Crawford (1971: 84). *P. Tebt.* IV 1108 (120/119 or not long before) reveals that twenty-five *machimoi* ran their 7-aroura allotments themselves, against twenty who rented them out (there are only six cases in which we are not able to decide). These figures are more significant than those for 119/118 which Dorothy Crawford had at her disposal in 1971.

[15] Here too *P. Tebt.* IV 1108, which precedes by one year (or a little more) *P. Tebt.* I 62, offers the same ratio of 2:1.

[16] With a very high proportion of uncultivated or not cultivable parcels, which seems especially to affect the leased-out allotments.

[17] Cf. above, n. 12.

[18] On the documents from Tholthis, see Crawford (1971: 76, 171–2); Uebel (1973: 538–9); and Chapter 15 below.

could create. The Greeks, in the country, are often absentees, often passers-by, and this explains how with time an Egyptian rural middle class acquired some importance through the durability and the density of its occupation of the soil. But, in the face of a certain 'absence' of the Greeks, it is still necessary to take into account a binding presence of an invisible 'Greek framework' of the country, bound to language and to ways of thinking and managing in the administration, especially at the level at which decisions were taken. Official documents in the Greek language, as we see in the Kerkeosiris papyri, record agricultural life in all its perspectives. The ways to approach the authorities of the metropolis, both in the documents and in the deliberations preceding the decisions, are Greek ways, and not only in language. This 'Greekness', moreover, found support on the spot in the permanent or temporary presence of a certain number of Greeks, often prestigious people if not necessarily very popular. More by its expertise than by its insufficient density, the Greek population of the countryside took its part in the processes of Hellenisation of some Egyptian social types, when as cleruchs, civil servants or businessmen, the autochthonous first became members of the Greek system,[19] before passing to a more or less complete partnership in the Greek dominant class.

---

[19] See, for instance, the case of Menches, discussed in Chapter 8; or the expression *Hellênes georgoi* ('Greek cultivators'), which appears in *P. Tebt.* IV 1107. 279 and seems to indicate small Egyptian cleruchic tenants of crown land (Shelton, *P. Tebt.* IV, p. 95), an expression which I would explain by the fact that those cleruchs are from then on active elements in the royal Greek system, the native cleruchy being exactly one of those zones of progressive Hellenisation revealed for instance by cases of mixed filiation or double names adding a Greek element to an Egyptian one.

Chapter 11

THE CAVALRY SETTLERS OF THE HERAKLEOPOLITE IN THE FIRST CENTURY

෧

In Ptolemaic Egypt the first century BC constitutes a period relatively poor in papyri, although the documents from the Herakleopolite are gradually improving this situation. This scarcity has certainly impaired our vision of what the realm was by this time. Dynastic events and the increasing influence of Rome are so prominent that they tend to obscure the importance of a certain number of social developments that we would like to clarify. The relative shortage of written documents has given the impression that outside of Alexandria those seventy years constitute only a languishing and rather dull transition period between the disturbances of the second century and the implementation of the Augustan order in Egypt. In this hazy context, one imagines only too easily the continuation of some theoretical linear processes, such as a decline of the power of the throne, an increasing power of the Egyptian clergy, or other current working hypotheses suggested by a rather superficial reading of, among other documents, the edicts of Euergetes II or the asylum decrees from the first century (see Chapter 19).

If we except that epigraphical dossier, the last reigns of the Ptolemies are illustrated in the main, as I have said, by papyri from the Herakleopolite nome. Two groups of texts, one concerning the transfer of katoikic allotments and the other petitions to the *strategos*, published in *BGU* VIII and X respectively, have been particularly exploited. More recently, William M. Brashear published a set of Ptolemaic papyri where the same nome is strongly represented, particularly by one long list of lands or holders of lands.[1]

Analysing this last addition to our evidence, we are inevitably tempted to compare it with another well-known body of documentation, relatively close in time (end of the second century) and in space (the neighbouring southeast part of the Fayyum), namely the land-surveys from Kerkeosiris. Brashear noted a difference between those

---

[1] *BGU* XIV, pp. 134–219, nos. 2436–50. For a good *status quaestionis* of the problems aroused by those texts, ibid., pp. 220–55.

land-surveys – as they were analysed by Dorothy Crawford, then by Shelton and myself[2] – and the Herakleopolitan file – as it appears in the Berlin papyri. To the complexity of the picture suggested by the Kerkeosiris material, and to its instability from one year to the other, seems to be opposed a certain stability in the Herakleopolite.[3] In my view, however, it is necessary to reverse this comparative evaluation of the two sets of documents, and perhaps to the detriment of our Herakleopolitan documentation, whose fragmentary character Brashear already underlined.

The publication of *Tebtunis Papyri* IV made possible a global analysis of the lands of Kerkeosiris and also of the population settled on those lands: the people who possessed it and those who were working on it, on the royal land, the sacred land or the cleruchic domain. Certainly considerable fluctuations appear at Kerkeosiris, on the one hand in the rate of exploitation of the soil, and on the other hand in the percentage of plots directly exploited by Greek or Egyptian cleruchs. Those fluctuations in fact disguise two constants: (1) the tendency of the Egyptian *machimos* to cultivate his *klêros* himself, whereas the Greek *katoikos* shows rather a tendency to rent out his *klêros*; (2) the more evident vulnerability of the Egyptian *machimos* during an absence due to mobilisation.[4]

The real weakness of the Herakleopolitan land registers of *BGU* XIV is the fact that they only supply a very partial image of the agricultural area in question and are very often centred on cleruchic allotments, thus on the category already predominantly represented in our papyrological evidence.

A doubt arises at once: are we allowed to extrapolate to the general category of the granted lands, to all holders and farmers of such lands, the data that the hazards of preservation and discovery have concentrated significantly only in a socio-economic environment as particular as that of the cavalrymen *katoikoi* of the first century? This problem arose earlier when the previous Herakleopolitan evidence concerning transfers of katoikic plots[5] seemed to reveal the birth of something close to private landed property at the end of the Ptolemaic period. In 1928, Kunkel published some

---

[2] Crawford (1971); J. C. Shelton, in *P. Tebt.* IV, pp. 2–18; see Chapter 10, pp. 124–30.
[3] W. M. Brashear in *BGU* XIV, pp. 254–5.
[4] Chapter 10, p. 129.
[5] *BGU* VIII 1731–4 and 1735–40. On a similar group of texts from the Oxyrhynchite see G. Messeri Savorelli, in *P. Oxy.* XLIX, pp. 165–73 (intro. and comm. to *P. Oxy.* XLIX 3482).

contracts for transfer, or several oaths which cover such transfers.[6] Only Rhodokleia's request, presented by Wolfgang Müller in 1958 at the Congress of Oslo, added significantly new elements.[7] The earlier documentation allowed Claire Préaux to propose major conclusions in 1939,[8] conclusions that were only slightly amended by the subsequent analysis of Wolfgang Müller. Even before the discovery of the land registers, this set of documents also received some additional light from contemporary cleruchic wills[9] and from *BGU IV 1185 = C. Ord. Ptol.* 71.

Claire Préaux showed how much the progressive extension of the cleruchic tenure when the army no longer served on active duty in lucrative wars meant a decrease of the royal income. This was, however, partially compensated on the economic level through cleruchic taxes and incentives to exploit (if not necessarily to exploit oneself) granted lands as far as they were cultivable.[10] On the social level, even if it was limited to some regions of Egypt,[11] this extension and stabilisation of the cleruchic tenure could only give birth to a social group with its own interests, a group whose relations with the king were all the more ambiguous in that they had been disrupted by dynastic quarrels and by reactions of competition or even hostility towards the body of the civil servants. The constitution of a closed group was, moreover, favoured by the structures of the cleruchy, and particularly by the mechanism of the privileged succession reserved to the sons of the cleruch and by the phenomenon of the cession (*parachôrêsis*), which we will meet later in the discussion. The latter often appears in the background of some land registers,[12] but two aspects have especially drawn the attention of historians: on the one hand, the apparent opening to something like private property, which one could dispose of more or less freely; on the other, the active

[6] Kunkel (1928: 285–313).

[7] *SB* VIII 9790 (Herakleopolite, mid-first century BC); editio princeps: Müller (1961: 190–3).

[8] Préaux (1939: 463–80): 'Évolution du droit clérouchique'; see also Préaux (1938: 41–57). Cf. Rostovtzeff (1941: II, 891–2; III, 1546–7).

[9] The most interesting case, although it is situated outside the Herakleopolite, is the Demotic will from Panopolis of the *katoikos* cavalryman Heti, published by M. Malinine, *Revue d'Égyptologie* 19 (1967) 67–85, pls. 3–5, an 'acte de droit grec écrit en langue égyptienne' (J. Bingen, *CdÉ* 43 (1968) 421–3).

[10] Préaux (1939: 467, 470).

[11] This limitation may be illusory, because the phenomenon appears in practically all the zones for which we have some documentation dating from the first century BC.

[12] Specifically mentioned in the surveys *BGU* XIV 2441, 2443, 2444 and 2449, the phenomenon of the *parachôrêsis* played probably the same role in other passages of these texts or in other Herakleopolitan documents.

appearance of women, Greek women,[13] in the process of succession to or of disposal of the *klêros*. At a minimum, an exceptional position or superior right was conferred on the wife of the cavalryman *katoikos*, because the *prostagma* of amnesty C. Ord. Ptol. 71, I (towards 60 BC) stipulates that the benefit of amnesty granted to some cavalrymen *katoikoi* was explicitly granted 'along with their wives and children'. This surprising provision anticipates the empirical adaptation of the common rules for a limited but important group: the old mounted militia of the realm.

In fact, for a long time scholars believed that a purely legal analysis of the *parachôrêsis*, the privileged cleruchic succession, or of the cleruchic will was inadequate. It did not cover the social conditions and the economic factors which certainly must have influenced the law at least as much as some theoretical connection between the royal power and the holder of a precarious possession did. With the benefit of a new document, Wolfgang Müller was able to point precisely to the wives of cleruchs as a disrupting element in our analysis, an element also present in our land registers.[14] He showed first that, in cases seemingly easy to explain even before the new evidence of 1958, the status of a woman able to vindicate rights to a *klêros* was actually only that of the representative of an orphaned son of a cleruch and was a coincidental support to the privileged succession by that son.[15] But Müller wondered if Rhodokleia's request, dated mid-first century BC, did not confirm, through an intestate succession, the existence of an almost free disposal of cleruchic land at the end of the Ptolemaic period. The cavalryman *katoikos* Menippos died intestate (as it seems) and had no male descendant. His daughter indicates that she inherits the rest of Menippos' estate and that the *logistêrion* of the cavalry recognised her claim on a *klêros* of 10 arouras 'by virtue of the royal decree'. The precise object of the request is not known, and it would have interested us because the request to the *strategos* was

---

[13] This is certainly one aspect of some larger autonomy, even if only from a relative perspective, of Greek women, compared with the situation of the domestic group in the Hellenistic period, as Karabélias (1982: 223–34) noticed on the specific level which we find in our texts and particularly in Rhodokleia's petition. But in fact, as we shall see, the main problem is not situated in the abstract analysis of the different individual situations which seem to develop freely in *parachôrêseis* and cleruchic wills, but in the fact that these situations do not modify the status of the katoikic *klêros* or its primary function of maintaining *katoikoi* cavalrymen.

[14] Let me quote at random the transfer of a parcel (actually of uncertain status) from Berenike to Erotion with the formula one finds for the devolution of the *klêros* of a cleruch, still alive, to his son (*BGU* XIV 2441.4).

[15] See n. 7.

probably caused by someone contesting her rights; in addition, or alternatively, it may have aimed at an ability to enter later into possession of the entire holding of her father.[16] In any case, however, I believe that the document does not allow us to go much farther than what we learn from the above-mentioned *parachôrêseis* of mothers of orphans. Did Rhodokleia, besides the fiscal responsibility of the *klêros*, have a right of free disposal which would eventually remove the *klêros* from the closed circle of the cavalrymen *katoikoi*? Did she really possess any alternative other than to choose between the usufruct of the *klêros* or the cession to a cavalryman *katoikos*? Nothing allows us to imagine any explanation that goes beyond a status as temporary holder of a cleruchic estate or, better, of the usufruct of the *klêros*, which seems to characterise the status of the mothers of orphans belonging to this group.

However, the case of Rhodokleia illustrates two other aspects of the cessions of Herakleopolis, aspects that we find more or less evident in the land registers. The first one is the partial character of those deals. Documents like *BGU* VIII 1731–40 concern plots from 1 to 18 arouras, not a large amount compared to the official endowment of a cavalryman *katoikos*, and even of his actual endowment.[17] None of these documents concerns the global transfer of a domain from a holder to a new one.[18] Secondly, all the transfers mentioned in the Berlin papyri go from a member of the katoikic class to a cavalryman *katoikos*. It is not impossible that this fact is linked with the circumstances of the grouping of documents in the archives at the time when they were sold as waste paper and transformed into mummy cartonnage. But the new documentation of *BGU* XIV invites us to more scepticism.[19]

In the registers, where the presence of cavalrymen *katoikoi* is probably more general than the mutilation of the documents and the conventional brevity of such indications allow us to guess, both of the two above-mentioned aspects are present, although they are more differentiated.

---

[16] Müller (1961: 192) (text reprinted as *SB* VIII 9790).

[17] For both it is difficult to evaluate the area concerned, if not specified by the document, because any area could be one parcel in a set of plots of a cleruchic holding, or the residue of such a set partially given up.

[18] This partial character of the transfer of land is certainly the usual case, because it became a stereotype in the Oxyrhynchite form of the oath (*P. Oxy.* XLIX 3482; *P. Fouad* 38): 'If I violate my oath, also the remaining parts of my allotment are to be taken back by the crown.'

[19] As the small dossier from Oxyrhynchos does, especially *P. Oxy.* XLIX 3482 (transfer + oath; 73 BC), documents not used in this chapter.

Let us take the section of Ptolemaios, son of Philon, a member of the 'old cavalry settlers'.[20] He possesses an allotment of 105 arouras, which is already allocated to his son Philon. From that total, 60 arouras are let to a group of farmers, respectively 20 arouras sown in wheat, 20 arouras in barley, and 20 arouras in fodder crops. A further 40 arouras were made over to three persons with Greek names, probably other cavalrymen *katoikoi*, as Brashear reasonably thought.[21] We find there respectively 15 unproductive arouras and parcels of 10 arouras and 15 arouras, both of grain land. The missing 5 arouras are probably a plot planted with trees, which is partially exploited and taxed as such, and which also contains the house of our gentleman farmer.[22] The file of the other 'old' *katoikos* is even less gratifying: Apollonios, son of Theodoros, possesses a *klêros* of 100 arouras of which he has let 20 arouras to Tryphon, who 'exploits' the plot himself. The rest is an orchard of 2½ arouras, which perhaps had become desert,[23] and 77½ arouras either desert or left uncultivated.

We are able to study one of those cases in the perspective of *klêroi* exploited by a third party. Cleruchs using the rent of their land as a source of income are a well-known phenomenon. Papyri from Herakleopolis published in the past had already supplied several particularly interesting references. For instance, the petition *BGU* VIII 1858, famous for the mention of a state of anarchy (*pragmatôn anarchia*),[24] was drafted by farmers who call their harvest 'the products of the land we have sown in accordance with the leases of katoikic *klêroi*'. Indicating by these words the type of collective exploitation they practise, they seem to use a commonplace and easily understandable reference. In *BGU* VIII 1861, a cleruch, probably a cavalryman *katoikos*, asked for a loan of seeds 'for the sowing of the allotment which belongs to me'. With such a formulation, he seems apparently to be a case of 'himself as cultivator'. Nevertheless the *strategos* asks him to put him in touch with the cultivators, obviously to be sure that the *klêros* is effectively cultivated. The cleruch reacts, rather disconcertingly, by asking the *strategos* to arrange for the *topogrammateus*, during his tour on the spot, to summon the farmers who exploit the *klêros*.

---

[20] *BGU* XIV 2441.135–42.

[21] *BGU* XIV, index *s.v.* Let us note that Sophon, father or son of one of the three men, was a policeman (*BGU* XIV 2441.218).

[22] *BGU* XIV 2441.147.

[23] If it is indeed the orchard of cavalry land which, in ll. 62–3, lies in the *klêros* of an Apollonios, called, I believe by mistake, son of Theodotos.

[24] Cf. Müller (1961: 184–6).

The registers supply numerous interesting types of exploitation of katoikic lands. It is possible here only to point out some newly attested situations. In *BGU* XIV 2444.83–92, lands with wheat adjoin a sanctuary in Tekmi and perhaps were part of sacred lands allocated to a settlement by the king. About 66 arouras had been granted to the cleruch Apollonios, but they were partially entrusted to his daughter Herakleia (24 arouras) and to his son Herakleides (6 arouras); the larger part of the *klêros* appears under the name of the father, but was transferred for the most part to an Apollonios who is probably his elder son or his grandson assuming the obligations of cleruchic service. This set of plots, which is not presented as a domestic joint possession but seems to have been the object of a division *inter vivos*, is transferred in its entirety to a Diodoros, certainly a cavalryman *katoikos*, but is exploited, also in its entirety, directly or indirectly, by one Hierax, said to be the cultivator. This illustrates the complexity of the statuses recognised for various persons connected at different levels in the katoikic system with the exploitation of the katoikic area. They have rights and duties which the royal authority recognises simultaneously. By contrast, we would normally have supposed that rights and duties disappeared when transferred to another holder. Whatever the nature of this transfer of rights, everybody remains involved at least in the land-surveys. But all this becomes even more tantalising if we make the highly probable identification of this Hierax with the homonym who occurs in several texts of the same dossier. A more astonishing and risky, although certainly possible, identification is with the *eklogistes* Hierax of the parallel Herakleopolitan dossier of the *strategoi*, in which, as an *eklogistes*, this Hierax is a major agent of the royal administration.

Let us take first the three men called Hierax in the same group of documents. In *BGU* XIV 2448.11, Hierax is cultivator for the *klêros* of a *phylakites*, a small *klêros* of wheat land, whereas in the accounts *BGU* XIV 2432.5 and 2436.12, he pays rents or money taxes for plots of 52 and 41 arouras. Put together, those figures (something like 100 arouras, 25 to 30 hectares) show once more the ambiguity of the term 'cultivator', the man whom the authorities recognise as responsible for the exploitation, whatever status he possesses and whether he is a large or a small agricultural entrepreneur. It is attractive to join to our texts two requests of the year 51/50. In the first, *BGU* VIII 1821, the nephew and steward of the *eklogistes* Hierax, put in prison due to a conflict with the *logeutes* or tax collector of a nearby village, indicates that his uncle's land runs the risk of not being sown. In *BGU* VIII 1831, the other request to a *strategos*, a cavalryman *katoikos* complains about the behaviour of a third party, an owner of cattle, who endangers the sowing of 130 arouras 'belonging' to the *eklogistes* Hierax, of whose domain he is the cultivator.

If the land register and the two series of documents quoted above are linked, as I am sure they should be, mutual relations appear between the class of the high civil servants and that of the cavalrymen *katoikoi*, both exploiting the main basis of production of the country, the grain land. Their relationships may on occasion be disturbed by local difficulties due to conflicts of authority, conflicts which eventually one tries to settle by a problematic appeal to the *strategos*.[25]

The *parachôrêsis* is a current practice in some of our Herakleopolis surveys. It appears, next to the direct exploitation of the *klêros*,[26] as one of the modalities of the cession to a third party of the cultivation of a cleruchic parcel.[27] Therefore it would be dangerous to simplify the analysis of the katoikic transfer by seeing there a mode of hidden sale of the land, or a solution to an eventual incapacity of the cleruch to assume the fiscal burden of his *klêros*.[28] Indeed, seeing how complex the data relative to the *klêros* are, I have the feeling that the katoikic holding of land has not yet evolved in the late Hellenistic period to have the more or less clandestine status of free disposal which katoikic land seems to have acquired later in the Roman period. At no moment does the cavalry land seem to be at the disposal of just anybody. The competition between the king and the holder of granted land for the mastery of the tenure, an ancient and permanent phenomenon in social history, is not the original element of this dossier. What seems to me to be original, on the contrary, is the fact that, by the mechanism of the *parachôrêsis*, the class of the cavalrymen *katoikoi*, taken as a whole, does not lose the global power of disposal over the soil which was granted to the horse militia. The cleruchic will appears as an individual project of distribution of a katoikic fund and of the domestic goods of the *katoikos*, including

---

[25] Cf., for instance, *BGU* VIII 1832 or 1834.

[26] Such direct exploitation seems more wide-spread than at Kerkeosiris among the cleruchs of a certain rank, but it is necessary to keep in mind the ambiguous character of the word *georgos*, cultivator.

[27] The difference from the periodic collection of a rent is that here only one part (not specified in the act of transfer) is credited to the patrimony of the cleruch, who gives up any further income from the plot.

[28] As shown by Préaux (1939: 477), fiscal deficiency could be a motive for abandoning part of the *klêros*, but nothing allows us to see this as the most frequent reason for the cessions. The fiscal clauses of the *parachôrêseis* aim especially to establish clearly the actual or future fiscal obligations of each party.

the dowry of the wife and the dowries to be foreseen for the daughters, a project of distribution which is perhaps regularly asked for by the cleruchic administration.[29] In the same way, the *parachôrêsis*, beyond the more or less fictitious legal act of an apparent transfer, appears to me on the socio-economic level as part of a permanent reorganisation of the katoikic space according to the persons and according to the status of the land.[30]

In a Greek society where the royal function had been in some sort of crisis for a hundred or a hundred and fifty years, the group of the cavalrymen *katoikoi* gradually ceased to be only a military structure, a militia of a more or less controlled elite, as it seems still to be in the Kerkeosiris surveys. It becomes, under the cover of katoikic regulations, a closed environment, a group which from now on defines itself by an autonomous economic power (even though this is in a perpetual state of revision for each member of the group), defines itself at least as much by its organised presence on the soil as by military availability to serve the king. Some decline of the links with the king (if there really was any decline of those links after the crisis of the second century) did not compromise the katoikic influence on the land or, indirectly, that of the king. The formal, purely institutional and legal aspects of this influence later survived in the particular conditions in which katoikic transfer was recorded under the empire. But from a socio-economic point of view, there was no alienation, much less dispersal of the land globally entrusted by the king to his cavalry settlers. Therefore, when this situation came to an end with the collapse of the dynasty, cavalry land remained an entity in itself as a territory, precisely because it had not been liquidated or really affected by the *parachôrêsis*. Without the king, this survival was limited to an accumulation of individual parcels, and in the end to an almost freely transferable possession, but in the anachronistic forms which were proper to the cession.[31]

---

[29] One can, indeed, wonder whether those cleruchic testamentary partitions are not a prerequisite obligation linked to the status of *katoikos* and whether legal provisions in case of intestate succession (for example, the *prostagma C. Ord. Ptol.* 71.16–19) do not make up for the deficiencies of the cleruch.

[30] *P. Oxy.* XLIX 3482 illustrates this phenomenon of reorganisation of the katoikic territory. The cavalryman Theon, with the agreement of his wife, makes over to the cavalryman *katoikos* Dionysios some plots of land which are certainly contiguous to those Dionysios already possesses near Senepta. The operation had at the same time the result of distributing, in equal parts, the allotments which both *katoikoi* possessed in this place.

[31] Within the framework of this chapter, I have not been able to examine other contributions devoted to these registers, or the *parachôrêseis* of other classes of cleruchs, or the problem of the cession of private land.

Chapter 12

TWO ROYAL ORDINANCES OF THE
FIRST CENTURY AND THE ALEXANDRIANS

◌

Edited for the first time by Gustave Lefebvre in 1913,[1] the double *prostagma* issued by Cleopatra VII and Ptolemy XV Caesar in 41 BC (*C. Ord. Ptol.* 75–6, from Herakleopolis)[2] is interesting first because this text fits into a rich papyrological documentation of the conflicts between the privileged classes and the fiscal administration, with a surprising parallel in *P. Tor. Choachiti* 4 (= *UPZ* II 191). Another royal edict, *C. Ord. Ptol.* 67 (Ptolemais, 46 BC),[3] issued some years before by the same queen, but with another coregent, probably Ptolemy XIV,[4] may be compared to our inscription.[5] The latter document and *C. Ord. Ptol.* 75–6 are sent for release to the same Theon, perhaps a royal *hypomnêmatographos*, if this office still existed in the late first century. *C. Ord. Ptol.* 75–6 present, in addition, the interest of reflecting in their different parts contrasted facets of what I would call 'epigraphic prose', or, if one prefers, different levels of the rhetoric of power in the late Hellenistic period, at least as it appears in the documents.

The earlier of the two *prostagmata* of Herakleopolis (ll. 11–35; 15 March 41 BC) has the shape of a decision issued by royal justice with its supporting reasoning, its procedural apparatus, and its technical

---

[1] Lefebvre (1913). Egyptian Museum, Cairo, inv. 45236. I have collated the text on a photograph (Centre de Papyrologie et d'Épigraphie grecque, Université libre de Bruxelles).
[2] Lenger (1964: 210–15, nos. 75–6; 1980: 210–15, nos. 75–6; and 382). *I. Prose* 45 (the re-edition of the inscription by A. Bernand depends on Lenger 1964).
[3] Cf. Lenger (1990: 17). Photograph in Svetlana Hodjash and Oleg Berlev, *The Egyptian Reliefs and stelae in the Pushkin Museum of Fine Arts, Moscow* (Leningrad 1982) 282, no. 204, p. 279. *I. Prose* 36. Cf. Bingen (1994: 13–21).
[4] For the successive coregents of Cleopatra VII, see Heinen (1969: 188–9); Criscuolo (1989: 325–39); and Hölbl (1994: 205–27, esp. 213–14, 219, 224), for Ptolemy XV Caesar. Cf. Chapter 5 above.
[5] W. Schubart, 'Bemerkungen zum Stile hellenistischer Königsbriefe', *APF* 6 (1920) 324–47, especially studying the royal epistolary style during the Hellenistic period, compared these two inscriptions (pp. 341–2). But his attempt is weakened by the fact that he compares the royal *prostagma* which introduces the main *prostagma* and the *prostagma* treating the substance of the decision.

Figure 12.1   Stele with C. Ord. Ptol. 75–6 *(photo Marie-Thérèse Lenger)*

vocabulary, accompanied by an ordinance by proclamation, duly called *prostagma* in l. 4 of the second *prostagma*, in fact the decree which foresees the execution of the judgement and its generalisation through publication throughout Egypt. The whole text is sent to Theon for that purpose.

```
11  Θέωνι.
12  τῶν ἀπὸ τῆς πόλεως, γεωργούντων δ᾽ἐν τῶι
13  Προσωπίτηι καὶ Βουβαστείτηι, ἐντυχόντων
14  ἡμε<ῖ>ν, (vacat) ἐπὶ χρηματισμοῦ τῆι ιε τοῦ Φαμενὼθ
15  κατὰ τῶν πρὸς χρείαις τῶν νομῶν, (vacat) ὃν τρόπον
16  οὗτοι παρὰ τὴν ἡμετέραν προαίρεσιν καὶ τὰ
17  πολλάκις ὑπὸ τῶν διοικούντων ἀκολούθως
18  ἡμῶν τῆι κρίσει ἐπιστελλόμενα ὑπὲρ τοῦ μηδὲν
19  πλεῖον ἀπαιτεῖν αὐτοὺς τῶν γνησίων βασιλικῶν
20  ἐπιβάλλονται παραπράσσειν ταῖς τε ἀγροικικαῖς
21  καὶ χωρικαῖς ξενιζούσαις ἀπαιτήσεσι (vacat) συνκατα-
22  ριθμεῖν, μεγάλως μεισοπονηρήσαντες κοινήν
23  τε καὶ καθολικὴν ἐπέξοδον πάντων κρείνοντες
24  ποιεῖσθαι, (vacat) προστετάχαμεν τοὺς γεωργοῦντας
25  κατὰ τὴν χώραν τῶν ἀπὸ τῆς πόλεως πάντας
26  μὴ γείνεσθαι συνεισφόρους τοῖς κατὰ καιροὺς
27  καὶ περιστάσεις ἱσταμένοις ἐν τοῖς νομοῖς
28  στεφά<ν>οις καὶ ταῖς ἐπιγραφαῖς, μηδὲ τὰ ὑπάρ-
29  χοντα αὐτῶν εἰς τοὺς τοιούτους ἄγ<ε>ιν μερισμούς,
30  μηδὲ τέλεσμα ἐπ᾽ αὐτῶν καινίζ<ει>ν, (vacat) διορθουμένους
31  δὲ τὰ ἄνωθεν (vacat) εἰς τὸ βασιλικὸν ὑποκείμενα τῆς
32  [τε σ]ιτοφόρου καὶ ἀμπελίτιδος σιτικὰ καὶ ἀργυρικὰ
33  γνήσια τελέσματα πρὸς μηδὲν ἕτερον καθοντινοῦν
34  τρόπον παρευρέσει μηδεμιᾷ παρενοχλεῖν. (vacat) γεινέσθω
35  οὖν ἀκολούθως καὶ προσεκτεθήτωι κατὰ νομόν.
```

```
13  Βουβαστίτηι   14 ἡμῖν   21-2 συγκαταριθμεῖν
22  μισοπονηρήσαντες   23 κρίνοντες   26 γίνεσθαι
28  ΣΤΕΦΑΠΟΙΣ tit.   30 KAINIZIEN tit.   34 γινέσθω
35  προσεκτεθήτω
```

To Theon. A complaint having been brought before us by people of this city, particularly those that operate agricultural domains in the Prosopite and Boubastite nomes – on the pronouncement of the judgement of 15 Phamenoth against the civil servants of the nomes – the object of the complaint being the way in which these last, against our policy and instructions many times communicated by those responsible for the finances, in accordance with our decision that no one is allowed to exact from these people anything more than the duly established royal taxation, manage to tax illegally, adding those people to the roll of the agricultural and local levies which do not concern them at all, judging, because of the hatred which in the past we dedicated to such abuses, along with a judgement aiming at the common and generalised eradication of those practices, we order that all the people of this city who operate agricultural domains in the countryside should not be involved in the 'crowns' and the other exceptional levies established in the nomes according to circumstances and moments of crisis; moreover, that their possessions should not be taken into account for such collective contributions, that any new regime of levy should also not affect them, but that, as far as they pay to the treasury the existing taxes in wheat and silver on the fields and on the vineyards as established in the past, nobody should bother them in any way or for anything under any pretext. Thus let it be done accordingly and let it be posted in every nome.

To make things easier, I have left aside an external element which enlightens us to some extent on the thinking of the originators of the inscription. Blank spaces strictly structure the 'prose' or syntax of the decrees, and also the argumentation of the various parties involved in this fiscal conflict which was settled in Alexandria.

The text of the main decree passed on to Theon opens with the identity of the plaintiffs and the date of the pronouncement of the judgement; there follow the grievances of the plaintiffs and the reasoning of the judgement (ll. 12-24). This last section (ll. 24–34) is introduced with the verb *prostetachamen*, 'we have decreed', which indicates at once that the verdict is situated at the supreme level of decision: there is no opening left for appeal, or for delegating the local authority to investigate and to decide.[6] Already in the statement of grievances, the plaintiffs argue that these concern malpractices committed against the general policy of the sovereigns and against the instructions of the higher financial authorities, which correspond to royal policy. We certainly find here part of the line of argument produced by the applicants; but this is summarised in the judgement with all the more complacency by the queen as it introduces the justification of the verdict and absolves the sovereigns and their higher administration of any collusion with the oppressive local agents of the treasury.

What sort of people are these applicants? The legal action was brought before the queen and the king, against royal officials active

---

[6] The same composition of the ordinance in two levels is found in *C. Ord. Ptol.* 64 (95 BC): a royal order motivated by a substantiated report from the *dioiketes* precedes the basic *prostagma* γινέσθω οὖν ἀκολούθως.

in the Prosopite and Boubastite nomes, by persons who were exploiting estates in those two nomes of the Delta. Adopting a suggestion of
Pierre Jouguet,[7] Lefebvre judged that the plaintiffs, as far as they are
called 'people of this city, particularly those that operate agricultural
domains in the Prosopite and Boubastite nomes', were 'natives of
Alexandria, but not citizens'. Since then, this view has been generally
adopted with some variations,[8] particularly by M.-T. Lenger, who
thought them 'farmers coming from Alexandria, established in the
Prosopite and Boubastite nomes. They do not enjoy the civil rights
recognised to the citizens of Alexandria; they belong however to a
class of privileged people.' In the last edition of the inscription, *I.
Prose* 45, A. Bernand adds an unexpected historical dimension to this
ambiguous status when he calls those people 'farmers born in
Alexandria, established in the Prosopite and the Boubastite nome;
this population, trying to extract a profit from the fields of the *chôra*,
was better trained and less "deprived" than the natives and could
constitute a considerable source of support for the queen, who
dreamed of a modernisation of Egypt'.

I have no access to the dreams of the queen, but it is necessary to
say here that, just as the leader of a group of Egyptian farmworkers
addressing Zenon proudly asserts,[9] in Egypt the experts in agriculture
were the 'natives', not the Greeks, and they certainly were not people
coming from a Greek city. If, as Bernand says, those 'natives' were
'deprived', it was only when the irrigation water did not arrive or
when the implements for production were missing, but that is the
result of failure on the part of the prince or, in some cases, of
the Alexandrian capitalist to invest enough money in his domain in
the country. Conversely, for P. M. Fraser, the phrase 'from the city'
covers simultaneously the citizens of Alexandria and the non-citizens
living in Alexandria.[10] I do not see how we could extend to the latter
the fiscal privileges which must by definition have been connected to
Alexandrian citizen status. I fear that Fraser extrapolates too widely
from the documentary evidence when he sees in those Alexandrians

---

[7] Moreover, basing his opinion on Jouguet (1911: 8 n. 6; 10; 48 n. 2).

[8] For instance, Chalon (1964: 159) calls the οἱ ἀπὸ τῆς πόλεως of Cleopatra VII's *prostagma*
      'natives who are not citizens' (see further n. 18). Erich Berneker, *Die Sondergerichtsbarkeit
      im griechischen Recht Ägyptens* (Münchener Beiträge 22, 1935) 62 speaks about
      'Kleruchen', but this implies for those people a military status which is absent from the text.
      Moreover, we shall see that the fiscal status of those Alexandrians is more advantageous than
      that of the cleruchs.

[9] Cf. *P. Lond.* VII 1954.7–8; cf. *P. Cair. Zen.* IV 59376.17–29.

[10] Fraser (1972: II, 230, n. 297).

'agricultural workers and small-holders in the Alexandrian *chôra* and in the nomes of the Delta, who were being taxed unjustly by local officials' and explains the gesture of the queen as an attempt to improve the lot of 'lower-class Alexandrians', to win them over 'to her side and consequently to that of Rome'.[11]

Nothing of the kind appears, even between the lines, in the Herakleopolitan inscription and in the motives we can perceive in the lawsuit of Alexandria.[12] I believe that it is now imperative to abandon the subtle but erroneous distinction which Jouguet introduced in 1911 between *Alexandreis* and 'those from the city', that is, between 'Alexandrian citizens' and people with a lower status, 'non-citizens born in Alexandria'.[13] The preposition *apo*, 'from', marks their origin and not relocation; it regularly indicates in our papyri membership in a town, a metropolis or a village, without implying that one is living elsewhere for one reason or another, and especially not suggesting that one has lost one's status of origin, with one kind or another of *deminutio capitis* compared to the *Alexandreis*. I am even convinced that *apo tês poleôs* is used here only because the lawsuit was held in Alexandria.[14] Undoubtedly, the verb *geôrgô*, 'cultivate', generally indicates in our papyri the activity of working directly on the soil, but it applies to any farmer, including the non-resident landlord who has his fields worked by local farmers or by hired people.[15] Moreover, I do not see how to define the activity of such a landlord any other way. For that reason, there is no objective basis not to consider the plaintiffs as full Alexandrians by right.[16] Maybe some of them never visited

---

[11] Fraser (1972: I, 127).

[12] Fraser himself notices (1972: II, 231, n. 299) how little we know about the actual relations existing between the queen and her subjects in this period. I find in this an additional reason to submit our document to a new and closer scrutiny.

[13] I shall not enter here into the problem of the variable degrees of citizenship among the inhabitants of Alexandria. El-Abbadi (1962) showed that the problem is much less complex than is supposed from a terminology which is more floating than discriminative. Cf. Delia (1990: 7–11).

[14] For the same reason the prefect Tib. Julius Alexander uses in Alexandria the word *polis* to indicate this city.

[15] For example, in *P. Tebt.* III 782 (towards 153 BC); cf. above, Chapter 8, p. 109. The *geôrgountes tên chôran* who assailed the prefect Tib. Julius Alexander with their recriminations at his arrival in Alexandria belonged to this category.

[16] The use of the particle *de* means essentially that the term 'those from the city' does not imply a status in itself connected with the working of agricultural lands, but the *geôrgountes* form a subset of the broader category of those 'from the city'. Moreover, in ll. 24–5, in τοὺς γεωργοῦντας κατὰ τὴν χώραν τῶν ἀπὸ τῆς πόλεως πάντας, the partitive genitive τῶν ἀπὸ τῆς πόλεως necessarily seems to me to indicate a group among the Alexandrian citizens, unless one wants to create a third category: the 'natives' who have no agricultural activity.

their farms, and, if others settled in a more or less permanent way in the country, one does not see why they would have been reduced for that reason to a non-citizen's lesser status, 'privileged' or not. They correspond roughly to the 'landowners from the city' mentioned in an inscription from the Delta dating probably from the beginning of the empire.[17] Hardly a century later, the great edict of Tib. Julius Alexander (AD 68) illustrates the importance of the farming of the Egyptian countryside by the Alexandrians, and particularly in the *chôra Alexandreôn* ('territory of the Alexandrians') and the Menelaite nome. Now on this point, if it is really granted that the prefect of Egypt was inspired by Cleopatra VII's ordinances,[18] the Roman edict resolves our problem without ambiguity: the *engeneis Alexandreis*, a group of citizens of Alexandria, enjoy their fiscal privileges in the *chôra* even though they settled there because of their economic activity (ll. 32–4). *Pace* Bernand, would it not be a strange policy for the queen to involve Alexandrians in the 'modernisation' of the country (as far as Cleopatra ever thought of modernising anything) by depriving them of their most precious treasure, their full citizenship, their source of prestige and of privileges?

Moreover, the Alexandrian status alluded to by the plaintiffs, who were probably Alexandrian people of means, explains the favourable, spectacular and energetic reaction of the queen much better. We are in April 41. In his small treatise on the Nile, today embedded in his *Quaestiones naturales*, Seneca reveals an important fact: 'Two years in succession, under Cleopatra's administration, during her tenth and eleventh years, [the Nile] did not have the flood',[19] in other words in 42 and 41 BC, during the summer.[20] Our edict comes after a first failed

---

[17] *APF* 5 (1913) 162, no. 8, dated with some reservations in the Augustan period by Fraser (1972: II, 231, n. 299).

[18] τοὺς ἐυγενεῖς καὶ ἐν τῆι [χώ]ρᾳ διὰ φιλεργίαν κατοικοῦντας. On ἐγγενεῖς, see Chalon (1964: 159–60). Wishing to reconcile the text of the Roman prefect (who makes no distinction among the Alexandrians) and the ordinances of Cleopatra VII, Chalon (picking up Lefebvre's remark (1913: 111)) tries to save the character of 'non-citizens' which he attributes to the ἀπὸ τῆς πόλεως by considering that it is 'obvious that the immunities granted to the natives concern *a fortiori* the citizens'. This would be on behalf of Cleopatra a strange way to fix the law *e silentio* – a silent *a fortiori* indeed – while it would have been for her a splendid occasion to recall by analogy the existence of those privileges for her 'genuine Alexandrians'.

[19] *Q.N.* 4a.2.16: *Biennio continuo regnante Cleopatra non ascendisse decimo regni anno et undecimo constat.* In the decree in honour of Kallimachos (*SEG* XXIV 1217, according to Hutmacher 1965), whose date is lost, the mention of the double ἀβροχία and of the resulting σιτόδεια allows us to date this bilingual inscription in the year 39.

[20] Normally, the flood is identified by the regnal year at the end of which the Nile is rising; cf. P. J. Sijpesteijn, *ZPE* 65 (1986) 151–3, and P. Heilporn, *CdÉ* 65 (1989) 287–9. Although

flood, presumably in the middle of a crisis for the realm and its fiscal returns. The agricultural producers were put in jeopardy by the drought; the civil servants would inevitably try to extend the rolls of taxpayers illegally by subjecting privileged domains to the common fiscal regime of the soil. On the other hand, for the queen, at the same moment, some months after the battle of Philippi, the situation outside Egypt was all the more unsettled for her in that, voluntarily or not, some of her people had helped Cassius, the loser.[21] Had Cleopatra already received her summons to appear at Tarsus in front of Mark Antony, the new power in the East? In any case, she needed the support of the Alexandrians, especially the Alexandrians who meant something in the political games of the palace by virtue of their wealth. Tired of the abuses of the administration in the nomes, they felt that they were now in a position of strength: surely the queen would condemn her own agents with virtuous indignation, when in fact they were probably pressed – by her – to feed royal finances exhausted by a too ambitious foreign policy. How grandiloquent the assertion (we shall see later) that the protection of the Alexandrians is a fundamental political policy (*prohairesis*) of the throne and that it is as fundamental to have those admirable subjects protected from fiscal exactions, not only in the two nomes concerned by the trial but everywhere in Egypt. This confirms, moreover, the political power of the party which attacked the royal administration in front of the queen.

The solemnity of the lawsuit, of the stage setting around the Alexandrian complaint, as I would put it, offers a significant contrast with the dry administrative treatment of a quite similar affair, handled brusquely and without any rhetoric in 111 BC: the complaint of the *pastophoroi* of the Memnoneia against the abuses they suffered at the hands of a fiscal administration which refused to take their privileges into account.[22] The *epistrategos*, who, it is true, here plays the role of viceroy in a distant Thebaid, contents himself with copying out the petition of the *pastophoroi*, adding three lines for the *epistates* who

---

D. Bonneau (1964: 311, 329) put those two years without flood in the summers of 42 and 41, later (Bonneau 1972: 149, 231) she proposed years 43 and 42. She considered then, as far as one can judge, that Seneca or his source uses the year at the beginning of which one could notice in a definitive way that the harvest was compromised, the year in fact when the fatal consequences of the water shortage were developing, including in fiscal matters. But this higher dating would make even more anachronistic the link which, if Seneca is right, was made between the two years of poor harvest and Antony's and Cleopatra's 'misbehaviour'.

21 Cf. Hölbl (1994: 214–16).
22 *P. Tor. Choachiti* 4 (*P. Tor.* 7; *UPZ* 191).

is in charge of the Pathyrite (ll. 17–19): 'Do not let the civil servants introduce any innovation or collect from the aforementioned *pastophoroi* any taxes beyond the original customs'. In spite of the similarities in the answers of the authorities, our *pastophoroi* did not enjoy either the royal splendour of the lawsuit in Alexandria, or the heavy reaction of authority and its epigraphic climax.[23] There is a world of difference between the Egyptian plaintiffs of Pathyris and our Alexandrians, who are definitely not the second-rate people affected by some downgrading that modern scholars have made them out to be.

For the rest, the object of the lawsuit is clear and indeed was commonplace in Ptolemaic and Roman Egypt. The Alexandrian landlords of granted land asked and obtained that, because of the privileged status which was always accorded to them, they remain exempt from exceptional taxes like the *stephanos* (crown) and *epigraphê* (harvest tax).[24] It is interesting to note that, among the holders of the royal land, these exceptional taxes, imposed κατὰ καιρόν, as is sometimes specified, hit cleruchs in particular. In a document contemporary with our edicts, the *epigraphê* appears even as a tax that cleruchs divide among themselves.[25] Claire Préaux explained how the crown of the cleruchs, collected when one was obtaining an allotment or, later, for a dynastic event, was coupled with an annual land tax.[26] Everything indicates in our ordinance that the officials of the treasury tried to tax lands granted to the Alexandrians as if those fields or vineyards were part of the cleruchic or katoikic land. This explains a visible redundancy in the royal decision. After having forbidden the inclusion of the Alexandrians on the roll of these exceptional taxes, it adds 'or that their possessions be taken into account for such personal taxes' (ll. 28–9). Here, the queen counters the likely argument of the civil servants, who, certainly referring by analogy to cleruchic and particularly katoikic land, thought that these taxes fell on the granted land and not the holders of the land. However, let us not exaggerate the royal concessions, which in fact follow a careful jurisprudence on the

---

[23] The *pastophoroi* had to introduce their complaint again the next year, *P. Tor. Choachiti* 5 (*P. Tor.* 5–6; *UPZ* 192–3, 110 BC). The copy which was sent back with the decision of the *epistrategos* underneath was drafted in terms similar to those used in the year 111 (*P. Tor. Choachiti* 5b). The later note ordering obedience to the previous decision seems to me, in consideration of the delays, a confirmation of the decision of the *epistrategos* after appeal against it by the defenders.

[24] See on those terms Préaux (1939: 132, 184, 400, 414–15).

[25] *BGU* VIII 1785; cf. Préaux (1939: 512).

[26] Préaux (1939: 395).

subject. We have already noticed the same carefulness in the orders issued by the *epistrategos* Phommous with the key words 'do not innovate' and 'original customs'. The respect for the lawful situation plays in and from both directions: the traditional taxes which burden these lands have to be paid.

The social importance of the parties involved in the lawsuit of Alexandria appears still more clearly in the exceptional device of a second ordinance generalising the execution of what has been provided. In ll. 1–10 of the stele, an epistolary *prostagma* confirms for the second time (12 April 41) by its solemn procedure the importance of the royal reaction.

> *Βασίλισσα Κλεοπάτρα θεὰ Φιλοπά< τ >ωρ καὶ βασιλεὺς*
> *Πτολεμαῖος ὃς καὶ Καῖσαρ θεὸς Φιλοπάτωρ καὶ*
> *Φιλομήτωρ τῶι στρατηγῶι τοῦ Ἡρακλεοπολίτου*
> 4 *χαίρειν.* (vacat) *τὸ ὑποκείμενον πρόσταγμα σὺν τῶι*
> *χρηματισμῶι μεταγραφήτωι τοῖς τε ἑλληνικοῖς*
> *καὶ ἐνχωρίοις γράμμασι καὶ ἐκτεθήτω ἔν τε τῆι*
> *μητροπόλει καὶ ἐν τοῖς ἐπισημοτάτοις τοῦ νομοῦ*
> 8 *τόποις, καὶ τἆλλα γινέσθω τοῖς προστεταγμένοις*
> *ἀκολούθως.* (vacat) *ἔρρωσο.* (vacat) *ἔτους ἐνδεκάτου*
> *Δαισίου ῑγ̄ Φαρμοῦθι ῑγ̄ .*

5 *μεταγραφήτω*   6 *ἐγχωρίοις*

Queen Cleopatra the Goddess Philopator and King Ptolemy also called Caesar, God Philopator and Philometor, to the strategos of the Herakleopolite, greeting. The ordinance below with our judgement is to be copied out in Greek and native letters and exposed (or 'explained') in the metropolis and in the most notable places of the nome. And otherwise things are to be in accordance with the ordinance. Farewell. Year 11, Daisios 13, Pharmouthi 13'.

In the case of the *prostagma* issued a few years earlier, in 46, and sent to the same royal *hypomnêmatographos* Theon, the latter was simply ordered to transmit the royal decree to 'those whom it may concern'. Theon only drafted a covering letter notifying every person who might be interested in the existence of the *prostagma*.[27] We would have expected that, in the same circumstances, Theon would have provided for follow-up to the ordinance of 15 March 41 simply by way of a circular letter. But, as Paul Collomp noticed,[28] the royal authority was not satisfied in 41 by sending the copy of the *enteuxis* of the Alexandrians, endorsed by a laconic 'let it be done' (*ginesthô*)

---

[27] On the procedure followed in that case, see Bingen (1994: 16).
[28] *Recherches sur la chancellerie et la diplomatique des Lagides* (Paris 1926) 196.

ordinance. In the judgement, the queen proclaimed her will to eradicate everywhere[29] the abuses brought to her attention by the plaintiffs and to protect the Alexandrian landholders throughout the whole *chôra*. The transmission of the royal verdict is governed by a circular executive ordinance.[30] By decree the texts will be sent to all the *strategoi*. The name of Theon, the administrative recipient of both decrees, does not appear any further at this stage of the process.

I am persuaded that the Herakleopolitan inscription supplies us with good material for new reflections on the nature of what we could call 'epigraphic prose', as far as there is any reason to use such an expression. This is not because the language of the decrees represents a specific moment in the evolution of Greek prose, but rather because I am struck by the difference of style and even of register of language which appears between the *prostagma* for execution in the third-person imperative (ll. 1–10 and 34–5) and the motivated judgement from the royal court in Alexandria, under the cover of a 'we have ordained'.

The first decree, drafted in a sober chancellery language, is purely functional and moreover traditional in the matter.[31] It is the style and language we find in the instructions of the *epistrategos* Phommous already quoted and also in the text from Ptolemais which the same Theon had distributed. On the contrary, in ll. 15–34, the statement of the grievances (ll. 15–22), the reminder of the royal philosophy which justifies the verdict (ll. 22–4) and the verdict itself (ll. 24–34) all differ from the first decree by their verbosity and avoidance of any technicality in the language. A minimum of technical terms had to be kept, like *stephanos*, *epigraphê*, *merismos*, and 'innovate' (*kainizein*). Otherwise, the text is the object of a surprising effort, not necessarily very felicitous, to give more impact to the discourse, at second-degree drafting, by using circumlocution or metaphor. For example, consider the long circumlocution μὴ γείνεσθαι συνεισφόρους τοῖς κατὰ καιροὺς καὶ περιστάσεις ἱσταμένοις ἐν τοῖς νομοῖς στεφά<ν>οις καὶ ταῖς ἐπιγραφαῖς (ll. 26–8). It ends with two inevitable technical terms, but the rare compound συνείσφορος appears here for the first time, avoiding the repetition of συνκαταριθμεῖν (itself quite recent)

---

[29] It is likely that it was for reasons of convenience (simplification of the inquiry? exemplary character of the abuses? importance of the Alexandrian individuals concerned?) that the complaint concerned only two nomes.

[30] The anonymity of the addressee, the '*strategos* of the Herakleopolite', reveals the general character of the order to transmit the royal decrees throughout Egypt.

[31] Some royal *prostagmata* are reduced to the sole word *ginesthô*, 'let it be done'.

τοῖς στεφάνοις καὶ ταῖς ἐπιγραφαῖς, these two technical terms being announced through the implicit element εἰσφορά in the rare word συνείσφορος.

But, to our surprise, this rhetoric does not express itself in a conservative 'language of the school'; it is not a display of classical discourse. Language here has its roots mostly, as we shall see, in the Greek which is in the making at that moment in Alexandria, one of the main centres of the new community, and which is also the Greek of the period which was to follow. In ll. 22–3, κοινήν τε καὶ καθολικὴν ἐπέξοδον is a good example. The word ἐπέξοδος is quite rare. It exists in its basic meaning with all the strength of the two independent prepositional prefixes ἐπί and ἐξ in Thucydides 5.8 ἐπέξοδον ποιεῖσθαι πρός τινα, 'march out against an enemy' (*LSJ*); still, the use of the double prefix, rather limited in pure classical Greek, was appreciated by Thucydides, who betrays as he does so often in his writing the will to create a specific literary prose. In the metaphorical use of the word we find in l. 23, the basic notion of exit does not exist any more; the double prefix is a whole where ἐξ has a subjective value (the attack made in depth) which emphasises κοινήν τε καὶ καθολικήν. Now this use of ἐπέξοδος, before long to become a commonplace word for 'punishment', occurs only in imperial *koinê*, in papyrological contexts among others, as punishment coming from the authorities.

In l. 21, ξενιζούσαις ἀπαιτήσεσι adds a rather close example. The verb ξενίζω possesses two semantic branches. The first, illustrated by epic, tragedy and comedy, especially in the active voice, but also by prose (here especially in the passive), covers the idea of hospitality. The second, well attested in the *koinê*, including the New Testament, marks what is felt as strange, unusual, incomprehensible. This profane term, rather than covering too precise a notion of illegality, suggests in a smoother way that the problem is about exactions which seem illegal only because they do not take account of the status of the Alexandrian holders of royal land. Moreover, ἀπαίτησις adds something to this careful subtlety of the authority. The word is rare, and, as ἀπαιτεῖν in l. 19 confirms, it is a rather colourless word.

The participle μισοπονηρήσαντες (l. 22) has essentially a Hellenistic and imperial connotation. The writer adds to it μεγάλως, a strangely pompous substitute for σφόδρα. The use of παραπράσσειν (l. 20) appears at the moment when the word is shifting over to the connotation 'to exact money illegally' (*LSJ*) and heralds the imperial age. This last phenomenon is present even in words at first sight as harmless as ἀγροικικαῖς (l. 20), 'rustic' *LSJ*, with references from

Cephalio, Athenaeus or the Scholia to Nicander, or χωρικαῖς (l. 21), which also dates from the imperial period.

The word προαίρεσις is not new in the meaning of 'political choice' and the interest here lies rather in the appeal to a general royal policy at the point when the sovereigns have to settle a particular case. But semantically more amazing is the expression which marks the exceptional character of some levies: κατὰ καιροὺς καὶ περιστάσεις. I proposed a translation 'according to circumstances and moments of crisis', opposing levies κατὰ καιρόν and crisis taxes. Naturally, one could wonder if we have not here simply a hendiadys for the banal κατὰ τὰς τῶν καιρῶν περιστάσεις, which would describe levies 'due to the difficulties of the moment'. Indeed, this grouping of words exists as such, ἐν τῆι τῶν καιρῶν περιστάσει, in Hermias' fourth petition in 119,[32] just as it is found in the *Jewish Antiquities* (16.8.6), but is also in the κατὰ τὰς τῶν καιρῶν περιστάσεις of Polybius (2.55.8) and in various Hellenistic inscriptions, for instance in Tomi, *Syll.*[3] 731.2, διὰ τὰς τῶν καιρῶν περιστάσεις.[33] On the one hand, one cannot escape the feeling that this monolithic group has doubtless more or less unconsciously influenced the use of the pairing καιρός-περιστάσεις,[34] but the unusual coordination of the two elements in the judgement of Alexandria, even if it was encouraged by the technical use of κατὰ καιρόν to describe some taxes, is more than a stylistic effect. Through a kind of second-order editing, by dismantling the familiar τῶν καιρῶν περιστάσεις, it gives more weight to a technical distinction, traditional taxes and crisis taxation, reduced at the same time to one concept: off-limits when taxing Alexandrian landlords.

One might like to reduce our stylistic problem to the coexistence of variants of the tendency which marks Hellenistic epigraphy of adopting in the course of time more and more elaborate speech. But our problem here is, on the contrary, the coexistence of two very different levels of Greek prose. Can we then explain this difference of verbal expression between the two parts of our inscription by the fact, however incidental, that it would be merely the echo of the stylistic effects practised by lawyers and judges in Alexandria, a rhetoric that

---

[32] *P. Tor. Choachiti* 11.17 (and 11 bis.14), where P. W. Pestman (p. 137) sees an allusion to the rebellion of 131/130 and to the disturbances which followed until the arrival of refugees in the Theban area in 116. Cf. earlier U. Wilcken, *UPZ* 160.17 and 161.14, with comment.

[33] Quoted by *LSJ*, in relation to the simple κατὰ τὰς περιστάσεις, 'in critical times', of Polybius.

[34] The ἐπὶ παντὸς καιροῦ καὶ περιστάσεως of Polybius (1.35.10) is situated on a quite different semantic level.

the chancellery did not use except eventually in the court? The problem seems more general. This thought-out speech, which gives more weight to the expression by some emphasis, by handling it in the second degree, by adding emotional elements, is a type of speech which we know well. Even if it is often less clearly marked than here, we find such language in petitions, in *enteuxeis*, in ordinances of authority or exhortations of the latter to its civil servants.[35] Really, even without treating the general problem of the rhetoric of power during the Hellenistic period, we notice that our inscription alternately presents the 'language which organises' and the 'language which persuades'. In the summary of the lawsuit in Alexandria, there is still an echo, as I said, of the language of persuasion used in the speeches of the applicants and of the defenders as well as in the considerations of the verdict, which is at the same time a plea for the royal policy towards the privileged Alexandrians. This political declaration of principles appreciably broadens the reach of the judgement and aims to persuade the applicants of the excellence of the sovereign. We are thus caused once again to notice that the queen addresses herself to weighty people, members of the economic elites of Alexandria, and not to obscure citizens or non-citizens in distress somewhere in the *chôra*.[36]

---

[35] A random sampling easily allows us to discern this duality of the speech, when going through papyri 110 to 113 of Wilcken's admirable *Urkunden der Ptolemäerzeit*. A thought-out speech in *UPZ* 110, an appeal of the sovereign to the good feelings of the civil servants, contrasts with the purely functional Greek used for the specifications of tax farming in *UPZ* 112. In the letter sent by the king to Dionysios (*UPZ* 113), one sees the letter gradually sliding towards the 'speech of persuasion' when it develops views on administrative morality. *UPZ* 114 presents the same opposition of language as the Herakleopolitan inscription, between the order to execute and the statement of the royal policy to be executed. It is clear from this sample how vain it is to separate inscriptions and papyri in any study of the prose of Hellenistic documents.

[36] Three technical appendixes in the original article have been omitted here; the reader is referred to the first publication for them.

PART III: THE ROYAL ECONOMY

Chapter 13

THE REVENUE LAWS PAPYRUS: GREEK TRADITION AND HELLENISTIC ADAPTATION

ๆ

> I do not mean to suggest that the ancients were like Monsieur Jourdain in Molière, who spoke prose without knowing it, but that in fact they lacked the idea of an 'economy' and, a fortiori, the conceptual elements that together constitute what we call the 'economy'.
>
> Moses I. Finley, *The Ancient Economy* (1973: 21)

For a millennium, from Alexander the Great to the Arab conquest, a Greek-speaking population played a determining role in Alexandria and in Egypt in the administration and the economy of the country. It developed in Egypt, on a socio-cultural level, the pattern of a privileged minority which continued to practise, with more or less distinctiveness, the language and cultural heritage which defined the group. Thanks to this Greek presence and to the dryness of the climate of Middle and Upper Egypt, for more than a century we have had available to us a large number of Greek and Latin documents on papyrus. It is one of the tasks of papyrology to make this documentation, of infinite variety and richness, known to others. But – and this is the foundation of all documentary criticism – attempts at interpretation need to be carried out with a two-fold spirit; first generalising, extrapolating the information provided by the documents, as far as possible; but at the same time, being as conscious as possible of the limits that must be set on the meaningfulness of an isolated text in a very fragmentary documentation. This two-fold critical problem will be present in the analysis offered here of what is usually called the 'Revenue Laws Papyrus' and which its first editor called, in a more concrete but also more restrictive fashion, the 'Revenue Laws' of Ptolemy II Philadelphos. What, we shall ask, can one legitimately infer from this text? How far can one generalise these data in order to extract, rightly or wrongly, the general lines of the economy and royal management of Hellenistic Egypt?

Published in 1896 by B. P. Grenfell,[1] the document that I present here evoked lively interest from the beginning, not only because of its extraordinary size for a Ptolemaic document and the density of the information that it provides, but also for three other reasons, each of very different character. The first was the early date of the document. As its latest elements dated from year 27 of the reign of Ptolemy II Philadelphos, or 259 BC,[2] it is the oldest text of comparable length from Ptolemaic Egypt. The second reason is that a couple of decades after its publication, a very rich body of Greek papyri of nearly contemporary date was juxtaposed to it, the find usually called the archive of Zenon.[3] There are evident, but still ambiguous, connections between the Revenue Laws and the so-called Zenon papyri, not the least of which is certainly the personality of the *dioiketes* Apollonios, the chief minister of the kingdom. Indeed, he was the authority upon whom depended the matters regulated by the Revenue Laws papyrus, but he was also the holder of a gift-estate of more than 2,700 hectares, which Zenon managed for a time and near which no doubt the papyri of Zenon were found by clandestine excavators.

The third reason, finally, is that during the first half of the twentieth century, more and more precise analyses of the economy of Ptolemaic Egypt were progressively developed in the works of Ulrich Wilcken, Michael Rostovtzeff and Claire Préaux. With them came a sketch of the supposed theoretical economic thought of the royal government of Egypt. Now this analysis and this sketch were profoundly influenced by the interpretation set forth by each scholar of the Revenue Laws

---

[1] *Revenue Laws of Ptolemy Philadelphus* (Oxford 1896); re-edition of the text based on the original: J. Bingen, *Papyrus Revenue Laws: Nouvelle édition du texte* (SB Bh. 1; Göttingen 1952). Corrections to the text are recorded in BL 4 (1964) 71; 5 (1969) 86; 6 (1976) 121.

[2] In fact, it consists both of documents copied in the year 27 (259/258) and of older documents (year 25 or year 26) brought up to date in the year 27 (cf. col. 1: adaptation of the titulature to that which was introduced in 259; col. 24: year 27, old titulature; col. 38: note about updating on 31 August 259). Some sections, particularly the last, cannot be dated precisely, but they seem contemporaneous with the others.

[3] On these archives, one may consult the synthesis of Préaux (1947). Since then, some further papyri of the find have been published without significantly modifying the conclusions of this work. The most important of these additions, T. C. Skeat, *Greek Papyri in the British Museum (now in the British Library). VII: The Zenon Archive* (London 1974) contains numerous papyri which were used earlier by Préaux and indeed by Rostovtzeff (1922). Cf. also Swiderek (1954, 1956). Although this group of papyri, one of the finest that Egypt has produced, forms an exceptionally rich and varied documentation on the settlement of Greeks in the countryside, on the various relationships which could arise among them or between Greeks and Egyptians, on the agricultural landscape of new lands, etc., every analysis of this body of material must take into account the very particular character of the institutional, social and economic situation that governed the development of the *dôrea* of Philadelphia.

papyrus. I will take for illustration perhaps the most characteristic work: Claire Préaux's *L'économie royale des Lagides*,[4] a synthesis in which definitions of the royal power's hold over the new social and economic situation in Ptolemaic Egypt, and that power's limits, are always built on a foundation of the exhaustive use of the documents. What do we see? When the book tackles the problem of the king's resources, the author establishes first the necessity for a managed economy in Ptolemaic Egypt (pp. 61–5), then she immediately begins her inquiry with the study of the oil monopoly, that is, with the most important and most original part of the Revenue Laws papyrus (pp. 65–93).

Now since 1939, under the strong impulse of some historians of the ancient economy, we tend to look quite differently at the ancient economy and particularly at the understanding of the economy by people in antiquity, both as a subject for reflection and as an arena for action. Surely it is time to take another look at a text that has been seen as so decisive for the study of the Ptolemaic economy.

Let us first look at the material side of things. What is called 'the Revenue Laws papyrus' appears in our editions as a whole of 107 columns plus some fragments.[5] Ever since the original edition's title page, the strong idea has been put abroad that this is a single and homogeneous document: 'Revenue Laws of Ptolemy Philadelphus Edited from a Greek Papyrus in the Bodleian Library'. And this singular 'papyrus' designates in the preface of 1896 the combination of two rolls which actually form this whole. For in fact it is a matter of two rolls, acquired under different circumstances,[6] even if there are good reasons to connect them. In fact, the problem of external criticism which the two physical objects containing the text pose to us does not stop at the level of the possible division of a single document into two parts, but instead directs us to the contingent circumstances thanks to which the two rolls make known to us seven or eight documents, which were originally independent and were gathered only when they were already outdated. This is a classification procedure

---

[4] Brussels 1939.

[5] The state of preservation of these columns varies considerably. Some are almost complete; of others there survives nothing but a few scraps.

[6] The first roll was purchased in Cairo by Flinders Petrie in 1893. Grenfell bought the fragments that form the second roll in 1894/1895, partly in Cairo, partly in the Fayyum. For the second roll, he speaks in his introduction of a 'sister roll wrapped around it' (meaning the roll acquired in 1893). Grenfell notes (p. V) that 'both the external and the internal evidence point to its provenance having been the Fayoum', an affirmation that must be founded in part on the circumstances, which have remained unknown to posterity, of the acquisition of the document.

well known to papyrologists: one glues pieces one wishes to keep, one to another, thus creating more or less homogeneous rolls, suitable for being classified and consulted.[7]

But this bibliological observation is of importance, even if there was a single discovery that led to two purchases in 1893 and 1894/1895. It establishes that the text does not represent the remains of a manuscript intended, in its entirety and from the beginning, as the regulation of the royal revenues. It was not a code. What we call 'the Revenue Laws papyrus' is a collection of documents made for administrative or private use.[8]

These documents, which have a particular common character, were brought into being by the practice of selling contracts for tax farming and for licences to carry out some of the economic activities of the country. The farming of taxes is a practice attested in classical Greece, particularly in Athens. When was it introduced into Egypt after the Macedonian conquest? We do not know exactly, but it was used, as it seems, to a very large extent by the year 259, the date of the Revenue Laws. The contract of tax farming connects two parties, the king and the farming companies; the duties and rights of each of these parties had to be laid out in governing documents,[9] which will have governed various implicit tax-farming contracts between the king and the farmers following an auction. 'These governing documents', I wrote in 1952, 'enumerated specific obligations on the part of the farmers, of the officials, and of the king's subjects; they provide penalties for infractions and negligence. They define the royal revenue that is contracted, define the controlling law and the various activities under the contract, reveal the means provided by the king to ensure the best payment of the revenues guaranteed by the contract and describe the eventual recourse to those guarantees or, in the contrary case, the cession to the tax farmers of excess receipts.' In short, the

---

[7] The documents were assembled in the same offices where they were collated and had served as bases for revised texts of the regulations. At least, the second document contains, in column 23, a note of revision in the same hand and probably of similar content to the note in column 38.

[8] The first of these hypotheses now seems to me the more probable, although it may be hazardous to try to separate the official and the private estates in a situation where Apollonios is involved in the problem.

[9] Some of these texts open with the formula *pôloumen* ('we offer for sale'), followed by the object of the contract (cols. 57–9; col. 73). They do not seem to differ in their content from other sections which have only an objective title (for example, col. 80, *nomos dekatês*: 'law of the tenth') or beginning with a date using regnal titulature (cf. col. 1; col. 24). In cols. 57–9, the text introduced by *pôloumen* appears under the title *diorthôma tou nomou epi têi elaikêi* ('regulation of the law governing the oil contract'); cf. below, n. 35.

king describes, in each of the separate sets of regulations, how he is going to make the holders of the contract fulfil its obligations and, as a counterpart, how he is going to make his own agents and his payers make the contract as profitable as the king has given the contractors to expect it will be in his announcement of the auction. Such is the analysis of the contents that I proposed for these texts in the re-edition that I gave of the Revenue Laws, and this analysis, based in part on the bibliological analysis of the group of documents, constituted a deliberate step backwards from some of the positions taken by earlier scholars, who saw in the Revenue Laws an attempt at fiscal or even economic codification. To be sure, the phrase *nomoi telônikoi*, which in Greece was already given to such sets of regulations, may have suggested the idea that the collection of these regulations, once gathered here, would form a systematic code, as Rostovtzeff believed.[10] But in reality, *nomos* indicates only that these texts emanated from a political or royal authority and that each of them was of a general and permanent authority for the matter that it dealt with. And one could hardly fail to mention that *telônikos* showed that the legislator had fiscality in mind in legislating.

At this point in the discussion we should take stock of the problem. How are we to define the economic context of the two parties to the contract, the king on one side and the tax-farming companies on the other, in third-century Egypt, two or three generations after the annexation of Egypt by Alexander? Here we bump up against a first difficulty. Nothing allows us to follow with any exactness the evolution of the Macedonian administration, or of the influence of the monarchy and of the Greek immigrants on the Egyptian economy during the first generations of the Graeco-Macedonian immigration. We have some sense of how Alexandria was developed both as an urban centre, a base of royal power, and as a cultural centre. We can work out that the very superficial regime of the Macedonian military occupation was transformed bit by bit into a civil administrative regime and a system of cleruchic settlement.[11] During this period the vast landed domains,

---

[10] Rostovtzeff (1922: 165–6): 'The whole document seems to be an attempt at a codification of the rules which regulated those parts of the State economy which were organized as incomes of the State collected by tax farmers . . . The "Codex" was published by order of the king by the dioiketes Apollonius . . . We may assume that Satyrus, the predecessor of Apollonius, was the author of the Νόμος ἕκτης [= second document], and that Apollonius was the author of the codified Νόμοι τελωνικοί [= first document] and of the Νόμος ἐλαικῆς [= third document].'

[11] This period will become progressively clearer as a result of the publication of the Greek papyri of the fourth century found at Saqqara and by the systematic study of the Demotic

which the Macedonian king, then the first Ptolemy, found themselves
endowed with, simply because they were the successors of the older
pharaohs and of the Persian kings, was organised. We have good
reasons to think that the Greek kernels already in place in Egypt before
Alexander the Great, particularly in Naucratis and Memphis, put their
knowledge of Egypt and of the Egyptians at the disposal of the conqueror and the new Graeco-Macedonian immigrants.

We have the same difficulty in describing the economic condition
of Egypt at the arrival of Alexander and the socio-economic situation
of the Egyptian population at the beginning of the Hellenistic period.
Egypt was certainly no longer as a whole an agricultural society with
Bronze Age techniques. The Delta and Memphis had for a long time
had contact with Persian and Greek cultures, and already in the
fourth century, at least in the Delta, the presence of mercenary soldiers paid in coined money must have generated some local forms of
economy in which coinage had a certain role. We can probably get a
tolerable sense of Egyptian society and economy in the fourth century,
thanks to the bas-reliefs with inscriptions from the funerary temple of
Petosiris at Hermopolis.[12] This archaeological document is described
in Chapter 16. As a whole, it gives us the picture of an Egypt in which
the local priestly aristocracy carried on both the management of a
complex and extensive sacred domain and an important part of the
civil administration of the nome. The priestly household included at
its core extensive agricultural operations, but also artisanal production and the leasing of houses and of boats. The great priestly domain
managed by a high priest is probably the product of a certain political and administrative void present in Egypt over the three centuries
leading up to Petosiris. It is at the centre of our picture of the large
socio-economic unit that the Egyptian nome had been and would continue to be: a large temple, an urban core grown up around the
temple, with a countryside and villages dependent on it. This socio-
economic unit was to be taken up by the Ptolemies as the main administrative division of the country (see Chapter 8 for this process). But
the nome would undergo profound modifications in the grip of royal
power; in fact, the king's administration would turn the control of the
arable land inside out, taking back the management of the royal land
and controlling the working of the temple land.

documents of Upper Egypt from the same period. For a characteristic text of the first period
of Macedonian military occupation, see the 'Off limits' notice published by Turner (1974,
1975).

[12] Lefebvre (1923–4).

In the picture of an Egyptian economy in which a well-organised local royal power reappears in the face of this clerical structure, the practice of tax farming supposes the presence of a third element: a mobile economic potential, based on a monetary economy – a class of men capable of assessing the royal revenue that they were going to underwrite in monetary terms, and capable of putting together the credit facilities necessary for this purpose. We should not suppose that this phenomenon was limited to the scale of a class of large Greek capitalists. Much of the time it must have been a matter of very modest and localised operations. But in any case, the fiscal farming that the Revenue Laws describe, just like the existence of farmed royal banks which were closely connected to the tax farming, demonstrates the existence of a relatively independent Greek economic potential. On the planned-economy model that some scholars have developed for the economy of Egypt, the king would have deliberately incorporated this independent economic element into his system of the exploitation of the country. On the contrary, I think, it is more likely that this potential developed in Egypt precisely because there was a situation in which the monarch had to leave this field to men other than his own agents, or, more simply, was incapable of imagining that there was any other means of running the country that he possessed.

We do not need to resolve this matter; rather, we shall pass on to the analysis of the four best-preserved parts of the Revenue Laws:

1. the *nomos*, both regulations and contract conditions, concerning the farming of the taxes in money (columns 1–22);
2. the *nomos* concerning the *apomoira* on wine and orchard products, a tax paid either in kind or in money (columns 23–37);
3. the declaration of the auctioning of, and the governing document for, the *elaikê* – what is usually called the oil monopoly (columns 38–72);
4. the declaration of the auctioning of the farming of the banks and the royal cash receipts (columns 73–8).

The first of these documents (columns 1–22) is directly to our point. It is a document concerning the character of which Rostovtzeff went astray (above, n. 10) when he saw in it a general text bearing on the entirety of Ptolemaic farmed contracts. If one wishes to see in the Revenue Laws a systematic code, one is fatally led to suppose – as he did – the existence of an introductory chapter describing the rules common to the entire group of subjects treated in the code. If, however, one looks at the text without any such prejudice and bearing in mind that originally this first part of the text was not joined to the others, columns 1–22 take on an entirely different meaning. Their title is, unfortunately, lost, if indeed there ever was one.[13] But it is evident that the document concerns only one of the domains capable of being let out on a contract,[14] although it is true that it is the most classical area of tax farming: the farming of taxes paid in money.[15]

The first half of this set of rules (columns 1–15, the first hand) is very mutilated; but one can see that it was concerned with problems connected to the collection of taxes and the organisation of farming companies. We know that the peculiar trait of this collection system was that it was carried out in Egypt by the royal tax collectors, while the farm was there to fix the amount of the tax, control the collection and accounting, and determine whether the total was greater or smaller than the sum bid. The second half of the rules is, by contrast, well preserved. It concerns the carrying out of monthly balances and of the general balancing of accounts for the collection of taxes. It provides also precautions to be taken when farmers take on several

[13] To the extent that the mutilated condition in which the papyrus has reached us allows us to judge, the first column began with a regnal date (*basileuontos*, etc.), which appears in ll. 1–4. That is also the way that the second ordinance begins (col. 24). Just like the information provided by the papyrus itself and by the handwriting, this shows the independence of these two sets of regulations before their 'posthumous' gluing together. Cols. 1–22 could not play the role of general regulations capping the ensemble of fiscal and economic regulations except by virtue of the place they received in the process of assembling the different regulations end to end.

[14] There is one provision which could be taken to suggest that cols. 1–22 formed a preamble applicable to the entirety of the legislation concerning farming contracts. It is located at the end of the long section on partial and final balances (cols. 16–20, headed with the title *dialogismos*, 'reckoning'). We read, in fact (20.12): [Δια]λογιζέσθωσαν δὲ πάντες κατὰ ταὐτὰ ὅσοι τι [τῶν βασιλ]ικῶν π[ωλ]ήσουσιν ('Let all of those who shall sell any part of the royal revenues carry out their balancing of accounts in accordance with the same provisions'). One could understand (especially if one accents κατὰ ταῦτα, 'in accordance with this') that the accounting procedures described earlier were to be generalised to all of the other farmed revenues, thus also to the taxes in kind transmuted into cash and to licences to exploit an economic activity; and thus cols. 1–22 could appear as a general preamble. But such an interpretation does not impose itself. These two lines may make allusion only to the necessity for all of those farming a money tax to follow the same accounting norms. Moreover, this 'generalisation', as a preamble to a 'code', would find no other echo in the rest of what remains of the first twenty-two columns.

[15] At first sight, the expression οἱ ἐν τῶι ἐμπορίωι λ[ο]γευταί, 'the accountants in the emporium' (9.1–6), could even suggest the notion that the first text was concerned only with a particular money tax. But nothing in the rest of the document confirms this notion. The auction offer (*pôloumen*) of UPZ I 112 (203) contemplates the entirety of the farming of the money taxes, but provides particular rules for some of them. We should note that in the passage cited earlier, the expression ἐν ἡμέραις δέκα means 'within ten days' (following the award of the contract), and not 'for ten days' as U. Wilcken proposed (*Chrest.*, p. 299, n.).

contracts, to avoid confusion during the balancing of accounts and in profits and losses (columns 16–22). These procedures are described in detail. Here, for example, are those related to the general balancing (18.17–20.10). At the end of the contract's term, all the members of the tax-farming company are to present themselves before the *oikonomos* (a financial official) before the tenth day of the next month. The *oikonomos* carries out the general balancing of accounts in their presence. Setting forth the total of the tax for which the farming contract was awarded, he notes to the credit of the account the tax receipts, any debts to the treasury which can still be recovered, and any difference to be made up by the contractors, as well as the part of the difference that each of those responsible for the contract will have to pay. Beyond that, to the debit of the fiscal account, he indicates whatever the contractors and their sureties have already paid when monthly balancings have been in the red. The text also clarifies the situation of the tax-farming company in the possible farming of other taxes,[16] and it establishes the process that allows the recovery of arrears during the course of the first month of the following term. Thus within thirty days, the royal treasury and the farming company will have settled their account: either, if the receipts exceed the contracted amount, the farmers receive the surplus; or, if there is a deficit in the receipts, the contractors and their sureties (we would say their insurance company) are to pay the difference to the royal treasury.

These contracts for farming the money taxes, as described in the first document and as they appear in numerous other documents from ordinary practice, are a matter for astonishment and reflection. The entire process is Greek, in the sense that it is linked to the monetary economy. The taxes in money, even more than the use of coinage, were foreign to the pre-Hellenistic Egyptian economy. What is of interest to us here is that the cultural and political world in which the new form of tax farming has been conceived was Greek even if developed in the context of a monarchy. Certainly there was a transfer – Claire Préaux was prepared to go as far as speaking of a 'graft'[17] – of

---

[16] Col. 17.15 contains an allusion to the recovery by the *oikonomos* of provisional profits transferred prematurely to another contract which is in deficit and which belongs to the same contractors. I would restore (despite the lack of parallel papyrological texts): πρότερον δὲ ἐκ τοῦ αὐ[τομάτου ἀ]ποκαθιστάτω, that is, 'of his own initiative' (cf. Xenophon, *Anabasis* 1.3.13) the *oikonomos* may proceed to re-establish a favourable balance in the first contract. It is not impossible that the same expression occurs in l. 8 of the same column, but the context is too mutilated to allow certainty.

[17] Préaux (1939: 450). The sections (pp. 450–9) that Préaux devoted to tax farming, to its new role and to its contribution to Ptolemaic law, are fundamental for the problem discussed

an institution that worked in Greece. There was a transfer of Greek technical terminology, known to a considerable degree from inscriptions and the orators. At the same time, an accounting technique born in the monetary economy of Greece was transferred. We observe as well the complexity of some mechanisms that bear witness to this monetary economy. I would, for example, point to the financial associations that made it possible to render business undertakings more profitable by reaching a level at which competition was less; or, another example, the use via the system of sureties of short-term credits covered by these sureties, an insurance mechanism that deserves recognition in turn. All this is familiar to the Athenian economy of the fourth century.

But, transferred into the new contexts of a traditionally very different economy, this institution underwent a fundamental adaptation which brings up a paradox: the collection of the tax is no longer carried out by the tax-farming company, although that was its role in classical Greece. Collection is the exclusive prerogative of royal agents, at the level of the direction of the finances of the nome with the *oikonomos*, at the level of the inspection of the finances with the *antigrapheis*, and at the level of local collection with the *logeutai*, not to mention other local agents.[18] As Claire Préaux noted, one could thus imagine Ptolemaic royal taxation functioning without the tax farmers, even though they bore the entire weight of collection at Athens.[19] Then why keep them? It has been suggested that the farming system was assigned a new function, that of insuring for the king's benefit against fiscal risks. It would thus exist in order to protect the treasury against fiscal vagaries in a society where the monetary economy was poorly established and where execution of the debt against the defaulting taxpayer was usually without much financial benefit for the creditor.[20] This role is undeniable, but it

here. See earlier Wilcken, *Grundz.* (1912), p. 182 (I translate): 'Just as other Greek institutions which were transplanted to Egypt at this time were changed in the climate of absolutism, so also was tax farming taken over from the *polis*.' Wilcken perceived the phenomenon of transfer but located the cause of its evolution in a political vision, characteristic of its time, that is no longer acceptable.

[18] A text earlier by some years than the Revenue Laws, *P. Hib.* I 29 verso (= *W. Chrest.* 259), has seemed to show the direct collection of a tax by the farmer and his turning over of the receipts to the royal bank. Do we see here an earlier stage of the fiscal contract in Egypt? It is impossible to say, because the text is incomplete, and even if the text were secure, it could describe a specific situation. Moreover, we cannot be certain that this regulation was intended for the countryside.

[19] Préaux (1939: 450).

[20] Préaux (1939: 451).

already existed in Greece. It is unthinkable that the first Ptolemies deliberately gave only this role, and such a limited role, to the tax-farming companies. They would not have survived, either because the real compensation for such a risk incurred by the king would rapidly have made the enterprise unviable, or because the farming companies would have covered themselves sufficiently against such a risk to the point of significantly harming the royal treasury.[21] Nothing in my view demonstrates that this Greek institution was deliberately and straightaway remodelled to conform to the new economic base on which taxation was going to be applied.

Here I would willingly apply the term 'graft of an institution' devised by Claire Préaux to speak of the transplantation of the Greek tax-farming practices of the fourth century to the Egypt of the first Ptolemies. But I do not see in the paradoxical transformation the institution of farming underwent the result of a choice by the Ptolemies, but rather the results of the natural degradation of an institution which, in the nature of things, was connected with the task of collecting the taxes in a newly conquered Eastern country, where there existed a long tradition of direct collection of rents and tribute. At the beginning, probably, no one thought – no one could have thought – that some other formula would be better.[22] I would insist on this last point, because I think that this is only one facet of the necessary revision of the image we have of an essentially creative and voluntarist Hellenistic royal thinking. It is true, as we have seen, that they do not simply adopt a system of truly direct collection of taxes, carried out by royal officials. But the farmers intervene directly, and often by themselves, in the setting or estimation of the dues to be paid. And particularly the employees of the tax farmers, by their presence and desire to make the contract as profitable as possible, and by their right to prevent fraud, help and control the royal collection organs at every level. They participate actively in the accountable management

---

[21] The economic fluctuations of the offers from tax-farming companies were well known to the Greeks. See, for example, Xenophon, *Ways and Means* 4.40; cf. P. Gauthier, *Un commentaire historique des Poroi de Xénophon* (1976) 9–12, 172–3.

[22] The difficulty of escaping inherited structures is well illustrated by the piece of bravura in the *Poroi* of Xenophon, his great project for the public exploitation of the Laurion silver mines (his Chapter 4), even if the purely rhetorical development of the problems does not give him much authority. Struck by the revenues of the great owners of servile manpower hired out to mining entrepreneurs, the author simply imagines that the city will use a one-time tax to acquire masses of slaves and will let them out either to mining concessionaries or to the tribes, turned for this purpose into mining companies. The entirety is based on two myths: the inexhaustible character of the Laurion mines and the innocuousness, even advantage, of supersaturating the silver market.

of the farm. Thus the farmers, large or small (we should not forget that the impressive formulae of our regulations could be applied to tiny fiscal entities), continued to play a part of the role granted to them by the Greek tax-farming system, at the level of collection, beyond the role of insurance against fiscal risk that they also continued to play. The whole seemed sufficiently useful to the king for the farming system to survive for quite some time.

Why did the Greek farming system lose within two generations the actual collection of the taxes? We do not know the first stage of Ptolemaic taxation. But by analogy one can imagine some of the causes of the institution's transformation. When we look at the development of Apollonios' large estate, as it appears in the archive of Zenon, we are struck by the permanent mobilisation of royal agents, even for forays into what to our modern eyes would be considered private enterprise. The usual explanation is that the finance minister abused his position in order to use the activity of officials for his own private benefit. That view certainly contains some truth, which would probably not have scandalised his contemporaries. But there are other reasons for the intervention of royal agents. The expansive economy of Egypt in the time of the first immigrants required, because of a shortage of manpower, a permanent and probably somewhat anarchic mobilisation of all the Greeks wherever they were and for whatever need presented itself.[23] This must have been especially true for the only more or less coherent Greek network, more or less complete in the Egypt of the pioneers, the network of royal officials. The paradox of the evolution of the Greek tax farming system in Egypt shows the pressure of factual socio-political situations and not, in my view, of any theory of the organisation of power implanted in new conditions. To use overly simplistic terms, I have the impression that no one imagined a new type of tax farming intended for integration into a planned system, but rather that it was the inadequacy of the farming system in the face of the Egyptian realities of the Hellenistic period that led to the use of mechanisms without having the imagination needed to remake them consciously.

The inadequacy of the classical tax-farming system to the mechanisms of Ptolemaic taxation cannot, however, be reduced only to a manifestation of a lack of adaptive ability. There was also a problem of territoriality. The activity of classical tax farming was relatively

[23] Alan Samuel (1966) showed how by the press of circumstances the royal administration, for want of men, displays obvious clashes between the tasks that people were supposed to carry out and those that they actually carried out.

tightly defined, both by the geographical limits of the city and by the nature of the taxes farmed. In Egypt, the nome appears as the territorial unit at the scale of which the royal bureaucracy and the tax farmers generally interact, both for the auction and for the final settlement.[24] This is the unit that our regulations usually envisage, and it this that explains the fact that they regularly speak of the farm as if of a farming company with its associates and guarantors. Easy enough to manage at the level of the nome metropolis, the farms could not, for want of personnel, be organised for each type of tax for the entirety of the nome without being assisted on an ongoing basis by the local royal civil service. In the nature of things, collection, which demanded the highest degree of local presence in the area involved, must have been removed from, or perhaps was never a responsibility of, the tax farmers in Egypt.

We shall linger only briefly on the second document (columns 23–37), that which concerns the collection of the one-sixth tax on vineyards and orchards, destined for the cult of Arsinoe Philadelphos.[25] As an annex to the regulations we find the circulars by which in the year 23[26] Ptolemy ordered that the sixth paid to the temples be directed to the cult of his deceased sister and wife,[27] and generalised this levy to all vineyards, whatever their status,[28] with the exception of those located on sacred land. It is a doubly concerted act; it links the development of the dynastic cults to the sacred revenues

---

[24] Some of the dispositions of the Revenue Laws, for example the placement of *antigrapheis* or controllers in Alexandria or Pelusium by the farmers of the oil-production contract, with a view to keeping an eye on the traffic in Syrian oil (54.15–19), even suppose an association of the tax farmers of several nomes or indeed of all of them.

[25] On the vineyards, their extremely various status and their taxation, see Préaux (1939: 165–87).

[26] Cols. 36–7 = Lenger, *C. Ord. Ptol.* 17–18.

[27] Actually, *UPZ* I 156 shows that there was a retrospective imposition of the tax on the harvest of year 22 (cf. Revenue Laws 36.7). The second circular (November–December 263) provided for an account of the deliveries and payments made to the temple on account of the *apomoira* for the years 18–21, 22 or 23 with the three-fold aim of establishing a list of the temples which benefited from them and of those who delivered the *apomoira* to them (cf. 33.19–20), of fixing *a posteriori* the amount of the tax for the year 22 (and perhaps also for the year 23), and of documenting these matters for the royal bureaucracy and, secondarily, for the future auctioneers of the *apomoira* contract.

[28] There was a privileged rate of a tenth (col. 24.5–10) for cleruchs in the countryside, in so far as they worked their own allotments, as well as for certain land in the Thebaid, probably land reclaimed from the desert by irrigation, and some land of a particular status that we cannot now recover ('those which are managed like that of Simaristos'). There was a tax exemption for young plants; it is not provided for in what survives of the text, but it appears in other documents like *P. Col. Zen.* I 13 (cf. *P. Cair. Zen.* II 59236, not for the *apomoira* but for the *epigraphê*).

which will be simultaneously favoured and controlled by the king; and it channels to the profit of the royal treasury the growth of this revenue stream connected to the growth of vineyards on reclaimed land. What interests us in this reform is that the economic fact in this case clearly precedes its exploitation for taxation and that it is in itself the automatic corollary of Greek expansion. That expansion created a demand for wine and took place on lands where vineyards were profitable, indeed were sometimes the only profitable possibility. This should not be forgotten in evaluating the mechanisms for the collection and the transformation of the harvest which, *mutatis mutandis*, are found in what is called the oil monopoly.

In principle, the first fruits (*apomoira*) of the vintage are paid in wine, those of orchard products in cash. The enactment of the year 27, as we know it in the second document of the Revenue Laws, reveals some classic features of tax farming. It fixes the tax: for the wine, concretely, ἐκ τοῦ μέτρου, 'coming out of the press'; for fruits and vegetables, by verifying the estimate that the producer offers.[29] But the tax farmers are no longer anything but witnesses to the collection of taxes and to the system organised by the royal bureaucracy to transform the tax in kind into amounts of money credited at the royal bank to the account of the farming contract, just like the taxes paid directly in money. The *oikonomos* establishes storehouses, makes sure that storage jars are available for the wine-growers, reimburses them for the purchase of containers (at the expense of the contract), and sees to the sale of the products delivered for the tax in kind.

These dispositions do not create production. They only translate an old fact by way of new mechanisms, the collection and fulfilment of the first fruits in wine received by the temples, and a new fact, the placement of the royal bank's receipt of wine under the aegis of the contract. The latter, as in Greece, was supposed to ensure the king the monthly minimum income that it had guaranteed (col. 34.4–6) and to find itself credited at the end of the exercise with any surplus realised or debited with the shortfall and forced to pay it off.

The third document (columns 38–72) regulates the 'monopoly' of oils.[30] It gathers texts written by several hands and, at least for the most part, was the object of a revision that modified and added to

---

[29] Col. 24.11–13; 29.2–21. The process of estimation (*syntimêsis*) and of setting a fixed equivalent for the *apomoira* seems to have been extended to the tax on vineyards; cf. Préaux (1939: 177). It does not seem possible, as Grenfell wished, to interpret the mutilated tariff of col. 31 as an order providing for conversion of the *apomoira* on wine into cash.

[30] Cf. Préaux (1939: 65–93).

it,[31] carried out in the offices of the *dioiketes* Apollonios on 10 Loios of year 27, or 31 August 259 (column 38).

This set of regulations is the most famous of the series, but also that which has evoked most intensely the hypothesis of a planned economy, in which the expansion and division of production are conceived as the purpose of deliberate alterations in the economic situation. The production of oil, an important element in both nutrition and lighting, was on this view modelled and carried out by the monarchy on centralising premises. In working with this text, more than any other, and erring in the direction of modernism, scholars have introduced ideas as foreign to the ancient economy and to the people of antiquity as the 'national economy', the 'directed economy' or the 'planned economy', which have often been used to define the Ptolemaic economy.

But does the *elaikê*, the oil monopoly, really deserve this honoured position? Although it is by its very nature grafted onto agricultural production – sesame and castor – which, one may well admit, is to a large extent carried out on royal land and on other land controlled by the bureaucracy, the *elaikê* remains in its essence, to my eyes, an essentially fiscal organism.[32] To be sure, the socio-geographic circumstances of the problem, as I will explain, give a specific form to the enterprise. But, even if the regulations for the *elaikê* present indirect economic implications, their real place is in the area of taxation of a widely used product and not in that of a thought-through redesign of production, and not above all in that of a deliberate policy of concerted pressure on the economic situation.

For the *elaikê*, we possess a complete set of regulations, i.e., beyond the regulations published in the year 27 (columns 39–56); we can still read the 'amended' proclamation of the auction in the the year 259 of the *elaikê* for a period of two years (columns 57–8 and 59–72).[33]

What does this last document teach us, presented as it is as a *diorthôma* (correction) of the regulations on the *elaikê*?[34]

---

[31] These modifications and additions figure largely above the lines or between them, sometimes in the margins, sometimes even on the back of the roll, where there was room to fulfil the order ἔξω ὅρα ('look on the back').

[32] Cf. my timid earlier attempt at this subject in Bingen (1946).

[33] It appears in two copies, except for the statistics about the amount of sown land under the authority of the agricultural administration. These appear only in an annex to the second copy of the *diorthôma*, a copy glued later after column 58.

[34] The question of the nature of this *diorthôma* arises at once. Is it a new version of the regulations, or an amendment to some of its provisions? The first hypothesis seems excluded by the limited character of the measures provided by this *diorthôma*. Rather, its structure leads us to think of the amendments to Athenian *nomoi* (laws) as we know them, for example, from such relatively clear texts as the amendments to the law on coinage (375/374: *Hesperia*

First,[35] it informs us that the farm of the *elaikê* is offered for sale for the entirety of the countryside (that is, excluding Alexandria) for two years, on the basis of a document made public earlier, in which one could perhaps have seen the list of land areas sown with oil-bearing crops.[36] Next comes a passage mutilated in both copies, in which we can pick up only an allusion to the tax (*telos*) of a quarter on sesame and castor.

The provisions that follow are of too technical a character to be discussed here. But two general principles emerge from them:

1. The statistics that the king puts at the disposal of the auctioneers are informative. But if, upon testing, the amounts of land promised and those actually sown turn out to differ, the royal administration will provide to the contractors sesame or castor harvested elsewhere or, failing that, the counterpart in oil, including potentially oils of lower quality (in which case financial compensation in the form of a credit will be provided). The vagaries of the contract of the *elaikê* thus bear less on the area planted with oil-bearing crops than on the yield of the harvest and the level of oil in the crops.[37]

2. There is constant reference to the tax on sesame and castor. Even if in reality, for the farming contract, the transfers from nome to nome and the calculation of the amount of the tax mainly represent

---

43 (1974) 157–8) or those to the law on tyranny (337/336: *SEG* XII 87). These begin by recalling the general article that is being completed (ll. 3–8 in the first case, 7–11 in the second), and then the new provisions are put forward. In these texts, as in our two columns 57–8 = 59–60, one is struck by the difference between the fundamental character of the beginning of the text and the technical and specific nature of what follows. Either the formula πωλοῦμεν ('we offer for sale') etc. reprised the start of the general proclamation of the offer of the *elaikê* at auction, or it referred in its missing lines to the more general text. The document described as ἐκκείμενον in 57.5 = 59.5 (see the following note) is perhaps this document – if it is not instead, as I am tempted to believe, the description of land areas for the current year. The lacuna that chops off the start of 57 = 59 is a particularly grievous loss for the interpretation of the contract for farming the *elaikê*.

[35] Here is the passage as restored by combining the two versions (57.1–5 and 59.1–5): Διόρθωμα το[ῦ νόμου ἐ]πὶ τῆι ἐλαικῆι. Πωλοῦμεν τὴν ἐλαικὴν τ[ὴν κατὰ] τὴγ χώραν ἀπὸ μηνὸς Γορπιαίου τοῦ [κζ (ἔτους)? Αἰγ]υπτίων Μεσορὴ εἰς ἔτη β κατ[ὰ τὸ ἔκθεμα?] τὸ ἐκκείμενον [- -. ('Corrected version of the law concerning the oil contract. We offer for sale the oil contract for the country from the month of Gorpiaios of the twenty-seventh year, that is Mesore of the Egyptian calendar, for a period of two years, according to the edict made public . . . ').

[36] See, however, the reservations expressed in n. 34.

[37] The surplus of an exceptionally abundant harvest is credited to the benefit of the treasury. This provision (58.8–9 = 60.15–17) appears also in the amendment and seems to be a measure tending to diminish the variability of the farming contract, but this time to the detriment of the farming company. None the less, it is impossible to establish with certainty the actual bearing of this provision.

complications at the level of control and accounts, the privileged mention of this tax shows that the *elaikê* remains a fiscal organism and, in the legislator's mind, has not evolved into an economic one.

In its main lines, but only in its main lines, the treatment of the *elaikê* recalls that of the *apomoira* on wine. Here too, the basic fact is that the farm concerns a tax in kind, in the present case the *telos* on the production of two oil-bearing crops, sesame and castor (column 39.13–18). Here too, the contractors are put in possession of statistics about areas planted, the basis of the auction; here again the harvest is to be transformed (into oil) and sold by the efforts of the royal administration, but at the expense of or at least with the expenses charged to the debit of the contract (cf. columns 54.20–55.14), which has a right to superintend all of the operations. Here too, finally, any negative or positive balance of the contract is established on the basis of receipts in cash from retail sale of the product (column 55.1).

But everything is much more complicated in the case of oils than in that of wine. This is partly the result of profound differences between the production of wine and that of oil. The areas planted in sesame and castor appear to be much greater; they are unequally spread through the countryside, something that is also true of vineyards, but they seem less connected to the areas of Greek settlement and, above all, less easily controllable than vineyards, which are perennial plantings that mature slowly rather than annual crops on arable land. Grapes are processed near the vineyard and relatively soon after harvest. Oil, by contrast, does not have to be made immediately after harvest or in proximity to the fields; it is also more expensive and somewhat more complicated, and it is thus the domain of specialists, the *elaiourgoi*. Trade in wine was apparently untaxed; the retail sale of oil was regulated. This regulation, moreover, posed a very specific problem to the royal administration, which had to supply the retail trade: the zones of production were limited to certain nomes, but from these had to come the supply to be distributed to all nomes and to Alexandria. If the nome was the territorial unit from the point of view of the treasury and the contract, it was the receipt of the product for sale in all the nomes that formed the basis for the final accounting.

There was another fundamental difference. Because the retail trade in oil was contracted out,[38] the state had to supply the holders of the

---

[38] Cf. Préaux (1939: 81–90), whose interpretation of the king's motives involved in the variations in the price of oil I do not follow.

concession in accordance with its contractual obligations (while it could unload the wine from the *apomoira* by any and all means). Moreover, because the oil contract covered the entire production of these oils and not only the 25 per cent collected as tax, the government had to find a common system to handle both the more limited quantity of oil derived from the tax and the much larger total quantity of oil produced for consumption.

The regulations of the year 27, with the numerous emendations evinced by the corrections (cf. above, n. 34), show that the fiscal mechanism that we call the oil monopoly was still in the process of being organised. A solution to the problem of the lack of geographical congruity between the zones of production and the zones of consumption (columns 41–3; cf. columns 60–72) has been sought; prices have been modified, rules have been laid out for oil of lower quality, the surveillance and taxation of oils imported from abroad have been improved. But these are minor alterations. The essentials all existed before the year 27. Some details, like the use of the process of advance estimate (either of the harvest standing in the fields, or of the quota for retail sale), a typically Greek procedure,[39] show that the system contained in the oldest state of the text had already evolved from its initial form. But we cannot really evaluate this development, because, contrary to what happened for the *apomoira*, we cannot imagine what the origin of this tax of a quarter of the harvest of sesame and castor was. A traditional rent? An innovation of Ptolemy I Soter or of Ptolemy II Philadelphos?

Right away, we shall see that the responses given to the difficulties and contradictions already described were characterised by two traits by the year 27: first, by the across-the-board intervention of tax farmers and bureaucrats in the totality of the oil-bearing crops, and not only in those products paid as taxes in kind;[40] and second, by the control of the entire process of the making and distribution of oil.

[39] The process of *syntimêsis* or joint evaluation of the standing crop by the three parties involved (production, tax farming, administration) (col. 42.11–20) seems at first glance to duplicate the calculation of the actual amount of the tax at the moment of the harvest (col. 39.13–18). But the *syntimêsis* does not seem, in these regulations, to function as the basis for setting the amount of the tax. It may have been only a means of avoiding later diversions of a part of the harvest. On the opposition (in practice, not only in theory) which separates the mentality of the Greek, familiar with the estimation of the standing harvest, and that of the Egyptian peasant, who holds to the concrete process of setting on the harvest floor the share of each individual and of the king, see Chapter 17.

[40] The generalisation seems to go farther still. The privileged categories of producers, like the *ateleis* or the holders of *dôreai*, were also supposed to deliver their harvest of sesame and castor. Since they receive for it a lower price (6 drachmas per artaba instead of 8 drachmas),

In other words, through a significantly increased scale of action by the interested parties, the matter moves from the strictly fiscal character of the enterprise to a level of massive and protected exploitation of an economic activity. How far has the traditional management of an economic matter been turned into a tool of economic expansion? Yet the tax is not a simple trick in the final accounting of the farm. We have already seen that the amended text of the auction proclamation for the year 27 (columns 60–72) deals fundamentally with the *telos* (tax) on sesame and castor.[41] The process unfolds in a series of stages.

First stage: all of the production of oil-bearing seeds is required to be sold by the producers to the farm, at the same time that these same producers deliver the tax of 25 per cent of the crop of sesame and castor, thus a quarter of the production.[42] The regulations provide only a few minor exceptions to the rule: for example, the seeds kept for sowing for some categories of land and sesame seeds from sacred land intended for production in the temple of oil for its own consumption. Apart from these exceptions, the entire harvest of the oil-bearing crops is sequestered immediately in sealed storehouses. Any fraudulent diversion of oil-bearing seeds is severely punished, as is all negligence on the part of functionaries who are responsible for the proper execution of the royal orders.[43]

Second stage: a series of orders is issued concerning the making of oil.[44] These are of two sorts: on the one hand, the royal administration undertakes to provide for a certain number of oil factories, to supply them with staffing, tools and raw materials; on the other hand, the administration is also supposed to prevent the bad organisation

it looks as if they too pay the *tetartê* (25 per cent tax). Wickersham (1970: 45 n. 2) has looked again at this problem of two prices, observing that by receiving 8 drachmas per artaba and delivering a quarter in addition as tax, the peasant actually received 6.4 drachmas net per artaba, including tax. The calculation is correct and follows to the letter the rather laborious formulation of column 39.13–18 (with a tax in kind defined, Greek style, in money!); it shows a situation in which the peasant seems to occupy a more privileged position than the privileged Greek. The comparison of the two tariffs suggests to me that the calculation of the tax is inclusive and should be interpreted from the concrete point of view of the Egyptian peasant: three measures to be paid for, one measure for the tax, which brings us back to an average of 6 drachmas, as Grenfell earlier supposed.

[41] This *telos* does not appear in the numerous later sources concerning the production, manufacturing or distribution of oil products.

[42] Cols. 39–40.8; 42.3–43.19.

[43] Including the accuracy of information provided in the *diagraphê tou sporou* (the sowing schedule); see below, p. 178; cf. col. 41.3–13; 43.3–10.

[44] Cols. 44–47.9; 49.1–50.5; 50.20–51.19; 56.19–21. Cf. Préaux (1939: 73–81) and *P. Tebt.* III 703.140–58.

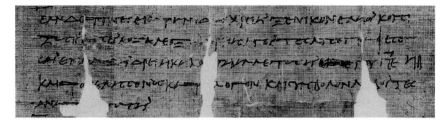

Figure 13.1   P. Rev., *col. 52, lines 13–17 (after* Revenue Laws of Ptolemy Philadelphus, *ed. B. P. Grenfell, Oxford 1896, pl. X)*

of work, the flight of oil-workers and access by outsiders to the equipment, and neither compromise the output of the oil factories nor facilitate clandestine manufacture. In the same spirit, the importation for private use of oil coming from other nomes or from Alexandria, or from abroad via Alexandria or Pelusium, is drastically limited.[45] Actually, the 'manufacturing' stage concerns the contract only in an indirect fashion and from two points of view: it protects the farm from a bad outcome caused by lack of manufacturing or by illicit competition, and it permits the farm to calculate any premium from manufacturing due to it. The Revenue Laws, moreover, describe the organisation of manufacturing only partially. Here more than elsewhere, the limited character of the objectives pursued by our document becomes clear. It is not concerned with a code for a royal industry of oil-bearing products.

Third stage: provision is made for the transfer of the oil to commercial channels, either to wholesalers or to retailers in the metropoleis of the nomes or in villages.[46] The organisation and control of these operations depends here again on the responsibility of the royal officials. At the end of the cycle, a licensed retail trade corresponds to the monopoly of the purchase of oil-bearing seeds that rests with the farm. Perhaps following a formula that we know well for brewing and laundry, for example, the countryside at least must have seen frequently the conjunction of a tradesman, usually Egyptian, and a low-level concessionary who assumed the (remunerated) risk of moving a certain quota of oil. Once again, it is the obligation assumed by the farming contract to cover the transformation of the tax into a sold product that causes the regulations to describe

---

[45] Cols. 52.7–53.3; 54.6–19.

[46] Col. 40.9–20 (orders that are part of the preamble of the regulations on the *elaikê*, cols. 39 and 40).

between the first and fourth stages some problems connected to manufacture and sale; the farm is not in fact actively involved in these, but it has considerable interest in their being carried out. The state undertakes to protect them also at the level of sale, something it does the more easily in that it must control, for its own benefit, the innumerable tax burdens affecting the artisanry, retail commerce and consumer products.

Fourth stage: at first monthly, and then at the end of the contract, the officials and the farmers of the *elaikê* proceed to establish the balance-sheet for the contract, including the valuation of any unsold surplus and contractual allowances provided for the farmers as a result of production.[47]

Despite the very schematic character that I have given to this operation, the complexity of the enterprise, or at least its apparent complexity, is obvious. For some of the operations, particularly the entire portion concerned with the transformation of the taxes in kind, are partly tricks of writing. Moreover, still on this point, we must put things into perspective and remember that this scheme was applied partly to very modest operations, from a quantitative point of view, a minor cultivation at the village level, a small oil-factory behind a shop. But it is understandable that in the attempt to theorise the subject, historians have been able to turn such businesses into such unhappily modernising phrases as 'nationalised industry' or 'planned industry', or have thought themselves able to discern the king's wishes to create production structures aimed at making the kingdom self-sufficient in oils and at finding ways other than taxation to exploit local consumption as fully as possible.

It is easy enough to see what aspects of the rules concerning the *elaikê* most readily suggested to modern historians a stage of managed, or even planned, economy going well beyond the relatively traditional ideas present in Greece, like the resources available in taxation, or the empirical methods of managing an immense royal estate characteristic of the Orient.

The first of these aspects, and that which is easily located very close to the idea of a planned economy (that is, an economy going beyond

---

[47] Cols. 54.20–55.14. Cf. col. 53.12–26. For an attempt to evaluate the profits of the farming contract, considered to have been constituted in the main by reimbursement of the expenses of manufacturing (45.6), see Wickersham (1970). He may not have given sufficient weight to our ignorance of the total cost of the operations covered by the contract. The reimbursement seems to me only one of the elements that allow the farming company to make an offer at the auction of the *elaikê*.

the authoritarian running of the royal domains), is the διαγραφὴ τοῦ σπόρου (*diagraphê tou sporou*), the sowing schedule. The Revenue Laws papyrus refers twice to this document. Moreover, the auction proclamation of columns 59–60 includes as an appendix a summary statement, nome by nome, of the amount of land sown in sesame and castor, and provides for the quantities intended to be exported to other nomes.

This statement, the προκηρυχθεῖσαι ἄρουραι ἐν ἑκάστωι νομῶι ('arouras proclaimed in each nome'), that is, the areas publicly listed for each nome before the auction, was certainly a summary of the *diagraphê tou sporou*, laid out for each nome for each crop, for the land subject to the *diagraphê*, probably the royal and sacred land. The nature of the *diagraphê tou sporou* has been the object of a substantial controversy, which is right at the heart of our assessment of the Ptolemies' 'economic thought'. For those scholars who have supposed that this *diagraphê* originated in Alexandria on the basis of pre-established requirements, the word is connected most often to the idea of directed, or nationalised and centralised, production. This would be the first stage of a planned process of production, manufacture and sale, with anticipation and manipulation of consumption. The offices in Alexandria, on the basis of prior reflection on economic imperatives, would calculate the areas of oil-bearing crops needed and would allocate them among the nomes that produced them. The instructions would be sent to the local administrations, which in turn would be responsible for seeing to the execution of the central directives.

This 'centrifugal' interpretation of the *diagraphê* was undermined by the appearance of specific documents, particularly *P. Yale inv.* 1647,[48] which show that the *diagraphê tou sporou* was developed at the nome level by the local officials. Pierre Vidal-Naquet devoted a monograph in 1967 to this idea, which he clarified very fully.[49] The *diagraphê tou sporou* was, in his view, a schedule detailing the obligations of the peasants and villages in the matter of sowing. The *diagraphê* was established before the sowing and is thus not a simple descriptive document concerning the state of planting. It was developed by the local administration and was binding, at least in theory, for the tenants of the land.

[48] C. B. Welles and J. A. S. Evans, *Journal of Juristic Papyrology* 7–8 (1953–4) 35–41; text reprinted as *SB* VI 9257 (Arsinoite, 232). The text was re-edited as *P. Yale* I 36 (pp. 104–6, pl. X).
[49] Vidal-Naquet (1967).

Following a process the reverse of what was previously supposed, then, the *diagraphê* travelled from the countryside towards Alexandria, where the financial administration could supply to prospective bidders in the auction a table of the areas sown, for such information was indispensable in order to contract for the *elaikê* of a nome. I would go even further in seeing the *diagraphê* as a type of economic intervention.[50] What we must see in it, at least in part, is the traditional approach of the management of the royal estate,[51] an estate that extended in this case to practically the entirety of the arable land, certainly the royal land and probably the sacred land of the nome, which the *diagraphê tou sporou* most probably covered. The fact that the king remained, in his own domain, the master of the choice of crops was not a new development, or especially a theoretical contribution of Greek power. It has even less to do with the normal relationship between proprietor and tenant than with the old practices of large Near Eastern estates. On this basis, to be sure, the king could have had a policy of preferring certain crops,[52] but this choice was conditioned to a large extent by opportunity and local tradition. Nothing shows that it was connected to any wish emanating from Alexandria, or to any creative economic thought going beyond the empiricism of the agricultural management of classical Greece or the pre-Hellenistic Orient.

Other traits of the *elaikê*, with less good reason, have also contributed sometimes to turning the oil monopoly into a witness to a planned or state economy. One example is the royal control of the price of seeds and oils. It is true that some wages and reimbursements and some prices have been modified in our text with respect to a new

[50] The late N. N. Pikous also refused to see in the *diagraphê tou sporou* an argument in favour of the existence of a planned economy in the Ptolemaic kingdom. See Pikous (1969) with the review by H. Heinen, *CdÉ* 45 (1970) 186–8.

[51] Here I concur with N. N. Pikous (see previous note), quoted in Heinen's review (p. 188): 'The elements of planning that one could infer from the contents of some business papyri reflect simply a general situation encountered by every proprietor of every period who tried to profit from his land as rationally as possible from his point of view and in accordance with the objective conditions of his possibilities. It was the same purpose that the efforts of the Ptolemaic government had in mind in managing the land that was in its immediate control.'

[52] We should not go to the other extreme, of denying the king and his advisers a wish to create, renew, rationalise and adapt their profit-seeking to the setting. We have a splendid dossier of four letters written by Apollonios on 27 December 256 (*P. Cair. Zen.* 59155–8), where there appears, among other things, the royal suggestion – for Apollonios, an order – of practising a double harvest of wheat, and Apollonios' own order to plant resinous crops which would be 'useful for the king'. Certainly there was creativity in management, but the *quantitative* level of execution is alien to a planned economy.

year. The lowering of reimbursements provided for oil-making artisans and for the farming company (col. 45.2–6), the modifications of
prices for stock to be taken back at the end of the contract (col.
53.12–17) or for deliveries destined for Alexandria (col. 53.18–26),
are not economically significant. The first modifications are partly
connected to the alteration in the way the reimbursements to the
farmers and the paid workers are calculated: in effect, these will be
fixed according to the production of oil, and no longer according to
the sale of the oil. The others are simple changes of accounting procedure in the relationship between the financial entries to be credited
to the farming company or to the treasury in the final reckoning. It is
a financial problem, and not an economic problem, even if the reform
tends to increase the treasury's profit margin on the sale of oil.

More weight could be given to the increase in the sale price of *kiki*,
or castor oil, from 30 drachmas per *metrêtês* to 48 drachmas, the
same as the price of sesame oil. This increase seems the more significant in that it is out of line with quality, for the two oils were not of
the same quality. But it must be pointed out that this equalisation of
prices already existed in Alexandria (col. 40.14–20), and there is thus
some reason to hesitate in interpreting this action. In any case,
nothing shows that these modifications are the result of a systematic
economic analysis or of a wish to influence the market for oils
prospectively by means of price. These may be simple corrections,
adaptations, which are connected to the empiricism and familiarity
with the market that every agricultural producer had. Agricultural
products have always undergone variations in current prices. These
were indeed a source of speculation, but that does not allow us to say
that such speculation is the result of economic science, or that the
variations in price in the Revenue Laws can be explained systemat-
ically by royal speculation or by the king's wishes to modify the
market. Finally, these changes, particularly the first set, may also be
nothing more than rectifications needed to correct defects in earlier
farming regulations. Such defects could have been revealed by inadequate bids from the farming companies, or by their exaggerated
profits, or even by excessively frequent deficits on their part – deficits
that could only worry the treasury. Long-established Greek experience came into play here.[53] Just as the farming companies readjusted
their bids, the treasury must also have adjusted the conditions of
auction of tax contracts.

[53] Cf. n. 21 above.

Similarly, the status of the oil-making artisans or *elaiourgoi* has been a matter for reflection. We know that these people were obliged to work, and could work only, in their own district, in their own nome. There is no reason to linger on this point, because the manufacture of oil is in fact an activity outside the farm, even if it was useful and prudent for the farmers to follow it closely. What in fact were the *elaiourgoi*? Were they the remains of indigenous family artisans, whom the intrusion of the Greek monetary economy must have weakened? Were they on the contrary part of the sub-proletariat that temporary agricultural workers formed in antiquity? Do they represent wandering teams working for a period of some days? Or are they instead small employers with their own employees? Whatever the case, their employment as *elaiourgoi* brought them into a particular controlled structure:[54] they were the *elaiourgoi* of the nome, it was forbidden for them to work in any other nome, and those who might receive them elsewhere could be arrested (col. 44.8–18). It is in this respect, to be sure, that their status has received the most attention, but this is a social and legal matter, rather than a question of the economy of Egypt; it is thus outside our focus at present. Actually, we are acquainted with this type of constraint for other types of Egyptian workers as well, for example beekeepers. Although the latter practised an important economic activity in which royal control was essentially fiscal, and one cannot speak of a monopoly,[55] and although they were free, they were connected with a poorly defined association at the level of the nome[56] and could be arrested and shipped back from a neighbouring nome if they went there with their hives.[57] Nothing allows us to presume the existence of any connection, hereditary or otherwise, to their occupation or to the place, going beyond a personal obligation. And, in the rural society of Egypt, does not the entity '*elaiourgoi*' represent a factual rather than legal situation? What explains the

---

[54] They are referred to as ἐν ἑκάστωι νομῶι καταταχθέντας ('stationed in each nome') (44.8–9), using a verb (κατατάσσω) that implies simultaneously the idea of a category and that of a particular assignment. *P. Hib.* I 43, a little older than our amended version of the *elaikê* regulations, attests that the *elaiourgoi* formed a group that could be readily mobilised by the agricultural administration of the nome.

[55] Cf. Préaux (1939: 233–8); Sullivan (1973); *P. Lond.* VII 1977 (253), along with Chapter 16 below.

[56] In *P. Cair. Zen.* III 59467, the beekeepers form an organised group, which describes itself as οἱ ἐκ τοῦ Ἀρσινοίτου νομοῦ (*hoi ek tou Arsinoitou nomou*: 'those from the Arsinoite nome'). The memorandum *P. Tebt.* III 853.26 (c. 173) reveals the existence at Krokodilopolis of a ἱερὸν τῶν μελισσουργῶν (*hieron tôn melissourgôn*, 'sanctuary of the beekeepers').

[57] Cf. *P. Cair. Zen.* III 59368.

prohibition on the *elaiourgoi* from working in another nome than that in which they are engaged to exercise their craft is that the nome formed a fiscal unit as well as an administrative one, covered by its own farming agreements and its own contracts for business. The bee-keeper who leaves the nome, or the *elaiourgos* who deserts his, abandons the royal structure which puts them to work for various reasons and causes losses to the tax-farming contractors whom they are supposed to help in carrying out their farming contract. But nothing allows us to suppose that the creation of their status dates from the introduction of tax farming into the Egyptian economic setting. From the analogies that we find among the oil-making artisans, the bee-keepers and perhaps the goose-rearers,[58] we can deduce that their status was traditional, just as the nome was a borrowing from the past. It is only natural that the farming system and Egyptian artisanal structures found themselves face to face in the text in which the king had to give the contractors a guarantee that the seeds would be transformed into oil in a timely fashion.

The oil monopoly thus appears, as I argued already in 1949, as another example of institution-borrowing: the transfer into a new setting of a classic type of tax farm. But, under the two-fold pressure (resulting from the conditions under which oil-bearing crops were grown in Egypt) of assuring the transformation of the tax revenue in kind from seeds to oil and of avoiding the manufacture and sale of oil from undeclared seeds, the fiscal farm evolved more profoundly than in the case of another tax in kind, the *apomoira*. It saw itself in effect provided by the king with such substantial means of protection (like the purchase of the entire crop or the suppression of unsupervised manufacture) that the economic structure of the production and sale of oil felt the consequences. But it would be difficult to believe that the practical dispositions linked to the revenues of the classical city, whether they concerned taxes or mining concessions, did not also have some influence on the purely economic aspects of the matters they involved. Those elements that produced the idea that the 'monopoly' of oil was a prototype for a state economy (that is, the systematic survey or even mandating of plantings, the concentration of the harvest, the organisation of manufacture and distribution, the manipulation of prices) seem in the end like a series of happenstance

---

[58] *BGU* VI 1212, D = C. *Ord. Ptol.* 83 (221–205), despite its mutilated condition, indicates for the goose-rearers a status displaying similarities to that of the *elaiourgoi*, although there is no mention of any geographical limitation on their right to exercise their profession.

aspects of the difficult adaptation of the tax-farming system to the broad-acred cultivation of an Oriental type, if not already simply a result of the size of the royal domain and of the lands that the king controlled directly.

The fourth document that has survived in this group is that concerning the contract for farming the royal banks.[59] These are the organisations where the royal revenues in money were received, credited to the account of the tax contracts, accounted for and as needed expended on order of the royal administration. The concession, which allowed the holder to handle the royal receipts, also included money-changing and commerce in coinage. The bank concessions were authorised to carry on other banking activities like lending, but without having the monopoly of these activities. It was in such operations that they could put the royal money sitting at their disposal to profitable use.

The text is badly damaged and barely permits us – with only limited assistance from other sources – to depict precisely the functioning of these farmed banks. We know that they were organised hierarchically, from the 'banks of the cities and villages' up to the great royal bank in Alexandria. Several documents from practical operations define the role that the bank played in respect to tax farming. The tax contract had an account, debited at the beginning of its term with the value at which the contract had fixed the revenue that it was guaranteeing. The tax contract deposited the required sureties for the amount guaranteed and the transfer tax. The taxes all had to be paid, whether directly or indirectly via collectors, to the bank, which credited them to the contract's account. Taxes paid into other hands would not be credited to the farming company. This subject needs no lengthy discussion. For a very long time, the direct Greek ancestry of the Ptolemaic royal bank has been recognised, with a particular relationship to the Athenian model. In Egypt, obviously, that outcome was required by the fact that the monetary economy, the foundation of banking activity, was itself of Greek origin. In 1899, Ulrich Wilcken accepted this point in connection with the accounting technique of the banks. Since then, the points of contact with the classical bank have multiplied. Claire Préaux showed how the terminology of the bank, the form of bank records and, by means of the records, the role of the bank as witness all display continuity with the roles of the classical bank.[60]

[59] Cf. Préaux (1939: 280–97).
[60] Préaux (1958). Cf. Bogaert (1968: 89–90).

This continuity of forms may even go as far as direct borrowing from Greece, if we accept that by the end of the fourth century Athens already possessed a *dêmosia trapeza* (δημοσία τράπεζα, 'public bank'), a bank that handled the city's money.[61] It is even possible that the public banks of the Greek cities attested in the Hellenistic period had ancestors in the classical period. But let us leave this problem aside and limit ourselves to the point that we have already been able to establish: the system of farmed banks, like the other organs that we have analysed earlier on the basis of the Revenue Laws, postulates the existence of a Greek social group with the right and the power of economic initiative, a business setting capable of mobilising either money or sureties to become involved in the countryside. This is true even in economic matters where the role of the royal administration seems to be important, or even decisive, among the jurisdictions of the Egyptian economy.[62] Thus the Revenue Laws demonstrate the presence of a 'third body' of some importance, beyond the military and civil organisations of the monarchy and beyond the peasant and artisan mass of the Egyptian population. It would be too simplistic to see in the 'king's Greeks' and those of the 'free diaspora' two watertight groups. The *dioiketes* Apollonios, a businessman exploiting landed estates and small industries in Palestine, in Alexandria or in the countryside, shows the double character of some of the immigrants. Zenon, first Apollonios' business agent and then his manager, after having been on close terms with the royal administration during his management of the *dioiketes*' affairs, would in his turn become one of these 'independent' Greeks.

If we recapitulate the contribution of the four documents that I have analysed in this chapter, we cannot avoid posing one question at the start of any synthesis that depends on the Revenue Laws: did the king deliberately associate himself with this world of handlers of money and credit, big and small, in order for them to collaborate in the systematic creation of a new type of economy? Or did these independent elements, immigrants to Egypt under various rubrics, instead naturally claim a place in a system of 'royal' type, which remained sufficiently Greek because of the monetary economy for them to have found in it enough to satisfy their own desire for self-enrichment, a natural dynamic among immigrants?

---

[61] Bogaert (1968: 88–91).

[62] I have tried to define the role of another group of independent Greeks in agriculture in Chapter 15.

But is it not the case that these questions really are questions only for modern scholars? Surely the economic forms that we perceive in Ptolemaic Egypt are the fruit not of any historic choice, but of an accumulation of events and an evolution, in which no one thought of creating a new economic type as a result of theoretical analysis of what might produce the greatest return from the great Egyptian household managed by a king and his Greeks. We can scarcely attempt here, on the basis of this one document, to present a new synthesis of the Ptolemaic economy. Rather, let us concentrate on relocating the problem, because of the role that this document has played in the genesis of the idea of a 'planned Egyptian economy' and in all of the political and historical developments that have been imagined on the basis of this text.

To be sure, the monetary economy transplanted to Egypt underwent influences exerted on it by its substantial change of scenery. From the unpredictable, small-scale agriculture native to most of Greece and the traditional Mediterranean landscape of olive trees, vineyards and cereal fields, the Greeks moved to vast flood plains supplemented with irrigated areas, organised in large units under traditional bureaucratic control, whether it was royal or sacred. They moved from a constellation of microeconomies to a limited number of much larger and more homogeneous entities. In the nature of things, the economies that developed in the Greek kingdoms of the East were distinguished from those of Greece by the new status of the relationship between land and community. Royal management of the land by an agricultural bureaucracy and the financial administration must have been largely based on the management of the land by the pharaohs or by the temples, but also on that of Achaemenid and even Macedonian estates. To my mind, however, there is no proof that this management of the king's *oikos* went beyond the bounds of a wish to exploit the estate as much as possible, or, on a parallel front, that the search for income for the treasury went beyond exploiting a tax-based system to picking up modern economic forms, like planning, state economy, centrally administered economy and the like, that have so often been credited to it.

The entire picture that can be sketched, beyond the king's control over the land, which is an inheritance from the pharaohs and from the Achaemenids, brings us back instead to economic traditions at home in fourth-century Greece. Specifically, the terminology of fiscal and financial structures, the techniques of accounting in terms of money, the institutions transplanted – for better or worse – like tax farming or the cleruchic system, witness to this continuity. To be sure, they inevitably underwent transformations in contact with the new geographical and social realities, un-Greek as those were. What is most important for us, however, is that these Greek traditions survived, and that even in some depth. It is agreed today that the ancients' concept of economics was limited to a certain number of specific behaviours, and that they had no concept of a separate category of 'the economy' or 'economics' as such.[63] The Greek cities essentially sought to guarantee their revenues by taxation or where possible by the indirect exploitation of natural sources of wealth like mines (following fiscal models even there). Their commercial policy was conceived in terms of the importation of the materials necessary for survival or in terms of military imperialism based on the same idea of acquiring goods and security. No one tried to remodel his own economy or to remodel the economies that were exploited, in order, for example, to create new types of wealth or export-oriented zones.[64] Classical Greece in particular does not appear to have done these things on the basis of theoretical considerations. I do not believe, no matter what has been said about the Ptolemies' mercantilism, that they displayed any economic behaviour which, apart from the management of newly reclaimed farmland, really went beyond the lines of the empiricism of the Greek city: fiscal exploitation and – but this goes beyond our subject here – the concern to be guaranteed the needed imports of foodstuffs, of metals, of wood and of men.

There are other points of contact between the fourth century in Greece and Ptolemaic Egypt that have emerged as a result of the analysis of the Revenue Laws. In bringing to a close her study on the transmission of banking from Athens to Egypt,[65] Claire Préaux sketched in a few lines a more general reflection, towards which my last point brings us. The bankers who were so important to fourth-century Athens, she remarks, were foreigners. That puts a finger on one of the fundamental aspects of the Greek economy in the fourth century, a period of the destruction and restructuring of Greek society. We witness at this point the progressive disappearance in the Greek city of the prestige and power of the citizen-farmer. This disappearance is perhaps the result of the crises from which the civic body had suffered; it is above all the result of the competition of a new type of prestigious Greeks, because these held the initiative in

---

[63]   Cf. Finley (1973: 21–2).
[64]   Cf. above, n. 21.
[65]   See above, n. 60.

many non-traditional activities. It was the foreigner, a merchant or banker, the metic, who was needed all the more because the need for money was ever more pressing. When, at the end of a war which had weakened Athens, Xenophon ventured in his *Poroi* to reflect out loud on the ways of bringing Athens back to prosperity, he proposed favouring the immigration of metics, the source of economic activity and of a tax base, by various types of measures. The Greece of the fourth century thus gave birth to an experienced and powerful class of mobile individuals, who were a model of action and became indispensable to the city. It was at the same point that another type of mobility of action outside the framework of the city imposed itself on the Greeks, that of the mercenary soldier. Seen from the point of view of expatriates, mercenary service was actually a deliberate and honourable economic activity; if one thinks of the model brother of Menander's *Aspis*, he has nothing of the *miles gloriosus* in him. To be sure, the mercenary's ideal remained his return to his home city, but in reality, ever since the fifth century a competing idea, that of colonising barbarian soil and creating a new existence in a new framework in the middle of an exploited population, had been present.

When Alexander, and in his wake the Ptolemies, took control of Egypt, a monetary economy, or at least the forms of a monetary economy, entered along with them. This was not a decision they took; no one thought that there was any other economic model in which an active life for Greek settlers was possible. In the same way, the Ptolemies and their advisers, faced with the need to organise the Graeco-Macedonian conquest and the immense and fertile lands that it had opened up to the conquerors, of necessity thought about the economic life of the country in the institutional terms and with the economic habits born in the Greek city of the fourth century. The contribution of Athens, through the influence of Demetrios of Phaleron and others, must have stamped not only the institutions and law of Alexandria but also, indirectly, the life of the countryside. At most, something must have been added to this from the Macedonian royal experience (which in economic matters is unknown to us), and some specific ways of managing these new lands inherited from the pharaohs must have come with the land. But, as I have already stressed, what seems to me just as fundamental in the Revenue Laws is that they show the importance that mobile and at least partly independent financial strength had taken on – strength that belonged to the Greek who was already successfully detached from his home city in the economy of metics or of mercenaries. We should not think of the Greek 'financier' in the Egypt of Ptolemy Philadelphos as a banker who has transferred capital with him from Greece, the islands or Asia Minor to Alexandria. This must have been the exception. In a rich region suddenly opened to the monetary economy, there were opportunities for profit for those with initiative, experience and aptitude for handling risk. The American millionaires of a century ago had not brought their capital with them from Europe (although they did, to be sure, borrow from European investors). The lack of manpower, the need for the Ptolemaic monarchy to ensure itself the assistance of as many Greeks – the only people suitable for handling Greek-style management – as possible, explains why this introduction of financiers was a success and continued even in a framework where the real authority was the king, who controlled the land. The equilibrium that came into being between these two powers was not the result of a royal wish to attach these men to a modern economy that the king was creating; it was born rather of an adaptation of deep-rooted tendencies in the Greek world of the fourth century to the realities of a new political system and a new agricultural situation. The king, the mercenaries, the bureaucrats, and also the independent Greeks who came to Egypt to make their fortune were all equally, through their language, ways of thinking, analysing and deciding, the unconscious bearers of these tendencies, in which the economy was only one element integrated with others. It is not one of the least of the paradoxes of the Revenue Laws – the source of the modern idea of an economic power autocratically reconceived by the king – that they can appear on the contrary as a witness of the unity of the Greek destiny. This witness appears at the beginning of the long and slow wear and tear that was to lead the Greek mentality to its slow death ten centuries later, under the weight of a country and a foreign population which inexorably blurred the meaning of words and institutions, and the spirit that they embodied. This wear and tear on Greek words and institutions can already be seen in the Revenue Laws.

Chapter 14

THE STRUCTURAL TENSIONS OF PTOLEMAIC SOCIETY

However privileged papyrology may be among the documentary sources for the Hellenistic period – only a few great epigraphical sites can offer anything comparable – it remains true that this documentation presents discontinuities of various sorts. These are the more embarrassing in that we have too few historical sources to be able to draw from them a synthesis of the evolution of Ptolemaic Egypt or a balanced image of it. The discontinuities are first geographic: we jump from one site to another, and these sites are most often isolated points, whose typicality for their period is hard to discern. To these geographic discontinuities are added chronological ones. Even when a site is, exceptionally, known from several points in the Hellenistic period, it is difficult to bridge them, as we find with Tebtynis between the papyri of the third and second centuries, or at Herakleopolis, between the cleruchic documents of the third century and those of the first. To these discontinuities we could add the cultural gap between Greek and Demotic documentation, a discontinuity aggravated and misplaced as a result of scholarly specialisation.[1]

These considerations, well known as they are, cannot be treated as of merely academic concern. Indeed, these discontinuities are a kind of mortgage on any structural study of the Ptolemaic world. In setting out in this chapter to approach one of the most difficult points of such a study, we need to look at two preliminary points.

The first is that these discontinuities are not purely a defect in our documentation that can allow us to avoid issues. They are also a fact, and not entirely a matter of chance; they can and should be in themselves a matter for reflection. Indeed, even the chance of discoveries, the most arbitrary element – at least at first glance – in the creation of

---

[1] Other disconcerting discontinuities could be mentioned, for example those between the relatively well-known rural settings and their neighbouring urban milieus, or indeed in the situation of a single individual – an official, for example, whose official activity may be well known to us but whose private circumstances, like origin, education, recruitment and connections, may escape us entirely.

discontinuities, is something arbitrary only in its negative effects. It can even be significant, as when, for example, it connects the greatest extent of cleruchic settlement and the conditions of the preservation of papyrus. On the contrary, these discontinuities, like those between Greek and Demotic documentation, or between Greek documents of the same provenance but different dates, reflect indirectly the problems of socio-economic structures, problems connected in many cases to the very particularities of the Greek settlement in Ptolemaic Egypt, to its vicissitudes, and to the vagaries of its relationships with the Egyptian population. These are therefore sometimes significant discontinuities, in which it is, none the less, worthwhile determining the more or less hidden fundamental continuities. That, in a sense, is the journey on which this chapter is setting out.

From that base comes the second remark which further undergirds my view that we have here a significant theme for reflection: the problem appears in an entirely different light in our papyrological documentation of the Roman period. To be sure, the papyrological documentation of the imperial period – and this remains true for the Byzantine era – presents the same problems of geographic discontinuity, and up to a certain point, it suffers also from chronological discontinuity. Soknopaiou Nesos, Tebtynis, Oxyrhynchos and Hermopolis cannot be superimposed or juxtaposed. And yet, and this is what appears to me a starting-point for reflection, the documentation of the early empire presents itself to us in Egypt as an entity of converging sources, a body of legal, administrative, social and economic facts, which can be integrated relatively easily. The image that we have of Roman Egypt is, so far as structures are concerned, a coherent image, even if we have to admit that we know regions like the Theban region and above all the Delta relatively poorly for this period.

One could of course object that the sources from the imperial period are much more numerous and give us a much tighter web of information. It is possible, however, to come to an explanation of a very different sort. There is between these two bodies of documents in the first place a fundamental difference of coherence in the overall behaviour of the local dominant classes. Parallel to that, there is an equally fundamental difference in the socio-economic structures of the two periods, with the one offering little scope and the other a sufficient scope for the coherent development of directing classes.[2] Yet

---

[2] I do not intend to attach any necessarily favourable prejudgement to the coherence of behaviours or of socio-economic structures, as these might be nothing more than the sclerosis of a

Egypt remained what it had been, a land with wide-spread cultivation of wheat.

How can we make specific what seems at first like a subjective approach to the papyrological documentation? I intend here to approach this question with a summary evaluation of the structural tensions that operated on Ptolemaic society, and especially its component of Greek culture.[3] To this end, I shall discuss three groups of documents belonging respectively to the third, second and first centuries. The choice of these groups is in a sense arbitrary, but it has the merit of allowing me to confront at least one type of the numerous difficulties that threatened the harmony of the Ptolemaic royal system. For all social behaviours are complex, and we will get only as far as the beginnings of the investigation.

I could for the third century base the inquiry on the papyri called the 'Revenue Laws', in order to emphasise the conflicts of interests that the king tried to balance by means of his regulations, although he was in fact the source of the conflicts. I am thinking here particularly of the conflicts between the interests of the agricultural administration, the financial administration, the controllers who supervised this financial administration, the more or less independent businessmen who farmed the royal revenues, the small local contractors, and all the guarantors who were involved in the tax-farming system of the third century. But such a source is too specialised and still too stamped with its Greek models.[4] It does, however, place squarely in front of us the problem of competitive accumulation by Greeks in a limited economic sphere, without any noticeable increase in productivity generated by their presence.

The 'archive of Zenon'[5] appears to us more and more like a cluster of complex economic activities and less like the papers of the estate of 10,000 arouras of the *dioiketes* Apollonios. The work of Claude Orrieux in particular has brought into focus the part of the archive that reveals the lucrative personal activities of Zenon and others.[6] Zenon, a Greek from Caria, appears first in Palestine and Alexandria

---

group or a system. The Ptolemaic 'incoherence' certainly created some positive outcomes for the big contractors and near-feudal landholders of which Roman Egypt would be ignorant.

[3] The tensions in the 'integrated cultural system' of the Egyptians and factors of disintegration in this system are treated in Chapter 18.

[4] For a discussion of these texts, see Chapter 13.

[5] For an extraordinary point of departure and survey of the archive, see Pestman et al. (1981). The classic syntheses are now old: Rostovtzeff (1922), early and much-debated, and Préaux (1947). See also the more recent attempt at synthesis by Orrieux (1983).

[6] Orrieux (1981).

as the confidential agent of a powerful personage. As Apollonios'
agent he soon becomes responsible for the development of 2,700
hectares of new land in the Fayyum. In this role he succeeded
Panakestor, another Carian Greek, who was the true reclaimer of the
domain at Philadelphia. In this entire rich body of documents, the
fragility of the relationships that existed between these Greeks –
whoever they were – and the arable land, the unshakeable foundation
of economic power in Egypt, becomes apparent. And yet this is a
milieu in which the solidarity around the king is particularly perceptible and effective. To be sure, the deeper reason for the fragility of
these relationships rests precisely in the status of the arable land,
which is essentially the property of the king, and to a lesser degree of
the temples. That is, the Greeks, Macedonians and Thracians whom
immigration had brought to Egypt, whether they were soldiers or
royal officials or not, found hardly any reasonably broad scope for
action, outside of Alexandria, except for the army, bureaucracy or
occasional tertiary activities. Everything seems to indicate, moreover,
that these activities could often be very remunerative, especially under
the early Ptolemies. Think for example of the higher civil and military
careers or, in the golden age of the monetary economy, of the exploitation of the new economic order by banking and the more important
tax-farming contracts. All the same, we must not allow ourselves to
be excessively hypnotised by the Theocritean representation of an
Egypt of inexhaustible riches, where the wealth of the palace of a rich
king is the symbol of everyone's wealth. But our purpose here is not
to define and evaluate this economy.

The 'archive of Zenon' marks for us the limits of the hold of
Graeco-Macedonian circles on the land. The domain of Apollonios,
even though he was the *dioiketes* and a good master, belonged to
Apollonios only by a revocable title. It matters little for us to know if
the *dôrea* was lost to him because of his death or because he fell into
disgrace, or simply because he got rid of an estate the profitability of
which was insufficient. In any case, his involvement with the estate
must be recognised as short-term. And this temporary character has
repercussions on every level of the Greek intervention on the *dôrea*.
Panakestor is a bird of passage, who probably left the estate to enter
the king's service,[7] or because he was dismissed by Apollonios for
Zenon's benefit. Zenon himself had an ambiguous relationship with
the same land. He was the agent of Apollonios, but very quickly he

---

[7] Cf. *PSI* V 502.5.

launched himself into the direct exploitation of other land. As soon as the allocations of *klêroi* in the neighbouring estates began, Zenon started to lease a significant part of their land from the cleruchs, and he set out to work them with Greek or Egyptian foremen or by turning them over to deputies.[8]

What I would emphasise in this type of activity is that they created a hierarchy of economic interests in land which was subject to instability as a result of royal actions and with which Greeks, on various bases – cleruchs, agricultural entrepreneurs, foremen, businessmen, but also royal functionaries – had involvements which at first sight appear complementary, but which in reality were redundant and competitive. Because of the short-term character of their status and their basis for involvement, it is evident that these activities could quickly come into conflict with one another, the more easily because growth in the land's productivity must have ended rapidly. This omnipresent latency of conflict was permanent among the Greeks who were trying to develop remunerative activities in the weak and purely parasitic field of action that an agrarian economy based on royal property left to them.

I will cite just one example, but a symbolic example coming from the archive of Zenon,[9] one taken from among the conflicts between free Greek entrepreneurs and Greek bureaucrats, whom Claire Préaux studied in her excellent work on the detrimental economic and social effects of the responsibility of officials.[10] A Greek named Demokrates was involved, perhaps rather incidentally, in the traffic in wheat. He bought 50 artabas of wheat from Egyptian harvesters. Now the toparch Philokles had these 50 artabas seized on the grounds that they were actually due to the king from the peasants. We do not know just what the source of the conflict was. Perhaps the purchase of wheat was fraudulent despite Demokrates' protestations. But if there was fraud, it is because there was social tension produced by the restriction of access to wheat. Perhaps also, as Préaux suggests, the toparch was in dire straits because he had not managed to gather enough wheat to complete the deliveries that he was responsible for making as a bureaucrat, and he knew that only illegal action would save him temporarily.

---

[8] The lists of beneficiaries of regular grain payments in Reekmans (1966) or in Orrieux (1981: 319–23) probably give only a partial picture of the accumulation of men attached to the working of the estate.

[9] *P. Cair. Zen.* III 59322.

[10] Préaux (1939: 444–50, 514–33), with a clear exposition of the conflictual consequences of the responsibility of officials.

The critical lesson to be drawn from this incident, for which it would not be difficult to find other parallels, is that the types of activity which were left open to the initiative of these two Greeks, the small businessman Demokrates and the bureaucrat Philokles, were limited to relationships easily capable of becoming conflictual. Indeed, they are parasitical in contradictory ways on the royal agricultural economy. Put in other terms, the Graeco-Macedonian milieu is united against the Egyptian milieu, the more united in that it is simultaneously privileged and in a minority; but because of the narrowness of the manoeuvring room left to the Greeks by the economic system and the instability of the situations in which many of them found themselves, that milieu had more or less active tensions. And these tensions were complicated; even in the petty conflict of Demokrates and Philokles, the tension abounds. If Kriton, who was protecting Demokrates, intervened with Moschion, the toparch's superior, and if the letter wound up with Zenon, the *dioiketes'* agent, it was in order that he might intervene and take the tension higher, so that the matter might either be suppressed or keep going and get settled at yet another level.

We might imagine that these tensions must have taken on considerable proportions in the second century, when Egypt was faced with a period when the equilibrium among the various components of the Ptolemaic system was ruptured, above all by two factors: dynastic disputes and indigenous movements. These, in turn, are probably not the causes, but some of the external signs of a profound dysfunction in the Ptolemaic royal system.

Here we must take another short cut, by taking *P. Tebt.* I 5 as our sample for the second century.[11] This text has the advantage of locating our Greeks in rather more generalised perspectives, yet at the same time more directly centred on the will of the royal power, than the archive of Zenon. We shall see that this important text brings to light above all the conflicts which undermined the cohesion of the Ptolemaic royal system rather than offering for these conflicts any solutions rooted simultaneously in Greek solidarity and a harmonious organisation of the ethnic and social components of the kingdom.

P. Tebt. I 5 brings together at least forty-six royal ordinances attempting, as Rostovtzeff put it, to 'pacify the country' by a series of

---

[11] Republished as *C. Ord. Ptol.* 53, along with fragments from other copies as *C. Ord. Ptol.* 53*bis* and 53*ter*.

measures of amnesty or of confirmation of former rights. It dates from the year 118, at the end – more apparent than real – of a dynastic crisis. This assembly of measures has evoked various judgements. Grenfell and Hunt, with that tenderness for a document that often characterises a text's first editor as he brings it into the world, saw in it proof of the enlightened wisdom of Ptolemy VIII Euergetes II and disproof of the image given of him in the ancient historians.[12] Since then, the analysis of this document has led to very divergent assessments.

Before seeing how *P. Tebt.* I 5 fits into our inquiry, we may turn to one of those assessments, in this case that offered by Claire Préaux to the congress of papyrology in Florence in 1935. She raised the question there of the ineffectuality of the Ptolemies' edicts,[13] with *P. Tebt.* I 5 as one of the major elements in any analysis of Ptolemaic policy. Certainly her paper seems today strongly marked by the historical approach to social phenomena in Ptolemaic Egypt. Now that, under the influence of the later work of Rostovtzeff and Préaux, we tend to give pride of place to the sociological approach to historical phenomena, the paper has rather aged. None the less it is striking to discover in this paper of the youthful Préaux – she was not yet thirty – among its premises an affirmation that 'the weakness of the laws is the sign of a lack of harmony among the political entities which make up a state'. It is an astonishing prescience that led her to state as a starting-point what I have been trying to establish as the conclusion of an investigation made from a different point of view. And yet we were both basing ourselves on *P. Tebt.* I 5, which was one of the major sources of Préaux's article.

Thanks to the richness and variety of the matters treated in this papyrus, the document is probably more important for what it teaches us today about the ills of the regime than it was then for its actual consequences, whether immediate or deferred, for the troubled situation of Egypt at the end of the second century. Above all, we must not treat it as a provisional end of a period – or even of a sort of internal Hundred Years War – following the battle of Raphia.[14] In reality, this assemblage of ordinances is not original and does no more than repeat, at least in part, *prostagmata* issued in the past. For example, *P. Tebt.* I 6 (*C. Ord. Ptol.* 47) not only already protects in 140/139 a

---

[12] *The Tebtunis Papyri* I (London 1902) 19ff.

[13] Préaux (1936).

[14] On the prudence with which the historian must interpret the presence of Egyptian soldiers in the Ptolemaic army and particularly at Raphia as a determinative factor in an 'Egyptian nationalism', see the synthesis of Peremans (1983).

sanctuary against the robberies and abuses that *P. Tebt.* I 5 was to forbid in a general manner later on, but the earlier text makes explicit reference to a royal ordinance of still older date on the protection that the king gave to the sacred revenues. A series of *prostagmata* concerned with the protection of the rights of sanctuaries, *P. Tebt.* III 699 (*C. Ord. Ptol.* 43), of 145/144, is not necessarily the ordinance to which *P. Tebt.* I 6 is alluding, but what little remains of it offers significant verbal reminiscences of the amnesty decrees of 118. These repetitious edicts point up simultaneously the structural character of the disorders and the inability of the government to remedy with new burdens the tensions which the amnesties and prohibitions describe precisely. *P. Tebt.* I 5 is the most complete witness to the totality of 'ordinances of amnesty and supplementary *prostagmata*' that Ptolemy VIII Euergetes II had issued in his name and in the name of Cleopatra his sister and Cleopatra his wife, and of which the copies or extracts were discovered in the papers of the *komogrammateus* Menches.

The text begins with a series of amnesty measures, first of all with a general amnesty for all crimes, no matter how grave, from unintentional acts of negligence right up to grave crimes which have been the object of judicial investigation or even conviction. Two almost obligatory exceptions are made, murder and pillaging a sanctuary.

Next comes the general amnesty for those who have abandoned their domicile as a result of some accusation, particularly those accused of brigandage. Finally, in a whole series of *prostagmata*, the sovereigns renounce collecting arrears of taxes, licences and debts to the treasury. These measures betray resignation and inability to recover these arrears from those in debt to the king or from their guarantors: the sureties, the tax farmers and the royal financial bureaucrats. The amnesty is here the only means of resolving the intolerable tensions among these groups, tensions which turned into sources of anarchy once Ptolemaic structures were subjected to exceptional pressures.

Without going into textual detail, it is of some interest, in trying to locate these areas of tension, to compare what the royal ordinances provide for the clergy, on one hand, and for the various culturally Greek groups on which the crown had to be able to depend, on the other. The matter is the more interesting in that the entire policy of the Ptolemies in the second and first centuries has traditionally been presented as being, at least in part, one of concessions to the Egyptian clergy – in order, it is claimed, to secure their indispensable assistance in keeping the peasants, artisans and native soldiers exploited by the foreign power and its agents in passive obedience. Now one can hardly deny that there was a good-neighbour policy between the Ptolemaic kings and all or part of the Egyptian clergy. That is, after all, a commonplace trait in royal policy. But to see this Egyptian clergy as a permanent competitor for power, a competitor to be bought off at any price, is a dangerous extrapolation from the sources. Even in the most extreme form that any actual break between the upper clergy and the monarchy really took, namely the secession of the Thebaid at the start of the second century with obvious priestly involvement, we are dealing much more, in my view, with an act of response to a certain political and military void, a failure by the Ptolemaic occupier, rather than with a nationalistic religious dynamic. The real rebellion of the Thebaid, after all, under Ptolemy IX Soter II, ended with the destruction of the Theban priestly power.

Analysed from this point of view, *P. Tebt.* I 5 hardly looks like evidence for important concessions made to the temples by the Ptolemies. We look in vain for such in the texts. If we look through the entirety, we find that the decrees re-establish, or rather try as best they can to re-establish, the temples, both Egyptian and Greek, in their ancient rights. *Prostagmata* 13 and 14 (ll. 50–61) imagine that the sacred land and the revenues of the sanctuaries will remain the property of the temples, and that no one will have the right to appropriate the lands, their management, or the sacred revenues in general. *Prostagma* 14, indeed, shows the totally conservative character of measures that are in any case short-lived: a prohibition against taking possession by violence of that which is dedicated to the gods, prohibition of torture, prohibition of cornering sacred lands or the revenues of temples and religious associations.[15] To be sure, *prostagmata* 15–19 and 21 provide amnesty to priests for certain misdemeanours, particularly of a fiscal nature, but these concern the past, and in no case do they represent the conversion through the *prostagma* of an abuse into a privilege. Finally, if *prostagma* 22 (ll. 83–4) confirms the inviolability of places that were *asyloi*, that is still not a matter of the decree's enlarging the zones of asylum. In no way does this package of measures contain any new concessions to the clergy. This conclusion is all the more troubling because, when the king was legislating at the same time on the subject of officials and cleruchs, his attitude

---

[15] See also *prostagma* 10 (ll. 36–44), where the sovereigns order those who have trespassed on sacred land to leave it, without having to do anything other than pay the dues for the last year of their usurpation.

was different: he was forced to swallow a part of the usurpations committed by these last. Certainly, in observing that the cleruchs and other occupants of various types of land have seized royal land, *prostagma* 10 (ll. 36–48) by no means ratifies these usurpations of grain land, grazing land and land planted in oil crops. But the edict clears the usurpers of liability for their cultivation and unpaid dues on these lands, and indeed it goes still further. In making the delinquents pay only the dues for the past year, the sovereigns allowed them a legitimate place on the usurped lands even if this means their coming back into the Ptolemaic system of the king's land, into the system of access granted on revocable terms to grain land which remains the king's property.

This is paradoxically confirmed by *prostagma* 25 (ll. 99–101), where the sovereigns ratify the trespasses and usurpations more or less regularised by purchase from the treasury when it is a matter of houses, vineyards, orchards or boats,[16] that is, of types of property not reserved to the king, zones in which the system tolerates private property, i.e., sovereign access to secondary means of production. It is sufficient to analyse the constituents of this 'free' zone to observe that these abuses mainly concerned the group of those who were culturally Greeks.

A notable contrast is presented by *prostagma* 11 (ll. 44–8), which contents itself with guaranteeing to cleruchs and native soldiers the peaceful possession of the plots that had been given them according to the rules. At the most, it shelters them from a technique which must have been widely used during the time of troubles: the confiscation of their land on the basis of one or another accusation.

The edicts addressed to functionaries reveal yet another psychological approach on the part of the sovereigns to the abuses committed by the agents of royal power. Dorothy Crawford has shown how the theme of the 'good official of Ptolemaic Egypt' – perhaps both an old Egyptian theme and a political philosophy? – is in official documents and in petitions an ideology of power, but above all the rhetorical opposite to the customary delinquency of local authorities and the vague response of an authority which shirks its responsibilities.[17] The ordinances devoted to the misdeeds of abusive authority have the attraction of remonstrances. The picture that emerges from them is too much that of what one cannot do, even if one is the *strategos*, for us to be able to speak

---

[16] The text makes no reference to the irregular character of the acquisition of these goods, but only that can explain the need for an ordinance like this.

[17] Crawford (1978).

accurately of a code of good conduct. But the aim is general and does not imply in its form that the officials in office have committed abuses. No sanctions are foreseen, except for the *sitologoi* and controllers who use false measures when the taxes in kind are being collected. The penalty of death reminds us here that this abuse affects the royal revenues, in particular those that are essential to the survival of the royal system in Egypt: the revenues from the land. We will return to this point.

The portrait of delictual behaviour by royal bureaucrats is striking: usurpation of royal and sacred land, extortion of money (including by torture), contributions raised for personal benefit, illegal requisition of housing, requisition of supplies for the benefit of the official, including domestic animals, fine cloth or boats, and organisation of a private judicial system founded on arbitrary arrest.

It is probable that the natives of every rank as well as the temples were often the victims of the abuses carefully described as acts not to be committed.[18] And many documents tell us that it is in this population that one finds most of the victims of these abuses. It is of more direct concern to us here to note first that even the very highest officials are the objects of these reprimands. That implies organised abuses or, to put it another way, the existence of networks competing with the king for benefiting from the revenues of the arable land and from its resources of manpower and goods. But it is also interesting to note that, if the priest and peasant as victims of abuses seem almost to be a recurrent stereotype in the sequence of edicts (and probably for good reasons), a considerable number of these abuses were felt also by the Greeks – and here too there are numerous instances in the documents. In any event, the edicts tried in this way to resolve the tensions among Greeks, debtors and creditors, collectors and payers, producers and parasites, strong and weak. The fact that the ordinances express these tensions among Greeks very unclearly is probably the result of the fact that the government did not perceive them as clearly as the illegal relationships, so easily described, of the Greek administrator and the Egyptian subject.[19] None the less, these tensions existed. We have seen this reality for the third century, and we will see it still in the first century.

---

[18] *Prostagma* 23, already exceptional in mentioning a penalty, although it bears on officials, makes explicit reference (with the euphemism *prospiptei*) to the existence of abuses.

[19] An analogous vagueness makes it possible to ignore the tensions inside the zone of Egyptian culture with its various groups. To be fair to the person who drew up the ordinances, it must be pointed out that actually neither the abuses, nor the losses undergone, nor the conflicts can be defined by the overall relationships of one cultural group with the other.

One final remark about the second century: the land that is protected by sheltering the royal cultivators from extortion of money, confiscations, requisitions or mere encroachments on the royal domain is also very present in the ordinances. That represents self-protection by the crown, for all these abuses are fundamentally an illegal means of profiting from the only large-scale production in Egypt, that which the king kept for himself as far as he could. Now this protection is indispensable. Even in the papers of Menches there are several complaints, in complete agreement with one another, from the royal peasants of Kerkeosiris. On 23 August 113 – thus five years after *P. Tebt.* I 5 – a cavalry settler, a former resident now transferred to another cleruchic location, and a Greek of the village, along with several armed men, attacked and looted the houses of these peasants (among them, one Demas son of Seuthes), in the absence of the latter, who had gone off to work or to collect rents. We have only the version of the villagers of Kerkeosiris concerning this raid, which was perhaps a settling of accounts or a punitive expedition rather than an act of brigandage or an episode of intimidation. The incident, probably commonplace, is particularly meaningful because it is the exact contemporary of the normalised picture which the same archive of Menches gives us for the area of Kerkeosiris in the period 120–113. In the statistics, we discern the peaceful operation of direct working of land or of the leasing of the plots of the Greek settlers and the Egyptian *machimoi*, of sacred land and of the royal land with its peasant lessees. There are just two shadows on this sunny landscape: the abundance of infertile land and, rather variably, of land which has not been cultivated. And it is in this setting, with its well-maintained land registers, that this raid of the king's men into the dwellings of royal peasants breaks out, one of the types of delicts described in the ordinances under the heading of brigandage. But this type would normally develop into a conflict with other of the king's men or into some non-cooperation which harms the king while discreetly preserving Greek solidarity.

The Herakleopolite papyri of the first century present similar situations of conflict, some of them episodic and violent, others latent and more profound, connected to the economic competition between Greeks of different statuses or between these Greeks and the king. The dossier of the cessions of katoikic land, the *parachôrêseis*, is discussed in Chapter 11.[20] But it cannot be left completely aside here,

---

[20] These acquire a new dimension as a result of the land registers published by W. Brashear in *BGU* XIV.

because it is at the heart of our problem. These documents are used by the holder of a katoikic allotment (even a woman) to cede the katoikic land by recording it in the records of the cavalry office under the name of a different cavalryman on a permanent basis. Since Kunkel in 1928, it has been supposed, with various nuances, that such a mechanism corresponded to a power, more or less limited to military circles, to bequeath or alienate royal land originally granted on revocable title to the cleruch. We would thus be seeing here, following a normal evolution of all revocable possession towards quasi-property, the competition of the king and of the settler for granted land being resolved for the king only in the sense of his retention of a fiscal grip on the harvest of the allotment,[21] with the loss of the power of disposing of the land. Actually, the *parachôrêsis* sometimes affects relatively minor amounts of land and is executed solely for the benefit of other settlers. It seems to me that the *parachôrêsis* is on the one hand, from an economic point of view, a permanent adjustment of katoikic space (of cavalry land, as it happens), and, on the other hand, in the mind of the person ceding the land, as a form of having the katoikic allotment worked by a third party, a kind of permanent lease with the total rent due up front.[22] There is thus no need to see in the *parachôrêsis* a new element in the competition of the king and the cleruch for arable land. In reality, this competition had long been unequal because of the difficulty of recruiting new mercenaries and because of the need to privilege the sons of cleruchs who might one day be able to take up the relay. The interest of the *parachôrêseis*, on a social level, is to show how the old soldiery of cavalry settlers, settled on the king's arable land, had become a closed society; by this very fact it is in effect able to maintain as a collectivised entitlement the rights to the land that the king had originally granted on an individual basis. Probably a study of cleruchic wills would reach a similar result.

The land registers and petitions to the *strategos* of the Herakleopolite open broader perspectives on the structural tensions of the population of Egypt and on the permanence of a royal system which played a part in those tensions.

On the qualitative level, the land registers of *BGU* XIV give the impression that there was a great variety of types of connections

---

[21] This would change hardly anything for the king, from an economic point of view.

[22] The cession contract does not mention any financial compensation, but that does not mean that none can have been paid in some form or other, or even that such payment was not normal.

between the population and the arable land, ranging from private land to several types of direct or indirect working of farms. From a quantitative point of view, however, the land registers show something quite different. The royal land, the queen's dowry, and the lands dependent on the *idios logos* (another branch of the government) make up the bulk of the arable land, and their surface area is generally of a different order of magnitude from that of other categories of land. But this accounting points up as well the permanence of tension-producing factors already noted in the third and second centuries.

First, there is instability in who actually works the land, an area in which the settler was privileged. The case of the *metepigraphê* (transfer) of *BGU* XIV 2441 (ll. 115–24) is exemplary in this respect, even if the interpretation of this text, with its very dense style, is not entirely certain. A *dioiketes* Ptolemaios left his son some land of poor quality and unclear status, made up of dispersed plots cultivated by various Egyptian peasants. These lands were recovered from the son by the *idios logos*, and before long transferred by this royal office to a certain Heliodoros, perhaps a high official or an officer. This was a quick turnover, but one which shows us officials and even very high officials among the groups competing for control of the working of the arable land. In Chapter 11 I discuss the case of Hierax, another high official, the *eklogistes* of the nome, who took on lease various plots of land, amounting altogether to a significant amount.[23] He declares himself as the cultivator, even though he does not live on these lands. His nephew, a cavalry settler, acted as his managing agent for one of the estates and was arrested after a conflict between Hierax and a village collector. The latter confiscated (or stole, depending on one's point of view) a load of seed-grain. The same year, another cavalry settler who operated 130 arouras for Hierax in another village noted that he was in conflict with a Greek who had pastured his sheep on Hierax's fields. In each of these two cases, the *strategos* – the highest official of the nome – is asked for justice. Thus five levels of Greeks, involved in rural operations or in the maintenance of order in the countryside, oppose or join with one another on the king's land. It is not hard to see the advantage that a high official would have in this contest.

The figure of Hierax is comparable to that of the protectors of the temples, officials and higher officers, who appear in the

---

[23] Around this person cluster, in my view, a number of texts: *BGU* VIII 1821 and 1831; XIV 2432.5; 2436.12; 2444.83–92; and 2448.11.

contemporaneous asylum decrees as mediators with the king. The competition between the Greeks for the part of the rural economy that the king left them did not prevent some of them from forming a wealthy caste. For in the documentation of this period, one suspects more often than one can demonstrate the existence of powerful lineages, servants of their own interests as well as those of the king.

Separated in time and space, each with respect to the others and also with respect to the entirety of our Ptolemaic documentation, these three samples which we have chosen, all different from one another, do not seem at all to be foreign bodies in this documentation. Our three forays cannot by themselves cover the complex social and economic phenomena that troubled human relationships in Egypt and often weakened the royal system, even to the point of endangering it. But among the channels that we can follow in an attempt to flush out the structural causes of these tensions, there is one which appears like a filigree through the three groups, particularly in the first and third, and which turns up in hundreds of other texts as well: the problem of insufficient access to arable land for the Greeks and, particularly, access to wheat. All through the three centuries of the Hellenistic kingdom, the restrictions put on the working of the land by the very system of the royal agricultural economy were in contradiction with the overall dynamic of Greek immigration, which was a profit-seeking economy. Private land was poorly developed and remained a small factor compared to the commercial and artisanal activities that the Greeks could exploit. And this private land does not seem to have included grain land or land growing oil-bearing crops.

It was thus by indirect means that the Greeks played their part in the overwhelming bulk of the economy of Hellenistic Egypt that wheat represented. A Greek could be a royal official, a cleruch, an agricultural entrepreneur occupying a slot between cleruch and peasant, a business agent who, like Zenon, would be a parasite on rural society with numerous employees and servants dependant on him. But these constellations revolving in and around royal agriculture were only rarely stable. Those who could snatch a bit away from the king, for example the settlers, were not necessarily the active elements in the economy. Thus the land was unable to play the role of the stabiliser of society that other means of possession and working of the arable land, at once simpler, more direct and more open, were able to play in the Roman period. This explains the difference in coherence that I mentioned at the beginning between the documentation of the Ptolemaic and imperial periods.[24] The paradox of the Ptolemaic economy lies in its having installed, and often installed rather ineptly, a series of microcosms of competition (officials, cleruchs, managers, etc.) in a broadly based agricultural system of a royal type, partly inherited from the pharaohs and the Achaemenids. These microcosms had to live, directly or indirectly, off this land, along with the king and the royal peasants who alone were able to make it productive. Royal prestige could without undue difficulty impose a *modus vivendi* on the competitive appetites, thus tempering the solidarity of the minority in control, a solidarity embodied in the royal organisation of the territory. If the king's authority weakened, if dynastic struggles caused loyalty and the unity of values to be two-edged, if the economic response that the system was able to give to everyone's needs was insufficient, then the latent tensions among the competing Greeks and the tensions between the cultural groups living together would manifest themselves in conflicts and abuses. *P. Tebt.* I 5 is only indirectly an echo of the tensions created by the system, but it practically gives an inventory of the flood of these tensions when equilibrium is broken and of their unleashing at the worst moments of dynastic quarrels.

I would like to draw two further conclusions. First, in establishing the persistence of these tensions and the problems which they created in the Egyptian rural world, we are measuring the inability of the Ptolemies and their entourage to let the categories and ways of Greek thought – a poorly functioning monetary economy or the cleruchic system, for example – to evolve, pinned, as they were, to an organisation of the arable land which was exploited essentially outside these ways of thought.

Moreover, to end in a minor key, the different perspectives that functional analysis and structural analysis give us of the place that this group occupied in society and economy are demonstrated once more. In 1966, Alan Samuel, in a brilliant inquiry into the organisation of the nomarch's bureau, rightly came to the conclusion that the royal administration was suffering in the third century from a lack of qualified staff; this would explain numerous accumulations of roles and evident clashes between the theoretical organisational charge of functions, as it appears, for example, in the Revenue Laws, and the reality on the ground as it is obvious to us in the everyday documents

---

[24] It would be interesting to look more deeply into the problem of onomastics in the Fayyum. Naming was both stable and relatively localised in the Roman period, but at first sight it does not offer the same characteristics in the Ptolemaic period.

of the time.[25] On the contrary, the structural analysis of the Greek cultural group reveals, in the countryside, a problem of competition between the immigrants in the exploitation of the insufficient economic margin that the king's enormous grip on the land and on the land's revenues left them. These two facts are not contradictory.

---

[25] Samuel (1966).

Chapter 15

THE THIRD-CENTURY LAND-LEASES FROM THOLTHIS

☙

The publication by Wolfgang Müller of *BGU* X drew my attention to a set of Ptolemaic documents that fitted into the general framework of studies I was carrying out on the social components of the population of Hellenistic Egypt. In this chapter[1] I deal with a small group of texts limited in time, restricted to a single village and confined to one type of juridical transaction, the leasing and subletting of cleruchic holdings.

In fact, the nucleus of the texts we will be considering consists of a series of land-leases and receipts for rents drawn up at Tholthis in the Oxyrhynchite nome during the seventh, eighth, ninth and tenth years of Ptolemy IV Philopator. These documents come from mummy cartonnage, the yield of which is scattered over several collections, especially those of Berlin, Hamburg and Frankfurt.[2]

From the methodological point of view, it is both interesting and dangerous to centre our attention on such a small and uniform group of texts. It is interesting to study it separately mainly because I feel that as far as the third century BC is concerned, we tend to consider the documentation for that period as a whole, whereas in fact it covers a century of deep change in the way the Greeks behaved in the Nile valley, from the first military occupation to the progressive development of a Greek urban bourgeoisie. But it is not without danger to consider a small sample as a valid model only because it is homogeneous, even if we restrict its application to a limited period and area. Let Tholthis be taken as an example. All our documentation on third-century Tholthis comes from cleruchic circles. Does that imply, for instance, that there were large numbers of cleruchs at Tholthis, or that

---

[1] First delivered as a paper at the papyrological symposium held at the University of Illinois at Urbana in April 1976.

[2] *BGU* VI 1262–5, 1268–9, 1277–8; *BGU* X 1943–50, 1958–62, 1965, 1969–70; *P. Frankf.* 1, 2 (= *BGU* 1264), 4; *P. Hamb.* I 26 = II 189; *SB* III 6302–3; *P. Hamb.* II 188 + *P. Iena inv.* 905 (published by F. Uebel, *APF* 22–3 (1974) 111–14); *P. Hib.* I 90, II 263. There are many other documents of this period from Tholthis or in general from the Oxyrhynchite nome.

the land there consisted exclusively of cleruchic holdings? Further-more, do our land-leases represent the normal way cleruchs were han-dling their holdings? No matter what degree of improbability we assign to any of these possibilities, we can agree that Tholthis provides us with the possibility of studying the socio-economic conditions underlying cultivation of a certain number of cleruchic holdings.

With that restriction, we may establish that our land-leases from Tholthis point to one type of cultivation of *klêroi*: the surrender of the holding to third parties with part of the yield of the land coming back to the titular holder as a rent in kind.

A first significant feature of this group of contracts covering years 7 to 10 of Philopator is the fact that the lessor in the contracts is always a cleruch, with one half-noteworthy exception. This exception is a woman, but she is the mother of a cleruch, who is her *kyrios*, or legal representative, in this affair.[3] These cleruchs, including this last one, are all either privates of one military unit, *idiôtai* of the troup of Philon, or cleruchs 'not yet under a commander' (οὔπω ὑφ᾽ ἡγεμόνα). The lessees, by contrast, are always individuals designated as *tês epigonês*, 'of the descent', sometimes in partnership with one or two Egyptians or, in one case, with a cleruch 'not yet under a comman-der'. Can this opposition, cleruch as lessor vs. *tês epigonês* as lessee, be interpreted according to the classical social model whereby on the one hand, from the economic point of view, the holder of the land, here the cleruch, would be the strong party, while the lessee, here a *tês epigonês*, would be the weak party, condemned to short-term con-tracts and to producing at least in part for another person, the lessee? That would be an erroneous interpretation.

Let us briefly consider the status of the different parties at issue here. First of all, there are the holders of the land, the cleruchs who are part of the military or who are waiting for a military involvement; there are the *tês epigonês* (and on this point I agree with most of Oates's conclusions),[4] who are non-Egyptian civilians claiming a non-Egyptian origin, through a real or fake foreign origin – unlike the newcomers from Greece or elsewhere whose status was acquired by virtue of their birth abroad.

An analysis of the contracts indicates that the strong party, eco-nomically speaking, lies among the *tês epigonês*. This appears quite clearly, for almost half of the contracts involve either advance

---

[3] *BGU* X 1944.
[4] Oates (1963: esp. 60–1).

payments of rent or a loan to be repaid or subtracted from the rent. This brings us back to something familiar to the papyrologist: the various sorts of contracts which cover financial transactions warranted by the right of use, whether a house, fields or the work of human beings. The activity of the *tês epigonês* Aristolochos son of Stratios is indicative. Sometimes he acts alone,[5] sometimes with partners, among them a cleruch 'not yet under a commander',[6] but, and this is important, a cleruch who is going to give up his military title in order, in turn, to become a *tês epigonês* in a later transaction.[7]

At the end of the seventh year, during the month of Peritios,[8] Aristolochos and Straton rent Zopyrion's *klêros*, according to a lease not in our possession. Zopyrion is a private from Philon's troop. At the same time, Aristolochos agrees with Zopyrion to an advance payment of rent. Repayment of the loan is entered into the rent accounts not only for the eighth year but also for the ninth. Several months later,[9] in Hyperberetaios in year 8, Aristolochos acts alone. He now supplies another cleruch (a Macedonian 'not yet under a commander') with wheat, and this as an advance to cover future rents. At the same time, he signs a lease for the *klêros* of this cleruch. An additional element comes into play here: the contract is concluded several months before the traditional time for doing so. It is clear that at this very moment the holding was leased to someone else; the loan therefore includes a long-term option on the *klêros*. In this document of year 8, the rent in wheat (*ekphoria*) is to be taken for and from the crop of year 10, and the balance is eventually to be carried over to year 11. This contract is important because it helps dispel our original uncertainty as to the meaning of the first part of the document. One might have interpreted the advance payment of the rent for the coming year as an additional requirement set by the lessor. But in the second case the advance payment is to be recovered over a long term, and this indicates that the traditional lessor/lessee relationship does not exist between the two parties. Instead, their relationship is that of a creditor (the lessee) to a debtor (the lessor), or rather the relationship of the one who has economic means to produce (the lessee) to the one who has not. In addition, shortly afterwards, at the beginning of year 9, Aristolochos and Straton carry out a similar operation for

---

[5] *BGU* X 1959, *P. Hamb.* II 188 + *P. Iena inv.* 905.
[6] *P. Hamb.* I 26 = II 189, *BGU* X 1958, *BGU* VI 1265.
[7] *BGU* X 1944.
[8] *P. Hamb.* I 26 = II 189, *BGU* X 1958.
[9] *BGU* X 1959.

the *klêros* of a different cleruch, a 'Persian' who is a private in Philon's troop.[10] They advance him 100 artabas of wheat as rent not for year 9 but for year 11. Furthermore, we have two leases concerning other transactions of Aristolochos.

The first, *P. Hamb.* 188 + *P. Iena inv.* 905, is an ordinary one-year lease for the *klêros* of a *triakontarouros* (30-aroura cleruch). In the second document (*BGU* X 1944), Aristolochos signs with Straton. But in the meantime, as I have already pointed out, Straton has become a *tês epigonês*, and there is a third partner who is also a civilian. All three together lease, for one year, the land I mentioned earlier, the *klêros* belonging to a woman whose *kyrios* is her son, a cleruch of the troop of Philon.

The group contains other documents accompanying such loans guaranteed by the right of cultivation of the plot and by the rents. They show two other variants at Tholthis. *SB* III 6303 is a cession with loan of a piece of land by a private in the troop of Philon to two *tês epigonês*. This lease exceptionally covers a period of two years. By contrast, in two other cases, lease and loan are combined in one document. This time it is a question of an advance payment (*prodoma*) in silver. In one case, *P. Frankf.* 1, a *tês epigonês* lends 60 silver drachmas to a cleruch not yet under a commander and leases the latter's entire *klêros* according to the usual terms: no loan of seeds, a duration of one year, harvest in year 10, and payment of the rent in Dystros of year 11. The loan in silver has to be repaid by the lessor before the rent is paid to him in wheat; otherwise the sum will be subtracted from the rent at the price of wheat on the threshing-floor. *BGU* VI 1262 is a similar document, very probably from Tholthis. Each of these contracts confirms our picture of the socio-economic relationship between the cleruch (weak party) and the *tês epigonês* (strong party), at least in our group of documents.

Is the *tês epigonês* to be considered the actual cultivator of the holding he leases, whether alone or in partnership? Does he use his economically stronger position to secure more land to be directly cultivated by himself? This would be strange, and nothing in the Tholthis contracts leads to the idea that this so-called lessee intended to work on the fields he leases.

In the Tholthis documents it seems that a situation I have noted elsewhere for the Fayyum at Tebtynis can be found here as well. The *tês epigonês* of the contracts, at any rate, often seems to be a middleman

---

[10] *BGU* VI 1265.

who puts the land into the hands of Egyptian peasants. I should first like to examine the problem in the light of a contract from a neighbouring village, Takona, found in the same cartonnage made from the documents of cleruchs from the troop of Philon. *BGU* VI 1266, dated in the year 203, presents us with the case of a *tês epigonês* who has leased a *klêros* that is found under the name of an orphan. He shares his rights to cultivate the *klêros* with three partners. There are several important factors in the provisions of the contract. First of all, we know one of the partners as a lender of money and wheat. Secondly, the profits and costs are divided among the four partners as follows: ⅕, ⅕, ⅕ and ⅖; this indicates that the share of profit obtained is not a function of direct common cultivation of the fields, but of differentiated investment in the transaction. The third factor, which elucidates the second, is that the contribution which each partner is required to make concerns the supply of seed and operating expenses. We are dealing with a small-scale capitalist group intervening between the cleruch, or holder of the land, who either does not want to cultivate it or is unable to do so, and the peasant who has no means of production of his own, and who will till the land with heavier rent requirements than those provided in the lease between the *klêros*-holder and the civilian middleman.

This general phenomenon of the absence from the land of an important portion of the Greeks who are involved in administration and cultivation of land is found elsewhere, and I have tried in Chapters 8 and 11 to discern this phenomenon and its counterpart, the effective role of Egyptian peasants on cleruchic land and on royal land leased by Greek middlemen, mainly on the basis of the Tebtynis papyri. This phenomenon does not appear as clearly in the Tholthis contracts, but that is mainly the result of the nature of the documents resulting from transactions between Greek cleruchs and Greek middlemen *tês epigonês*. Even so, on that level, Egyptians are not absent from the Tholthis documents. In some of the contracts we find an Egyptian directly associated with a Greek as a lessee,[11] the latter being always a *tês epigonês* except in one case where the associated lessee is a cleruch. But are the two associates, the Greek and the Egyptian, on the same level? One might theorise that the Egyptian associate also belongs to the category of middleman with a certain capital, and we cannot exclude that possibility. But, from what we know about the

---

[11] *BGU* X 1943, 1946, 1947; *P. Frankf.* 2 (cf. *BGU* VI 1263 and 1264); *P. Frankf.* 4. Cf. *P. Hib.* II 263.

role of Egyptians in agriculture, it is far more probable that in many cases the Egyptian is associated with a Greek middleman not because he contributes his own capital, but because he brings to the partnership his own labour or that of a team of Egyptian peasants.

Furthermore, some of the texts advance our understanding of the role of Egyptians in the agricultural structure of the *chôra*. *BGU* VI 1269, for instance, probably from Tholthis, shows how a *tês epigonês* Greek sublets to an Egyptian part of a *klêros* he leased from a cleruch.

In short, in the Tholthis land-leases a socio-economic system appears in a clearer light than was the case in the study of the situation in Tebtynis in Chapter 11. There, in fact, our attention is focused on Greek/Egyptian relations, taking into account the frequent absence of the Greek from the soil and the physical presence of the Egyptian in the fields, with all of the consequences this situation could have, even if most of the Egyptians were exploited by the absent Greeks. The Tholthis file makes it possible to be more precise in this description. The cleruch has the privilege of holding part of the available good soil. A class of Greek civilians, settled in the *chôra*, has at its disposal some economic means with a certain flexibility in using these resources. The Greeks may grant loans in money or in wheat, but they can also use their capital to involve themselves in the cultivation of the soil, whether cleruchic land, as in the Tholthis documents, or royal land. This involvement is accepted, and even sought, by cleruchs. For various reasons, one of which is their military engagement, cleruchs may not have been able themselves to cultivate the fields they received or to exercise direct control over the cultivation of this land by Egyptian peasants. Perhaps a certain degree of indebtedness on the part of the cleruchs may have hastened the development of this situation. This is nothing new, and we could extend the dichotomy between cleruch and free Greek, whether free Greek originating from Greece or from Asia Minor or free Greek *tês epigonês*, to other periods of the third and second centuries. And we are immediately reminded of the versatile activity of Zenon after the end of his tenure as Apollonios' manager in Philadelphia.

In conclusion, I would like simply to emphasise that the social dichotomy that I have demonstrated between cleruchs and, we may suppose, civil officials, on the one hand, and Greeks not in the service of the army or administration, on the other, is a tendency, not a rule. For instance, *BGU* X 1943 reveals more complex structures. Hermias, a cleruch not yet under a commander, has a *klêros* of 30 arouras. This *klêros* is leased to another cleruch, Pyrrhos, also not yet under a commander, who in turn leases the *klêros* to a *tês epigonês* associated with an Egyptian shepherd, accompanying the lease with a loan of seeds. In this case, a man not yet under a commander, in fact a cleruch with loose ties to the army, acts as a middleman between the landholder and the Egyptian and his Greek associate, who has at his disposal movables to invest in production. Here too we could easily find parallels in the third-century documents of other provenance. The case of Pyrrhos would be an exception only if we were to take as a rule the relationship we found in Tholthis between a certain number of cleruchs and a certain number of men *tês epigonês*. I was not searching for a rule, but I have tried to bring into the foreground a double facet of the social structure of Egypt at the end of the third century.

It would be a broader topic to insert this relationship into the inter-action of two socio-economic elements: (1) on the one hand, the inability of cleruchs fully to assume the role of a production factor in the cultivation of the soil they had at their disposal; (2) on the other hand, the existence of a Greek (including Macedonian and Thracian) population with the means to take the economic initiative and to intervene in cultivation, even though they had no personal access to landholding. Taken on an even bigger scale, this could be the begin-ning of a new approach to the study of the various levels of Greek population in Egypt in the third century. Two factors have condi-tioned papyrologists in this matter: first, the omnipresence in our doc-uments of the king's administration and the king's holding of the land; second, the myth we have created of a Ptolemaic state economy. Analysis of groups of texts, such as the land-leases drawn up at Tholthis, will make increasingly evident the number of Greeks who were neither officials nor cleruchs, and will indicate that they were an important element in the development of the Greek community settled in the *chôra* into the society of Greek notables that we see in the Roman metropoleis.[12]

---

[12] Cf. Préaux (1947), where private types of economy developed by some Greeks are alluded to rather than specifically studied and described. See also the not quite satisfactory approach to the problem in Rostovtzeff (1941: I, 328–32), on 'tax farmers', 'Greek bourgeoisie' and 'foreigners of lower standing', with such statements as the following: 'In any case a Greek bourgeoisie was in the course of formation in Egypt. The Ptolemies were aware of the fact and opened the doors of their new economic system to this new class.' Was the door ever closed? And was the class really new?

PART IV: GREEKS AND EGYPTIANS

Chapter 16

GREEK ECONOMY AND EGYPTIAN SOCIETY IN THE THIRD CENTURY

ᥩ

In 332, Alexander the Great conquered Egypt without difficulty. The Delta and even the Nile valley were well known to the Greeks, who had long traversed them as mercenaries or landed as merchants. Some permanent settlements, like the city of Naucratis or the Greek quarter of Memphis, certainly aided the Macedonian's invasion, along with no doubt the Egyptians' dislike of the common enemy, the Persians. When he set off again, Alexander left behind him both a Graeco-Macedonian army of occupation and a new city, Alexandria, which was destined to grow beyond all expectation – Alexandria, the city of Sarapis, which from the beginning and for a thousand years to come lived with a double destiny: Hellenism and the rule of Egypt.[1] A generation or two later, Egypt had become a Macedonian kingdom in which Egyptians and Greeks lived with some other, less numerous ethnic groups.

One of the most interesting directions of papyrological research has been the study of the connections that we can discern in the Ptolemaic period between the dominant Greek minority and the Egyptian majority. Here we will try to set forth some of the consequences that the intrusion of new economic forms connected to the wide-spread Greek settlement in Egypt, particularly a monetised economy, had for various indigenous social groups.

Such an investigation, to be sure, demands by way of preliminaries a definition of just what the Greek and Egyptian populations were. One approach to this problem – the only really productive one – has been the critical study of the names of the thousands of persons mentioned in the papyri. In this connection I would single out the work of the 'School of Leuven', above all the *Prosopographia Ptolemaica*, its crowning achievement. In particular, I would cite a series of articles by Willy Peremans in which he considers the proportions of

---

[1] The second half of the fourth century has become somewhat better known as a result of excavations at Saqqara. Cf. Turner (1974, 1975).

Egyptians and Greeks discernible in various areas of the economic
and administrative structures of the Ptolemaic kingdom.[2] This attention to concrete detail – and there are other scholars who have
pursued similar paths – is all the more important in that, parallel to
these studies but in a more speculative vein, during the past generation a fundamental working hypothesis, that of the mixing of cultures
in the Greek Hellenistic East, has been dismantled by Claire Préaux
and other scholars. Thus the notion of the interpenetration of two
societies and two cultures has been largely replaced by the idea of the
coexistence of two largely autonomous socio-cultural entities, even if
there are noticeable areas of osmosis, such as religion, and even tran-
sitional zones from one group to the other.

Turning our attention back to the studies aimed at discerning the
relative positions of the Greeks and the Egyptians in Ptolemaic society,
we cannot help noticing that, in general, the vision put forward of these
two groups has often been global and dichotomous. The discourse is
generally of 'Greeks' or 'Egyptians'. But other types of investigations
have established the heterogeneous character of each of these groups.
To be sure, the studies of Peremans mentioned earlier aimed principally
to discover whether the use of onomastic criteria in the sociology of
ethnic groups was legitimate for the entirety of the Hellenistic period.
But it only adds to the value of this complex inquiry to have established
that relations between Greeks and Egyptians took different forms in
various socio-cultural levels or professional activities.[3]

What impact did the opening to a monetary economy have upon
Egyptian civilisation, a civilisation based on an agriculture characterised by extensive irrigation and the dense occupation of rural
space? Two preliminary remarks are necessary. First, it would be mistaken to schematise matters too strongly by opposing an Egypt still
in the Bronze Age and practising a natural economy to the sudden and
total presence of an economy conceived and realised in monetary
terms, both at the level of management and transactions and at the
level of fiscal control. Some Egyptian milieus were already familiar
with systems of exchange different from their own well before

[2] *Ancient Society* 1 (1970) 25–38 (general remarks); 2 (1971) 33–45 (civil and financial administration); 3 (1972) 67–76 (army and police); 4 (1973) 59–69 (clergy, notaries, courts); 5
(1974) 127–35 (agriculture and stock-raising); 6 (1975) 61–9 (commerce, industry, transport,
home life); 7 (1976) 167–76 (Alexandrian society). To these can be added Peremans (1975/6).
[3] This pattern appears also in the analysis by Swiderek (1954). Although the *dôrea* of
Apollonios was an exceptional case, the data from which cannot be generalised except with
caution, this documentation is useful for our purposes, particularly when it concerns the
activity of Zenon after he had left Apollonios' service.

Alexander, as a result of the Persian occupation and a considerable Greek presence. Even if it was intended to pay the Greek mercenary or trader, the Athenian tetradrachm had circulated and no doubt served more purposes than just hoarding when it arrived in Egyptian hands. Moreover, Egyptians had for centuries at least valued dowries and purchases, particularly of real estate, in quantities of precious metal and may even have been paid in such transactions with silver or gold. Secondly, we must not forget that in Greek and then Roman Egypt the monetary economy never encompassed more than a part of the total range of exchange and obligation, particularly salaries. Payments in kind, particularly in wheat, but also in oil, wine and other foodstuffs, remained one of the most striking realities of the economic life of Egypt, especially the countryside.[4]

What then was the situation with Egyptian society at the beginning of the Hellenistic period, and particularly in the domain of the economy? The scarcity of documentation for the fourth century and the very limited character of our insights into Egyptian society in the third century are both obstacles. At most, we perceive the continuity of traditional structures both socially and economically, structures the stability of which rested on the prestige and power of the clergy, even when it was persecuted, on the predominance of unchanging exploitation of the land, and on the limited role of urban activities and especially of the urban artisanry.

In the fourth century, both under the last pharaohs and under the management of Alexander's agent Cleomenes of Naucratis, the sanctuaries and their higher clergy appear to have been major economic players, and their wealth drew the attention of the royal power. Up to a certain point, an archaeological discovery offers us some hope of understanding the Egyptian economy at the beginning of the Hellenistic period and, more especially in its most prosperous element, the sacred land. The tomb of Petosiris, found in the desert cemetery area at Tuna el-Gebel west of Hermopolis, dates in its oldest parts from the last third of the fourth century or a bit later, while the

---

[4] I have been able to demonstrate (*CdÉ* 26 (1951) 378–82) that in the third century AD, in the great estates of the Arsinoite, the accounting of salaries was carried out in monetary terms, even though only products were actually disbursed – wheat, oil, wine, etc. – the balance of the accounting being brought about by outlays of goods through fictitious sales. This has been challenged by D. Rathbone, *Economic Rationalism and Rural Society in Third-Century A.D. Egypt* (1991) 112–14, esp. n. 39. Moreover, the rapid spread of bronze money in Egypt, both as currency and as a unit of account, is connected to the difficulty of assuring a sufficient volume of silver currency in circulation.

Figure 16.1   *Tuna el-Gebel, tomb of Petosiris, view (photo Roger S. Bagnall)*

pronaos is perhaps somewhat later still.[5] This tomb is that of a high
priest who held important hereditary offices, a representative of the
old religious aristocracy. If he directed, as the representative of the
god Thoth, the god's domain, to the point practically of appearing as
its proprietor, he was also a man with the ear of the pharaoh and, at
the same time, one of the upper administrators of the nome, because
he was royal secretary at the same time that he was high priest and
administrator of the god. The gracious and luxurious monument
which was to immortalise the merits of the high priest has memori-
alised the worldly management of Petosiris as much as his spiritual
work. A telling detail: Petosiris recalls that he restored the temples
and their domain when they had been ruined by a foreign invasion,
probably the second Persian invasion of 347. The sacred estate
formed a complex and coherent entity, a bridge between the nome
capital and its hinterland. The land of the estate, directly managed by
Petosiris and his agents, produced both flax and grains, probably both
wheat and barley. The vineyards, orchards and gardens ran alongside
meadows with large and small quadrupeds and fowl, or with papyrus
marshes, while fishing and hunting were organised to supplement the
food resources. Other sectors of the estate's activity – jewellery-

---

[5] Lefebvre (1923–4); cf. Guglielmi (1973: esp. 218ff).

Figure 16.2 *Tuna el-Gebel, tomb of Petosiris, relief scene from pronaos (photo Roger S. Bagnall)*

making, coppersmithing, woodworking (including luxury ebony work), perfume-making – are only a selection of high-level artisanal activities. The economic triptych is completed by the estate's possession of ships and numerous city houses which it leased out.

To be sure, both texts and figurative representations may have been influenced by artistic traditions[6] and by the embellishment of reality,[7] rather than by any desire to translate faithfully the worldly realities over which Petosiris presided. But the image that they give us is confirmed by what we know of the priestly estates in the early Hellenistic period. The Satrap Stele, in announcing the restoration of substantial territories to the clergy of the northeast Delta, describes its large estates with their villages, cities, population, fields, animals, birds and flocks.[8] The range of resources of the temple estates appearing in our

---

[6] Although Guglielmi's (1973) book shows the traditional character of the themes depicted on the temple walls, the author insists above all in his conclusions on the new spirit and the new realities which appear both in the reliefs and in the texts.

[7] In the glorification of the tasks carried out by the high priest, there may have been some exaggeration of his temporal power. And the image of a sacred domain with a coherent society and its differentiated social classes in perfectly harmonious relationship thanks to Petosiris' leadership is marked by panegyric euphoria. But that detracts only from the perfection, not the existence, of the structures described.

[8] Bouto, 311–310: K. Sethe, *Hierogl. Urk. griech-röm. Zeit* I (1904) 11–22, no. 9; translation in E. Bevan, *History of Egypt under the Ptolemaic Dynasty* (London 1927).

sources adds to Petosiris' account other natural products, like wool, honey and oils, and other artisanal activities, like textile production, dyeing, tanning, brewing, basket-making, pottery manufacture, brick-making and oil-making. The cult foundations, gifts, and rents from the leasing of land all constitute other fruitful and traditional contributions.

The importance which the great sanctuaries, with their estates and their influence over their neighbouring cities and their nomes, possessed at the beginning of the Hellenistic period must not be underestimated; the Ptolemies chose the places with major temples as the capitals of the nomes, the basic element in their administration of Egypt.[9] The structure described by the high priest Petosiris probably ensured the continuity of local power during the first decades of the Ptolemaic era. But this theocratic organisation of the nome evolved profoundly. The Macedonian power passed from a regime of occupation to one of direct administration, particularly in taking the royal lands under its control, and the sacred land also was administered under the king's oversight. It is hard for us to judge the reaction of the great temple estates to the new economy. Our knowledge of the third century comes above all from papyri originating in new lands or in zones where Greek cleruchs were settled. When in the second century, particularly in Tebtynis and in the Theban region, texts concerning the temples or the king's attitude towards them become more numerous, the political and economic conditions of Egypt had changed greatly. But it is clear that both the kings' grants to the temples and all of the forms of royal management over the temple economy had the consequence of creating receipts and expenses in money for the priestly class. The royal bank became the necessary intermediary for numerous fiscal and economic interventions. Certainly the importance of wheat, the traditional relationships between the temple and its environs, and even inside the estates the internal network of exchange and consumption, will have reduced the temple's dependence on the new forms of the economy. All the same, the distorted distribution of our sources clearly leads us to give an inadequate picture of the economic evolution of the sacred estates during the third century, even though we sense that they remain a characteristic economic entity.[10] Fortunately, our sources do open perspectives

[9] See Chapter 8.

[10] The pages devoted by Claire Préaux to the place of the temple estates in the Ptolemaic economy and to the relationships that can be identified between the clergy and the king remain fundamental: Préaux (1939: *passim*, esp. 480–91).

– more limited, perhaps, but actually very fruitful – on the problems that the monetary economy posed for the Egyptians, whether directly or indirectly.

A sampling of texts shows the inevitable, even insidious character of the extension of the monetary economy into the activity of the Egyptians. The craft of beekeeping was an ancient calling, a skill more important for the ancients than for us. The papyri acquaint us with Egyptian apiculture at various levels of operation. From *P. Petrie* III 43 (3) we learn of the existence of fields of hives belonging to a temple. One text from the Zenon archive (*P. Cair. Zen.* III 59467) illustrates the operation of apiaries by associations of *melissourgoi* [beekeepers], who owned the donkeys necessary for transporting the hives. Another text from the same archive (*P. Mich. Zen.* 29) shows us a widow who owns a few hives, while yet a third (*P. Cair. Zen.* II 59151) reveals the other end of the spectrum, with a man named Samos who owned 5,000 hives spread over several nomes. However traditional these hive-owners were, and however diverse among themselves, they were all none the less caught up in the monetary economy, whatever complications it might bring them. The beekeepers owed the king a cash rent, called *phoros* in Greek; and this *phoros* was considerable, both because of the omnipresence of apiculture and because of the commercial value of the honey.[11] On the other hand, commerce in honey was unregulated, and the product was readily convertible into cash. Is the importance of money in this traditional activity to be explained by fiscal pressure or by the existence of a large market of Greek consumers? It is difficult to say, although a text like *PSI* V 512 seems to indicate that Egyptian beekeepers developed some experience in collective price-fixing. But other consequences of the new economy disturbed this craft more seriously. The honey market was profitable, and Greeks invested money in hives which they leased out to Egyptian beekeepers, thus inserting themselves into the business with an eye to a profit which they can only have thought of in monetary terms. Thus we see Sostratos, a virtual tycoon as Claire Préaux called him, owning a thousand hives let out to various beekeepers (*P. Cair. Zen.* III 59368). With financial means at his disposal and the ability thus to acquire the means of production by a simple investment decision, the Greek intermediary adds his profit to the burden of the royal *phoros* paid by the Egyptian beekeeper. It is true,

---

[11] I cannot deal here with the question of the nature of the *phoros* or, according to the answer one gives to that question, the character of the royal property rights in the hives. Cf. Préaux (1939: 235).

however, that sometimes the rental on hives was paid in honey rather than in money.

On the other hand, the beekeepers' dossier shows that their difficulties arose as much from the new tax structures of the country as from its new monetary economy, even though the two are linked. The hives needed constant care, and in a country like Egypt, they needed to be able to be moved. Only a profound knowledge of the terrain and of bees will have made it possible to decide the distance and frequency of such movements. This was the trump card for the small Egyptian beekeeper, that which made him indispensable. But the beekeeper ran up against constraints coming from the Greeks or from his king. For one thing, it was no simple matter to reconcile the transhumance of hives and the impermeable barriers that royal decrees had created between the nomes in many domains, in order to give a geographical basis for tax farming and to protect the tax farmers. Sostratos points out (and takes care to note that it was without his knowing) that the beekeepers who rented his hives went to the Herakleopolite nome. The local *oikonomos*, familiar with administrative geography but not bee geography, immediately arrested the beekeepers, thus compromising the survival of the bees. Here we encounter one of the most commonplace consequences of the lack of conformity on the part of the Egyptians with the new rules imposed on them and the incongruity of the rules with the realities of agricultural work: imprisonment, most often for debt, i.e., for lack of sufficient available cash. A passing notable managed to get our beekeepers out of prison; we may imagine that here, just as the beekeepers themselves did in other circumstances, the king's interests in not seeing the royal revenues ruined along with the hives will have been the crucial argument.

But the beekeepers also collided with the feverish needs of the Greeks for transport animals. The Greeks did not hesitate to requisition donkeys wherever they found them, particularly those idle between two trips with hives. But failure to move the hives at the right moment would rapidly ruin the beekeeper. This conflict turns up in more than one text, and it is not the only collision between the new economy and the beekeepers, for at Philadelphia the extension of irrigation and clearance by fire threatened the hive-keeper with destruction if he did not get out of the way. Meanwhile, the same feverish drive for production drove the same Greeks to keep separate the transport animals that would have allowed the beekeepers to move away. We thus see a rural activity confronting at the same time and with difficulty the problems created by the need to have cash, the problems generated by the way in which the king exploited the country – among others, the Greek system of tax farming – and finally the difficulties arising from the unequal competition between the profit motive among the Greeks and the traditional networks of the old Egyptian economy.

The members of the rural workforce were, moreover, the less capable of adapting because they were socially destitute. I have studied elsewhere (see Chapter 17) the frustrated reaction of uprooted peasants, their flight in the face of forms of agricultural management imposed by the Greek landholders but incomprehensible to the peasants because of their abstract character. Particularly for the peasant, it was difficult to amass the small sums of money needed to pay the cash taxes. Consider, for example, the report to Zenon (*P. Cair. Zen.* I 59130) in which we see a peasant arrested for failure to pay the salt tax (*halikê*). The order is given for his release on the arrival of the tax farmers, so that he can get on with his agricultural work. But the report is accompanied by a more general order from on high: 'Stop picking on the peasants of Tapteia [a Memphite village] in the matter of the salt tax.' Apollonios (the *dioiketes*) is aware of the impossibility of these people's coming up with the sums demanded of them and the uselessness of throwing them in prison. But does he not see how far his own attitude is full of contradictions? For as *dioiketes* he will have to give the tax farmers the choice of flaying the delinquent taxpayers or making up themselves for the taxpayers' deficiencies. These contradictions are, up to a certain point, the very image of the incompatibility of the two economies which circumstances have brought face to face in Egypt. Be that as it may, we find in this papyrus the consequences of this confrontation: imprisonment and recourse to protection from the powerful.

The same problems appear on the level of the artisans. The Revenue Laws papyrus shows how the production of oil-bearing crops, the activity of oil-makers and the retail commerce of oil were heavily adapted to a money-based fiscality and were managed in Greek style. The artisanal traditions, which must have been family-based, are jostled, pushed towards instability by the system of annual or biannual renewals of concessions, and weakened by the intrusion of tax farmers and royal functionaries. These latter, the strangers in the house, have become its master. Technically speaking, the culture of the oil crops and the making of oil continue to be carried out in the main by the same peasants and same craftsmen as they were before these activities were remodelled with an eye to the fiscal exploitation of the product along Greek lines, that is, in terms of coined money. Just as with the beekeepers – and it is easy to find analogous situations in other artisanal activities, like brewing or weaving – the new economic structures imposed on the Egyptians, particularly on the less wealthy classes, additional constraints which translated into greater economic dependence on the Greeks.

There are, to be sure, factors which modify the excessively simplistic picture that such an analysis suggests concerning the relationship of some of the Greeks and the less privileged Egyptian social strata, or the all too systematic element in the idea of a general upsetting of Egyptian society by the intrusion of the monetary economy for the profit of the Greeks and their king.

As I mentioned earlier, wheat remained alongside coined money an important factor in Egypt in payments and receipts, and even in the principal amounts of loans and in short-term hoarding. One may suppose that thanks to this fact the traditional economy was less disrupted by the Greeks on the royal and temple lands cultivated by the peasants. Indeed, for the Greeks the extensive irrigated culture of cereals and the secondary activities of cultivation and animal-raising connected to it were a new phenomenon, which only the Egyptian peasant, however exploited he may have been, could handle knowledgeably. In Chapter 15, I analyse a phenomenon visible on wheat lands given by the crown to military settlers: the intervention of independent Greeks (those referred to with the descriptive phrase *tês epigonês* in the documents)[12] between the cleruch, who was unable to work his parcel of land, and the Egyptian peasant. This intervention of a small capitalist in the wheat economy is not only a phenomenon of supplementary exploitation of the peasant at the level of the new economy but also a phenomenon of interaction between dissimilar groups of Greeks. For the rest, even if the practice of short-term leases diminished the stability of peasant life on grain lands, even if these lands witnessed some rude collisions between Greek and Egyptian mentalities,[13] the image that we can form of this peasantry cannot be too different from a picture of the countryside before the Greeks. That does not mean that this picture necessarily conformed to the idyllic imagery of the tombs of the pharaonic period or of the tomb of Petosiris.

---

[12] Cf. Oates (1963).

[13] Cf., for example, at Philadelphia *P. Lond.* VII 1954 or *PSI* V 502 (see Chapter 17).

Other factors contributed to moderate the weakness of some classes of Egyptians vis-à-vis the new economy. First among them, as I mentioned earlier, was the irreplaceable experience of the peasants and artisans. They do not fail to mention this, as the archive of Zenon shows, and sometimes with a barely concealed scorn for the Greek who is in a position of authority over them. This competence, however modest, had additional weight because the Greeks were relatively few and desperately needed to join forces with these peasants and artisans, if only to take advantage of their activity.[14] And this experience was real. Just as the Egyptians had their place in the royal administration where their competence was useful, even in very high positions like that of the royal secretary of the nome (like Petosiris),[15] the Egyptians kept their places in the cities, just as in the countryside, on the economic level. Moreover, if the economic and social structures of ancient Egypt were disturbed by the monetary economy and the profit-motive of the Greek immigrants, the Egyptians themselves often adapted well in commerce or industry.[16] The dossier of the beekeepers shows how, under the pressure both of the market and of fiscal requirements, individuals were integrated into the new economy, whether willingly or of necessity, and with greater or lesser success.

One constraint that the new economy imposed was the need for sureties, a source of economic dependence. It is thus perhaps not without interest to introduce here another dossier, that of the Demotic sureties preserved in Lille, published by Françoise de Cenival.[17] These texts date from the reign of Ptolemy III Euergetes, except for a few from the reign of Ptolemy II Philadelphos. The documents come from the Arsinoite, from the Themistos division. They contain guarantees

---

[14] Let us not forget that the idea of replacing indigenous peasants or artisans with a Greek population would have been entirely foreign to a Hellenistic government. There are, none the less, cases of competition at an individual level. This must have been relatively commonplace among artisans in the metropoleis and the villages. There are even instances on arable land. The best-known example comes from *PSI* IV 400 (cf. Préaux 1939: 135). Agathon proposes to Zenon to take over 60 hectares cultivated by an Egyptian farmer named Petobastis. For Agathon, however, it was probably a matter of inserting himself between the landholder (Zenon) and Petobastis or other Egyptian farmers who might have replaced Petobastis. Even here there is no real interchange of Greek and Egyptian.

[15] Cf. Samuel (1970). The image offered by Samuel needs some modification. The higher functions held by Egyptians are in the area of the secretariat or agriculture; they are absent from management positions, particularly that of *oikonomos* (p. 450: Ammonios is a Greek name).

[16] Cf., for example, at Krokodilopolis, in the dossier of the petitions to the king (*enteuxeis*), a wool-merchant (*P. Enteux.* 2), an expansionistic weaver (*P. Enteux.* 5) and wine merchants (*P. Enteux.* 34).

[17] *Cautionnements démotiques du début de l'époque ptolémaïque (P.dém.Lille 34 à 96)* (1973).

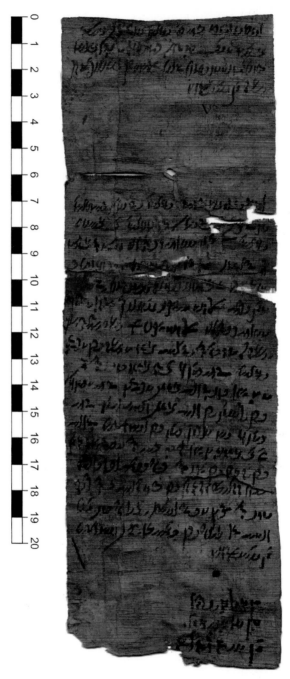

Figure 16.3   P. Lille dem. *55, surety for a brewer, 262* BC *(photo courtesy of Institut de Papyrologie, Sorbonne)*

for obligations of payments and obligations to appear, two types of surety which were added to the previously known model of the guarantee for the appearance of a prisoner freed on bail. They also offer for the first time examples of second-level sureties. I do not have the competence necessary to treat the problem of whether this type of contract, the documentation for which falls in the third century BC, was Persian or Egyptian in origin, or perhaps a purely Ptolemaic development.[18] We may remark that whatever the type of surety, it often concerns very modest sums. In this we find one measure of an economic level at which guarantees for even minor sums must be spread around several persons. To be sure, this is the same manner of using sureties that exists among the tax-farming companies and their sureties, and even at this more exalted level the causes are much the same, bearing in mind the different financial dimensions: the insufficiency of the money in circulation and of individual financial resources. What is interesting is that we can identify here a modest response to the pressure of recurring requirements for cash obligations, and up to a certain point, a response born of that group solidarity which we often find in our Ptolemaic documentation, be it among Greeks or among Egyptians.

The brewer Hereteboïs, from the village of Apia, assembled a group of at least six persons at the beginning of the fiscal year in 262 in order to provide the guarantee he needed; each individual guarantees 5 drachmas. Elsewhere, oil-makers used sureties in the same amount. Among this group, in one of the documents (*P. Lille dem.* II 50), a member of the priestly class (*pastophoros* or *neokoros*) was perhaps involved in the making of oil, because the verso of the papyrus indicates that he is a *koskineutes* (winnower). The dossier of Keltoun, a brewer at Philagris, is more complicated. Among his sureties appears a lower Egyptian priest as well as donkey-drivers – one of whom is even a Greek, presumably of humble circumstances. The case of the Greek Artemidoros is no less remarkable: at Philagris, he appears to carry out simultaneously the role of tax farmer for natron and that of laundryman. Even better than the previous examples, this combination shows that no matter how much the theoretical structures envisioned in royal legislation, with its Greek origins, separate craftsmen submitted to professional licensing from tax farmers collecting from this occupational group, in the microeconomic reality of the village, everything could be made concrete in a

---

[18] Ibid., pp. 137–50: 'Les cautionnements, étude juridique'.

single man and the sureties whom he can find. And this man, in the clearest example that the surety dossier offers us, is a Greek.[19]

Altogether, the dossier reveals a more or less satisfactory Egyptian response to the problem of Greek fiscality and its 'monetary' pressure, which otherwise would endanger the artisanry of the village. But the dossier also displays the limits of this reaction. First, we are dealing with a rather low level in the economy; second, the documents hardly provide an opportunity to see how successful the guaranteed person was in satisfying the king's demands, not to speak of the guarantors' success in escaping foreclosure. Finally, the use of sureties, which cannot have come without cost, increased further the burden of the royal hold on artisanal activity. More than ever we regret at this point the absence of any documents concerning the interaction of wealthier strata of the Egyptian population with the new economy.

All the same, our picture of the specific relationships to which the entry, even very partial, of the Egyptians into a monetary economy gave rise has become much sharper. For the Egyptians, this move was an important source of dependence. It allowed the Greeks to acquire a privileged role in the Egyptian economy by a series of processes: acquisition of the means of production; the necessity imposed by the new economy for poor Egyptians to turn over part of the fruits of their labour to an intermediary; random needs to adapt themselves to taxation in money; and, finally, recourse to the protection of more important people, either Greeks or priests. In parallel, and following analogous mechanisms, language, the bearer of modes of thought and of the keys to the new management of the country, the vehicle of *de facto*, if not legal, privileges, similarly created hierarchies in the relationships of some groups of Egyptians to some groups of Greeks. Although I cannot go into detail here about this point, it should be noted that despite the absence of any true racial policy on the part of the Ptolemies, language and the monetary economy profoundly marked the social structures of the third century. But even at this point the adaptive facility of some Egyptians announces the evolution of this same biracial society which was going to occur during the second half of the Hellenistic period, and its slow development into the 'Egypt of the notables' of the imperial period, where it is the possession of land which marked definitively the structures of Graeco-Egyptian society, rather than the problem of the availability of currency.

---

[19] Ibid., pp. 250–2.

Chapter 17

GREEKS AND EGYPTIANS
ACCORDING TO *PSI* V 502

అ

One of the fundamental problems of papyrology is that posed by the cultural contact that arose from the settlement of Greeks in a traditional Egyptian milieu. Those Greeks, even after losing their original social roots, were bearers of political and economic traditions ready to be used in the particular dynamics of immigration. The problem, like any sociological problem, is complex, because neither the Greek nor the Egyptian milieu was homogeneous and closed. Except in some domains, however, mixing of their cultures was not extensive. Cultural 'borrowing' was instinctively limited by the privileged minority; it was also restricted, unconsciously, by an Egyptian majority which used a certain cultural solidarity to resist its own incapacity to compete with the Graeco-Macedonian minority. Greek settlements did not follow any fixed formula, and even the new polis of Ptolemais surely did not imitate the types of installation achieved in Naucratis or Memphis in very different historic conditions. The initial period of military occupation was followed, except for the more or less urbanised areas, about which we are poorly informed for the Ptolemaic period,[1] by the rather classic stage of cleruchic settlement and that of the development of a royal network of administration of the country, a network directed from above in the milieu of the court in Alexandria. The monopoly which the Greeks possessed, of what I would call 'the dialectic of administration and of monetary economy', gradually assured to the *Hellênes* of the Macedonian royal system at first the occupation of power, then a dominant position in the use of land and availability of capital. We know that the Greek population, which gradually became urbanised, evolved at the beginning of the Roman empire, as it lost its last cleruchic structures, into a hierarchically organised society where access to the Greek language and education became more than ever the technical support for administration, management, and preservation of social privileges.

---

[1] See Chapter 9.

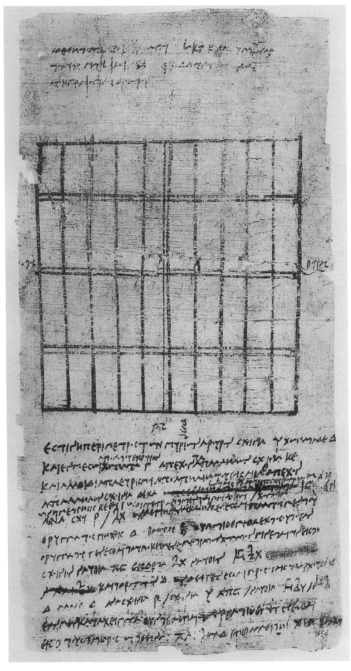

Figure 17.1 P. Lille 1, *with plan of irrigation works at Philadelphia (from P. Jouguet et al.,* Papyrus grecs I, *1907)*

Our papyrological documentation does little to shed light on the first contacts between two cultures as different as the one imported by Greek immigration and that of a battered, complex Egyptian society. We only guess the adventitious contribution of the earlier groups of Greek immigrants, settled in Naucratis or in Memphis. But, for the rest, everything is rather obscure, and the oldest documents, those of Hibeh or the Petrie papyri, enlighten us mainly on the probably rather traditional cleruchic stage, one aspect of the later stabilisation of a Greek population in Egypt.

The so-called Zenon archive, although revealing multiple exceptional relations between the *chôra* and Alexandria, and originating for the most part from the artificial environment of the gift-estate of the *dioiketes* Apollonios, allows us perhaps to observe from different angles certain sociological processes in the contact of cultures, I would almost say under the harsh lighting of a laboratory experiment. It is, for example, in this environment that, paradoxically, one finds an inscription which demonstrates an effort of acculturation absolutely without any successors in our Greek documentation, the stele dedicated by the *kynoboskos* Pasôs to Anubis for the safety of Apollonios and of Zenon.[2] It is conceived in the best Greek epigraphic tradition, but below a strictly Egyptian relief and under hieroglyphs. However, what is striking in this testimony of acculturation is that it is, as I said, without later followers, at least in the Ptolemaic period.

To this abnormal example of the close juxtaposition of the two cultures, I would oppose *PSI* V 502, one of the most impressive documents from early Ptolemaic rural Egypt. This papyrus confronts on the one side the most dynamic type in a diversified Greek environment, the most 'Promethean' one, according to the expression of the sociologist G. Gurvitch, and on the other side what, in an Egyptian environment just as diversified, represents the element most opposed to the new techniques of management which Alexandria wanted for this badly structured, displaced group, somehow deprived of a real traditional frame.

The sender of the letter, or better of what we would call a dossier, was a Greek from Caria, Panakestor, steward of Apollonios' new domain, which at this point had been under development for two years around Philadelphia in the Fayyum. He would soon leave the direction of the domain and hand it over to another Greek from Caria, Zenon son of Agreophon, the 'Zenon of the archives'. Zenon

---

[2] *SB* I 5796 = *SEG* XX 647 [now *I. Fay.* I 98]. Cf. Rostovtzeff (1941: 319 and pl. XXXIX, 1).

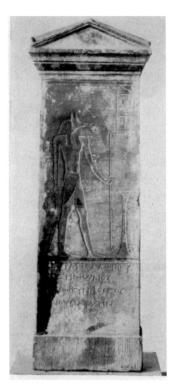

Figure 17.2   Stele of a kynoboskos, *I. Fay. I 98; Egyptian Museum, Cairo, Journal d'entrée 44048 (photo courtesy of Egyptian Museum, Cairo)*

is precisely the Alexandrian addressee of the letter which introduces the dossier. The other persons mentioned appear later: first the protagonist and mover of the drama, the finance minister Apollonios, in relation to whom Panakestor's position is very ambiguous; then a group of agents of the administration, whose exact role in the domain represents a rather obscure problem. There is finally a group of Egyptian farmers, who seem loosely organised, since at no time does a leader or a spokesman appear among them.

Looking at this papyrus, we are at first struck by an element important for external criticism: the dimensions of this letter are exceptional, 34 cm by 37 cm. With such a large sheet we are obviously dealing with quite an unusual matter. Moreover, later on Zenon brought this piece of evidence with him from Alexandria when he took over Panakestor's responsibilities in Philadelphia.

The first seven lines of the document sent to Zenon contain a double message which illustrates the contradictions of Panakestor's position in July 256. On the one hand, in the letter Panakestor asks, rather stiffly, that Zenon use his influence with Apollonios (the boss whom he is about to leave), so that the minister will hasten a royal decision concerning Panakestor. On the other hand, towards the end, this letter becomes a note introducing a dossier; in fact there are two letters, a correspondence exchanged between Apollonios and Panakestor in the latter's role of local agent of the omnipotent courtier. This file marks a complete disagreement between the two men on the occasion of the failure of a new agricultural policy imposed from Alexandria by the minister for the management of his domain in the northeast of the Fayyum.

Lines 8–10 of *PSI* 502 quote a brief letter of Apollonios dated 22 June. The powerful holder of the *dôrea* blames Panakestor sharply for having left him without any news about the evaluation of the crop, the *syntimêsis tou sporou*, and similarly, later on, about the harvest of the wheat. The rest of the complex document sent to Zenon is occupied by the long answer of Panakestor to the letter of Apollonios, a skilful although embarrassed justification. Hurt in his pride, the man succeeds all the same in remaining flattering enough and avoids saying that the failure was due to a poor grasp of psychology on the part of the absent master of the domain and to his lack of familiarity with the problem of the relations between Greeks and Egyptian farmers.

In fact, difficulties arose from the unprepared contact of two very different levels of culture. On the one side, as I said, the demanding dynamics of an active economy, particularly the dynamics in Apollonios' environment, more pressing than the average dynamics of Greek immigration in the army, the administration or among the cleruchs; on the other side, poorly organised farmers who represent in the complex social order of old, stagnant Egypt a particularly deprived group unexpectedly facing unknown techniques of management and virtual monetarist techniques, when they had little practical experience of handling money, and then only on a small scale. The whole business is based on the dialectic of the Greek immigrant. To use a rather improper image, I would say the Egyptians represent a farming community whose sickle, let us not forget, had just passed or was passing from the age of bronze to the age of iron.

What really happened? The affair is obscure and no interpretation that one may give to it manages to clarify the entirety of the data. In the new domain, plots of wheat-land were exploited under contract by Egyptian cultivators (*geôrgoi*), amounting as it seems to a rather extensive area. By entrusting them to Egyptian farmers, Apollonios made a sensible choice: those farmers, rough as they were, knew a lot about the cultivation of wheat under local conditions, and from the point of view of Apollonios they would succeed if supervised by Greeks who could make the decisions required by the special nature of the new domain and the ideal of profit which was the philosophy of the newcomers.

The agreement concluded in the past by Apollonios with the Egyptian farmers remained wisely in the range of simple, concrete procedures familiar to them. The rent to be handed to the master of the domain was one third of the crops, to be measured on the thresh-ing-floor. One measure goes to the master of the domain and then two measures go to the farmer. Such a setting of the rent as a proportion of the actual harvest did not follow a Greek model but is well attested in earlier Demotic leases. The rate of two thirds of the crop is rather favourable for the farmer; this is doubtless a consequence of the recent conversion of the land to agriculture.

When the harvest approached, particularly late in this case (maybe a second harvest of three-months' wheat), Apollonios, from his offices in Alexandria, unilaterally modified the method of estab-lishing the rent.[3] Instead of the concrete process of sharing the har-vested wheat, he now imposed a preliminary estimate of the future harvest with the crop still growing. He explained the matter to Panakestor in a *hypomnêma*. The document is lost, but, according to the later messages, we can easily imagine how it sounded, one more imperative lesson in the management of the domain, the sort the offices of Apollonios in Alexandria were constantly sending towards the *chôra* with a constant reminder of the necessary urgency of the demands. Maybe Panakestor was persuaded of this urgency, but he needed twelve days to gather people supposed capable of applying the speculative method of the new assessment. He waited twelve days more, then five days to establish what I would call the cadastre of the problem: a survey 'by cultivator and by crop'. Then our Greek, with the help of the *basilikoi grammateis*, tried to explain to the Egyptian farmers the decision of Apollonios and asked them to proceed either according to this *syntimêsis*, or to

---

[3] I do not think it is possible to reconcile the terms used in the document with the hypothesis of Rostovtzeff (1922: 75–9) that the wheat was already harvested. This would make things easier for some aspects of the problem, but in that case the attitude of the Egyptian farmers would be entirely absurd, the order of Apollonios quite odious and the survey of the grain-land imposed on Panakestor and the *basilikoi grammateis* totally inexplicable.

agree to a standard document (*entupê*) and draw up particular agreements according to this one.

The reaction of the farmers was negative, although prudent: 'We will first think about it.' Three or four days later, they withdrew into the temple, rejecting any form of abstract estimation of a crop still growing and threatening to abandon the fields at the risk of losing everything, recalling the agreement which both parties had signed. Extensive reprimands obtained nothing from them. Panakestor left the place to find help somewhere, but without success, and had to return to Philadelphia, to propose to the Egyptians that they should make individual counterproposals (*hypotimêsis*). What was the nature of these? We do not know, but Panakestor says he passed them on to Alexandria, then was occupied by other duties.

This story is unusual even if we neglect a series of points of detail that we cannot clear up with any certainty, like, for example, the exceptionally late date in the agricultural year when the different stages of the process happened.

The extent of the small revolution Apollonios wanted to impose on the farmers is not clear. Panakestor calls it a 'concession' or 'benefaction', *philanthrôpa*. In the environment of the Ptolemies, the word means 'decision', sometimes masking an arbitrary exercise of power, even the dishonesty of the operation. What really was this *syntimêsis*, particularly if, in spite of a late date (May and the beginning of June), it relates, as I believe, to an estimation of the crop before the harvest?

Foreign to the concrete division of the harvest on the threshing-floor that seemed appropriate for the Egyptians, the *syntimêsis* of a crop still growing, a speculative method, was part of the repertory of economic techniques practised by the Greeks. In Thasos, about the year 400 or somewhat later, a law regulated the purchase of the future crop of a vineyard.[4] Far from forbidding such a thing or revealing that this deal *ex abstracto* goes against Greek law and rules, the Thasian text, as Finley saw,[5] establishes the existence of a type of sale based on *syntimêsis*. At least people wanted to prevent abuses due to the unpredictable character of a premature *syntimêsis* and the losses which the treasury was risking. It is moreover in this spirit, and particularly for the fiscal consequences, that sale of the future vintage would eventually be forbidden in Roman Egypt in the *Gnomon of the*

---

[4] *IG* XII, Suppl. 347.1–6.
[5] 'The Problem of the Unity of Greek Law', in *Storia del Diritto nel Quadro delle Scienze Storiche* (Florence 1966) 140–1.

Idios Logos. The *syntimêsis*, on the contrary, is widely evidenced not only for vineyards, but also for orchards, kitchen gardens and oil in Ptolemaic documents of the third century, not least in the so-called *Revenue Laws*, a document contemporary with *PSI* 502 and coming from the offices of the same Apollonios, which is of purely Greek conception (cf. Chapter 13).[6] The fact that such a procedure is applied to wheat may seem more disconcerting, because, more than any other product in Egypt, wheat, once harvested, has a stable value with a role similar to that of the currency. The *syntimêsis* of the future harvest of wheat is also evidenced in Telmessos and in Hieron's law.[7] It is a Greek practice and, if it is mostly documented in the Hellenistic period, it is doubtless more ancient.

Regrettably enough for the historian, the *syntimêsis* imposed by Apollonios on his farmers is susceptible on a second level to two interpretations (besides some that we can reject without discussion), even if we do not decide whether it is an estimate of the crop still growing or an estimate of the harvest on the threshing-floor: (1) is it an estimate in artabas of wheat, such as appears, for example, for oil in the contemporary *Revenue Laws*? (2) Or is it an estimate of the value of the harvest in monetary units, as foreseen for the levy on orchards in the same *Revenue Laws*, and for vineyards in some Petrie papyri, or for the royalties on kitchen gardens in *P. Cair. Zen.* 59300?

Panakestor's file is not explicit on this subject; but in favour of the first hypothesis, the estimate of the crop or of the harvest in measures of wheat, there is an argument *e silentio*: the expression *pros argyrion*, 'in cash', appears nowhere. Moreover, the assessment of quantities of grain in money is not present in our general papyrological evidence. If this first hypothesis is correct, then, Apollonios' reform would have been only a technical reform of management. Moreover, it adds speculation on an economic mass available in the short term, by fixing its value before the harvest. The sole risk, small indeed, is that of some loss in a fraudulent evaluation. The procedure is in accordance with the atmosphere of acceleration of the demand of return, with the 'right away' clause which appears in Apollonios' letters in the month which follow our incident. This accords very well with the concept of economic management in accounting terms, which seems one of the characteristics of the Greek manipulation of

---

[6] Rostovtzeff (1922: 79) made the connection between *PSI* 502 and the legislation he studied later several times.

[7] In the *lex frumentaria* alluded to as *Hieronica* by Cicero, *Verr.* II 32.

Egyptian economic potential. Claire Préaux showed the dimensions and the versatility of the accounting methods of Apollonios' offices.[8] I demonstrate elsewhere[9] that, five centuries later, in Heroninos' archives, a complex of several large domains in the third century AD practised only a very restricted use of coinage for internal business in and between the domains, while the monthly reports of the management of each domain are drawn up according to a fictitious accounting in drachmas for a large part of the activities, including the wages.

The other hypothesis, the *syntimêsis pros argyrion*, would have an even more decisive meaning. First of all, it would uphold, in a more direct way, since it is expressed in silver, all the importance which I gave above to the adoption of a *syntimêsis* of the crop. Furthermore, it would add another motivation, speculation on the value of the wheat. We return here to a familiar aspect of the management of the domain, an aspect which Claire Préaux highlighted well, a penchant for gambling on the difference between prices imposed on the farmer and actual prices, a difference that explains how it happens that the domain eventually was sometimes lacking wheat.[10] In that case, the *syntimêsis* made compulsory before the normal harvest would have been perhaps a way of considerably increasing, even deceitfully, the profits on a late harvest, because a *syntimêsis* in silver implies the capture of the whole future theoretical harvest, whereas an evaluation limited to the rent paid to the master of the domain could be unfavourable to him.

Anyway, whether the *syntimêsis* is only a reform of the management of the domain, or instead adds to it a large-scale speculation, in either case this *syntimêsis*, with its abstract and unpredictable character, was not situated at the level of the objective treatment of the harvest, the only one where the Egyptian farmer was able to conceive his obligations. For him there was a breach of contract (this is, after all, indisputable), but, furthermore, Apollonios was imposing on him a discussion on a dialectical plane which escaped him, an abstract *syntimêsis*.

Here arises the problem of the reaction of the Egyptian farmers and the need to interpret the reaction of such a group. Flight, secession, *anachôrêsis* [withdrawal] and strike are frequent phenomena in our papyrological documentation; but what is interesting in *PSI 502* is specifically that the logical motivations of these other cases, with only

---

[8] Préaux (1947: 75–8).
[9] Bingen (1951).
[10] Préaux (1947: 63–4); cf. Préaux (1939: 139).

one exception, do not appear here. We do not find here a flight to avoid arrest, to escape a creditor or a tax inspector, or people moving away due to famine or lack of water. One thinks rather of a strike, a more organised but quite different notion, an act of suspension of contractual relations, entailing as penalty temporary losses that the other party will undergo.

It is, however, difficult to admit such an interpretation, at first sight rather attractive, for the reaction of our farmers. If we accept Rostovtzeff's thesis that the farmers refused to estimate the harvested wheat because the new process was unfavourable to the producer, we must admit that the reaction of the farmers was simultaneously a concerted and organised act and a completely absurd one. By abandoning the harvested wheat, they lost everything, and there was no loss for the other party. On the contrary, if the estimate was a preliminary *syntimêsis* of the crop, one can hardly speak more reasonably about a resistance which would end in the destruction of the harvest or in its seizure. Maybe Rostovtzeff was influenced here by the exactions of Verres in Sicily, while Apollonios' proposal at least seemingly leaves to the farmers the initiative of the *syntimêsis*. It is necessary for us to choose. Either this is a strike; but such a thoughtful act of resistance does not 'stick' to the data of the document; or else this is a flight, and a flight which is a purely emotional reaction. In the case of *PSI* 502, we cannot easily escape this last conclusion.

Flight is a characteristic reaction of an archaic group (in the ethnographic sense of the word) abruptly facing the intervention of a more evolved group, and particularly the intervention of a group which, being conscious of the innovative efficiency of human intervention, disrupts the existing order. It would be excessive to rate Egypt versus Greece in the third century as an archaic civilisation, prehistoric in ethnologist's terms, facing a civilisation integrated into history as a 'Promethean' one. But the sampling supplied by *PSI* 502, however extreme on both sides, highlights at the dawn of our papyrological documentation a contact of cultures which recalls, in a hardly forced way, the well-known pairing archaism/history.[11] On one hand, in the Egyptian farming community (a community of displaced farmers), an archaism by regression reflects this fundamental character of the archaism of ethnologists, the lack of consciousness of a possible insertion into any evolution, and, more concretely, inertia faced with the aggression of a new context. In contrast, the environment of

[11] Cf. Y. Cazeneuve, *La mentalité archaïque* (Paris 1961).

Apollonios, more than any other Greek environment we can imagine in Egypt, has this Promethean character of conscious insertion into history, the will, in the spirit of lucre developed outside the traditional framework, to be the basis of the future through original decisions which ignore tradition. The reaction of the farmers is characteristic of this archaism, the flight in the face of the unusual, and such a reaction, commonplace during first contacts with techniques that are still unassimilable, is well known among ethnologists. It is a refusal, a refusal to discuss, a refusal to accept the new rules of the game. And if those Egyptian farmers did not disappear into the forest (or rather, the desert, for them) as primitive Africans or South Americans did when facing commercial or fiscal techniques which they did not understand, it is because the Egyptian farmer was part of a tradition historically already evolved, and the altar appears instinctively to him as an effective protection. It is also because eighty years of proximity to the Greek immigrants gave him, if not a clear idea of how to use their techniques, at least a sense of the limits of their arbitrary power and appetites.

Certainly a conflict between a Promethean Apollonios and an archaic farming community, without political structure and particularly deprived on a social level, could only appear with such sharpness in the artificial environment of the *dôrea* and in the ideally experimental circumstances we find in *PSI 502*. But this conflict is probably representative of a certain number of the problems of acculturation which arose in a less sharply contrasted way after the settlement of the Greeks in Egypt, problems which were never completely resolved. Naturally, one should not generalise for all Egyptian circles the sociological type of the weaker party present in *PSI 502*. Some Egyptian groups possessed prestigious techniques (medicine, learning, and the religious authority of the priests), or practical techniques indispensable to the Greeks (secretariat, administration of the native communities). They were automatically protected from any form of regressive archaism, if not from possible communal conservatism. Their social structures made them able to face passive confrontation with or, in a more pragmatic way, more or less active integration into a system with its colouring of lucre proper to immigration, based on ways of thinking, discussing and administering of Greek origin. Nevertheless the gap between the two cultures was never entirely filled, and the future evolution of Graeco-Egyptian society was marked during several centuries by the indispensability of access to the Greek language and to the administrative and economic techniques of which it was the carrier and support.

Chapter 18

GRAECO-ROMAN EGYPT AND THE
QUESTION OF CULTURAL INTERACTIONS

❧

This chapter originates in an impulse from the general assembly of the International Council for Philosophy and the Humanities (ICPH),[1] held in December 1979, in New Delhi. At that gathering, Mr Conil-Lacoste, head of the Division of Studies on Cultures, presented the first results, essentially on the heuristic and methodological side, of the work pursued in his department since 1976 simultaneously by a working team, created with the hope of elaborating a programme of intercultural studies, and by a committee of coordination for those same studies. He invited each member federation of ICPH to participate in the project and to promote the various methods which might emerge from the achievements of the team.

There is no need to dwell at length on the quite different perspectives which these works opened up; but it is worth mentioning one instance, our deep-seated concern to question our own mentality in an effort to avoid an ethnocentric approach to the culture of the 'other' – a perennial fear in Greek papyrology, where, in front of Egyptian data, each of us is an ethnocentric Janus, a Westerner of the twentieth century and a Greek descended from Alexander. The programme also sought, more broadly, new practical approaches corresponding more tightly to the aims of UNESCO, such as identification of values that could be common to something like a general 'human culture', without endangering the creative specificity of each existing culture. One of these perspectives, or rather one direction of thought, might be to develop our knowledge of phenomena associated in the past with the coexistence of two different cultures. This historic sector would not only enumerate and analyse mechanisms of acculturation, as they are perceptible in what we know of antiquity, but describe as

---

[1] The beginning of this paper, as originally read at the final session of the XVIth International Congress of Papyrology, recalls the links existing between the Association Internationale de Papyrologues (AIP) and UNESCO. AIP is a member of the International Federation of Associations of Classical Studies (FIEC), itself one of the thirteen member associations of ICPH. ICPH is one of the major non-governmental consultative organisations of UNESCO.

well what might explain negative attitudes, such as refusal of or simply indifference or imperviousness to any influence coming from outside.

The world of classical studies soon presented to UNESCO a first response to this agenda, the proceedings of the Sixth International Congress of Classical Studies, which was held in Madrid in 1974, under the auspices of UNESCO and ICPH. The papers were published under the title *Assimilation et résistance à la culture gréco-romaine dans le monde ancien* (Paris 1976). Regrettably the Eastern provinces of the Roman world were rather neglected, and Graeco-Roman Egypt, of all places, was totally absent from that programme. This is at least paradoxical: Egypt is the only geographic and chronological space in antiquity which can contribute a splendid literary and documentary treasury in Greek and Latin coupled with what is by far the richest evidence from documents created by the native populations.

FIEC offered the possibility in New Delhi of filling such a gap, with the certainty of risk-free success, because papyrologists had long been concerned about, and indeed drawn in various directions by, the problem of the cohabitation of Greek and Oriental cultures. Important publications of that era had refined our thinking on the matter – the 1976 symposium of Berlin, for instance,[2] or many pages of Claire Préaux's *Monde hellénistique*.[3] FIEC proposed to UNESCO that one of the contributions from the Federation to ICPH's response be a report on the 'case' of Graeco-Roman Egypt. Regrettably, the timetable was too tight to organise a team project of this sort. My comments in this chapter are not a substitute for a report that never materialised,[4] but an attempt to settle some structural preliminaries to any descriptive study of cultural interactions in Egypt, and the critical imperatives such preliminaries contain.

On the one hand it is necessary to define the concept of 'culture', that is, to enumerate the values according to which a collective identity gets organised and become apparent. On the other hand, we were asked to analyse the concept 'culture' in its double objective and subjective reach: one can describe the global creation of a particular community, but one can also look for the consciousness which this group

---

[2] *Das ptolemäische Ägypten* (Mainz am Rhein 1978).

[3] Préaux (1978). Since then, of course, more studies on ethnicity and cultural interactions have appeared.

[4] It was published later as 'Voies et limites des interactions culturelles: le cas de l'Égypte gréco-romaine,' in *Douze cas d'interaction culturelle dans l'Europe ancienne et l'Orient proche ou lointain* (UNESCO 1984) 25–43.

has (more or less confusedly) of its cultural identity, whether it is the 'lived-through consciousness' of the distinctive reality of the group, its ethnicity, or even the mythologised consciousness of its identity. Now, this profusion of methods and matters for inquiry means, for papyrologists, applying them to the cohabitation of some peculiar form of Hellenism and of some peculiar 'Egyptianity', or rather applying them to the 'Greeks' and 'Egyptians' we find in our documents, as well as to the 'Egyptians' that Demoticists and Coptologists rediscover through 'their' documents. The subjective and relative character of our perception of these groups, separated by no impenetrable barrier, is aggravated in an inquiry of a merely historical nature: the number and range of possible methodological approaches are limited by the incomplete character of the literary, documentary and archaeological sources at our disposal, even though we are able to place them in a historical and geographical context exceptionally well known by the standards of antiquity. My first reaction to tackling such a task involved some fear: as soon as one leaves the well-marked-out domain of documentary philology or that of concrete ancient history to try the methods and techniques we use for the socio-psychology and sociology of cultural cohabitation, our documentation appears only as a partial sampling and sometimes not really a significant sample.

The project of the the UNESCO experts, however, turned out to encompass a very broad idea of what culture is, 'including all domains of human behaviour like technology, art, thought, social organization, economy'. That reassured me. For papyrologists, the Greek formula of a fiscal receipt in the Thebaid, Edfu's purely Egyptian Ptolemaic temple, the status of grain-land, Archimedes' screw, even the camel introduced into the rural circuit, are omnipresent parameters of culture, meaning as much as Homer's place in the books of the Greek pupil in the Fayyum or as the remains of literature written in Demotic. Still, it is necessary to order these parameters, and to make the most of heterogeneous evidence.

In Egypt, the study of the interactions that might be discerned between Greek culture and the autochthonous Egyptian one from Alexander the Great until the early Roman empire concerns a particular case: the coexistence of two basically different complex cultures in the same territory. However, this case presents itself at the same time in the form of the unequal relations of a privileged and dominant minority and an autochthonous majority which has a lesser capacity to organise its own future, this majority and this minority corresponding approximately to the two cultural groups in question. But it shows also an exceptional character: two quite heterogeneous evolved cultures living with their own pasts and ethics (even if one could, in the event, find some 'decline' of particularism in both cases). But, precisely because of their long coexistence, we will have to be attentive not so much to the actual zones of osmosis between the two groups as to the most evident feature in the relations between these two coexisting communities: a marked reciprocal 'opaqueness', which sometimes goes as far as rejection of the 'other'.

It is not necessary to recall here the historic conditions which brought about in Egypt this coexistence of two cultural identities, the Egyptian cultural complex, which is the autochthonous substratum of our problem, on the one hand, and the Greek cultural complex on the other, which is a 'foreign' and even 'disruptive' factor, in the sense that the Graeco-Macedonian minority organised and exploited the country. One detail, however, will immediately show that mere historical analysis sometimes highlights purely formal data which have no weight when compared to the underlying socio-psychological data. The ancient historiographical record is unambiguous: Alexander, we are told, came to Egypt not as an aggressor, but as a liberator from the Achaemenid oppression. At first sight, this should have made relations between the two groups relatively smooth, apart from an emotional element which might have been negative for the Egyptians. They were not under Graeco-Macedonian dominion because they were defeated; the Greek was not a loathed invader and thus a sacrilegious population that divine vengeance would strike sooner or later.

A generation later, Ptolemy assumed the Macedonian royal diadem, but also the pharaonic crown of Upper and Lower Egypt; and this inaugurated the ambiguous relationship between the king and a new bicultural Egypt, which was no longer a satrapy in a foreign empire, even though the king had his capital in Alexandria, a non-Egyptian entity. Certainly, such historic circumstances could easily give consistency to the fiction already admitted during the short reign of Alexander the Great, namely that the Macedonian king was also the pharaoh, indispensable to the gods and people of the Nile valley. This is an important element in our problem. This situation also made contacts easier, if not at the level of real cultural exchanges, at least between an Alexandrian milieu curious about exoticism and the higher Egyptian priesthood disposed to give answers to their questions.

But these favourable circumstances – the arrival of the Macedonians as liberators, their role later as a guarantee of independence – were only superficial factors. They could figure on the walls of some Egyptian temples in a mythology of the Macedonian king as destroyer of the sacrilegious foes of Egypt and as son of the gods, but they were incapable of removing the intimate feelings soon directed against outsiders linked in the eyes of the natives to the idea of administrative or economic abuses committed by the immigrants or their offspring. Surely such behaviour must often have been taken by the Egyptians to represent an assumed right to oppress on the part of the Greeks and to be a mark of the contempt in which the foreigners held the natives. However, when the decline of the monarchy enabled the first revolts, at the end of the third and in the second century, the rebellions appear too readily to us as signs of a cultural cleavage, when in fact the dichotomy is one between privileged and exploited; we too often use the word 'nationalist' to define such movements.

If the 'Ionian', even though he was a liberator, remained a foreigner for the Egyptian, how did the Greeks perceive their settlement in Egypt and the setting up of their permanent political and economic dominion over the autochthonous population?

Here too, we have to make a distinction between historic developments and the evolution of mentalities. History supplies us with some parameters to which we easily assign greater importance than they deserve, for instance the widely held idea that the Greek immigrants thought they had a leading place in the *chôra* by right of conquest. Conquest only accelerated immigration into Egypt, but the major part of this immigration was later than the generation of the conquest. Even for the Ptolemies, Egypt was 'spear-won land' only to support their rights against the other successors of Alexander. At a minimum, our analysis of Greek behaviour in Hellenistic Egypt cannot be based on some legal dialectic the Greeks supposedly used to justify their presence or their privileges. We should instead take into account the 'purely existential' character of this Greek presence in Egypt: the Greek was there because, for one purely personal reason or another, he was there, happily for him in a coherent Greek structure legitimised by royal power, where he was a member of the ruling minority only because he was a Greek and because he was there. On the other hand, Greek immigration into Hellenistic Egypt, especially if the immigrant came from the islands, from Asia Minor or from Cyprus, carried on an old tradition of crossing the sea to get to Naucratis, Memphis or some other Greek settlement, or simply to enter the service of some pharaoh or of the Achaemenids as mercenaries. It is possible to spot some influence of these immigrants in pre-Alexandrian Egyptian culture, for instance, in the field of art, coinage or techniques, but these traces are limited to specific and secondary aspects and are not really signs of a decisive cultural force.

Conversely, we may ask how far Greek immigrants had a persistent sense of Greece's past cultural indebtedness to Egypt. I do not think they were aware of the existence of the utopian image a certain Greek intelligentsia had developed in the archaic and classical period, the *Mirage égyptien* of Christian Froidefond (Aix-en-Provence 1971). In contrast to the mischievous Egyptian of the xenophobic Aristophanes, Egypt and especially the Egyptian priestly class were for the Ionian thinkers, and then from Herodotus to Plato and Aristotle, a source of the sciences, wisdom and philosophy, and even of an incomparable model of devotion and morality. Certainly, there was in archaic and classical times some perception by the Greeks of old cultural transfers, even though this perception quickly became a stereotyped theme of literary utopia. This may have influenced relations between Alexander and his Alexandrian successors and the Egyptian clergy and explain some of the interest among intellectuals, like those of the Museum, in some aspects of Egyptian culture. Surely, however, the average Greek immigrant of the Hellenistic period cannot have acknowledged, even very confusedly, any intellectual debt he owed to Egypt, except maybe in religious matters. Such feelings had no place in his decision to emigrate to Egypt, nor did they influence much his behaviour as a member of the leading class in the realm of the Ptolemies.

If one considers the paradox of such a long coexistence of Egyptians and Greeks in Ptolemaic Egypt and the rather superficial character of the instances of acculturation in the first centuries, it is necessary to establish two preliminary points at once:

1. Neither group formed a homogeneous community. Memphis was not Thebes. Soknopaiou Nesos, which remained essentially Egyptian, was not Krokodilopolis with its Greek elite. Even in partial subgroups, like the Egyptian priesthood or the Greek civil service, different levels existed, sometimes competitive or even antagonistic. It would be dangerous to simplify any proposition.
2. Even if we consider closed cultural entities, these communities were never totally impervious. In fact, zones wherein some osmosis was possible were rather limited: marriage, the army, some branches of the administration, the isolated world of women (from the lady of the house to the maidservants). But even in such

cases the cultural ambiguity would often be temporary. A mixed marriage would probably, sooner or later, insert the new domestic cell into one of the two groups rather than the other. The zone of mixed activities is not significant on the cultural plane: even in the imperial period, urban or village culture seems at first sight Graeco-Egyptian in many aspects, but nothing indicates that such a situation favoured major cultural transfers, even if we must admit that in a millennium both groups certainly evolved, indeed evolved in the immediate vicinity of the other as one major parameter of their evolution.

Finally, it should also be underlined that neither group had a real missionary vocation that would lead to the use of persuasion or force in cultural or religious matters. P. M. Fraser showed that the brilliance of the cult of Sarapis, an Alexandrian cult with an Egyptian origin, is not due to some desire to convert somebody or to shape a community. In fact, as often, the spread of the cult around the Mediterranean illustrates a religious need waiting to be filled, not a dynamic missionary movement like Christianity, Islam or Marxism.

The reason for which the two old cultures which coexisted in Egypt did not give birth to a truly mixed culture, in other words to a process of deep mutual acculturation, lies at the same time in the different structures and dynamics of the two groups and in the lack of interest of either in abandoning the fundamental cultural signs of its own group. This last factor is perhaps obvious for the privileged group, but the absence of interest in the other, where changing offered chances of social and economic advancement, is more significant. Moreover, each of these two groups represented an integrated system, a system in which the parameters of the expression of cultural identity (language, literature, education, religion, etc.) were closely bound to the organisation of the legal, economic and social space of the group and its different components. Integration of the Egyptian or of the Greek system in the Egyptian *chôra* never reached the relative unity and omnipresence of Islam, for example, but these systems are no less remarkable for both their own coherence and their mutual incompatibilities.

In the early Hellenistic period, the integrated cultural system which regulated the Egyptian-speaking population seems to have been based essentially on a priestly structure. This population was easily and functionally situated in a religious universe, rich in explanations of the world, in rules for life, models of society, and promises of survival for the group and for the individual. That made to a certain extent for a monolithic system. Proliferation of divinities, the local character of the cults, multiplicity and competition of the religious authorities, are only superficial appearances of dispersal and diversity. What was fundamental was the unity of the deep devotion of the Egyptians and the coherence of the global answer the religious system and its clergy offered to them. That was particularly precious for a community which had a lot of reasons to feel underrated.

When Alexander the Great 'liberated' Egypt and handed back to the temples the treasures taken away by the Persians, the Egyptian clergy was coming out of a rather short period of persecution. None the less, at the beginning of the Hellenistic period, there was a densely organised network of sanctuaries with its own hierarchy, most of them in settlements which were to become the nome metropoleis, where they functioned as general-purpose socio-economic organising factors for the region around. The upper clergy was the holder of the traditions and guaranteed the survival of the group, maintaining theological education and scribal traditions, practising the sciences, mathematics and medicine. But this clergy had also the prestige which the wealth of the sanctuary conferred, because a major temple was also the holder of a landed domain, which around the largest sanctuaries was very extensive.

Texts and reliefs of the funeral temple of Petosiris in Hermopolis are the classic reference-point for describing Egyptian sacred domains at the beginning of the Hellenistic period. But other sources confirm this image of a system where agriculture, breeding, craftsmanship in gold, copper, perfumes or wood, and the exploitation of real estate all were located in or near the large sacred domains in both rural and more or less urbanised communities. Along with the direct management which they assumed in the sacred domain, the clergy had at first some responsibilities towards the royal domain. Petosiris was not only priest and treasurer of the gods, he was also royal scribe, an office which would remain marked by its Egyptian origin when the first Ptolemies entrusted Egyptians with that high-level task. And the case of Petosiris is not isolated.

By its double function, the temple organised the native population at different levels and proposed to the people through their language and cults the fundamental lines of their cultural identity. The Egyptians instinctively filled in those lines when, for instance, bullied farmers challenged the Greeks by declaring that only they, the Egyptians, knew how to manage agriculture. Surely this Egyptian world was neither homogeneous nor exempt from tensions or striking disparities, and it was certainly far from unanimous when rebelling, but it appears to us, as far we know it, to have constituted a well-balanced group. In fact Herodotus had already, when speaking about a society of castes and specialists, set out for his readers the image of an integrated, stable and immovable stratified community.

The Greek-speaking population settled in the Nile valley also formed an integrated cultural system, but according to quite different parameters. In the Greek system, for example, religion was only an adventitious element, even if it was omnipresent in daily life. Greek immigrants came from a religious environment which somehow managed to move from being a religion that saves the group to being a religion of the individual, with believer, clergy and the city less bound by global imperatives. It was also a milieu with a rather superficial priestly organisation, even though the Ptolemies tried, with some success, to organise dynastic cults and to develop, for instance, a sacred Dionysiac network.

The Greek-speaking community which concerns us here is the Hellenism of the Delta and the valley, not that of Alexandria. Certainly Alexandria, the seat of royal power, was a privileged source of cultural influences in Egypt. This was true particularly for the Greek population of the *chôra*, for which Alexandria supplied a permanent point of reference on the intellectual level, from the point of view of administration and law, and in some degree of economic activities. But the Alexandria of the royal court, the Museum, Neoplatonism or religious syncretism, and later the Alexandria of early Christianity, the harbour open to the Eastern Mediterranean countries and soon to Rome and Italian businessmen, was another world. There the Greek community was a majority and coexisted with non-Egyptian communities, sometimes as culturally and economically important as the Jewish one.

The Hellenism of the *chôra* might appear as an entirely heterogeneous mixture of Greeks, Macedonians or Thracians, mercenaries, civil servants, or more or less organised businessmen, who had only the king as a common point of reference. I believe that such a limited viewpoint would be an error and that one can also consider the immigrants as an integrated cultural system, with its own hierarchy and social disparities. Here too the parameters of cultural expression, language, Greek traditional education and social behaviour, fit in with the parameters of the organisation of the territory, royal administration, law, tax system and cash economy, which were all based on a common economic and social dialectic in the Greek language. Particularly in the beginning, the 'Promethean' Greek milieu of the immigrants distanced itself from the Egyptian by a different relationship with the natural environment. But even when in the course of time and due to constraints of the geographic context the specificity of the Greek-speaking entities declined, the system kept some coherence because the privilege of the minority justified itself by its Greek culture and defended itself by this same culture. This coherence of a Greek-speaking elite among the 'Egyptian' population of inner Egypt was later to be institutionalised by the Romans, even if by that time the socio-cultural character of Egypt had evolved.

Some fundamental aspects of Hellenistic Egypt may seem to cast some doubts on the relative imperviousness of both cultures. First and most salient is the behaviour of the Greeks towards the Egyptian gods. Our modern mentality makes it difficult to imagine the religious feeling of a Greek living in Egypt. His education was partially built upon a literary normalisation of the ancestral religion – the gods of Homer – but for him the local Egyptian temple was a close reality, where the divine took on an exotic look. To what point did the Greek become integrated into this religious exoticism, as the funeral customs we observe strongly suggest? It is all the more difficult to offer an answer in that the situation surely varied from place to place and according to social situations.

Even Egyptian gods worshipped by Greeks do not yield a simple answer. Sarapis, for example, who was very early reshaped as a purely Alexandrian divinity, was a popular source of Greek names, but not of Egyptian, and he is absent from the decorated walls of the Egyptian temples, except as an Osiris. The case of Isis is hardly more significant for the acculturation of the Greek immigrants. Like the cult of Zeus Ammon, that of Isis had its Hellenised versions even before Alexander the Great. Isis's polymorphy, with her 10,000 names, with the theology of her omnipresent divinity as prime mover, might seem to create a common religious zone for faithful Greeks and Egyptians. Nevertheless, we do not easily imagine the place of a devout Greek in Philae's Egyptian sanctuary, which they certainly visited with a faith evidenced in their numerous *proskynêmata*. Isis holds a rather important place in Greek onomastics. But a sounding in the privileged classes from the *chôra* in the imperial period moderates this observation: among gymnasiarchs, at the pinnacle of Greek society, one observes a high frequency of names derived from Apollo, Dionysos, Herakles and Sarapis, too high a frequency to involve an exclusive identification of the first two with Horus and Osiris. It is only in the second zone of frequency that Isis appears, at the same level as Alexander, Zeus, Ammon (the Greek series of Ammonios independent from the Egyptian series of Amounis and derivatives) or simply Ptolemaios. In fact Isis is even favoured when compared with the other Egyptian divinities, who are entirely absent from the higher frequencies. Even in Hermopolis, one of the places which inspired the prestigious idea of an Egyptian science patronised by Thoth/Hermes, and one of the places where Graeco-Egyptian hermeticism would develop, one notices that it is only in the third century AD that names formed on Hermes appear in the group of gymnasiarchs, the Greek closed elite par excellence.

The network of the Egyptian temples could fulfil relatively easily the religious needs of the Greeks, which can scarcely have been met by the few Greek festivals or cult centres, with the exception of the gymnasium. The assimilation of Egyptian and Greek gods was indeed an old Greek tradition, which a reading of Herodotus could sustain. On the other hand, more or less consciously, the Greeks always confusedly combined the phenomenal access to their abundant polytheism and the ontological feeling of divine essence. The exoticism of the cult could be perceived as some local appearance to be transcended. Nevertheless, if the religious domain is the one where the Greek gradually borrowed the most from the Egyptian, basic Egyptian religion had no place in the education of the young Greeks in Egypt. And looking from the other side, we know that Greeks were not always welcomed in the Egyptian temple: a sanctimonious recluse in the Serapeum of Memphis complained – perhaps disingenuously – that he was persecuted there because he was a Greek.

The king and the royal cult might seem to have aspects common to our two integrated systems, being potential sources of mutual cultural transfers. But even here there was a dichotomy. The king-pharaoh was not the *basileus*, the fundamental symbolic element of the Greek integrated system and at the same time the concrete mover of the Greek organisation of the territory. E. Winter showed recently that the Egyptian royal cult was purely functional: the king was the supreme priest, who either in person or at least through his representative, the local chief priest, needed to be represented in order to ensure the perpetuity of the rite. Representations of the king alive show him as an officiating priest or as consecrated king. Even in Memphis, which had privileged links with the Macedonian dynasty, religion was distant from the Greek royal cults of Alexandria or Ptolemais, heroic traditions without any other theology than the symbolism of royal protection in the Greek integrated system. Even though the Egyptian royal cult made some concessions, as when deifying Arsinoe Philadelphos, and the relations of the clergy and the Alexandrian monarchy had political and economic aspects which required a common dialectic, one finds but few traces of ideological concessions on the part of the clergy. Two centuries had to pass before the leap year with a sixth epagomenal day was introduced into the Egyptian calendar, and even then only into the profane world, where it was not observed.

In fact, among the classic parameters of cultural interactions, language, education, literature, religion and the like, in most respects what prevailed was several centuries of relative opaqueness, impossibility or refusal of excessively visible cultural borrowings. And this opacity and separation exceed even these classic parameters. In 1979, H.-J. Wolff reminded us that the cultural dualism of Ptolemaic Egypt found its strongest expression in the legal domain, where Greek law and Egyptian law lived side by side without any real mutual concession.[5]

In the organisation and exploitation of the countryside, to be sure, cultural interaction was more effective, but in so uneven a way between the two groups that it mostly meant the cultural aggression of the privileged group in matters where the invaded group presented traces of archaism. In Chapter 16 we saw how, in Egypt, the cash economy, so familiar to the Greeks, was imposed on the Egyptian, with a double objective: first, to raise money and find guarantees for that money, if only to pay taxes or acquire licences for manufacture or sale; and secondly, to express in terms of money the estimation of the future product. Certainly the natural economy, particularly at the level of taxes and rent in wheat, retained an important role; that was unavoidable in an extensive rural economy, which maintained to a certain extent the tribute economy of the Achaemenid period. But massive payments in kind to the treasury which were not compensated in cash only worsened the Egyptians' difficulty in developing liquid assets and finding credit. The monetary economy stressed the dependence of the Egyptians and disrupted traditional relationships in the Egyptian community.

Let us take another factor and another instance where sociological analysis draws us to the opposite extreme from merely historical interpretation. The growing difficulty of obtaining mercenaries from

---

[5] *Das Problem der Konkurrenz von Rechtsordnungen in der Antike* (SBHeid. Philos.-histor. Klasse, Jahrg. 1979, 5) 49.

abroad, and the decline of a monarchy exhausted by the expensive splendours of what we may call a grandiose third century and probably weakened by dynastic problems, eventually forced the Ptolemies to enlist Egyptian troops. We should resist the notion that this last factor was the initial cause of the concessions that Ptolemies are said to have made later in the second century for the benefit of the Egyptian clergy. This is not the point to revisit the latter question (on which see Chapter 19). But let us first observe that this evolution is also manifested in the regularisation by the king of usurpations and exactions on the part of the Greek cleruchs and officials and, eventually, the existence of a sort of Greek military and administrative feudalism in the *chôra*, especially in Upper Egypt. Our point of departure is different. The settlement of Egyptian *machimoi*, detached from their ancestral homes, on lands which they effectively cultivated in a cleruchic system of a Greek type created a new native milieu more or less removed from traditional Egyptian society. The parallel development of an Egyptian civil service at the level of the village, of which Kerkeosiris' Menches is a model, is another centrifugal evolution of this same society. The emancipation of an Egyptian came initially at the expense of the autochthonous integrated system.

The signs of the decline of this system, particularly in its priestly structure, become more and more visible. In the first century, epigraphic documentation about the right of *asylia* of the temples has raised among historians the problem of the authority of the king (but the king is not the Greek community) and of a virtual autonomy of the Egyptian clergy. Those texts were interpreted as definite signs of the weakness of the first and the growing power of the second. For me this is without doubt an illusion. The concession of the right of *asylia* by the king means in fact that the temple was no longer naturally protected by a social consensus (see below, Chapter 19). Moreover, it is revealing of the growing weakness of the sanctuaries, at least the minor ones, because in those documents the temple often needs to be rebuilt or restored. Other alterations seeming at first blush to have more profound effects on cultural relations gradually emptied the Egyptian integrated system of part of its substance. I shall only briefly quote two of them: first, the growth of private property or stable possession of granted lands, and, secondly, at the same time, the tendency of the Greeks to concentrate in urban areas to become a class of propertied notables living more or less in absence from the rural world (see above, Chapter 8). Such a new network of relations between the two groups modified the two systems, endangering somewhat further the Egyptian system with its temple-based foundation, but scarcely weakening the Greek system, which preserved the fundamental cultural parameters of expression: the language of power, economic management and traditional Greek education.

The Romans completed the destruction of the Egyptian integrated system, which was already weakened by the wreckage, under Ptolemy IX Soter II, of a religious centre as important as Thebes. The Egyptian imperial cult of the emperor-pharaoh languished in pure formalism, even if the emperor was omnipresent as such on the walls and the stelae of the temples. It had no connection to the official imperial cults, cults which put state religiosity in the metropoleis at the scale of the empire. But the Roman attack against what remained of the Egyptian priestly system also took much more effective forms. Sacred property, movable and landed, was inventoried and controlled, when it was not simply amputated for the benefit of the public domain. The privileged personal and fiscal status of the priests became controversial. The priestly class, which was simultaneously the guide and organiser of the Egyptian cultural system, gradually weakened and before long disappeared as an interlocutor for the central power.

The reason was that the system did not find any functional place in the new order established in Egypt by Augustus and his successors: a society organised into a hierarchy with Romans, Alexandrians and a fringe of privileged Greeks on one side, and non-privileged, mostly but not only Egyptian-speaking people on the other. Even the Greek integrated cultural system, with its dominant position, which had evolved since the beginning of the Hellenistic period, now in the new structures of Roman Egypt disintegrated into a society of traditional Greek culture with big or small worthies, a local society based on landed property and dedicated to municipal management. It achieved a surprising preservation of Greek literary culture even in the early Byzantine metropoleis. The cultural parameters of social expression, the Greek language and education in the gymnasium, far from being affected, became (but only for part of the Greek-speaking populations) the elitist parameters of the organisation of the privileges, while in the past they had been only the expression of privileged action in a socio-political royal system.

In fact, one cannot speak any longer of an integrated Greek cultural system in early Roman Egypt. The higher Roman civil service, the Roman army, the increasing intervention of privileged Alexandrians in the economy of the *chôra*, more than a handful of veterans' settlements: these are the elements which broke the global character of the cultural structure. The Greeks of the *chôra* no longer had their *basileus*, they had an emperor. When, in the early Roman empire, neither of the two cultural groups which coexisted in Egypt was any longer an integrated system, they certainly became more permeable, as we can see in numerous domains. All the same, cultural interactions in fact slowed down. Linguistic cleavage remained essentially a social cleavage, with the classic reactions of the cultural self-protection of the privileged classes and the cultural crystallisation of the resentment of the non-privileged. Even the cultural turnover of the tetrarchy and the early Byzantine period did not change things too much. In any event, this increasing permeability of the two groups comes too late to supply us with any model of bilateral cultural interactions. Cultural exchanges outside of Egypt had long existed on the scale of the empire; Alexandria was very early involved in the new currents of the culture of the Roman East. The Egypt of the emperors, with its two cultures, had access to that intellectual and emotional mixture.

This period goes beyond my subject, and in evoking it here I risk simplifying too much, using a symbolic marker of the disintegration of the old global cultural system based on the language, religion and Egyptian scribal tradition. I refer here to the death of Demotic writing and the creation and spread of the Coptic alphabet, but especially the opening up of Coptic written expression, in spite of some continuities with the Egyptian past, to larger cosmopolitan currents like Christianity, gnosticism and Manichaeism. Here, we are far from the closed Egyptian world of the Hellenistic period. Empire created the conditions for the arrival in Alexandria of currents coming from the East, as the Graeco-Macedonian explosion had done for cultures coming from the North. What created the conditions of reception in the countryside of cultural contributions from outside, particularly on the religious and artistic level, is the disappearance of the integrated character, that is, the global function of the traditional Egyptian cultural system. The evolution of the Greek milieu, the product of the very present Alexandrian reference in the culture, preceded the Coptic alteration of society, without being so radical. But the same mechanisms operated in both cases: not the competition of classic aspects of the culture, but the undermining of secondary cultural mechanisms, what I called the cultural parameters of organisation: the Greek organisation of the country, which, in the Hellenistic period, slowly undermined the clerical pillars of the Egyptian cultural system; the new Roman hierarchical organisation of Egypt, which abolished the integrated character of the culture based on the Greek expression of the state organisation, and made this cultural group more available for influences coming both from its immediate Egyptian neighbourhood and from the outside world.

Chapter 19

NORMALITY AND DISTINCTIVENESS IN THE EPIGRAPHY OF GREEK AND ROMAN EGYPT

෨

This chapter, originally written for a colloquium in Bologna devoted to Egypt's place in the larger framework of ancient history, considers the attitude and concerns of the historian facing a pair of connected phenomena: on the one hand, the body of Greek and Roman inscriptions found in Egypt, a huge set of texts which by their mere existence imposes on scholars a duty to have them published and duly commented, and, on the other hand, the potential of this epigraphy to be used as a specific item of evidence, subjected to the normal rules of documentary and historical criticism, but according to a particular methodological approach dictated by local institutional and cultural conditions.

I will discuss this problem within the traditional chronological range of 'papyrology', the millennium which begins with Alexander the Great's arrival in Egypt and ends some decades after the Arabic conquest. But we should not forget that before the arrival of the Macedonian conqueror, in the archaic and later in the classical period, Greek inscriptions were set up or cut on monuments as far south as Nubian Abu Simbel, and that in Naucratis and in the area of Memphis Greek inscriptions as well as coin hoards witness to either the temporary presence of Greek mercenaries or merchants in Egypt or their first permanent settlements in the Delta or in the Nile valley. Furthermore, the survival of some Greek epigraphy after the seventh century AD, a ghost of Hellenism, in Christian Nubia and Ethiopia represents an interesting cultural phenomenon, in which one will find stereotyped Greek inscriptions which allow us to estimate the role of Coptic Egypt or of Palestine and Sinai in the development of Christianity in Northeast Africa. However, whatever their interest is, neither pre-Ptolemaic Greek epigraphy in Egypt nor its early medieval manifestation has a comparable density of existence and expression, nor especially such intimate relations with the socio-political structures of the ruling elements of the country, as we find, even if not without some blank areas, in the Greek and Latin inscriptions from Egypt dating from the period which mainly concerns us here.[1]

It is this considerable collection of documents, available to us after so many centuries and enriched every year by new finds, that we will investigate in this chapter. Perhaps the notions of normality and distinctiveness in its title are somehow provocative or even rather imprudent. In fact, they translate the ambivalent attitude which we should always maintain in documentary criticism: to what extent is the treatment of Greek and Latin epigraphic material from Egypt to be conditioned by the general approach we adopt for this specific type of ancient documents, and how far do we have to take into account, more than elsewhere in the ancient world, the distinctive conditions of environment and circumstances in which these inscriptions were conceived and engraved? We should add another parameter of documentary criticism, the particular conditions in which these same inscriptions were found, published, commented upon and employed by scholars during the past two centuries. These scholars were marked by their own cultural milieu and constantly faced with a larger number of parallel sources specific to Egypt, that is, the papyri and ostraca, than is true in other areas of the Graeco-Roman world.

Actually, even from this introduction it is easy to realise that these notions of normality and distinctiveness are quite relative and not at all mutually exclusive. If one thinks of such rich Greek epigraphic concentrations as Athens, Delphi, Delos, some Ionian metropoleis or even Rome, we immediately perceive how much the institutional, religious and economic local contexts gave a different colouring to each epigraphic thesaurus from these and many other sites. However, behind the differences from one site to another, existential constants also appear in the use of the epigraphic means of expression.

One of the basic approaches of documentary criticism takes into consideration the more or less open access the originator of an inscription foresaw for the text he was drafting. Carving on stone – and this is true for all languages – presumes the will to ensure a wide and durable access to the document. This is true even for the most modest funeral stele inscribed with a single name, that no doubt of a man who in his lifetime had neither history nor fame, and it is certainly true for the most ambitious imperial inscriptions engraved in

---

[1] The relatively poor epigraphy of late antiquity, with its own problems of 'normality' and 'distinctiveness', will not be treated here *in extenso*; see my paper 'L'épigraphie grecque de l'Égypte post-constantinienne', *XI Congresso Internazionale di Epigrafia Greca e Latina. Roma, 18–24 settembre 1997. Atti* II (1999) 613–24.

Behistun, Ankara, Adulis or elsewhere. It is a fundamental feature of epigraphy on stone or coins that these texts are purposefully created to be read for a long time and as often as possible. That makes these documents fundamentally different from those that aim at a restricted and short-lived access and conservation, like tablets in Linear B, shards of Attic ostracism, and documentary papyri or ostraca from Egypt, to keep for the moment to the Greek domain. This general characteristic of epigraphy applies without any restriction to Greek inscriptions in Egypt, to the monumental decrees of the Ptolemaic sacerdotal synods as well as to the signatures of more or less obscure travellers in the royal tombs or to the most humble of the Christian stelae in Antinoe or Nubia.

If one turns to the other component, or the other trap, in the heading of my paper, the distinctiveness of the Greek and Latin epigraphic phenomenon in Egypt, we encounter at once, at least from the point of view of interpretation and of the representative character of the document, two situations unique in the epigraphy of antiquity.

In the first place, in Egypt, Greek epigraphy is practised next to an epigraphy of considerable volume in the autochthonous language in its various forms. Egyptian is written in Coptic in the Byzantine period; in earlier times it could be Demotic, but the prestigious hieroglyphic epigraphy is dominant in the Ptolemaic age and survives honourably in the first centuries of our era. Those who have had the privilege of visiting the impressive Ptolemaic temples of Upper Egypt and seeing them with an epigraphist's eyes are overwhelmed by these bastions covered with figures and with texts, real kaleidoscopes of rituals a hundred times renewed in words and images by the king-pharaoh worshipping the local divinities. At the point these inscriptions were put up, hieroglyphic epigraphy was in full renewal, not decadent, even though it displays a sophisticated dead language. This renewal of its means of expression has, to be sure, a large element of esoteric acrobatics, but that does not diminish the innovative character of the developed subjects, even when they are ritualistic. We meet the same renewal in some historic stelae which glorify the king-pharaoh as well as in private stelae which praise the behaviour of individuals. There, for example, the Egyptian woman is valued with new specific accents which sometimes echo the spirit of some Greek metric epitaphs. Still it would be pointless to search there for any Greek influence or, at least, it is beyond the capabilities of a Hellenist to discern it. The evolution of hieroglyphic epigraphy during the Ptolemaic period is coherent in itself. What strikes me, as a devotee of the document and as a historian, is the parallel existence of two epigraphies foreign to each other with mainly different themes and means of expression, a gap which goes beyond the different structures of languages and systems of writing.

Although we meet some casual interconnections between the two epigraphic traditions, it is far easier to find types of inscriptions where the divergent approaches of Greek epigraphy and the autochthonous ones and the lack of mutual connections are clearly perceived. Part of the explanation is that the documents emanated from quite different epigraphic traditions. There we sometimes feel most sharply the gulf between the cultural systems which coexisted in Egypt. A group of late Hellenistic Greek documents illustrates this phenomenon because the way they are conceived is so stereotyped that it becomes significant. In this period, Greek decrees of associations or assemblies in honour of high protectors are followed by a list of names with their patronymics. In the Greek tradition, when the stone perpetuates the names of relatively important individuals, the list aims also to commemorate the right every single member of the group possesses to participate in deciding on the decree, even if such a right is tiny or purely nominal. There is another perspective seen in many Greek inscriptions, and not only among the *philobasilistai*, 'king-lovers', namely the desire to be directly or indirectly situated for eternity in terms of loyalty to the king, especially when the inscription illustrates the relationship of the king as benefactor to his beneficiaries or the vital solidarity which exists between them. We will later meet the 'on behalf of the king' (ὑπὲρ βασιλέως) formula particular to 'Egyptian' Greek epigraphy and the most meaningful manifestation of a cultural consensus. Such texts and such a mentality have no significant counterpart in Egyptian epigraphy.[2]

Among those Greek documents I would cite two inscriptions from Memphis that Dorothy Thompson (1984) has revisited. The first one is a decree of the *'politeuma* of the Idumaean servicemen and the Idumaeans of the city'.[3] This Semitic group, which met in the temple of the Idumean god Qos-Apollo, followed the quite typical Greek practice of proceeding by decree and perpetuating the role of each member by giving a list of names. The other is a decree of a community of founders, a κοινὸν κτιστῶν, the names of some of them

---

[2] For some echo of the ὑπέρ formula in the dying Demotic epigraphy of the early imperial period, see 'Parthenios de Coptos et l'Isis du Pimmeiômis', in *Pages* II 1–10, especially n. 5.

[3] *OGIS* 737 (*I. Prose* 25, erroneously understood as issued by the 'corps civique de Memphis'; cf. *CdÉ* 69 (1994) 158–9).

showing that they are Idumaeans (*SB* I 681). We find there the same Greek reflex to immortalise through a list of names the body that had the capacity to take such a decision. This type of inscription does not exist in the Egyptian language, because in that cultural group we find neither the same process of decision, nor the same feeling that the dedication ensures renown both to the honoured person and to the person or the group able to decide upon such honours. Moreover, the epigraphic reflex of the Idumaeans reveals their functional link with the Graeco-Macedonian cultural system, the world of the *Hellênes*. It corresponds to other trends towards self-insertion into this broader group like, for instance, the more and more frequent use of Greek names by the Idumaean colony as generations succeeded one another, as was noticed by Dorothy Thompson.

This global difference between Egyptian and Greek epigraphies makes all the more visible the fact that the king is often present on both sides, but he intensely illustrates the difference between the Macedonian king-*basileus* of Greek epigraphy and the king-pharaoh of the Egyptian hieroglyphic texts.

A second unique feature of our Egyptian documentary environment, at least at such a level of intensity, is the sharing of the same geographic space by epigraphic documents and by a mass of Greek, Latin and Demotic documentary papyri, ostraca and mummy labels.[4] This coexistence, unique in its extent in the ancient world, enriches both types of evidence. In some domains they are even inextricable. It is well known how much the study of ancient onomastics progressed thanks to Greek epigraphy under Louis Robert's leadership and to Latin epigraphy, among others by the activity of the Finnish school. In Egypt, for onomastics as for prosopography, there is a single encompassing documentation. As soon as we meet Egyptian names, we have to consider on the same level all the evidence in Greek and in Egyptian, a tendency which is now wide-spread and where the Leuven school has played a leading role.

Examples are not lacking where epigraphy and papyrology throw mutual light on their documents. Let us cite, for instance, in Coptos, the case of Paminis and his son Parthenios. For them there are three dossiers: Greek inscriptions, Demotic inscriptions, and a group of Greek ostraca found in Coptos but drawn up in the harbours of the

---

[4] It should not need stressing that papyrologists, in the broad sense of the term, treat inscriptions as part of the material for their studies, following models like Wilcken or Preisigke. Letronne, one of the founders of epigraphy, was also a papyrologist, whose editions, although now out of date, were praised by Wilcken.

Red Sea coast.[5] The first two series reveal the religious role of local Graeco-Egyptian worthies, particularly in the construction of a sanctuary; the last group documents their activity as forwarders of all sorts of goods to Myos Hormos, Berenike or the garrisons of the Eastern Desert. Only the conjunction of these three files transforms a ghostly dedicant and an insignificant trader into a valid sample of the Coptos bourgeoisie under the Julio-Claudians.

Are there Greek and Latin inscription types which are unique to Egypt? It would be 'owls to Athens' to deal at length in Bologna about the *proskynêmata,* or acts of adoration, to which our colleague Giovanni Geraci (1971) dedicated a model terminological and typological study, on which the following is dependent. But we cannot avoid at least mentioning this Greek epigraphic genre found only in Egypt, which almost has its model and the key to its interpretation in Demotic epigraphy. Witness of an acquired religious mentality, the *proskynêma* as religious practice had its roots in rituals Greek immigrants saw Egyptian people performing. Among Greek inscriptions, the type appears rather late, in the middle of the second century BC. Religion is the social domain where Greeks living inside the country most easily found intimate links with the native practices. Identifications of Greek and Egyptian divinities had been made for a long time, as we see in Herodotus, and the Greeks had always more or less consciously distinguished in their own pantheon the ontological access to the divine and the daily access to a lot of divinities, daimones and heroes. Assimilated Egyptian gods were plainly an exotic transliteration of a familiar religious environment, the divine character of which was not debatable. It is more interesting that with *proskynêmata,* an act of worship which one makes for oneself or for a distant person dear to one or even for one's superior, the epigraphic gesture takes on a new dimension, unknown to classical Greek epigraphy and borrowed from the Egyptian decoration of the temple or of the tombs: the inscription becomes the active substitute for its author after his departure. In this case, the desire to give a permanent utterance to words has the visited divinity in mind, not primarily the

---

[5] *I. Pan* 78 a, *I. Portes* 58–60. The article by A. J. Reinach-R. Weill, 'Parthénios fils de Paminis "prostatès" d'Isis à Koptos', *Annales du Service des Antiquités d'Égypte* 12 (1912) 1–24, gives a good general view of this trilingual epigraphic dossier, although since then it has been extended with some additional items; cf. *Zeitschrift für Ägyptische Sprache* 51 (1913) 75–88. For the ostraca, see the Coptos material in *O. Petr.* For the Demotic part of this epigraphic series, see A. Farid, 'Die Denkmäler des Parthenios, des Verwalters der Isis von Koptos', *Mitteilungen der Deutschen Archäologischen Instituts, Abt. Kairo* 44 (1988) 13–65. Add now Bingen, *Pages* II, cited in n. 2 above.

passer-by who stops to read the *proskynêma* and unconsciously renews in this way the first act of adoration.

Other inscriptions peculiar to the Nile valley have something to offer with more immediate impact for historiography. As a starting-point I choose the 'five-star' monuments of Greek epigraphy in Egypt, the large decrees voted at the conclusion of the priestly synods which regularly brought together delegates of the major Egyptian sanctuaries. Those impressive trilingual texts, Hieroglyphic, Demotic and Greek, represent a type of epigraphic production specific to Egypt. They are especially well known because two of them played a major role in Hellenistic historiography during the nineteenth century and even later.

After its discovery in 1799 in Rosetta, the decree issued in Memphis by the priestly synod of 196 BC (*OGIS* 90) immediately gave a serious impetus to the decipherment of Demotic; two editions of the Greek version were published as early as 1802. I shall not evoke here the role which this decree played later in the decoding of hieroglyphs and in the birth of the theory of mixed culture which from Droysen until rather recently conditioned studies devoted to the Hellenistic East. In 1866 another trilingual decree was found in Tanis, the one issued by the synod assembled in Canopus in 238 in the reign of Ptolemy III Euergetes. From the way both documents were drawn up it had seemed possible in the past to deduce from the later one a progressive Egyptianisation in the wording and substance of the sacerdotal decree. According to a trend which once seemed to impose itself on thinking about this period,[6] the decree of 196 appeared even as an early testimony of the decline of royal authority to the benefit of the growing power of the Egyptian clergy. Such a conclusion does not in my opinion stand up to a 'strictly documentary' approach to the problem. This analysis, I think, should precede any use of those texts as historical evidence. The whole problem is truly too complex not to be treated in an independent study, and I shall limit myself to a secondary but eloquent aspect of the data, the titulature used for the dating of both decrees.

Indeed, the differences which the two forms of titulature offer had their part in the traditional historical conclusions to which I alluded. The introduction of the decree voted in Canopus effectively shows a

---

[6] On the parallel case of *P. Tebt.* I 5, and for a questioning of the automatic interpretation of the same type, 'powerful clergy imposing concessions on royal power', see Chapter 14, particularly pp. 196–7. Later in the present chapter I propose an analysis of the same type for the decrees of *asylia* from the Fayyum.

pure Hellenic style with its series of Alexandrian eponymous priests:

> In the reign of Ptolemy son of Ptolemy and Arsinoe the Brother and Sister Gods, year 9, when Apollonides son of Moschion was priest of Alexander and the Brother and Sister Gods and the Benefactor Gods, when Menekrateia daughter of Philammon was *kanephoros* of Arsinoe Philadelphos, on the 7th of the month Apellaios, for the Egyptians the 17th of Tybi.

In the date of the Memphis decree of 196, the royal titulature is on the contrary loaded with Egyptian elements which precede the Alexandrian eponyms:

> In the reign of the young man who received the kingdom from his father, lord of the crowns, great of reputation, who restored Egypt and the affairs of the gods, the pious, who got the better of his enemies, the one who restored the life of men, lord of the thirty-years' feast, like Hephaistos the great, king like the Sun, Great King of the upper and lower lands, offspring of the Father-loving Gods, whom Hephaistos approved, to whom the Sun gave victory, living image of Zeus, Son of the Sun, Ptolemy the everliving, beloved of Ptah, ninth year, in the priesthood etc.

Here we particularly find versions of the great names of the Pharaonic titulature: 'in the reign of the young man' (Horus name), 'lord of the crowns', 'who got the better of his enemies', 'Great King of the upper and lower lands'. A series of other labels have an Egyptian origin – even if the names of the Egyptian gods are Hellenised – and Memphis occupies here a predominant place, not the least with 'the everliving, beloved of Ptah' closely linked with the name of the king – this time the great god of Memphis in his Egyptian expression rather than as Hephaistos.[7]

It is indisputable that the Egyptian titulature is here fully integrated into the Greek royal dating system which we found in its merely Greek display in Canopus. Quite understandably, this passage struck the Hellenists immediately and is still an element which we at least have to discuss. But are we entitled to infer from this fact a decline of the Macedonian monarchy and a heavier dependency of the king on the Egyptian clergy? I do not think so, and, as an epigraphist, I would react against a mode of comparison between the two texts which is far from being conclusive. As with every exercise of documentary criticism, we have to start by considering the place and the structural environment where the text arose. How far was this milieu different in 238 and 196?

---

[7] There is a convenient analysis and useful bibliography of this titulature in Koenen (1983: 155, n. 36).

Objectively it is not a case of evolution but one of difference of setting. Both decrees are issued by an assembly of high dignitaries of the Egyptian clergy. Next to them, Greek individuals, in the final analysis the representatives of the king, communicate what the latter wishes to see granted by the clergy and what he is ready to grant himself. Decisions summarised in the decree imply such a dialogue. Among those Greeks some secretaries were ready, if necessary, to help the scribes of the temple to draw up a beautiful trilingual decree.[8] However, we must take into account the fact that, assembled in Canopus, near Alexandria, far from its traditional dwellings, the synod of 238 felt the influence of the court, certainly more than it would have in Memphis, a place where, on the contrary, it was a rule to commemorate the royal filiation in the Egyptian way, the key to the legitimacy of the king-pharaoh. One might thus expect a different cultural tonality between the two decrees without needing to search for more general political conclusions.

On the other hand, the mixed Graeco-Egyptian titulature of the decree of 196 is not a new feature. We find one already, almost word for word, in the previous reign, in the so-called Raphia decree issued at the conclusion of an earlier synod in Memphis,[9] at a moment when it is difficult to suspect any concession by the triumphant king to the clergy. Moreover, such Egyptian titulature is already present in the hieroglyphic titulature of Ptolemy II. The beginning of the decree of Rosetta, far from defying the king-*basileus*, is, for the Egyptian milieu which inspired the wording of it, a recognition, formal or not, of the legitimacy of the king-pharaoh. Moreover the drawing up of the decree of 196 may be easily situated in the continuation of the coronation of the young Ptolemy V Epiphanes, celebrated some months earlier in Memphis by the same local upper clergy and probably the same delegates of the major Egyptian sanctuaries.

The wording of the decrees of both synods calls for one final reflection by the epigraphist, because the sequence of the elements of the

[8] The problem of the anteriority of the Greek text or of the Demotic one and what the historians should deduce from it seems to me a ghost-problem. It depends first on the linguistic capacities of the people who were drawing up both versions of the decree; on the other hand, these elaborated the decree from a file which contained pieces in both languages; finally, our perception of the matter, I think, can only be subjective. Since the symposium in Bologna, P. Derchain, *Le dernier obélisque* (Brussels 1987: 44), developed a very similar idea following a seminar in Cologne which he devoted, together with H. J. Thissen, to the comparative study of the three versions of the Memphis decree: 'There was no original Demotic or Greek text; the two versions must have been drawn up at the same time and depend one upon the other, according to the origin of the subject to be formulated.'

[9] Cf. Koenen (1983: 155, n. 36), and especially H. J. Thissen, *Studien zum Raphiadekret* (Meisenheim 1966).

inscription is edifying. The Memphis decree has the following structure: basic reference by a royal date – *psêphisma* (decree) – the promoters of the decree 'spoke': since . . . with good fortune . . . it was decided – followed by the decision-clauses of trilingual epigraphic publicity. Let us first notice the panhellenic arrangement of the Greek version of the decree of 196, at least in its structure and in the formulae which articulate this structure. If we except the omnipresent king and trilingualism imposed by the final clause, one would almost imagine that we were in Athens. More interesting is the fact that, apart from the insignificant variant in the decree formula (δεδόχ-θαι/ἔδοξεν), the wording already exists in the decree of Canopus. An epigraphic tradition of the priestly decree was obviously stabilised at an early date, and it is all the more remarkable to see it in 196 in a pre-eminently Egyptian environment. Rather than supposing that this environment was hostile to the king, in Memphis one should rather recognise a lasting complicity of the two powers, the king and the Memphite clergy.

I would like to end this part of the discussion with two conclusions this document suggested to me. Are we allowed to conclude that, contrary to what was done in Canopus, Ptolemy V Epiphanes made important royal concessions in 196 to the benefit of the Egyptian clergy? It is necessary first to take into account the general rhetoric of the mutual relations of king and clergy. This postulates *a priori* the munificent generosity of the former, the recognition of the royal piety by the latter. The Memphis decree adds the proclamation of the royal victory with priests openly dissociating themselves from the rebellion. If one examines closely the alleged concessions from the generosity of the king, one notices that they essentially guarantee the former rights and privileges of the clergy, which were ignored or violated by agents of the king or endangered during periods of unrest (as with *P. Tebt.* I 5; cf. above, n. 6). Amnesties and donations which complete those 'concessions' are part of the normal royal discourse during a coronation. In the same way, to perceive in the decree of Canopus more important concessions of the clergy than in 196 is only an effect of sacerdotal rhetoric in its counterpart of the decree. We do not know if the cult of the dead princess introduced into the Egyptian temple was as important as claimed in the declaration of the priests. As for the reform of the calendar and the introduction of a leap year every four years – surely a suggestion coming from some Alexandrian scholar – the Egyptian priests voted the change, and then did not implement it – nor did the king's own administration.

Figure 19.1   South temple at Karanis (photo Roger S. Bagnall)

In this light, the decree of Memphis appears to be part of a very different historical context from a supposed bargaining with the autochthonous clergy for some help for the young king. In reality, the king was actually reconquering parts of the realm lost more by a temporary local weakness of the royal power than by outside intrigues or internal revolts. This process of taking over the inheritance of the great Ptolemies appears to me much more as a moment in the evolution of the notion of Hellenistic kingship: the replacement of the legitimacy of the saviour by the legitimacy of the dynasty, even represented by a child, whom his ministers led eventually to the coronation in Memphis by means of a renewed foreign policy, the reorganisation of the army, and the reconquest of the realm.

I continue this review of the distinctive character of some Greek local epigraphic genres with a series of inscriptions which as much by phrasing as by contents are simultaneously purely Greek and yet indisputably documents unique to Egypt. A relatively homogeneous group of *asyliai* from the Arsinoite nome grant or confirm the right of asylum of some sanctuaries. These are grouped between 95 BC and the end of the Ptolemaic dynasty.[10] The series is sufficiently numerous and diversified to exclude the hazard of discovery as a significant factor. Moreover, those inscriptions form part of a wider group, some

---

[10] *I. Fay.* 152, cf. *C. Ord. Ptol.* 65 (Magdola, temple of Heron, 95 BC); *I. Fay.* 112, 113, cf. *C. Ord. Ptol.* 66 (Theadelpheia, temple of Isis Sachypsis, 93 BC); *I. Fay* 114, cf. *C. Ord. Ptol.* 68 (Theadelpheia, temple of Isis Eseremphis and temple of Herakles Kallinikos, 70 BC); *I. Fay.* 135, cf. *C. Ord. Ptol.* 69 (Euhemeria, temple of the Crocodile Gods, 69 BC); *I. Fay.* 136 (Euhemeria, temple of Amon, 69/68); *I. Fay.* 116, 117, 118, cf. *C. Ord. Ptol.* 72 (Theadelpheia, temple of Pnepheros, 57 BC).

ten analogous documents about the recognition of the right of asylum held by some sacred places, all from the first century.[11] Therefore the group may be considered as significant.

All six inscriptions from the Fayyum indirectly describe the procedure at the end of which a temple hopes to enjoy forever, at least theoretically, the safe possession of the right of asylum. It is easy to trace the genesis of the inscriptions. The first step of the procedure was a request to the king asking that the sanctuary and its people, including those that take refuge within, should be protected against any intervention and abduction and that the local authorities should ensure the application of this privilege. This request is quoted literally and at length in the inscriptions. The king complies with the request by issuing a very brief *prostagma* sent to the local authorities, ordering them to ensure the protection as described in the request.

One of these stelae allows us to follow concretely the epigraphic process implied by such a procedure. *I. Fay.* II 112 (Theadelphia, 95 BC) quotes in ll. 2–34 the request of the priests of Isis Sachypsis, who recall that their sanctuary was worshipped and honoured, but that it suffers a lot from sacrilegious humiliations. The epigraphist will note that the request asks not only that the right of asylum be granted to the sanctuary, but further that the priests be allowed 'to erect stelae of stone in the four cardinal points at a distance of fifty cubits around the temple', stelae that clearly show the text of the *lex sacra*: 'entrance forbidden for everybody who has no business'.[12]

We still possess two of those four stelae that the priests were allowed by the king to erect in the sanctuary of Isis Sachypsis. On both of them the order '*asylos* according to the decree for anyone who has no business' (ἄσυλον κατὰ πρόσταγμα ὧι μὴ πρᾶγμα) is inscribed above and is followed by the text of the request of the priests. The presence of this last document is indispensable to give content to the protection which must be ensured and to define the

[11] C. *Ord. Ptol.* 64 (Athribis, temple of Horus Kentechtai, 97/96, mentioning temples in Memphis and Bousiris as well as other temples which possess the right of asylum); *SB* I 3926, cf. C. *Ord. Ptol.* 67, cf. Add. p. 381 (Ptolemais, sanctuary of Isis erected by the *epistrategos* Kallimachos, 46). Cf. C. *Ord. Ptol.*[2] 70[2], 381–2 (Lower Egypt, sacred treasures, 63). *OGIS* 129. Cf. *SEG* XXXII 1954 (Lower Egypt, synagogue, 47–30, confirmation of an *asylia* granted by Ptolemy VIII Euergetes II). Some papyrological data may be added; among them *P. Tebt.* I 5.83–4 (118 BC) οἱ ὑπάρχοντες ἄσυλοι τόποι, cf. earlier *P. Tebt.* III 699.15–17 (135/134); G. Geraci, *Scritti Orsolina Montevecchi* (Bologna 1981) 163–9 (prohibition on buying, selling and occupying sacred premises, second century BC); *BGU* VI 1212.12–20 (allusion to a list of *asyliai* κατὰ τόπον for every nome, 46 BC).
[12] Cf. *I. Fay.* 114.46–51.

Figure 19.2 *Asylum stele* I. Fay. 116 *(photo after E. Bernand,* Recueil des inscriptions grecques du Fayoum II, *pl. 20 – reproduced with permission of IFAO)*

obligations of the officials of the king. Indeed, the royal *prostagma* which is transcribed beneath on both stelae is reduced to two words 'To Lysanias: do it' (*Λυσανίαι· ποιεῖν*) and the date. The name of the *strategos* Lysanias is actually the entire covering letter! The *strategos* Lysanias had to read the request of the priests to know more about his duty. Naturally he used the original text of the decision sent from Alexandria on a papyrus sheet, perhaps with a subscription by the king's own hand, which he kept in his archives. The four copies on stone came later as part of the follow-up to the decision and had another purpose in the minds of the priests: to confer eternity to the grant and to call to the passer-by forever to witness to what must or may not be done by the king's people. In other words, epigraphy.

I have dealt elsewhere[13] with the erroneous exploitation of those inscriptions, particularly for the history of the relations between king and clergy, a theme which – wrongly or not – is considered a major parameter of the internal situation in late Hellenistic Egypt. I raise there some objections against the traditional use of these documents as testimony for the existence of exceptional privileges granted to some sanctuaries, and especially as evidence for an almighty Egyptian clergy which in the late Hellenistic period could extract them from a weaker royal power. This myth, soon transformed into a dogma, was created by Rostovtzeff in 1920, under the double influence of the recent publication of the archives of Zenon and of our Fayyum stelae. Due to a surprising distortion of these last texts, the protection mandated by the inscriptions was transformed into a 'right to hide the strikers and exploit their labour for their own purposes. The old feudal system arose again.'[14] This extrapolation from the text, which nothing in the wording of the documents justifies, became an accepted view. It was not until 1978 that we find Claire Préaux refusing to accept such a role for these documents and their Rostovtzeffian interpretation.[15] All the same, that interpretation was given new support not long after by Françoise Dunand, with the statement:

> The capacity recognised for some temples in Egypt in the Hellenistic period to offer as a rule an inviolable protection to those that came to take

---

[13] Paper read at the VIIIth Congress of Greek and Latin Epigraphy in Athens in 1982. For an unknown reason it remained unpublished. Summary: 'Les ordonnances des Lagides sur le droit d'asile des temples', *Πρακτικὰ τοῦ η' διεθνοῦς συνεδρίου ἑλληνικῆς καὶ λατινικῆς ἐπιγραφικῆς* II (Athens 1987) 70.

[14] 'The foundation of social and economic life in Egypt in Hellenistic times', *JEA* 6 (1920) 161–78; cf. also Rostovtzeff (1941: 899–903).

[15] Préaux (1978: I, 378–9; II, 433–5).

refuge constituted for the clergy a powerful means for pressure and action; therefore, in the conflict which during the three centuries of the Ptolemaic dominion opposes clergy and monarchy, the question of the right of asylum appears to me to act somehow as a touchstone. One can indeed interpret the extension of the granting of *asylia*, in the first century BC, as a manifestation of the increasing influence exercised by the clergy on the population, and as one of the signs of the decline of royal power.[16]

And, by way of conclusion, she writes:

> But we may find there something that explains, after all, a policy seemingly against their own interests that motivates the sovereigns in the second half of the second and in the first century BC: in an Egypt shaken by revolts and ceaseless unrest, the clergy was probably the only organised force able to control the population and thus appears as the only possible support for the king who, forced to appeal to its influence, could only hope to win the priests over to his cause through dangerous concessions.

I do not know if such a clergy existed at that moment,[17] but the epigraphist vainly searches for one precisely in the inscriptions which are said to attest such a powerful sacerdotal class.

For that reason we should give more weight to the epigraphic aspect of the problem. Let us allude quickly to von Woess's *Asylwesen Ägyptens in der Ptolemäerzeit*, a reference dating from 1923 and still compulsory when studying *asylia*. Indeed, this good monograph has practically nothing to say on the matter of the internal history of Ptolemaic Egypt. A prisoner of his terminological constraints with their categorical concepts,[18] von Woess handled these late Ptolemaic decrees on the same semantic level as, for example, an amphictyonic *asylia* asked from Ptolemy Philadelphos or a petition of the Lydian town of Magnesia asking Ptolemy Philopator for the recognition of its rights of asylum. Such an approach fails to recognise that where we are investigating social relations, the specific characteristics of groups create local variations in the meaning of a word and, from the

---

[16] 'Droit d'asile et refuge dans les temples en Égypte lagide', *Hommages à la mémoire de Serge Sauneron* II (1979) 77–97. Cf. also, e. g., G. Casanova, *Aegyptus* 55 (1975) 119; but one could multiply recent references to what is accepted as common wisdom in the problem of the Fayyum *asyliai*.

[17] The large temples inaugurated in the late Hellenistic period, like Edfu or Philae, should not deceive us. Their construction started much earlier and with the help of royal endowments, in a period when such buildings were interpreted as a sign of the power and not the weakness of the king-pharaoh. But I certainly do not mean that in the later Hellenistic period, the large temples were on the edge of ruin.

[18] This monograph, however, remains fundamental for such notions as *hiketeia* [supplication], *skepê* [protection] and *asylia*.

epigraphic point of view, give the evidence about those relations a distinctive local flavour, even though the same word may be used. For *asylia*, von Woess bases his study, reasonably but none the less unsuccessfully, on a formal semantic approach to the problem of our *asylia* decrees. But, even before the publication of *Asylwesen*, more or less consciously adopted medieval models created among the scholars of the first half of the twentieth century – among them Rostovtzeff – the feeling that 'state' and 'church' were confronting each other in a zero-sum game, where the strength of one implied the weakness of the other. With such conceptions in our view of medieval history, it is hard to escape episodes like the Quarrel of the Investitures or assumptions about a mechanical opposition between monastery and castle, when we try to imagine the relations between secular power and clergy. Does this 'medieval' model really stand up to a purely documentary critical analysis of our inscriptions? More exactly, what can we learn from the arguments people used when drawing up the petition to ensure the epigraphic eternity of the royal answer?

From the seven sanctuaries[19] which are attested as obtaining concessions from the supposedly poor, weak king, two were devoted to Greek cults, of which one was located in an abandoned temple surrounded by a desert domain. Nothing allows us to think that the five other sanctuaries with Egyptian cults were prosperous (two of the temples were falling into ruins). Another major element in the genesis of our six inscriptions from the Arsinoite is not at all in accordance with the notion of a powerful Egyptian clergy facing a failing Greek kingship: the inscriptions mention that, except for the Isis Sachypsis temple (where Sarapis and the royal cult are associated with Isis), all the other requests are introduced on the initiative of Greek people or under their protection. When their legal position is specified, they are officers of the royal guard or chiliarchs. The inscriptions place the requests for *asylia* in an entirely different social context from the dogmatic dichotomy of tensions between 'state' and 'church'[20] in Egypt. Here, as often elsewhere, the rival and hostile centrifugal forces which pressed on the life of the sanctuary existed inside the Greek royal system – the army, which appears here as the defender of some sanctuaries, and the administration, whose servants are in particular cited as responsible for illegal exactions. Paradoxically, it is the same

---

[19] Of the six stelae, *I. Fay.* 114 concerns two sanctuaries.

[20] A term we should not use, because designating 'Egyptian clergy' in this fashion obliterates the fact that this priesthood was neither a homogeneous system, nor a unanimous one, nor even a united force.

Rostovtzeff who perceived – but this time regrettably without attracting a significant audience – the birth of the actual forces with which the monarchy had to cope in the late Hellenistic period: the 'Greek tycoons', the *condottieri*, often recent immigrants, the dynasties of high-ranking servants and officers.[21] Rostovtzeff concludes more precisely, 'It is highly likely that temples like individuals had their special patrons among the magnates of the day, under whose *skepê* they lived.' It is amusing for the epigraphist to discover that the same six inscriptions contributed to allowing this great historian to formulate two contradictory pictures of the weaknesses of the monarchy in the first century BC: on the one hand, the weak king has to buy the help of the clergy with fatal concessions to protect himself from the natives, and, on the other hand, the weak king gives up the task of organising an arbitrary portion of the realm to Greek structures more or less outside his authority.

A last detail of naive epigraphy: the stelae limit the territory 'in the four winds' [in four directions] to 50 cubits, about 25 m, all around the sanctuary. Do they protect more than the pocket-handkerchief territory where the priest is master at home and over his people, including those who would momentarily escape the exactions of the king's people? How could such a tiny area imply a space for a large rival economy and a significant autonomous domain?[22]

The analysis of the series of *asyliai*, taking them both in their epigraphic 'normality' (that is, as the last recourse available for ensuring a right, the open and permanent display of the institutional mechanism which created the right) and in their epigraphic 'distinctiveness' (isolating the inscriptions found in Egypt from their Greek pseudo-parallels) thus allows us to place the *asylia* decrees from the Fayyum or from elsewhere in their true perspective: the slow but inevitable decline of the influence of the temples, which depended more and more on the king to be restored to their traditional rights. With the progressive disintegration of the closed and uncontested cultural framework that Egyptian society constituted in the early Hellenistic

---

[21] See, for example, Rostovtzeff (1941: 896): 'It is no exaggeration to say that in the late second century BC and in the first Egypt was governed not by the king and by some of his honest and well-meaning ministers but by a clique of selfish, greedy, and lawless officials who formed a new, wealthy, and influential aristocracy of the kingdom.' It is necessary to take into account the tendency towards a causal stylisation of history which sometimes animated this great historian of the Hellenistic period. On the more general aspect of the problem, see Chapter 14.

[22] In the *prostagma* from Athribis, *C. Ord. Ptol.* 64 (96 BC), although the text is rather uncertain, it seems that the *asylia* is limited to the *peribolos* of the temple.

period, a framework more and more challenged by the growing responsibilities of the natives in the military and administrative system of the king, even at a high level, this decline meant that in the first century the clergy depended more on royal protection, but especially, just like the king himself, in a more present and more concrete way, on the protection provided by the new Greek civil and military aristocracies.

Another rule of documentary criticism, however, must be kept in mind. The appearance or disappearance of a particular type of text does not necessarily mean an institutional change. It can mean no more than a change in the requirements for publication, due for instance to new rules or a change in mentalities. The sudden appearance about the year 200 BC of the epigraphic records of manumissions providing 'freedom by sale to the god' in the Apollo sanctuary of Delphi does not mean that the practice of manumitting by this means dates from that period. There was simply some change, so far unexplained, in the way in which access was given to the text of the agreement, which from this point onwards was permanently open to all by means of an epigraphic publication, protected in this case by the sacredness of the place. In other words, faced with this series of six *asylia* decrees from the Arsinoite nome grouped in time and seamlessly inserted into a larger papyrological documentation, we should not neglect the hypothesis that a modification in the requirements for publication of the *asylia* might explain the abrupt appearance of those decrees, rather than some modification of the political conditions in Hellenistic Egypt. Actually some of the decrees, as we saw, have rather curious clauses of publication, but so far we have no evidence for any requirement of epigraphic publication. We must, I believe, look elsewhere for an answer to our problem. Allusions in the papyri to the registration of temples enjoying the right of asylum and the appearance of sanctuaries searching for a rather theoretical royal guarantee of this right reveal simply that the right of asylum of the temple was no longer to be taken for granted. As long as this right was not controversial, the royal decree was unnecessary. In the third century the protection of the temple was so widely recognised that debtors often had to enter into an agreement to give up a possible recourse to that protection. Formal recognition of the right of asylum and *asylia* decrees became necessary when the right no longer existed by consensus. The history of Ptolemaic Egypt during the second and first centuries is partly the history of the disintegration of such a religious consensus. Decrees of *asylia* testify not to the growing power of the temples, but to the disarray of at least some sanctuaries, which lost their undisputed authority and believed that the magic of a stele referring to the authority of the king could help them enjoy permanently a limited right of asylum. The 'documentary' analysis of our inscriptions shows that it is arbitrary to reduce the internal history of Egypt to difficult relations between the king and the heterogenous group we call by convenience the Egyptian clergy.

Any epigraphic inquiry has to consider the problem of formulae. The problem similarly exists in papyrology, and in spite of the limited access which was aimed at for most documentary papyri, the formula plays its role as a support of authenticity – for instance in contracts or in receipts for taxes – or positions the message in particular ways in social relations, as, for example, in private letters or oracular demands. In epigraphy, because of the required guarantees of authenticity and solemnity which the publication of many inscriptions needed to inspire, the formula was even more necessary. I have already referred to the existence of a stereotypical scheme in the Greek version of Egyptian priestly decrees, broadly borrowed from the decrees of the Greek cities. Similarly in the *asyliai* of the Fayyum, we could notice how the quotation of the petition on papyrus, which governed the request of the applicants (already in itself a solemn act), became a basic element of the inscription, along with other clauses like the sacred ordinance and the royal notation which completed the process of giving authority to the inscription.

I would like to say more about another formula used in some rather modest documents. It is specific to Egypt and is not without interest for the historian: the formula of inscriptions (generally dedications to a divinity, in the dative) initiated 'on behalf of the king' (ὑπὲρ βασιλέως), adding on occasion also other members of the royal family. Let me quote a modest example which reduces the problem to its simplest elements:

Ὑπὲρ βασιλέως Πτολεμαίου τοῦ Πτολεμαίου καὶ βασιλίσσης Βερενίκης ἀδελφῆς καὶ γυναικὸς αὐτοῦ Ἰμούτης Ἁρυώτου Ἴσει.[23]

On behalf of King Ptolemy, son of Ptolemy, and Queen Berenike his sister and wife, Imoutes son of Haryotes [dedicated this] to Isis.

Among the dedicants who use the formula 'on behalf of the king' we find the highest dignitaries of the country as well as people as

---

[23] I. *Philae* I 2, as emended in *SEG* XXIX 1665 (246 or after).

unknown as the man appearing in that short inscription from Philae.

The meaning of 'on behalf of the king' gave rise to controversy for a long time. Letronne thundered against those who tried to give to the preposition a temporal meaning ('under the king'), whereas, in his view, the preposition meant 'for the saving of', because it expressed the idea that a building or an inscription 'is the work of the people who live in the country or of the persons mentioned in the body of the inscription', whereas the nominative *basileus* would announce that it was the prince who ordered the operation.[24] Recently, André Bernand tried to clarify the meaning of the preposition, by using a supplementary peculiarity of *I. Philae* I 5 [*OGIS* 87] (210–205 BC):

Ὑπὲρ βασιλέως Πτολεμαίου καὶ βασιλίσσης
Ἀρσινόης, θεῶν Φιλοπατόρων, καὶ Πτολεμαίωι
τῶι υἱῶι αὐτῶν, Σαράπιδι Ἴσιδι Σωτῆρσι
4 Σωκράτης Ἀπολλοδώρου Λο[κρός].

On behalf of King Ptolemy and Queen Arsinoe, the Father-loving Gods, and for Ptolemy their son, Sokrates son of Apollodoros, Locrian, [dedicated this] to Sarapis and Isis the saviour gods.

In describing the royal family, the dedicant distinguishes (on Bernand's view) the king and queen, whose names are governed by ὑπέρ, grammatically from the long-desired child, the future Epiphanes. The latter is mentioned in the dative, as are the divinities to whom the inscription is dedicated. But the first dative is not at the same level as the following ones, as shown by the 'and' of line 2. Dittenberger adopted a drastic solution: this dative is an error for the genitive. On the contrary, Bernand, *I. Philae* I, p. 91, explains:

The dative draws our attention to the person in honour of whom the monument is dedicated. Indeed, the current formula indicates simply that the inscription is made for the king and the queen, that is 'in their place' and 'in honour of them': any inscription is so honouring the sovereigns, in the sense that the king (and, if needed, his wife and children) is supposed to make the offering to the god.

This leads Bernand to translate: 'In the name of king Ptolemy and of the queen Arsinoe, Gods Philopatores, and in honour of their son Ptolemy, to Sarapis etc.'. The late birth of a crown prince, the hope for dynastic continuity, would explain Sokrates' behaviour, asking for the blessing of the divinities in favour of the royal child.

[24] *Recherches pour servir à l'histoire de l'Égypte* (1823) XXII, n. 1, 2–3.

Such an explanation, admitting an ambiguous value for ὑπέρ, is attractive and, at first sight, finds parallels in many figurative stelae. For example, in the epigraphic dossier of Paminis and Parthenios from Coptos I have already alluded to (above, n. 2), the Greek inscription beginning with 'on behalf of' plus the name of the emperor and the hieroglyphic text were inscribed under a relief where the emperor dressed as a pharaoh is making an offering in front of Egyptian divinities. Do image and text substitute themselves for the emperor? We cannot exclude the possibility that in some circles (Parthenios was *prostatês* of the temple of Isis), people confusedly mixed the Greek vision of the emperor-*basileus* and that of the Egyptian pharaoh-intercessor. But even in this case this motivation is not a deciding factor. At first, one does not see how this substitution, dedicant-emperor, which does not appear anywhere to my knowledge in Egyptian rites, would not be perceived as an usurpation. Moreover, in many inscriptions, 'on behalf of' applies to the queen and to the royal children, who have no religious function. Finally, 'on behalf of' can even relate to persons foreign to the royal family, as in the famous dedication to Anubis by Pasôs, raiser of the sacred dogs, on behalf of Apollonios the *dioiketes* and his estate-manager Zenon (*I. Fay.* I 98, Philadelphia, mid-third century BC, see p. 232). This document should not mislead us by exceptional Egyptian elements. Generally at the beginning of an inscription the formula 'on behalf of the king' appears almost exclusively in Greek milieus. In fact, it is not the meaning of *hyper* which creates a problem; it means, as one would expect, 'in favour of, for the salvation and prosperity of', exactly as when a dedicant uses 'for himself' (ὑπὲρ αὐτοῦ), and also as later when expressions like ὑπὲρ σωτηρίας, 'for the safety', of the emperor appear. The problem lies in the Ptolemaic specificity of the very wide use of *hyper* in favour of the dynasty. Perhaps we find there a deep feeling of solidarity with the king, possibly also a sort of social correctness which crystallised in an epigraphic formula. The inscriptions reveal here by their specific Ptolemaic character a problem of mentality not easy to explicate, but whose Alexandrian origin is likely.

I have developed the various aspects of this chapter using Ptolemaic inscriptions. The same problems of documentary criticism arise in documents from the imperial period. In dealing earlier with the *asyliai*, I raised a problem, commonplace outside Egypt, but more disturbing in that country when the inscription is drafted in Greek, namely the predilection of the clergy for the epigraphic fashion of expressing their concerns. It is easy to explain, especially all around the ancient and more modern Mediterranean world, by the conviction that carving on stone, the memory of history, maintains beyond the wear of time the rights and privileges acquired by the house of the divinity. In the imperial period, a particular instance of this conviction intrigues me: the temple of Hibis in the distant Khargeh oasis, with its copies of three edicts issued by prefects of Egypt, and particularly Tiberius Julius Alexander's programmatic edict.[25] Normally an edict of the prefect is not intended to become a inscription. There is only one other prefect's edict which was the object of such exceptional publication on stone: the prescript of the prefect Lusius Geta exempting the priests of the god Soknopaios from compulsory cultivation.[26] The covering letter of this edict foresaw only the *ekthema*, 'publication', in the most convenient places, that is, short-lived posters on papyrus. The priests, acting on the scale of eternity, found it more prudent to inscribe their right on a stele set up in the sanctuary. Such was also the precarious publication on papyrus which, as far as we may guess, was provided for the three edicts of the temple of Hibis by the civil authorities. No doubt their display on the outer walls of the pylons was decided by the local clergy, and no doubt one of the axes of any interpretation of such edicts, which refer a lot to abuses by some authorities, should be the awkward relations between the sanctuary, its domain and its people all around, on the one hand, and the local civil and military servants of the emperor, on the other hand. Like the Ptolemaic *asyliai*, like Lusius Geta's edict, Tiberius Julius Alexander's endless inscription inscribed on the stone of the temple was for the priests a virtual shield against evil coming from outside.

That brings us to the conclusion of this discussion, in which inscriptions were put in the centre of human relations: conflicts of rights; admiration; affection or fear; purely formal initiatives or deep feelings, all of them sincere but misleading; human relations, even as far as the gods, who are supposed to read the inscription and to react to what is written and be as trapped as plain mortals by it. In inscriptions these relations are never innocent, and because the publication confers on the message the durability of the engraved text – *titulis manebis in aevo*[27] – these relations are ambiguous. An inscription will honour the dedicant as much as the man whose *virtù* is praised. Publication of the privilege thanks and threatens. We are the third party, and we too are faced with the ambiguity of our methods. The

---

[25] Chalon (1964); *I. Prose* 57.
[26] *I. Fay.* I 75 (AD 54).
[27] Found in Latin inscriptions and quoted by G. S. Susini, *Epigrafia romana* (Rome 1982) 16.

subtle game of *asylia* calls to mind the right of the one and the role of protector of the other, but the epigraphist will see it as evidence for the insignificance of the right and the relative weakness of the authority. Documentary criticism is a work of modesty, and the document, closely scrutinised, reminds us every day that it does not exactly say what it says or what we wish it would say, but instead what people wanted the reader to think, and, starting from there, we have to read between the lines what those understatements really meant.

Moreover, to the basic nature of the epigraphic document as permanent and open, the distinctiveness of the epigraphy of Graeco-Roman Egypt adds all the ambiguities of the relations between two cultures with their contradictory mutual behaviours and with a thesaurus of documents that five scripts left behind during a thousand years, to be rediscovered at random and used by us for a problematical systematisation.

CONCLUSION

'Hellenistic Egypt', though an apparently unproblematic pair of words, is in reality a troubling combination. It corresponds to a tiny slice of Egypt's history, barely three hundred years. After having been an isolated and passive unit in the larger entity of the Achaemenid empire, Egypt became, by virtue of its economic potential and human density, the lever of the power that a dynasty arriving from the north tried to exercise in the Eastern Mediterranean from Alexandria, and then the basis for the dynasty's survival. During these three centuries, a long span by the standards of the other Hellenistic kingdoms, the country was directed from this city, a nearby but foreign world. From Alexandria, the Ptolemies could look to the east, the north or the west while organising and exploiting the south. Once one sets aside the dynamics of the first few reigns, however, this period looks in its unfolding like a transition – like all periods in human history, to be sure, but still leading us to ask in what areas this transition prepared, or failed to prepare, new dimensions for Egypt. By way of Alexandria and then of Fostat, indeed, Egypt was to become an integrated element in a much larger whole, first the Roman empire, then the Christian Byzantine East, and finally the Islamic world.

On our conventional time-scale, the Hellenistic period begins when a military migration, revolutionising the Greek practice of warfare, emerged from the southern Balkans and destroyed the Achaemenid organisation of the East while at the same time trying to assimilate it, for better or worse. Egypt was a peripheral part of this process, and submitted to the Macedonians without resistance. Ptolemy Soter made it the central and largest part of his kingdom. He also initiated a significant innovation, the permanent installation in Egypt of a foreign population, significant in number, given a controlling role, and the source of dynastic stability.

The Ptolemaic intermezzo came to an end at the conclusion of another military adventure, this one at first glance more limited. But this time Egypt, or rather Alexandria, was an active participant in the form of its queen and fleet. Although Cleopatra VII seemed up to that point to have secured the succession to the throne for a young Ptolemy and a more secure future for her dynasty, her new Alexandrian empire collapsed at one blow. The defeat at Actium definitively reoriented the larger Mediterranean world and unified it under Rome's authority. A bicultural Egypt was to undergo profound change, but this change did not come from within; it was the work of Rome and of Alexandria, and later still of the great religious movements of the Near East which marked the first millennium of our era. Here we must confront two questions: was this change anticipated by the evolution of the bicultural society that existed in the Egyptian countryside under the Ptolemies? And how far did the arrival of Rome instead destroy some of the main evolutionary trends under way in this society?

If we come back to the entity that we call Hellenistic Egypt and invert our perspective, looking from the point of view of the historian towards the ancient sources, and if we follow the paths available to us for renewing, generation after generation, the perceptions that a modern person can have of ancient societies, the countryside of Egypt is astonishingly distinct from the rest of the Hellenistic Mediterranean world, including Alexandria. Egypt owes this particularity to the fact that for this period it has furnished us with material that only it can put at the disposition of the historian or sociologist. This it does by the means of Greek and Demotic papyrology, these two disciplines born from the discovery of the Rosetta Stone but which found their names and identities a century later, after decades of hesitant initial steps. Elsewhere, from Cyrenaica to Bactria, and even in Hellenistic Greece, the historian has available either literary sources, which have only a partial – and sometimes partisan – view of the realities of their own time and the past, or epigraphy, most often the reflection only of particular instances, even where the text has a historical dimension, or of archaeological data whose riches are often accessible only in the light of a historical environment already conceived by the historian.

By way of parenthesis, it should be noted that when Hellenists have epigraphical sources for Hellenistic Egypt, these differ substantially from what is available for the remainder of the Greek world. Even if they concern only the pinnacle of Macedonian power and of the indigenous clergy (a characteristic fault of the great inscriptions), the trilingual synodical decrees offer straight away the general problem of the relationships between, on the one hand, power and the human networks produced by immigration and, on the other, the then uncontested spiritual leaders of Egyptian society, who had seen this immigration arrive and take a dominating role. Beyond the conventional rhetoric of the decrees, beyond even the implicit proclamation of the primacy of the Macedonian king honoured as an Egyptian pharaoh, these epigraphical monuments illustrate a more general point: the strange symbiosis of two religious systems. The Greeks integrated the local religious system into their own, thanks to a flexible phenomenology of the divine. This allowed them to admit the exoticism which the local rendering of the divine presented for them and even to find new inspiration in it. Indigenous religious practice, although enclosed in its isolation and particularism, none the less from Alexander the Great onwards was able to absorb royal cults which could readily be integrated into local orthodoxy.

But even this epigraphy of prestige, and even the archaeological remains (one thinks, for example, of the exedra of the poets and philosophers which Ptolemy I commissioned and connected by a dromos to the necropolis of the Apis bulls at Saqqara), cannot offer a view comparable to the opportunities for investigation provided by the exponentially growing numbers of papyri and ostraca put at our disposition since the last third of the nineteenth century. Both in diversity and in quantity, these have allowed us to study Egypt from inside all of its component parts.

To be sure, it has been widely observed that discoveries of papyri are distributed unequally in time and space. They have been abundant only in certain areas and even there only intermittently. For the Ptolemaic period, we have no wealth of information on the urban milieu comparable to that of the imperial period. This gap weighs heavily on the study of Greek circles. The royal organisation of the countryside required the existence of a Greek administrative and banking operation in the religious and artisanal centres of the nomes, but, when it comes to individuals, we are often in the position of postulating the existence of Greeks in urban settings only because of their absence from the rural environment where they had dealings. This Greek urban milieu, with its gymnasia and economic potentialities, was to become the basis of the Julio-Claudian reorganisation of the countryside and particularly of the system of magistrates chosen from among the Greek elite. This reorganisation, in turn, assured the connection between imperial power and the nomes.

The same imbalance is present between Greek and Demotic documents, both in their bulk and in their representativeness. This disequilibrium is in part the result of the unequal efforts devoted to these two branches of the papyrological sources over a long period. It is true that some recent gains of great value for understanding Ptolemaic society have been made by taking better account of the indigenous factor as revealed in the Demotic documents. The evidence from the Egyptian side, with all its distinctiveness, has thus come to be given a larger role in our understanding of the evolution of Hellenistic Egypt. But it remains true that the content even of the present volume shows that Greek documents, accessible to a larger number of scholars, have dominated our studies. My work has in this respect suffered from a characteristic weakness of its period. This situation, however, has not been without its advantages. First, it explains the relatively rapid fashion in which the Egyptian Hellenistic scene has come to be taken into account by Western scholars. This opening has been eased by the simultaneous publication of great Greek literary texts and biblical texts, which have been better able to attract attention than wet-nursing contracts or certificates for work on the dikes. This interest, moreover, was easily justified by the fact that the Greek documents were in large part the product of royal power and of its administration of the countryside. Documents coming from the king or addressed to him occupied an exceptionally important place in one of the longest-known bodies of Ptolemaic texts, the Memphite documents later collected in *UPZ* I. We may add that the place that Alexandria holds in the development of Western culture has been an additional excuse for carrying research beyond this city into the Egypt that furnished so many of our Greek texts.

The fundamental differences separating the indigenous culture from that of the immigrants, coupled with their relative impermeability to one another, make it legitimate to conceive of what I will call a specifically Greek 'space' in this kingdom. We shall also see that this space is defined in part by virtue of its being invaded by individuals of the parallel Egyptian space or by relationships, even matrimonial ties, between its members with those of the other community.

In that part of the ancient world which speaks directly to our modern Western world, there exists, besides Graeco-Roman Egypt, another zone which offers the researcher an analogous wealth of means of gaining access to a large part of the social components of the human environment, namely classical Athens. In Attica, the richness of the literature, of epigraphy and of archaeological remains compensate better than anywhere else for the absence of papyri and ostraca. Thanks to this wealth of material, Pierre Lévêque and Pierre Vidal-Naquet were able to devote to the reforms of Cleisthenes and the creation of an Athenian civic space a little book which marked an era, particularly in my own development.[1] Indeed, I consider that the Athenian political space managed to be lasting and effective because it was superimposed both on a coherent, even if diverse, geographical space and on a homogeneous customary space, essentially religious in character, while at the same time being confronted to an increasing degree with two competitive phenomena: first, in its own proper civic space, the mass of everything that was not the deliberative and fighting citizen body but which made up a large component of the customary space: women, slaves, children, the marginal zone of doubtful citizenship; and, on the other hand, the increasing competition of a different space, a non-civic but Greek space, with the growth of the economy of the metics and mercenaries, with individualisation in access to the divine, and with the proximity of a new political structure, the Macedonian royal space.

One is all the more tempted to use the same methodology in our critical approach to the idea of Greek space in Ptolemaic Egypt, in that Alexandria was created as a city with Athenian legal structures and yet without an Athenian civic structure. But this would be an illusion. The irruption of people from the North installed a royal and Macedonian Alexandria, destined to be a capital, on the edge of the sea. But for the study of the *chôra*, Alexandria is only a deceptive intermediary, even if the role played by the city as permanent cultural model for Hellenism in the nomes must not be forgotten. Alexandria was a space of its own, characterised by the ambiguity of its relationship with the king who was present in the city; it had only a limited autonomy, but it was sometimes able to stymie a king or his ministers. With the king, it shared the seat of the cult of the founder Alexander and of the civic cult of Serapis; and, when it obtained the privilege of exploiting the countryside, it used the monarch (Cleopatra, in the case that concerns us) as arbiter in its conflicts with the agents of the monarch in this other space, where Alexandria was a privileged exploiter. I should therefore say explicitly that when I speak of Egypt, I exclude Alexandria from it. For the Greek of the *chôra*, Alexandria represented a source of authority, a sort of model because it was in the shadow of the king, but it was all the same another world; and for the Egyptian, it was the alien centre of a foreign administration of power, an administration generally accepted as being in the nature of things and a necessity of life.

[1] *Clisthène l'Athénien* (Paris 1964).

Moreover, I will not tackle the problem of the Greek settlements in Egypt before Alexander, Naucratis and the Hellenomemphites, which we know poorly even though they played an important role in the first settlement of Graeco-Macedonians in Egypt.

The Egyptian countryside in the Hellenistic period presented the distinctive feature of juxtaposing two spaces, a 'Greek' space and an indigenous one. How can one escape the temptation of transferring to the Egypt of the Ptolemies, particularly to the Greek space which our sources privilege, the search for solidarities which govern the space of a community, their origin, their reason for existence or for their undoing, their mechanisms for changing this space?

To grasp a space, we must initially establish a first parameter: the zone of action left to the group in question by the power as it is organised. That is true for the group which in Attica occupied the civic space and which managed to reserve for itself the use and protection of political and judicial powers. This was a matter of a closed space, protected by the relatively exclusive status of citizenship. In the Hellenistic East, the royal structures of the third century created for the immigrants a space of an entirely different type, parallel to a space occupied by the original inhabitants. The only power they could exercise was delegated, and that could be exercised only by participating in the royal authority. In the *chôra*, the unity of the Greek space was not territorial but that of a community – a notion more complex than its simple name – which depends on having connections, more or less direct, with the royal management of the country, and on holding the status of immigrant or descendant of an immigrant. With time, this relatively straightforward coherence became less obvious than it had been at the outset under military occupation or, following that stage, in the period of the establishment of the administration of the land and the plantation by military settlers. At the same time, the space is the place where the collectivity and its individual members shared a body of social relations and the place where each located the legitimacy of his existence there, an essential notion for the immigrant or coloniser.

But this first category is empty when taken by itself. The group concerned would concretely fill all of the potentialities, often unwittingly, of which it was the support. It was a matter, above all, of a body of traditions, of competences, and of practices, which gave the group its coherence and success. This explains at once its new and often efficacious contribution, but also the deficiences of action in this space, altogether one of expatriation. Its members organise, for this is the role of a dominant group, but they could organise only within the limits of the modes of thought they brought from Greece and Macedonia. For example, coinage, thoroughly assimilated in Greece as a means of valuation, was imposed as indispensable, but in a region where monetary exchange was embryonic and until this point mainly concentrated on foreign mercenary soldiers. The farming of taxes was a Greek practice, which was now applied in an extensive agricultural economy to which it was badly suited. To this second parameter were at times added some further developments, where these traditions evolved locally – one thinks of the cleruchy – when they were confronted with the geographic and human constraints of the new space which was coming into being.

The third parameter is relationships with the other. It is particularly noticeable in a bicultural society in which a dominant minority and a majority with its own traditions of dealing with power and the setting cohabit. This parameter had some positive content, particularly when it permitted the recognition to others of a right to have equally a place of legitimate presence. For example, this recognition appeared right away in the relationship of complicity between the Macedonian royal power and the indigenous clergy, especially the Memphite high priesthood. The right of the other to exist and to act within the limits of the system never appears in our Ptolemaic documentation to have been contested.

But often this parameter is negative, first of all because it is after all a question of a relationship between dominant and dominated parties, and one that restricts access to the means of management of the country on the part of the dominated. The difference can take on precise connotations. For example, as we shall see, taxation on persons was from an early date heavier on Egyptians than on 'Hellênes'. Racist reactions are visible in some documents. However, despite the cultural impermeability of the Greek and Egyptian spaces, time and propinquity modified the relationship of the two spaces and made their disparities less sharply defined. That is particularly true in that neither of the two spaces was homogeneous and in that a wide variety of possible zones of osmosis was available.

The space which I am calling 'Greek' and its 'Greeks' appear, at first sight, like a simple description of inseparable container and content. But there is some ambiguity in the term 'Greek' in the context of Ptolemaic Egypt. The adjective *hellênikos* and the adverb *hellênisti* represent a clear and simple dichotomy, when they oppose one language and its alphabet to the Egyptian language and scripts. By contrast, it has long been noted that in Egypt the notion of 'Greek' presents some blurriness. At one point I posed myself the question of the place of Thracian immigrants in the royal system. Bulgarian scholars situated them towards the bottom of the scale in a Ptolemaic society which they saw as a single hierarchical entity. I found, however, that these Thracians were perfectly integrated into the dominant royal 'Greek' system, including their engagement in such aristocratic practices as the organisation of contests in honour of the king. In 1967, the fiscal dossier published in *CPR* XIII (see now Willy Clarysse and Dorothy Thompson's *Counting the People*) brought a new element to the debate on the notion of 'Hellene', which is a very rare word in the papyri because it is not used to designate individuals. We find, for example, in these documents of the third century, coming from the heart of the countryside of the Fayyum, that, among the men, a certain number were exempted from the additional tax to which the roughly ninety Egyptians were subjected; most of the exempt are seventy-two *Hellênes*. Hermann Harrauer remarked that this supplementary tax goes back in fact to the creation, which I mentioned earlier, of a heavier capitation tax for the Egyptians than for the Greeks. But what appears above all in the lists of names is that the term *Hellênes* has a simple discriminatory connotation and means nothing more or less than 'non-Egyptians'. The Semitic names which appear in these lists show that the term no longer had any of its original ethnic sense; rather, it had been extended to other groups of immigrants more or less integrated into the Macedonian royal system. Among these *Hellênes*, the Macedonians were an elite – the monarchy, right down to Cleopatra, proclaimed its Macedonian character – to the point that the ethnic became with time an honorific distinction. It was indeed the only one of the Greek ethnics to have survived for some time in the identity of its possessors during the first decades of the Roman reorganisation of the countryside. But we find in the lists of *CPR* XIII some 'Hellênes', like the Jews, less capable of being assimilated, particularly for religious reasons.

The unity of the Greek space was thus coupled with a set of particularisms. I would say that this unity was above all vertical, because it was tied to the functions in which men succeeded one another in the service of the king, without taking any account of their cultural particularities. Onomastics shows that groups like the Thracians or Idumaeans by and large gave their children Greek names. This behaviour reveals at once their integration into a social component of Greek language and a sign of solidarity in their official functions. But what I would call a horizontal element, tied to the family and communal setting, was opposed to this functional unity. Thracian families also kept the tradition of giving some children names coming from their ancestral home, names which often had a princely connotation. An even clearer example of horizontality can be found in the Memphite inscription *OGIS* II 737 (*I. Portes* 25). This decree was voted in 112/111 BC by an assembly that included both the Idumaeans in military service and the Idumaeans settled in the city of Memphis. The assembly was held in the sanctuary of the Idumaeans in honour of a *strategos* named Dorion, who seems to have had privileged ties with this temple. It thus joined together soldiers, who belonged to the royal system, and a civil component of the multi-ethnic city of Memphis, which does not appear as an element in the Greek space. These ties were probably favoured by the closed character of a Semitic religion, even if the group seems Hellenised. Mixed marriages, always numerous in a land of immigration, take us even further in the field of solidarities outside those of the royal system.

The Greek space was not impermeable. To look at the phenomenon in its extension over three centuries, the penetration of this space by Egyptians was continuous and certainly in large part carried out in the service of the king. Was this Greek space thus progressively denatured? I think, rather, that it was enriched by the contribution of Hellenised persons and those on the path of Hellenisation. From the beginning of the installation of the immigrant royal regime, it must have been necessary to call on the qualifications of some Egyptian elites. This was needed first because there were not enough men, and particularly enough competent men, but then because an entire network of local social and economic relationships, foreign to the Greek world, had to be created and put to good use, particularly in the domain of agriculture. From the start, we find thus Egyptians involved in the royal organisation of the *chôra*, and even at a high level, like the *basilikoi grammateis* and the nomarchs. We observe that this is a matter of executive positions rather than posts of conception or command. But even the simplest tasks entrusted to Egyptians in the royal system could offer them more or less easy access to the Greek space. This could at times even be exceptionally effective: we know for the years 124–101 the astonishing fate of the modest policeman Nektsaphthis son of Petosiris, who became progressively Maron alias Nektsaphthis son of Petosiris alias Dionysios, and finally, at the end of a career worthy of the army of Napoleon, Maron son of Dionysios, Macedonian, one of the cavalry settlers, bearing the prestigious ethnic which had become the mark of the royal aristocracy, and with a katoikic standing which assured him access to the land reserved to this class (cf. *CPR* XIII, p. 45). And then there are the Egyptian priests who in the first century of our era became *strategoi* of large territories in the south.

In the late Ptolemaic period, it is inside the Greek space that we see some structural changes in the royal system which would affect the structuring of that Greek space. These changes probably came about under the pressure of events and in part to remedy gaps in the organisation of the kingdom. They are not a sign of weakening either of the royal power or of loyalty towards the king. I would mention just two aspects of this development. Under the reign of Ptolemy VIII Euergetes II there appears the title of *autokrator strategos* for the Thebaid: instances are Lochos (*Pros. Ptol.* VI 15218, VIII, p. 10) and Parthenios (*I. Th. Sy.* 318), along with the *epistrategos* and 'city-founder' Boethos son of Nikostratos (at least if my restoration of the title in *I. Philae* I 15.6 is accepted). The title *autokrator* (absolute or plenipotentiary; in the Roman period, the equivalent of the Latin *imperator*) is astonishing in a Hellenistic monarchy. This delegation of the power of final decision-making and of the ability to delegate decision-making further (privileges of a Hellenistic king) to a top-level dignitary seems to have been limited in time. But it foreshadows the imposing figure of Kallimachos, who, by accumulating titles connected with the Thebaid, the Eastern Desert and the Red Sea, was practically viceroy of the south of the kingdom under Ptolemy Auletes and Cleopatra.

Other changes occurred at a humbler level. The most striking is the birth of a pre-feudal landed category, through the formation of a body of land reserved to the class of katoikic cavalry. I have explained that, far from being a matter of the development of private property, the transfers of katoikic plots take place inside this reserved domain. This status was sufficiently well established for these lands to remain under the empire a special category of property, even though the caste of katoikic cavalry had disappeared with the end of the monarchy which they had served. Similarly, the confirmations of asylum for temples which multiplied in the first century BC mention high officials or officers as protectors of the temples. These show the growth of power of the local authorities, but they also display the conflicts between those various local powers, which are well attested from the previous century and must have tended to split the Greek space. Just like the incursions of the Hellenised, these changes of relationships to the royal power must surely have modified the nature of the Greek space and its relations with the Egyptian space. These new facts left some traces in the imperial system in the *chôra*, but more generally they disappeared with the dynasty which brought into being a Greek space in Egypt and witnessed its evolution.

In the Roman reorganisation of Egypt, Romans and Alexandrians were marked off from the mass of 'Aigyptioi' of the *chôra*, including the Greeks and Hellenised Egyptians. Despite that lumping together of Greeks and Hellenised Egyptians, the closed and privileged class of the Greeks who were 'from the gymnasium' was to play an important role in the management of the nomes. We may wonder if this group may not have owed its origin to the existence, among the 'old Greeks' of the Ptolemaic *chôra*, of a reaction in the direction of defending their privileges in the face of the rise of the Egyptian 'new Greeks'.

The difficulty the Graeco-Macedonian minority experienced in performing all of the functions that fell upon the directing group produced an unknowing response from the Egyptian milieu. But the loss of substance that the latter community underwent through these transfers of competences, however limited, was continuous. The traditional indigenous governing strata, particularly the clergy, seem to have become weaker, while the written form of the Egyptian language progressively disappeared. But written documents can be deceptive. There was simply an alteration in the means of expression, in the face of an administration which was more uniformly Greek in language than had been the case under the Ptolemies. But the Egyptian language remained alive, and the durability of the Egyptian milieu would be reaffirmed when the new relationship between religion and written expression was overthrown by the arrival of religious movements from the Near East. Paradoxically, it was by losing its gods, for us so closely tied to the image of Egyptian culture, that the Egyptian language and an Egyptian culture were able to experience their Coptic renaissance. By that time, however, the Greek space, like the Egyptian, had ceased to exist in the form in which it is visible under the Ptolemies.

We might devote a few moments to the contrafactual supposition that Cleopatra was victorious at Actium, which would lead us to imagine that Egypt under her successors might have pursued further changes in its Greek component, gradually more and more enriched by a Hellenised population, in the middle of an Egyptian population which would have continued to lose, bit by bit, its old mental framework. But history is not made of imaginary continuities; rather, it is formed from the ruptures produced by humans amid the continuities.

BIBLIOGRAPHY

Except for a small number of works cited once for a particular item of evidence, books and articles are in the main cited by author and date, as listed below. Papyri and ostraca are cited by the abbreviations in J. F. Oates, R. S. Bagnall, S. J. Clackson et al., *Checklist of Editions of Greek, Latin, Demotic and Coptic Papyri, Ostraca and Tablets*, 5th edn (*Bulletin of the American Society of Papyrologists* suppl. 9, Oakville, CT, 2001); online version at http://scriptorium.lib.duke.edu/papyrus/texts/clist.html.

Inscriptions are cited as follows:
I. Fay. = E. Bernand, *Recueil des inscriptions grecques du Fayoum*. Leiden and Cairo 1975–81.
I. Louvre Bernand = E. Bernand, *Inscriptions grecques de l'Égypte et de Nubie au Musée du Louvre*. Paris 1992.
I. Métr. = E. Bernand, *Inscriptions métriques de l'Égypte gréco-romaine: recherches sur la poésie épigrammatique des Grecs en Égypte*. Paris 1969.
I. Olympia = W. Dittenberger and K. Purgold, *Die Inschriften von Olympia*. Berlin 1896.
I. Pan = A. Bernand, *Le Paneion d'El-Kanaïs: les inscriptions grecques*. Leiden 1972.
I. Philae = A. Bernand, *Les inscriptions grecques de Philae I*. Paris 1969.
I. Portes = A. Bernand, *Les portes du désert: recueil des inscriptions grecques d'Antinooupolis, Tentyris, Koptos, Apollonopolis Parva et Apollonopolis Magna*. Paris 1984.
I. Prose = A. Bernand, *La prose sur pierre dans l'Égypte hellénistique et romaine*. Paris 1992.
I. Th. Sy. = A. Bernand, *De Thèbes à Syène*. Paris 1989.
OGIS = W. Dittenberger, *Orientis Graeci inscriptiones selectae*, I–II. Leipzig 1903–5.
SEG = *Supplementum epigraphicum Graecum*. Leiden and Amsterdam 1923–.
Syll.[3] = W. Dittenberger, *Sylloge inscriptionum Graecarum*. 3rd edn. Vols I–IV. Leipzig 1915–24.

In addition, the following abbreviations are used:

APF = Archiv für Papyrusforschung und verwandte Gebiete.

BIFAO = Bulletin de l'Institut français d'archéologie orientale.

Bull. épigr. = Bulletin épigraphique, appearing annually in the *Revue des Études Grecques*; cited by year and section number.

CdÉ = Chronique d'Égypte.

FGr Hist = F. Jacoby, *Fragmente der griechischen Historiker.* Berlin 1923–.

JEA = Journal of Egyptian Archaeology.

LÄ = Lexikon der Ägyptologie, eds W. Helck and E. Otto. Wiesbaden 1973–.

LIMC = Lexicon Iconographicum Mythologiae Classicae. Zurich 1981–99.

LSJ = H. G. Liddell, R. Scott and H. S. Jones, *A Greek–English Lexicon.* 9th edn. 1940. With revised suppl. Oxford 1996.

Pages I = J. Bingen, *Pages d'épigraphie grecque: Attique-Égypte (1952–1982).* Epigraphica Bruxellensia 1. Brussels 1991.

Pages II = J. Bingen, *Pages d'épigraphie grecque II: Égypte (1983–2002).* Epigraphica Bruxellensia 3. Brussels 2005.

ZPE = Zeitschrift für Papyrologie und Epigraphik.

Bagnall, R. S. (1976) *The Administration of the Ptolemaic Possessions outside Egypt.* Leiden.

— (1982) 'Papyrology and Ptolemaic history', *Classical World* 76: 13–21.

— (1984) 'The origins of Ptolemaic cleruchs', *Bulletin of the American Society of Papyrologists* 21: 7–20.

— (1997) 'Decolonizing Ptolemaic Egypt', in *Hellenistic Constructs: Essays in Culture, History, and Historiography*, eds P. Cartledge, P. Garnsey and E. Gruen. Berkeley, pp. 225–41.

Bagnall, R. S. and P. S. Derow (2004) *The Hellenistic Period: Historical Sources in Translation.* Oxford.

Bearzot, C. (1992) 'Πτολεμαῖος Μακεδών: sentimento nazionale macedone e contrapposizioni etniche all'inizio del regno tolemaico', in *Autocoscienza e rappresentazione dei popoli nell'antichità*, ed. M. Sordi. Contributi dell'Istituto di Storia Antica 18. Milan, pp. 39–53.

Bernand, A. (1969) *Les inscriptions grecques de Philae I: Époque ptolémaïque.* Paris.

Bianchi, R. S. (1992) 'Alexander the Great as a kausia diademophoros from Egypt', *The Intellectual Heritage of Egypt: Studies Presented to László Kákosy.* Budapest, pp. 69–75.

Bingen, J. (1946) 'Les colonnes 60–72 du P. Revenue Laws et l'aspect fiscal du monopole des huiles', *Chronique d'Égypte* 21: 127–48.

— (1951) 'Les comptes dans les archives d'Héroninos', *Chronique d'Égypte* 26: 378–85.

— (1978) 'Les inscriptions de Philae des IIIe et IIe siècles avant notre ère', *Chronique d'Égypte* 53: 304–9.

Bingen, J. (1982) 'L'asylie pour une synagogue *CIL* III *Suppl.* 6583 = CII 1449', *Studia Paulo Naster oblata II.* Louvain, pp. 11–16.

— (1988) 'Alexandrina: recollection and project', *Diogenes* 141: 41–58.

— (1994) 'Le dieu Hèrôn et les Hèrôn du Fayoum', *Hommages à Jean Leclant III.* = Bibliothèque d'Étude 106/3. Cairo, pp. 41–50.

Bogaert, R. (1968) *Banques et banquiers dans les cités grecques.* Leiden.

Bonneau, D. (1964) *La crue du Nil, divinité égyptienne, à travers mille ans d'histoire (332 av.- 641 ap. J.-C.), d'après les auteurs grecs et latins et les documents des époques ptolémaïque, romaine et byzantine.* Paris.

— (1972) *Le fisc et le Nil: incidences des irrégularités de la crue du Nil sur la fiscalité foncière dans l'Égypte grecque et romaine.* Paris.

Bowersock, G. W. (1984) 'The miracle of Memnon', *Bulletin of the American Society of Papyrologists* 21: 21–32.

Braunert, H. (1964) *Die Binnenwanderung: Studien zur Sozialgeschichte Ägyptens in der Ptolemäer- und Kaiserzeit.* Bonner Historische Forschungen 26. Bonn.

Cannadine, D. (1998) *History in Our Time.* New Haven, CT.

Chalon, G. (1964) *L'édit de Tiberius Julius Alexander.* Olten and Lausanne.

Chauveau, M. (1990) 'Un été 145', *BIFAO* 90: 135–68.

— (1991) 'Un été 145: post-scriptum', *BIFAO* 91: 129–34.

— (1997a) 'Ères nouvelles et corégences en Égypte ptolémaïque', *Akten des 21. internationalen Papyrologenkongresses.* APF Beiheft 3. Leiden, I, pp. 163–71.

— (1997b) *L'Égypte au temps de Cléopâtre, 180–30 av. J.-C.* Paris.

— (1998) *Cléopâtre au-delà du mythe.* Paris.

Clarysse, W. (1985) 'Greeks and Egyptians in the Ptolemaic army and administration', *Aegyptus* 65: 57–66.

— (1991) 'Hakoris, an Egyptian nobleman and his family', *Ancient Society* 22: 235–43.

— (1995) 'Greeks in Ptolemaic Thebes', in *Hundred-Gated Thebes*, ed. S. P. Vleeming. *Pap. Lugd. Bat.* 27. Leiden, pp. 1–19.

— (1998) 'Ethnic diversity and dialect among the Greeks of Hellenistic Egypt', in *The Two Faces of Graeco-Roman Egypt*, eds A. M. F. W. Verhoogt and S. P. Vleeming. *Pap. Lugd. Bat.* 30. Leiden, pp. 1–13.

Clarysse, W. and G. van der Veken (1983) *The Eponymous Priests of Ptolemaic Egypt (P. L. Bat. 24): Chronological Lists of the Priests of Alexandria and Ptolemais with a Study of the Demotic Transcriptions of their Names.* Leiden.

Crawford, D. (1971) *Kerkeosiris: An Egyptian Village in the Ptolemaic Period.* Cambridge.

— (1978) 'The good official in Ptolemaic Egypt', *Das ptolemäische Ägypten.* Mainz, pp. 195–202.

Criscuolo, L. (1989) 'La successione a Tolemeo Aulete ed i pretesi matrimoni di Cleopatra VII con i fratelli', *Egitto e storia antica dall'Ellenismo all'età araba: bilancio di un confronto.* Bologna, pp. 325–39.

Criscuolo, L. (1990) 'Philadelphos nelle dinastia lagide', *Aegyptus* 70: 89–96.

Delia, D. (1990) *The Alexandrian Citizenship during the Roman Principate.* American Classical Studies 23. Atlanta.

Dunand, F. (1980) 'Fête, tradition, propagande: les cérémonies en l'honneur de Bérénice, fille de Ptolémée III, en 238 a.c.', *Livre du Centenaire de l'I.F.A.O. 1880–1980.* Mémoires publiés par les membres de l'IFAO 105. Cairo, pp. 287–301.

El-Abbadi, M. A. H. (1962) 'The Alexandrian citizenship', *JEA* 48: 106–23.

Ewans, M. (2002) *European Atrocity, African Catastrophe: Leopold II, the Congo Free State and its Aftermath.* London.

Finley, M. I. (1973) *The Ancient Economy.* Berkeley.

Fleischer, R. (1996) 'Kleopatra Philantonios', *Istanbuler Mitteilungen* 46: 237–40.

Fraser, P. M. (1972) *Ptolemaic Alexandria.* Oxford.

Gauthier, P. (1966) 'Les clérouques de Lesbos et la colonisation athénienne au Ve siècle', *Revue des études grecques* 79: 64–88.

Geraci, G. (1971) 'Ricerche sul Proskynema', *Aegyptus* 51: 3–211.

— (1979) 'La βασιλικὴ ἴλη macedone e l'esercito dei primi Tolemei. P. Med. inv. 69.65', *Aegyptus* 69: 8–24, pl. I.

Goukowski, P. (1978) *Essai sur les origines du mythe d'Alexandre: 336–270 av. J.-C.* Nancy.

Guglielmi, W. (1973) *Reden, Rufe und Lieder auf altägyptischen Darstellungen der Landwirtschaft, Viehzucht, des Fisch- und Vogelfangs vom Mittleren Reich bis zur Spätzeit.* Tübinger Ägyptologische Beiträge 1. Tübingen.

Habicht, C. (1958) 'Der Stratege Hegemonides', *Historia* 7: 376–8.

Haeny, G. (1985) 'A Short Architectural Story of Philae', *BIFAO* 85: 197–233.

Hauben, H. (1990) 'L'expédition de Ptolémée III en Orient et la sédition domestique de 245 av. J.-C.', *APF* 36: 29–37.

Hazzard, R. (2000) *Imagination of a Monarchy: Studies in Ptolemaic Propaganda.* Toronto.

Heinen, H. (1966) *Rom und Ägypten von 51 bis 47 v. Chr: Untersuchungen zur Regierungszeit der 7. Kleopatra und des 13. Ptolemäers.* Tübingen.

— (1969) 'Cäsar und Kaisarion', *Historia* 18: 181–203.

— (1989) 'L'Égypte dans l'historiographie moderne du monde hellénistique', *Egitto e storia antica dall'ellenismo all'età araba: bilancio di un confronto.* Bologna, pp. 105–35.

— (1998) 'Eine Darstellung des vergöttlichten Iulius Caesar auf einer ägyptischen Stele? Beobachtungen zu einem mißverstandenen Denkmal (*SB* I 1570 = *IG Fay.* I 14)', *Imperium Romanum: Festschrift für Karl Christ zum 75. Geburtstag.* Stuttgart, pp. 334–5.

Hölbl, G. (1994) *Geschichte des Ptolemäerreiches.* Darmstadt.

Huss, W. (1990) 'Die Herkunft der Kleopatra Philopator', *Aegyptus* 70: 191–203.

Hutmacher, R. (1965) *Das Ehrendekret für den Strategen Kallimachos*. Beiträge zur klassischen Philologie 17. Meisenheim am Glan.

Johnson, C. J. (2002) '*OGIS* 98 and the divinization of the Ptolemies', *Historia* 51: 112–16.

Jones, A. H. M. (1937) *The Cities of the Eastern Roman Provinces*. Oxford.

Josephson, J. A. (1997) *Egyptian Royal Sculpture of the Late Period, 400–246*. DAIK, Sonderschrift 30. Mainz.

Jouguet, P. (1911) *La vie municipale dans l'Égypte romaine*. Paris.

Karabélias, E. (1982) 'L'épiclérat à Sparte', *Studi in onore di Arnalde Biscardi*: Milan 1982–4, II, pp. 469–80.

Koenen, L. (1977) *Eine agonistische Inschrift aus Ägypten und frühptolemäische Königsfeste*. Beiträge zur klassischen Philologie 56. Meisenheim am Glan.

— (1983) 'Die Adaptation ägyptischer Königsideologie am Ptolemäerhof', *Egypt and the Hellenistic World. Studia Hellenistica* 27. Leuven, pp. 143–90.

Kunkel, W. (1928) 'Über die Veräusserung von Katökenland, auf Grund neuer Urkunden aus spätptolemäischer Zeit', *Zeitschrift der Savigny-Stiftung für Rechtsgeschichte* 48: 283–313.

Launey, M. (1950) *Recherches sur les armées hellénistiques* II. Paris. Reprint with brief updating 1987.

Lefebvre, G. (1913) 'Le dernier décret des Lagides', *Mélanges Holleaux*. Paris, pp. 103–13, pl. IV.

— (1923–4) *Le Tombeau de Petosiris*. 3 vols: I, *Description*. II, *Les Textes*. III, *Vocabulaire et planches*. Cairo.

Lenger, M.-T. (1964) *Corpus des Ordonnances des Ptolémées (C. Ord. Ptol.).* = Mémoires de la Classe des Lettres et des Sciences morales et politiques de l'Académie Royale de Belgique, Collection in-8°, 2 ser. 57, Fasc. 1. Brussels.

— (1980) Re-edition of Lenger (1964). Mémoires, 2 ser. 57, Fasc. 2. Brussels.

— (1990) *Corpus des Ordonnances des Ptolémées (C. Ord. Ptol.): bilan des additions et corrections (1964–1988). Compléments à la bibliographie.* Papyrologica Bruxellensia 24. Brussels.

Mahaffy, J. P. (1899) *A History of Egypt IV*. London.

Malinine, M. (1967) 'Partage testamentaire d'une propriété familiale (Pap. Moscou n° 123)', *Revue d'Égyptologie* 19: 67–85.

Manning, J. G. (2003) *Land and Power in Ptolemaic Egypt: The Structure of Land Tenure*. Cambridge.

Mélèze-Modrzejewski, J. (1983), 'Le statut des Hellènes dans l'Égypte lagide: bilan et perspectives de recherches', *Revue des études grecques* 96: 241–68.

Mihailov, G. (1968) 'Les Thraces en Égypte', *Linguistique balkanique* 13 (1): 31–44.

Montevecchi, O. (1997) 'Problemi di un'epoca di transizione: la grecità d'Egitto tra il Ia e il Ip', *Akten des 21. Internationalen Papyrologen-kongresses*. Stuttgart and Leipzig, II, pp. 719–26. = *Scripta selecta*. Milan (1998), pp. 391–400.

Mooren, L. (1975) *The Aulic Titulature in Ptolemaic Egypt: Introduction and Prosopography*. Verhandelingen van de Koninklijke Academie voor Wetenschappen, Letteren en Schone Kunsten van België, Klasse der Letteren, 37 no. 78. Brussels.

— (1977) *La hiérarchie de cour ptolémaïque: contribution à l'étude des institutions et des classes dirigeantes à l'époque hellénistique*. Studia Hellenistica 23. Leuven.

Muccioli, F. (1994) 'Considerazioni generali sull'epiteto Φιλάδελφος nelle dinastie ellenistiche', *Historia* 43: 402–22.

Müller, W. (1961) 'Bemerkungen zu den spätptolemäischen Papyri der Berliner Sammlung', in *Proceedings of the IX International Congress of Papyrology*, eds L. Amundsen and V. Skanland. Oslo, pp. 183–93.

Nachtergael, G. (1980) 'Bérénice II, Arsinoé III et l'offrande de la boucle', *Chronique d'Égypte* 55: 240–53.

Oates, J. F. (1963) 'The Status Designation: Πέρσης τῆς ἐπιγονῆς', *Yale Classical Studies* 18: 1–124.

Orrieux, C. (1981) 'Les comptes privés de Zénon à Philadelphia', *Chronique d'Égypte* 56: 314–40.

— (1983) *Les papyrus de Zénon*. Paris.

Pavlovskaja, A. I. (1973) 'O rentabel'nosti truda rabov v ellinisticeskom Egipte' [English abstract: 'The profitableness of slave labour in Hellenistic Egypt'], *Vestnik Drevnej Istorii* 126 (4): 136–44.

Pedech, P. (1984) *Historiens, compagnons d'Alexandre: Callisthène, Onésicrite, Néarque, Ptolémée, Aristobule*. Paris.

Peremans, W. (1937) *Vreemdelingen en Egyptenaren in Vroeg-Ptolemaeisch Egypte*. Leuven.

— (1975/6) 'Classes sociales et conscience nationale en Égypte ptolémaïque', *Miscellanea J. Vergote* (= *Orientalia Lovaniensia Periodica* 6/7): 443–53.

— (1983) 'Les Égyptiens dans l'armée de terre des Lagides', *Althistorische Studien Hermann Bengtson* (Wiesbaden): 92–102.

Pestman, P. W. (1967) *Chronologie égyptienne d'après les textes démotiques (332 av. J.-C. – 453 ap. J.-C.)*. Leiden.

— (1978) 'L'agoranomie: un avant-poste de l'administration grecque enlevé par les Égyptiens', in *Das ptolemäische Ägypten*, eds H. Maehler and V. M. Strocka. Mainz, pp. 203–20.

Pestman, P. W. et al. (1981) *A Guide to the Zenon Archive*. Pap. Lugd. Bat. 21. Leiden.

Pfeiffer, R. (1968) *History of Classical Scholarship from the Beginnings to the End of the Hellenistic Age*. Oxford.

Pikous, N. N. (1969) *Agriculteurs royaux (producteurs immédiats) et artisans dans l'Égypte du IIIe siècle avant notre ère*. Moscow.

Porter, B. and R. L. B. Moss (1939) *Topographical Bibliography of Ancient Egyptian Hieroglyphic Texts, Reliefs and Paintings VI.* Oxford.

Préaux, Cl. (1936) 'Un problème de la politique des Lagides: la faiblesse des édits', *Atti IV Congresso Internazionale di Papirolologia.* Milan, pp. 185–93.

— (1938) 'L'évolution de la tenure clérouchique sous les Lagides', *La tenure.* Recueils de la Société Jean Bodin 3. Brussels, pp. 41–57.

— (1939) *L'économie royale des Lagides.* Brussels.

— (1947) *Les Grecs en Égypte d'après les archives de Zénon.* Brussels.

— (1958) 'De la Grèce classique à l'Égypte hellénistique: la banque-témoin', *Chronique d'Égypte* 33: 243–55.

— (1961) 'L'Économie lagide: 1933–1958', *Proceedings of the IX International Congress of Papyrology.* Oslo, pp. 224–5.

— (1978) *Le monde hellénistique.* 2 vols. Paris. 2nd edn, 1988.

Quaegebeur, J. (1988) 'Cleopatra VII and the cults of the Ptolemaic queens', *Cleopatra's Egypt: Age of the Ptolemies.* Brooklyn, pp. 50–3.

— (1991) 'Cléopâtre VII et le temple de Dendara', *Göttinger Miszellen* 120: 49–72.

Rathbone, D. W. (2000) 'Ptolemaic to Roman Egypt: the death of the dirigiste state?', in *Production and Public Powers in Antiquity*, eds E. Lo Cascio and D. Rathbone. Proceedings of the Cambridge Philological Society, suppl. 26. Cambridge, pp. 44–54.

Reekmans, T. (1966) *La sitométrie dans les archives de Zénon.* Brussels.

— (1971) Review of Crawford 1971, *Chronique d'Égypte* 76: 384–9.

Ricketts, L. M. (1980) The administration of Ptolemaic Egypt under Cleopatra VII. Dissertation, Ann Arbor.

Rostovtzeff, M. (1922) *A Large Estate in Egypt in the Third Century B.C.: A Study in Economic History.* Madison.

— (1941) *The Social and Economic History of the Hellenistic World.* Oxford.

Samuel, A. E. (1966) 'The internal organization of the nomarch's bureau in the third century B.C.', *Essays in Honor of C. Bradford Welles.* American Studies in Papyrology 1. New Haven, CT, pp. 213–30.

— (1970) 'The Greek element in the Ptolemaic bureaucracy', *Proceedings of the XII International Congress of Papyrology.* Toronto, pp. 443–53.

— (1989) *The Shifting Sands of History: Interpretations of Ptolemaic Egypt.* Lanham, MD.

Schrapel, T. (1996) *Das Reich der Kleopatra: Quellenkritische Untersuchungen zu den 'Landschenkungen' Mark Antons.* Trierer Historische Forschungen 34. Trier.

Shelton, J. C. (1976) 'Land register: crown tenants at Kerkeosiris', *Collectanea Papyrologica: Texts Published in Honor of H. C. Youtie* I. Bonn, pp. 111–52, no. 15.

Skeat, T. C. (1960) 'Notes on Ptolemaic chronology. I: The last year which is also the first', *Journal of Egyptian Archaeology* 46: 91–4.

Skeat, T. C. (1962) 'Notes on Ptolemaic chronology. III: "The first year which is also the third"'. A date in the reign of Cleopatra VII', *Journal of Egyptian Archaeology* 48: 100–5.

Sullivan, R. D. (1973) 'A petition of beekeepers', *Bulletin of the American Society of Papyrologists* 10: 5–14.

Swiderek, A. (1954) 'La société indigène en Égypte au IIIe siècle avant notre ère d'après les archives de Zénon', *Journal of Juristic Papyrology* 7–8: 231–84.

— (1956) 'La société grecque en Égypte d'après les archives de Zénon', *Journal of Juristic Papyrology* 9–10: 365–400.

Teodorsson, S.-T. (1979) *The Phonology of Ptolemaic Koine*. Göteborg.

Thompson, D. J. (1984) (as D. J. Thompson Crawford), 'The Idumeans of Memphis and the Ptolemaic politeumata', *Atti XVII Congresso di Papirologia III*. Naples, pp. 1069–75.

— (1988) *Memphis under the Ptolemies*. Princeton, NJ.

— (2000) 'Philadelphus' procession: dynastic power in a Mediterranean context', *Politics, Administration and Society in the Hellenistic and Roman World*. Studia Hellenistica 36. Leuven, pp. 365–88.

Totti, M. (1985) *Ausgewählte Texte der Isis- und Sarapis-Religion*. Hildesheim.

Turner, E. G. (1974) 'A commander-in-chief's order from Saqqâra', *Journal of Egyptian Archaeology* 60: 239–42 with pl. LV.

— (1975) 'Four obols a day men at Saqqâra', *Le Monde grec: Hommages à Claire Préaux*. Brussels, pp. 573–7.

— (1984) 'Ptolemaic Egypt', *The Cambridge Ancient History*[2] VII 1: *The Hellenistic World*. Cambridge, pp. 119–74.

Uebel, F. (1968) *Die Kleruchen Ägyptens unter den ersten sechs Ptolemäern*. Berlin.

— (1973) Review of Crawford 1971, *Bonner Jahrbücher* 173: 533–9.

Vassilika, E. (1989) *Ptolemaic Philae*. Leuven.

Velkov, V. and A. Fol (1977) 'Les Thraces en Égypte gréco-romaine', *Studia Thracica* 4.

— (1978) 'Les Thraces en Égypte gréco-romaine: la littérature et la méthode', *Pulpudeva* 2: 46–52.

Vidal-Naquet, P. (1967) *Le Bordereau d'ensemencement dans l'Égypte ptolémaïque*. Pap. Brux. 5. Brussels.

— (1984) 'Alessandro et i cacciatori neri: le rôle de la chasse dans l'initiation des jeunes nobles, les privilèges du roi et les ruses de guerre dans l'histoire d'Alexandre, en particulier selon le récit d'Arrien', *Studi Storici* 25: 25–33.

Vleeming, S. (ed.) (1995) *Hundred-Gated Thebes*. Pap. Lugd. Bat. 27. Leiden.

von Reden, S. (1997) 'Money and coinage in Ptolemaic Egypt: some preliminary remarks', in *Akten des 21. Internationalen Papyrologenkongresses II*. APF Beih. 3. Stuttgart and Leipzig, pp. 1003–8.

Walbank, F. W. (1984) 'Monarchies and monarchic ideas', in *The Cambridge Ancient History*[2] VII 1: *The Hellenistic World*. Cambridge, pp. 62–100.

Weissenow, H. (1976) 'Bemerkungen zum Gebrauch von πατρίς bei Polybios', *Philologus* 120: 195–209.

Wickersham, J. M. (1970) 'The financial prospects of Ptolemaic oilmen', *Bulletin of the American Society of Papyrologists* 7: 45–51.

Will, E. (1982) *Histoire politique du monde hellénistique (323–30 av. J.-C.)*. 2nd edn. Paris.

—— (1985) 'Pour une "anthropologie coloniale" du monde hellénistique', in *The Craft of the Ancient Historian*, eds J. W. Eadie and J. Ober. Lanham, MD, pp. 273–301.

Zucker, F. (1964) 'Beobachtungen zu den Permanenten Klerosnamen', in *Studien zur Papyrologie und antiken Wirtschaftsgeschichte Friedrich Oertel zum achtzigsten Geburtstag gewidmet*. Bonn, pp. 101–6.

GENERAL INDEX

INDEX OF PASSAGES DISCUSSED

HELLENISTIC CULTURE AND SOCIETY

General Editors: Anthony W. Bulloch, Erich S. Gruen, A. A. Long, and Andrew F. Stewart